Usability Testing and System Evaluation

CHAPMAN & HALL COMPUTING SERIES

Usability Testing and System Evaluation

A guide for designing useful computer systems

Gitte Lindgaard

Principal Scientist in Human Communication
Applied Research and Development
Telecom Australia

CHAPMAN & HALL
London · Glasgow · New York · Tokyo · Melbourne · Madras

Published by Chapman & Hall, 2-6 Boundary Row, London SE1 8HN

Chapman & Hall, 2-6 Boundary Row, London SE1 8HN, UK

Blackie Academic & Professional, Wester Cleddens Road,
Bishopbriggs, Glasgow G64 2NZ, UK

Chapman & Hall Inc., One Penn Plaza, 41st Floor, New York NY 10119, USA

Chapman & Hall Japan, Thomson Publishing Japan, Hirakawacho
Nemoto Building, 6F, 1-7-11 Hirakawa-cho, Chiyoda-ku, Tokyo 102, Japan

Chapman & Hall Australia, Thomas Nelson Australia, 102 Dodds Street,
South Melbourne, Victoria 3205, Australia

Chapman & Hall India, R. Seshadri, 32 Second Main Road, CIT East,
Madras 600 035, India

First edition 1994

© 1994 Gitte Lindgaard

Commissioned by Technical Communications (Publishing) Ltd

Typeset in 10/12pt Sabon by Fleetlines Typesetters Limited, Southend-on-Sea, UK
Printed in England by Clays Ltd, St Ives plc.

ISBN 0 412 46100 5

A catalogue record for this book is available from the British Library

To Tom Triggs for teaching and sharing human factors

Contents

Preface

This book was not going to be written, at least not by me, but what can you do when you work in a company with more than 23 000 different computer systems, 76 000 users and 3 000 systems developers whom you are trying to serve with a very small human factors team? Having spent years 'proving the obvious', doing stuff that is 'totally unimpressive' and generally being regarded as a bit of a freak, it sure comes like a gift from heaven when people start asking questions about human factors, wanting to know more. What do you give them? There is plenty of very good material around, and most of what is presented in this book has been borrowed from numerous valuable sources, being products of other people's efforts. However, although we do have a plethora of articles, journals and conference proceedings at our fingertips, what seemed to be needed was something like a summary of some of the usability evaluation tools which have proven to be effective. That, I could not find anywhere. Our developers want to know 'how' to perform a certain test or design and run an experiment; they do not want to read an entire book on reliability and validity, or another one dealing with questionnaires, or experimental design. So, at the risk of failing to do justice to the magnificent work of all those who have shared their knowledge and understanding, reported their research, theories and thoughts in the literature, this is a modest attempt to provide a workable summary for people who are interested in HCI, but who come from a background other than psychology.

One always faces a dilemma when selecting material; it is like trying to eat an elephant in the sense that there is so much one would like to discuss, and so much that deserves at least to be mentioned. Naturally opinions differ with respect to what should and what should not be presented. First and foremost, I wanted to highlight some of the pitfalls, potential sources of error and traps that often invalidate otherwise good research and sensible usability studies. Much of the thinking and reasoning behind these sources of error seems to become implicit, almost second nature, to experimentalists, and at the same time, it is not at all obvious to those who have not been exposed to it. I hope sincerely that this book will help some people to be more aware of what to avoid and how to control unwanted influences in their further endeavours in HCI.

I also wanted to demonstrate that there is some rigour and systematic thinking and planning behind many of the tools and techniques psychologists use. This is perhaps a by-product of local culture in which human factors expertise is not well understood or indeed appreciated.

In addition to writing for developers who are already working in the field of systems design, the book is also intended for students taking HCI as an undergraduate or graduate subject. It is with this audience in mind that exercises are provided at the end of most of the chapters. A series of questions presented at the end of every chapter is intended for revision and for students to monitor their progress. Examples scattered throughout the book are intended to illustrate what is described in the text. It is hoped they will add clarity where I have not managed to compress the relevant literature well enough to bring out the essence of the points made. These examples come mainly from work we have done in our own laboratory. One could have relied on the literature there too, but the level of detail sometimes required to show what we mean is rarely found in nicely polished articles. Furthermore, I thought a bit of light-hearted humour could break up the otherwise fairly dry topics addressed here. Perhaps I am quietly hoping that the availability of some of the points and examples will increase for readers through the simple line drawings which are intended to underscore important or pertinent points in some cases, and just to provide a bit of fun in others. Above all, then, I hope readers will enjoy their way through the following text.

Many people have contributed directly or indirectly to this book. The Department of Psychology at Monash University in Melbourne laid a solid foundation for understanding a little of the complexity of human behaviour. The dedication of the staff to research and teaching has been, and remains, an inspiration to try a little harder all the time. In particular Professor Tom Triggs, to whom this book is dedicated, has devoted more than a normal share of energy and enthusiasm for his subject to his graduate students who all benefit so much from his efforts. Dr Anna Bodi, who had the courage to act as my PhD supervisor at a time when HCI was barely thought of, deserves my thanks. The Telecom Australia Research Laboratories has provided constant support in numerous ways. Mr Harry Wragge, the former Director of the Laboratories, has been very enthusiastic about this project, and I thank him for his efforts and willingness to allow it to happen. Dr Noel Teede and Mr Des Clark have also been right behind the project all along, for which I am grateful. My colleagues who have been involved in part of the actual production by providing comments, helping with printing, drawing up figures and taking more than their share of day-to-day responsibilities, have been terrific. Michael Phipps, Ronnie Flanagan, Jo Chessari, Liz Bednall and Bert Borg must be mentioned in this connection. The line drawings in the book were provided by Mr Gwilym Major, a local artist and student, who showed a great deal of enthusiasm and dedication to the project. I thank Gwilym for many hours of good fun and good work. My publishers have also been very patient and supportive, and I thank the anonymous reviewer whose thoughtful and supportive comments helped a great deal to improve the original manuscript and Dr Glyn Jones from Technical Communications (Publishing) Ltd., as well as Ms Eliane Wigzell at Chapman & Hall for their encouragement. I owe too much to my friends and family to put into a few words. Let it be said, though, that without them, this book would have had no meaning. Poul, Margit and Karin, thank you for your understanding and support. Finally, although one attempts to give credit to all the sources from which one draws in collating a manuscript such as this, it is just not possible to put names to the original owners of ideas and thoughts that one internalizes and uses. They range from academic and work colleagues to students who have participated as subjects in some of the studies reported as examples here. I am grateful to all of them.

Gitte Lindgaard

Glossary of terms

BNF: Backus-Naur formalisms

Card sorting: experts sort cards into groups that are similar and explain why they seem similar

CCT: (Cognitive complexity theory); a kind of user modelling which concentrates on learners, learning and transfer of learning from one system to another

CLG: (Command language grammar); describes the user interface in a grammar from the point of view of the user

Cognitive stumbling blocks: spots in the interface in which typical users tend to 'get stuck' (see also 'trouble spots', 'usability problems')

Conceptual walkthrough: diagnostic usability assessment tool, theory-driven, form-based thinking exercise

Confirmation study: performance-based assessment of usability defect seriousness, usually uncovered in a heuristic evaluation

Content analysis: analysis applied to written/printed material, concerned with measuring the amount of attention given to various concepts

Content validity: a measure of the degree to which the contents of a questionnaire, experiment or test measures what it intends

Contextual inquiry: method which aims to discover design opportunities by interacting with users and interviewing them at the same time during task performance. Subsequent flexible data analysis

Continuous variable: property whose measurement can take an infinite number of values

CORE: (Controlled requirements expression); a method which encourages analysts to consider their systems from different perspectives, including that of users

Correlation: degree of relationship between two or more variables; can be positive, negative or zero

Correlation coefficient: formula that helps predict value on one variable from knowledge of another, provided the relationship between these is known

CTA: (Cognitive task analysis); framework that specifies distributed processing architecture for human cognition and actions

Dependent variable: property on which an effect of an independent variable is measured

Design guidelines: Generic statements intended for a wide range of contexts; include recommendations, examples, lists and exceptions; must be translated into more specific statements before they can be applied

Design principles: general, quite vague statements which, like design guidelines, must be translated into operational, specific statements to be used

Design rules: design specifications for a particular application; require no further translation

Design standards: clear, but general statements about design requirements and constraints

Discrete variables: properties which can only take on certain fixed values

Ergonomics: the study of how people interact with their equipment and environment

Estimate: (= statistic); any measurable characteristic of a sample

ETSI: European Telecommunications Standards Institute

Experimental conditions: values of the independent variable which an experiment aims to measure

Extraneous variable: irrelevant properties which affect experimental results in ways not foreseen in the experimental design

Face validity: degree to which a test appears to measure what it claims to measure

Facilitator: statement/action that facilitates communication in an interview

Field experiment: intrusive study in the field where the experimenter manipulates parts of the environment and then observes responses

Field study: non-intrusive observation of phenomena in their normal context

Formative evaluation: evaluation of a computer system early in the design process

Global usability analysis: evaluation method which combines heuristic evaluations and task-completion to gain a global impression of system usability

GOMS: (Goals, operators, methods, selection rules); a theoretical approach to user modelling which predicts error-free performance of experts

HCI: Human–computer interaction

Heuristic evaluation: informal, subjective usability analysis of an interactive computer system, conducted from the perspective of intended, typical end users

HTA: (Hierarchical task analysis); empirical analysis of tasks, described in terms of goals, subgoals/subtasks, arranged in a hierarchy and expressed in terms of how a person performs a given task

Human factors: same as ergonomics, i.e. the study of how people interact with their equipment and environment

Hybrid studies: studies of an operational system involving both pen/paper and computer simulation

Hypothesis: testable proposition proposed as an explanation for the occurrence of some specified group of phenomena

Independent variable: property which can be can controlled in experiments

Inhibitor: statement/action that hinders communication in experiments

Interviewer bias: unwanted influence of an interviewer's views on interviewee responses

Iterative testing: test-modify-retest cycles

ISO: International Standards Organisation

Job analysis: specifies how a number of tasks carried out by specified users fit into the wider context of the person's job

KAT: (Knowledge analysis of tasks); a method for analysing task knowledge, producing a description of a person's knowledge of the current task

KLM: (Keystroke level model); a concept within the GOMS models; predicts task execution times for error-free behaviour at the level of keystroke analyses

KRG: (Knowledge representation grammar); a method for redescribing tasks in a particular format in a bottom-up fashion

Mean: arithmetic average of a set of measurements

Median: point above which one half of a set of scores and below which the other half of the scores lie in a distribution

Mental models: hypothetical constructs representing user-knowledge that guide behaviour from the owner's current understanding of the relevant domain

MHP: (Model human processor); a concept within the GOMS models; an ideal which allows the modeller to make predictions about the time it will take to carry out tasks

MIMS: series of handbooks published by the Intercontinental Medical Statistics Division

Mockup: full-scale simulation of a system, used particularly in the physical sphere

Mode: most frequently occurring score in a sample or population

Model: reduced-scale representation of some phenomenon

Multi dimensional scaling: expert judgments of similarity of items in a given task domain

Parameter: a measurable characteristic or property of a population

Pilot study: trial-run of an experiment or test, before a full test is run; allows the experimenter to adjust aspects of the experiment

Population: aggregate of people, objects or events

Pre-experimental training: experiment/task-specific training offered to experimental subjects to familiarize them with the experimental tasks before data logging is commenced

Primary user: (end) user who interacts with the system

Probing: method to encourage interviewee to expand on a statement

Protocol analysis: verbal record of performance, thoughts, ideas, by task performers, concurrent or retrospective

Prototype: incomplete simulation of a system, may be 'static' (= non-interactive, 'non-runnable') or 'dynamic' (= interactive, 'runnable')

PUM: (Programmable user model); an architecture, intended to be an analytical model of a computer user

Quasi-experiments: experiments in which the experimenter does not have full control over all variables

Question-asking protocols: method in which the analyst asks questions of a task performer during a task which is explicitly slowed down

Random sampling: sampling method by which every member of a population has an equal chance of being included in the sample

Range: distance from lowest to highest score in a distribution

Reliability: stability or replicability of sets of scores

Repertory grids: method for judging task similarity in which the analyst selects groups of task components and expert judges estimate similarity and differences between these

Research question: well-defined, precise statement of what is to be investigated in a study

Respondent: participant in a survey or interview

Sample: subgroup or subaggregate drawn by some appropriate method from a population

Sampling error: degree to which sampling scores differ from population scores

SDLC: systems development life cycle

Secondary user: receives output from the system but does not interact with it

Semi-structured interview: an interview in which some questions are pre-defined, but it also leaves scope for expansion and elaboration

SIGCHI: (Special Interest Group for Computer Human Interaction); a special interest group within the ACM (Association for Computing Machinery)

SRS: (System requirements specification); varies according to client's needs, standards, technical risks, motivation of stakeholders

Structured interview: all questions are fixed and arranged in a certain order for all respondents; most/all questions are close-ended

Subject: a test-user participating in an experiment

Summative evaluation: system evaluation at later stages in the development cycle

Survey: sampling method in which respondents fill in questionnaires

TA: (**Task analysis**): step-by-step identification of the demands a task makes of the operator, compared with operators' capabilities

TAKD: (Task analysis for knowledge description); a technique that aims to identify and make explicit all knowledge required for executing a certain task successfully and systematically

Task analysis plan: plan that outlines tasks to be analysed in a task analysis for all user groups

Task plan: describes how a person performs a given task

Tertiary user: 'background' people such as system maintenance staff, strategic IT staff

TKS: (Task knowledge structure); represents the knowledge people have of tasks they are currently doing or have previously learned

Unstructured interview: open ended interview in which only the overall goal is defined *a priori*

Usability: the ease of learning and using computer systems for novices as well as for continuing users and experts

Usability defects: problems in the software that hinder smooth interaction between user and computer (see also 'cognitive stumbling blocks')

Usability dimensions: quantifiable concepts which form the basis for defining usability goals

Usability evaluation: program of a series of tests, using different tools and techniques to measure system usability

Usability test and evaluation plan: plan specifying what is to be tested, when and costing of same

Usefulness: degree to which a system meets users' needs and task demands

User modelling: models of human behaviour to guide predictions, design choices and assumptions; make the reasoning underlying decisions explicit

User needs analysis: analysis of users and their tasks as they are currently done which are to be supported by the new system

User profile: describes a number of user characteristics that are relevant to the system and the specific target audience

Validity: assessment of the degree to which a test measures what it claims to measure

Wizard-of-Oz technique: simulation method in which two computers are connected and an experimenter types responses to subject entries which appear on the subject's screen; it looks as if the system is operational

Introduction 1

Man cannot discover new oceans unless
he has courage to lose sight of the
shore.

Andre Gide

Already in the late 1960s, it was predicted that 'the need for the future
is not so much for computer-oriented people as for people-oriented
computers' (Nickerson, 1969, p. 501). Time has amply demonstrated the
truth of this statement; the need to interact with computers is pervading
many aspects of daily life. Computers erected in hotel foyers, in
department stores, museums, on railway stations and in city malls
contain most of the information people need to find their way around a
place effectively, locating items, exhibits, conveniences, cafes and departments, determining the cost of fares and accessing timetables, and so
forth. People who are not a little bit computer literate will find themselves
severely hampered in their access to even relatively trivial information.
The observation also that human–computer interaction (HCI) is being
integrated into an increasing number of computer science curricula in the
world is encouraging. It demonstrates both a growing awareness of the
need to produce people-oriented computers and also that it is not a
simple matter to design systems that people like and find easy to use.

To someone whose area of expertise is the study of human behaviour,
it is not surprising that 'perfect' computers do not exist. Behavioural
scientists know well that human performance and behaviour is unreliable, full of surprises, mostly unpredictable, fascinating and so variable
that one cannot establish 'simple truths' about people that will hold in
a wide range of different conditions and circumstances. People are
sometimes tired, excited, bored, sloppy, or stressed and nervous; at other
times the same people are highly motivated, alert, curious, very careful,
attentive and accurate in their work; they daydream, are sleepy, feel
fantastic one day and terrible the next. Biological and motivational
variations within people make it difficult to predict the performance of
an individual on two different occasions, even when conditions, task
demands, stimulus materials and environment are held constant. Differences within and between people make it impossible with our present
knowledge to write cookbook recipes outlining how 'people' will respond
to particular sets of circumstances, certain types of stimuli or particular
user interfaces. The best we can do to ensure that our computer systems
are usable is to test them on real people who are representative of the
intended target audience.

'We cannot always predict how a system might affect people'

People, computers, and the way they interact are the foci of HCI. More precisely, HCI aims to understand how people interact with computers. In the long term, a better understanding of this can help us to describe, explain and predict how easy a particular future system might be to use even before it is designed and developed. This enables us to compare competing ideas of how future systems might look and be presented before a particular solution is committed to paper and a project is given the go-ahead. HCI seeks to develop theoretical models of human performance as well as devise effective tools with which to measure ease of use. While this book is mainly concerned with usability testing tools and techniques, some of the most important theoretical HCI models are also discussed.

1.1 A brief history of HCI

Back in the 1950s and 1960s, computer operators were part of the design team and adapted their behaviour to that required by the machine. Operators were mainly scientists, engineers and programmers who had a vested interest in becoming conversant with computers because these enabled them to process their research data, perform complex statistical and mathematical analyses, and write more programs. These early computers were slow, expensive and unreliable, so that interactive use was relatively rare.

Ergonomic considerations of computer consoles commenced in the second generation of computer dialogues (Shackel, 1959). However, these were mainly concerned with matching the physical aspects of computers to people's needs. The breakthrough later of batch processing systems forced designers to think about the human operator who, already then, was not necessarily the same person as the one who had designed the program. What is believed to be the first conference on HCI, the IBM scientific computing symposium on man-machine communication was held in 1965 in Yorktown. Batch processing opened computer use to a wider community which was less tolerant of technical problems. In this era, Mills (1967) remarked that 'the future is rapidly approaching when 'professional' programmers will be among the least numerous and least significant system users' (p. 168). In that same year, White (1967) noted that effective solutions to the problems of intelligible communications between the user and the computer are few and far between. 'The user of many systems gets the feeling that either the messages he receives were hung onto the system as an afterthought or that they were designed for the convenience of the system rather than the user' (p. 19).

Martin's (1973) 'Design of Man-Computer Dialogues' was the first book devoted to HCI in which the critical role of human factors considerations on the utility of computer systems was emphasized. Problems created by poor human factors principles were becoming more evident, arising from a concern with the growing casual and non-specialist user population in the early seventies, although the main emphasis was on programmers as computer users. This was still evident at the time of the first HCI conference in Gaithersburg, Maryland, 1982, at which SIGCHI was founded (Grudin, 1990). Papers pointing to lists of faults in many interactive systems appeared in increasing numbers (Chapanis, 1984; Ledgard et al., 1981; Nickerson, 1981). The personal computer came into vogue in the early 1980s by the availability of small low-cost stand-alone units with graphics capabilities which led to increasing use in psychological studies and to a boom in the associated literature. However, it quickly became apparent that psychology could not deliver ready answers to the many issues and problems emerging within HCI (Carroll et al., 1991). The most notable early contribution from psychology was the book by Card et al. (1983) which continues to be quoted widely and has formed the basis for much theoretical thinking in HCI. The decline in computer costs together with improved hardware and software capabilities led to increasing commercial interest in 'good' human factors as a marketing feature (Jervell and Olson, 1985; Perlman, 1984). The notion of a user interface quickly gained currency in a plethora of books, journals, symposia and conferences on HCI. During the 1980s attention gradually shifted from motor and perceptual aspects of HCI to focus on how people interact with computers. Rather than directing all attention to the individual user, researchers began to study how groups of people accomplish tasks, thereby widening the scope of HCI to a much broader framework which incorporates organizations, social and environmental aspects of computing (Bodker,

1989; Damodaran, 1991; Forester, 1989a; 1989b; Greif, 1991; Grudin, 1990; Malone, 1985; 1987; Ostberg and Chapman, 1988; Pratt, 1988) and the impact of computers on society at large (Forester, 1989c; Rosenberg, 1992).

1.2 Perspectives and methodology in HCI

It is often said that a 'complete understanding of HCI is a multidisciplinary enterprise' (Barnard, 1991a; Carroll, 1987; Grudin, 1990; Lewis, 1990; Norman and Draper, 1986), but scholars disagree with respect to how the field should develop to achieve this. Some hold that HCI is a discipline in its own right (Diaper, 1989) which, like a basic science, should ideally be theory-driven (Barnard, 1991b; Card *et al.*, 1983; Newell and Card, 1985; Polson, 1987; Polson and Lewis, 1990). Others argue that HCI is far too complex for any theory to be helpful (Landauer, 1991), that scientific theory is largely irrelevant to progress (Carroll *et al.*, 1991; Pylyshyn, 1991), or that progress comes from case studies based on observations of what users actually do (Holtzblatt and Jones, 1992; Whiteside and Wixon, 1987; Whiteside *et al.*, 1988). Given the divergence in opinions, people also disagree with respect to what should be studied, how it should be studied and indeed how HCI might contribute to producing better computer systems. Proponents of theory-driven approaches aim to model users, tasks, the knowledge required for users to complete their tasks, their task-performance, or the understanding users might have of their tasks and of the system with which they interact. Alternatively, they seek to represent the complexity of computer systems in a model, enabling them to predict the amount of learning users need to acquire to use a given system effectively. Theoretical models, it is hoped, will eventually have powerful predictive and analytic capabilities which ideally should enable designers to compare different systems or possible solutions before a particular design path is taken. Naturally, it is attractive to think that we might be able to demonstrate exactly where and how one system offers usability advantages over another, to represent relative complexity from the user's point of view and calculate user task-completion times before crucial design decisions are made. This may well be so ambitious as to prove an unattainable ideal. Even if it can be achieved, it will take a very long time before designers can rely on formal models alone in producing effective and efficient computer systems; the very best current theoretical models provide only a first, rough approximation of what will be needed to accomplish the level of understanding required to fulfil theoreticians' ambitions.

In the short term, HCI can help improve interactive computer systems in two important ways: first, it can guide a systematic, careful analysis of what information, tools and capabilities people need to achieve their goals, and second, it can provide tools and techniques with which to evaluate usability in an effort to remove flaws that hinder smooth interaction between people and computers. Usability evaluations can and do uncover many problems that would stand in the way of efficient and effective use of a given system, even though they are not driven by comprehensive theories, and although it is unclear just how the term 'usability' is derived (Whitefield *et al.*, 1991).

A model is a representation of some entity. In HCI the entities we deal with include the user, the designer, the system and the environment in which it is placed, the tasks it supports, and the manner in which these tasks may be accomplished. This chapter describes some user modelling approaches, and Chapter 2 discusses task modelling approaches. It is generally assumed that people store models of tasks and systems in memory. These so-called 'mental models' are believed to guide behaviour at the interface, helping people to predict and explain system behaviour from what they observe, from what they know or think they have learned. Mental models are apparently simpler than the entities they represent, and because they are incomplete, they tend to change over time as people's understanding of the entity evolves. This evolution is not a smooth, linearly incremental learning process, but one fraught with uncertainties, wrong inferences and confusions. Indeed, we know relatively little about the way knowledge increases, although researchers do agree that learning is inductive, takes place in a trial and error fashion (Einhorn, 1980) and that it is an iterative process (Hayes-Roth *et al.*, 1981).

Apart from knowing little about how mental models evolve, it is also difficult to tap into them and describe what they contain, how they are structured, accessed and used. This is partly because they are subjective, that is, 'owned' by individuals, partly because people do not have a great deal of insight into their own thought processes, and partly because mental models are hypothetical constructs. Much research is devoted to elucidate these and many other aspects of mental models, but this is not the place to delve into that literature which you may like to follow up yourself (Ackermann and Tauber, 1990; Booth, 1989, Ch. 4; Gentner and Stevens, 1983; Johnson-Laird, 1983; Kieras and Bovair, 1984; Norman, 1983).

The term 'mental model' is used interchangeably with 'conceptual model' and 'user model' in the literature, and opinions differ as to what exactly these terms mean (Booth, 1989; Murray, 1988). The term 'user model', for example, sometimes refers to a representation of the user embedded within the system (the designer's model of the user reflected in the system); it may represent an 'ideal model' which an 'ideal user' might hold, or it may refer to a model of the user's knowledge of the system and task (Booth, 1989; Hammond *et al.*, 1983). The most common use of the notion of 'user models' cover the designer's model of the user, the user's

1.3 User modelling in HCI

'Ideal case: system's model of the user = user's model of the system'

model of the task, the user's model of the system, and the system's model of the user.

User modelling can be useful in HCI in several ways, like matching system features to user needs, suggesting metaphors to improve user learning, guiding design decisions and making design assumptions and choices explicit, providing predictive evaluation of proposed designs, identifying different user populations, and guiding design of experiments and interpretation of the results. Not all of these objectives are achievable by using a single modelling technique, and different techniques yield different kinds of information. Modelling techniques provide means for quantifying certain aspects of HCI. Some models are performance oriented; others seek to map the functionality of user interfaces to assess user performance in ways other than task-completion times. They take the form of formal grammars for describing user tasks at the interface in the sense that they describe the interface using symbols, rules and conventions characteristic of a grammar. The number of rules needed to describe a given interactive task is taken to reflect the cognitive complexity associated with completing the task. There is a large family of techniques which have been used to represent the interaction, but we will only deal with the most prominent and best known of these to give you a flavour for user modelling. Descriptions of the techniques are quite brief; you should follow up any you might consider applying.

1.3.1 GOMS

A whole family of GOMS (goals, operators, methods and selection rules) models, developed by Card *et al.* (1980; 1983), characterize the knowledge necessary to make effective, routine use of software tools such as text editors. They aim to calculate and predict task-completion times for a range of interactive tasks varying in complexity. GOMS models apply Backus-Naur formalisms (BNF) to specify HCI, and a GOMS analysis involves writing a collection of methods that represent a task. Each method decomposes goals into subgoals and terminates in a sequence of operations which are primitive mental operations defined in a theory of user actions. Card and his colleagues (1983) argue that the design of an interactive system begins with a set of requirements which includes both structural constraints and performance goals. The designer's job is to specify a system that meets these requirements. The system specifications are readily checked against the structural constraints, but a description specification cannot elucidate the performance aspects of a system. Special models are therefore needed to portray performance. The authors argue that such models can be roughly categorized in terms of experimental models, database models and symbolic models. Experimental models portray the ways users interact with actual or simulated systems. Database models are stores of pre-measured or pre-calculated data so that performance values are obtained from look-up tables. Symbolic models are calculational, algebraic, or simulation models which can be represented on paper or in a computer and have no human component. In a symbolic model, performance values are obtained by computation. GOMS models are particularly useful for estimating the relative efficiency of competing systems designed for expert users doing repetitive tasks. One limitation is that they deal with error-free performance of experts which is not representative of novice behaviour: even experts make errors.

Within the GOMS philosophy it is assumed that users segment large tasks such as editing a manuscript into a sequence of small, discrete modifications such as 'delete a character' or 'insert a word'. These subtasks, called unit-tasks, are assumed to be quasi-independent. This means that their effects are approximately additive. Each operation is thus assumed to have a fixed execution time which can be summed to estimate task-completion times for various sequences of operations.

The model human processor (MHP) is an ideal which allows the modeller to make predictions about the time it will take to carry out tasks. It gives parameters for the capacity and speed of its constituent perceptual and information processors and their associated stores. The keystroke-level model (KLM) predicts task execution times for error-free behaviour. It does not attempt to predict the methods applied, but restricts itself to estimates of time. It comprises several primitive operators, and execution of a task is described in terms of a set of physical-motor operators. Execution time is simply the sum of time spent executing the various operator types. The model provides an efficient tool for calculating physical aspects of task execution including the mental preparation time associated with these physical acts. Examples of how to construct a GOMS analysis may be found in Kieras (1988), and applications of GOMS analyses, for example, in Gong and Elkerton (1990), Gray *et al.* (1990; 1992), John (1990), Lerch *et al.* (1989).

1.3.2 COGNITIVE COMPLEXITY THEORY (CCT)

CCT arose from the GOMS philosophy (Kieras and Polson, 1985; Polson, 1987; Polson and Kieras, 1985), but instead of focusing on detailed user performance, it concentrates on learning and transfer of knowledge from one system to another. In contrast to GOMS models, CCT examines learners rather than skilled users. Measures predict learning time rather than success in learning, or errors, and the conditions to which the model is applied are restricted in such a way as to limit naturally occurring problem-solving behaviour (Lewis, 1990). CCT makes no attempt to represent fundamental processes such as memory retrieval or reading comprehension because this would dramatically increase the complexity of the simulation (Kieras and Polson, 1985), and also because it is assumed that inclusion of these processes would provide little additional information about the human–computer interaction. CCT assumes that rules for learning are cognitive units which are all equally difficult to learn and are learned at a constant rate. It is also assumed that these rules are invariably recognized and applied in novel contexts. Quantitative models of users performing typical tasks are portrayed in the form of production systems (Anderson, 1981; 1983; Newell and Simon, 1972). A production system model generates a hypothesized series of cognitive operations and the sequence of user actions required to complete a given task being modelled. A production system is composed of a number of production rules and a working memory which contains representations of the system's current goals, inputs from the environment, and other information about the status of current actions. A production rule is a condition-action pair presented in an IF...THEN format where IF is the condition and THEN the action. If the condition is true, the production is said to fire and the action is executed. The assumption that productions are learned at a constant rate holds only for constrained learning conditions which are not typical for new users in new applications. CCT uses production rules to assess the complexity of user interfaces by counting the number of rules required in the new as opposed to the old technical domain (Johnson *et al.*, 1988). Some experimental evidence suggests that CCT models fit actual tasks completed by human subjects on a computer system (Polson, 1987; Polson *et al.*, 1987; Polson and Kieras, 1985; Polson *et al.*, 1986), although others are critical of it, arguing that counting the number of rules cannot explain all the problems users have in early encounters with a system because the type and content of knowledge is as important as the amount (Knowles, 1988).

1.3.3 COMMAND LANGUAGE GRAMMAR (CLG)

A CLG representation is a description of the user interface from the point of view of the user. Moran (1981) called CLG a grammar because it can be used to describe the user's conceptual model of the system in a fashion that is useful during the systems design process. An important feature of a formal grammar is that it is not restricted to physical inputs at the interface but can include a representation of the cognitive actions associated with the input (Fountain and Norman, 1985). Structurally, CLG specifies three components of the user interface: the conceptual, the communication and the physical component. The conceptual component contains the abstract concepts around which the system is organized; the communication component contains the command language and the interactive dialogue, and the physical component contains the actual devices with which the user interacts physically (Fig. 1.1). The CLG representation is made up of a sequence of description levels where each level is a refinement of previous levels. In this fashion, the task level describes the task domain addressed by the system, and the semantic level describes the concepts represented. These two, the task and semantic levels, describe the conceptual component of CLG. The communication component is made up of a syntactic level describing the command-argument structure and an interaction level describing the dialogue structure. The physical component comprises the spatial arrangement of the input/output devices and display graphics, and all remaining physical features are described at the device level.

Conceptual   Task level
                 Semantic level

Communication   Syntactic level
                 Interaction level

Physical   Spatial layout level
                 Device level

Figure 1.1: The level of structure of CLG as presented by Moran (1981 p. 6).

The level structure is imposed to separate the conceptual model of a system from its command language and to illustrate the relationship between them. The levels are arranged such that they map onto one another in sequence, thus enabling a top-down design approach. The conceptual model of the system is created first, followed by specification of the command language and, finally, the display layout. CLGs have been applied to represent the complexity of different interactive dialogues (Moran, 1981; Payne and Green, 1983; Reisner, 1981; 1982; 1987). Reisner, for example, (1981) showed how CLG could be used to derive a user-action language, that is, the sequence of cursor movements, key presses and so on, used to provide input into a computer system. Two colour graphics systems which differed in the user interface, but had identical functions, were compared in an assessment of usability of the two designs. Using CLG, it was possible to predict the relative ease of specific user functions, and later to substitute and confirm these predictions in laboratory experiments. Reisner used a BNF notation adapted to measures of complexity of an interface, mainly by counting the number of rules required to produce the necessary actions. This is similar to the approach taken in CCT.

1.3.4 TASK ACTION GRAMMAR (TAG)

A more recent grammar model is the task action grammar (TAG) proposed by Payne and Green (1986; 1989). TAG is concerned with the learnability of systems and the mapping of concepts. It claims to model competence rather than performance. It intends to provide a formalism for modelling the mental representation of an interaction language, allowing formal specification of that language (Johnson, 1992). However, as a competence model, TAG may not necessarily predict the performance of actual behaviour, but rather the knowledge an ideal user may have of the language. Since performance is a measure of some behaviour, and TAG does not translate into predictions of actual behaviour, the model cannot be validated by empirical observations of behaviour. It has two major advantages over other grammar models. First, the representation of what gets written into actions is shifted from machine commands to 'tasks' that the analyst assumes are perceived by the user. Hence, TAG concentrates on the cognitive aspects of the language. Second, the syntactic and semantic aspects of the interface language are aligned in the sense that semantic relations go hand-in-hand with syntactic relations. This means that the sequence of objects or statements is always the same, for example, 'find word', 'find file', 'find folder'. By imposing consistency, TAG aims to enable designers of interaction languages to identify errors of inconsistency in their design. Syntactic and semantic bases are derived from an analysis of the user's assumed understanding of the relationship between tasks to be carried out and commands required to effect these. Representations of the semantics of tasks result in predictions about ease of use and learnability based on measures of consistency within the interface language (Simon, 1988). Measures of complexity are derived by counting the number of rules required to rewrite tasks into actions.

1.3.5 COGNITIVE TASK ANALYSIS (CTA)

In an attempt to isolate ways in which the various interrelationships between theory, cognitive phenomena and system design may be made explicit, Barnard (1987) has presented a framework that specifies a distributed processing architecture for human perception, cognition and actions. The aim is to provide an explicit and integrated set of information processing resources. Barnard focuses on the nature, organization and function properties of conceptual processes together with their associated memory structures. This model could be regarded as an enhanced MHP as described by Card and his associates (1983), except that their model focuses on the properties of the processes rather than on functions. Barnard's model can be utilized for a cognitive task analysis that has a common basis for exploring the demands for representing knowledge as well as the information processing constraints involved in the use of the model. Within this framework the processes of perception, cognition and action are assumed to lend themselves to a useful analysis in terms of discrete and well-defined information modules. It is also assumed that mental representations stored in memory records can be separated from context-specific processes that construct and utilize these episodic memory records. Finally, the model assumes that the human cognitive system is highly capable of parallel information processing. The human information processing system can thus be partitioned into functionally independent subsystems each of which is devoted to a specific processing domain. In particular, a distinction is drawn between sensory, representational and effector subsystems. Sensory subsystems process incoming sense data and transform these into specific mental 'codes' representing the structure and content of incoming data. These encodings are handled by other subsystems that specialize in processing higher-level representations with specific properties. Propositional and implicational subsystems support the processing of more abstract semantic and conceptual representations. Effector subsystems process output from representational subsystems and compute appropriate instructions to control motor output such as articulation of a word or movement of limbs. Preservation of memory traces takes place in parallel with the relevant subsystem's processes. Hence, at this level of analysis, the human information processing system is described as sets of functionally independent subsystems.

Any given subsystem can only process information represented in a specific mental code. A single primary process, the copy process, creates an episodic record of all information input to the particular subsystem. Information is then recorded by a secondary process. Each such secondary process may be conceptualized as a functionally independent production system. If a particular pattern of conditions is met in the pattern of data input to the subsystem, then a particular process transforms it into an output representation. There is no general-purpose central working memory shared by the different resources, nor is there an executive controlling the pattern of activity. The subsystems are viewed as self-controlling via representations computed by specific processes and passed from one subsystem to another in a data network.

As a descriptive approximation of complex cognitive functioning, Barnard and his colleagues have shown how experimental results can be retrofitted within the framework of this model (Barnard *et al.*, 1982; Grudin and Barnard, 1985). Yet, it is unclear, as Barnard also says, just how such principles could be of practical utility outside the context of laboratory research.

1.3.6 PROGRAMMABLE USER MODELS (PUMs)

A PUM (Young *et al.*, 1989) is an architecture, intended to be an analytical model of a computer user, which in theory enables the designer to program simulated user performance in a range of tasks. The architecture is thus psychologically constrained, and provides a way of assisting the designer to consider the usability of a proposed user interface. This focus on usability as well as on the computer enables the designer to ascertain whether a user would be able to run, or execute, the program. PUMs do not attempt to calculate user performance in the manner the GOMS models do; rather, they are approximations, providing tools for building a model of users. PUMs are still at the research stage, and it is not entirely clear what they are, what they include, and what they might contribute to design. However, because they offer a new perspective which allows designers to incorporate the user side into a software program, we are likely to learn a great deal more about PUMs as the concept matures.

1.4 Systems analysis, design and HCI

Many different systems analysis and design methodologies exist which may be classified in numerous ways (Benyon, 1992a; Burch, 1992; Johnson, 1992, Ch. 6), but so far little attention has been devoted to data capture techniques (Diaper and Addison, 1992) although the traditional focus on the technical aspects of computers (Carter, 1991) is now seen by some to be inadequate (Gentner and Grudin, 1990; Winograd, 1990). Yet, although it is generally recognized that there is an urgent need to integrate HCI into information systems design (Benyon, 1992b; Burch, 1992; Damodaran *et al.*, 1988; Sutliffe, 1989), it is not clear how this might be done, although promising attempts are being made to try (Lim and Long, 1992a; 1992b).

Principles guiding the systems design and development process from a usability point of view have been summarized by Gould and Lewis (1985) who recommend

1. early focus on users and tasks;
2. empirical measurement;
3. iterative design.

Regardless of how one chooses to decompose the systems design and development cycle, these principles should always be adhered to in user-centred design. When it comes to breaking down the process into distinct phases to make it more manageable, there are many ways to 'skin a cat'. Gould (1988), for example, views the design/development process as a set of four phases, namely the gearing-up phase, the initial design phase, the iterative development phase and the system installation phase. In the gearing-up phase you learn about related systems, about user interface guidelines and standards as well as company policies and styles. During the initial design phase the user needs analysis is conducted, and

'Smart technology does not always impress users. . .'

a usability test and evaluation plan is developed. The iterative development phase focuses on repeated and continual usability testing until usability goals have been reached. Finally, Gould discusses a system installation phase which centres on techniques for installing the system, introducing it to users, employing the training materials and ascertaining the level of user acceptance.

The process model selected for this book is conceptually very similar to Gould's, but it uses labels describing the various phases which are perhaps more closely aligned to those adhered to in many systems design and analysis models and methods. It is a slightly modified version of one proposed by Shackel (1991a). As it is presented here, it divides the system development cycle into four phases, namely: feasibility, research, development and operation. Gould's 'gearing up' phase is very similar to the 'feasibility' phase described here; his 'initial design' phase is similar to the 'research' phase; the 'iterative development' almost identical to the 'development' phase, and Gould's 'system installation phase' is much like the 'operation' phase, except perhaps that the 'operation' phase also allows for initial investigations in the case of designing a follow-on, replacement system. Shackel's original model comprised five phases by incorporating a 'prototype' phase between the 'development' and 'operation' phases. It was decided that prototyping, both with rapid prototyping tools available (Hartson and Smith, 1991; Hix, 1990; 1991; Rantanen, 1991) and by applying inexpensive methods such as pen/paper studies, can and should be integrated into all phases at relevant points rather than being confined to a particular point in the development cycle. This model is similar to models of structured systems analysis and design models (Downs *et al.*, 1988; Page-Jones, 1988) and comparable to the systems development life cycle (SDLC) model described by Burch (1992), for example, which distinguishes between front-end and back-end phases. Front-end phases focus on system planning, analysis, design and evaluation, and back-end phases are concerned with installation and maintenance. Front-end phases encompass systems planning (feasibility), systems analysis (research), systems design (development), and a distinct 'evaluation' phase, and the back-end phases are similar to the operation phase. In the usability model used here, evaluation takes place throughout the entire process.

1.4.1 THE FEASIBILITY PHASE

The feasibility phase is the point at which the potential success of a proposed system is investigated. Some design methodologies distinguish between several feasibility factors such as technical, economic, legal, operational and schedule feasibility, each of which is investigated and reported in separate documents (Burch, 1992, Ch. 1). Usability might be regarded as yet another factor which overlaps with several of the others mentioned by Burch, except that the user's view is always central to usability considerations. A feasibility study in the usability framework may start with a bright idea that you want to pursue. You might want to offer support in an area of work or leisure in which no computer system exists, or you might be asked to replace an existing system. The purpose of the feasibility phase varies according to whether a system is to be upgraded, or whether you are trying to convince someone to fund the development of a brand new system (more detail about this in Chapter 7). During the feasibility phase a human factors investigation aims to define who the proposed system would be for, what tasks it should support, how it would fit into an existing organizational or other environment, what technology could or should be used, and what the system would cost to develop and install. The outcome of a feasibility study is a document or set of documents that outlines the system in broad terms and gives enough information on which to base a decision to go-ahead or to drop the brilliant idea altogether. The feasibility phase is thus the point at which a cost/benefit analysis should show how likely it is that the proposed system would be popular with target users and cost effective to use.

The cost/benefit analysis should stipulate the relative cost, merits and disadvantages of developing the system using different technologies; it should state how each technology would affect usage and usability in the short as well as in the long term. From a programming point of view, as well as from considerations of hardware costs, it might be more economical to require users retrieving data to enter simple commands from a keyboard rather than walking them through several menu layers presented on a touch screen. However, if the users need to wear thick gloves when they interact with the database, or if they have only one hand free with which to operate the system at that point of completing their task, then you can be sure that they will not want to fiddle with small keys on a keyboard. If you persevere and produce your keyboard command-driven system, chances are that it will be under-used, abused or not used at all once installed in the work place. Therefore, if you want to secure your system's longevity, you stand a better chance if you consider who the users are and how your system will fit into the work schedule in your cost/benefit analysis. Savings in programming time or hardware costs may not be worth the cost of producing a system people will refuse to use. So, consider carefully what you are proposing to give your target audience. Empirical measurement may be done at this stage, but because there is no commitment to go ahead with the system as yet, the tendency is to rely on more informal investigative tools.

1.4.2 THE RESEARCH PHASE

Once it has been decided that benefits outweigh the costs and that the proposed system should go ahead, the research phase commences. This is the point at which a thorough user needs analysis (Chapter 2) is carried out, and hardware/software platforms are selected on the basis of the outcome of this analysis. Typical user tasks are walked through in detail, and the global outline of the system should be drafted. The research phase is the point at which controversial issues that affect decisions about the design, layout, technology, hardware or software platform need to be clarified. The type of interactive dialogue to be employed is decided upon in the light of the tasks to be supported, the end user audience, and the location in which the system will reside. The level of freedom your design team has in deciding how the system should look and feel, what type of interaction it should use and so on, depends on a large number of factors, including company policies, budgetary constraints, and the need to fit in with existing systems. An organization might be committed to a particular presentation style, reflected in the structure and layout of the system and manuals as well as its choice of hardware. Some of these factors are obviously beyond your control, so you need to know the limitations within which you are to work before you launch into a research programme designed to define optimal system solutions and set the direction for the development of the system.

Usability goals are established and a usability test and evaluation plan is devised during the research phase (Chapter 8); specific issues are also most conveniently removed from the system context and investigated, perhaps in laboratory experiments (Chapter 6). At the end of the research phase, you will have a very accurate picture of the users, their system-relevant tasks, and the way in which the tasks are completed in the current system, be this system sets of manual procedures or a computer to be replaced.

1.4.3 THE DEVELOPMENT PHASE

During the development phase, iterative usability testing continues as per the usability test and evaluation plan. You should refer back to the user needs analysis at points earmarked and agreed by the project team. Regular reviews of progress in the systems development, and achievements along the usability dimension should be integrated into this phase. In project reviews, the project team meets to discuss how it is going. The status of the emerging system is assessed and compared with the project plan, the project time line, the functional specification and the user needs analysis. Review meetings are extremely important for several reasons. First, it is an appropriate forum in which to identify different possible and equally attractive, but perhaps incompatible, solutions and walk through these to assess their impact on other parts of the system. Second, review meetings are a forum for reaching agreement on occasional, unforeseen issues and problems, and for making explicit the course to be taken in the next phase. Third, regular meetings help to establish how the development is faring with respect to the time frame and the budget allocated. Fourth, they offer an opportunity to invite task experts, who may not be part of the project team, to comment and ask questions. Finally, regular review meetings help to tie the project team together as a 'proper' team. Unless all team members feel they 'own' the system, it can be very difficult to maintain a high level of co-operation, motivation and interest until the project is completed.

Given that the purpose of review meetings is to inform everyone concerned about all aspects of progress, it is valuable if you can also convince the management of the organization for which the system is intended, to be present at least at some of these meetings. Senior executives are very busy people, so you could, for example, invite them along to the first part of the meeting and provide a kind of 'live' executive summary. Alternatively, you might only invite them along when significant milestones have been reached, or you could stage special small presentations put together especially for the senior management.

1.4.4 THE OPERATION PHASE

The operation phase encompasses the fine-tuning of the system, co-ordinating it with user manuals, tutorials, help systems, and so forth. All components are assembled, tested as a whole, packaged, delivered and installed at the customer's premises. It also includes the day-to-day running, reliability and performance checks of the system. At this point, follow-up studies would be in place to give you feedback on how well your team achieved its target and the level of success of the system. A great deal can be learned from such post-installation studies but they are, unfortunately, frequently a luxury which few can really afford (Stewart, 1991a). Delivery, installation and implementation policies and procedures are important components in the overall project. However, they fall beyond the scope of this book and are therefore not discussed.

1.5 What is usability?

My introduction to computers can only be described as brutal! It was the kind of frustrating, confusing and intimidating experience that could mark one for life – maybe it has. After several days of trying to run a statistical analysis, I finally thought I had succeeded in compiling the FORTRAN program which the machine had patiently and persistently rejected without comment, when the terminal went clunk, clunk, clunk.

I held my breath in eager anticipation, but to no avail; after several minutes in suspense, it delivered a long list of error messages none of which made sense to me, culminating in a statement saying 'Limit of 10 errors exceeded. Replacement operator requested.' I was ready to give up there and then, and had not my thesis depended upon that and many subsequent analyses, I would have thrown in the towel or smashed the terminal.

The system, a Burroughs 6700, was similar to other mainframes at the time. It had no user interface at all; one modified lines in an existing program to suit the datafile to be analysed. I knew nothing about FORTRAN programming and was therefore ignorant about the importance of preceding certain lines within the program by exactly x spaces, about how the FORMAT statements work, about arrays and system variables, runner files, batch files, and so on. There were no user manuals, no help functions, no listing of numbers quoted as part of the error messages, and feedback from the system was either uninterpretable or insulting; the system gave absolutely nothing away that could have assisted a new user to gain some understanding of it! At the same time, the program was a very powerful and adaptable one – once you knew what to do and what the lines referred to. Someone had brought it back from another university and changed it to fit local purposes, but that person had long since left the sacred halls of learning, so no-one could help. Trial and error, dogged perserverance, numerous 'AHA' experiences, and sheer stubbornness finally brought results and my analyses

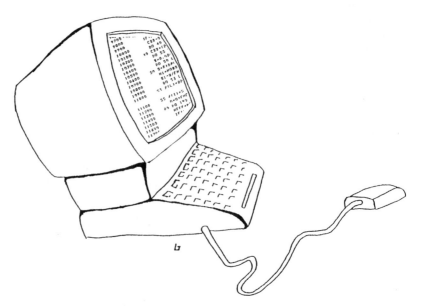

'The parsimony of FORTRAN may well be a virtue for experts. . .'

were duly processed, but by then I had wasted seven weeks of an awfully crammed honours year.

In that situation, I had plenty of task knowledge; I knew precisely how to perform the analysis manually, but this did not help very much in my efforts to learn how to deal with the computer. At the same time the system was very useful in the sense that it could handle highly complex data analyses; once it had been mastered, it was also easy to use. However, one could not by any stretch of the imagination have called it usable for non-experts.

The notion of usability is sometimes taken to mean both ease of learning and ease of use but, as Booth (1989) has pointed out, the two do not necessarily go hand-in-hand. A system can be easy to use without being easy to learn, as my experiences with statistical analyses suggests, and it can also be easy to learn but difficult to use. Many hierarchical menu systems do, for example, not allow users to enter keywords or search through a list of keywords describing the system contents, but force them to navigate screen-by-screen from main menu to target datum. Experienced users of such a system might tend to press keys in rapid succession without looking at the screen because they know what to enter at every level of the menu hierarchy. Suddenly they find that they are not where they intended to be, so – back to the main menu and start again. Systems such as menu-driven ones that hold the newcomer's hand, but fail to allow shortcuts for experts, can be very easy to learn but be cumbersome and obstructive to use. A usable system would, thus, be one which is both easy to use over time with increasing experience and easy to learn to use.

1.5.1 DEFINITIONS OF USABILITY

Eason (1984) has suggested that the major indicator of usability is whether a system or facility is being used. The Burroughs system was being used, despite its prohibitive lack of user support, and despite the fact that usage was discretionary; no one was forced to use it. However, that is probably one notable exception; generally, when people have a choice as to whether or not to use a given system and the system in question is as awful to learn to use as that one, it will never become popular. Therefore, perhaps a definition of usability should allow for both ease of learning and ease of use to represent what we want it to cover. Shackel (1986; 1991b) proposes that 'the capability in human functional terms to be used easily and effectively by the specified range of users, given specified training and user support, to fulfil the specified range of tasks, within the specified range of environmental scenarios' (p. 24) portrays a usable computer system. Chapanis (1991b) echoes this definition which is modelled upon Shackel (1981) by stating that 'the usability of a computer is measured by how easily and how effectively it can be used by a specific set of users, given particular kinds of support, to carry out a fixed set of tasks, in a defined set of environments' (pp. 362–63). So, there is some agreement that usability involves users, users' tasks, users' tools, and the environment in which users function. The major advantages of both of these definitions are that they allow usability to be expressed in quantifiable, and therefore in measurable, terms. Shackel (1986; 1991b) proposes four dimensions of usability – effectiveness, learnability, flexibility and attitude – all of which can readily be integrated into distinct usability goals and criteria.

These definitions are not the only operational usability statements around (Bennett, 1984; Booth, 1989; Dumas, 1989; Gould, 1988; Gould and Lewis, 1985), but they are useful for the purpose of this book which attempts to highlight the importance of specifying measurable entities. In discussing the usability dimensions identified by Shackel, Booth (1989) argues that flexibility is 'particularly difficult to specify, communicate and test in a real product development environment' (p. 111), and suggests that it be dropped from the list. However, it is reasonable to argue that one should select the dimensions that are appropriate to the users, the particular system and the environment to be considered in specified usability testing circumstances. Sometimes, flexibility is not the most important issue, or it might not be specifiable for a given system, as indeed Booth suggests; at other times it may be central to an evaluation. The same is true for other dimensions. Learnability, for example, is easy to measure, but it may not always be an appropriate measure of usability. When testing, say, a help system, users should not have to 'learn' to use help; here, one would primarily be concerned about the 'effectiveness' of help, that is, the ease with which relevant help information is located, correctly interpreted and applied to solve the problem at hand successfully. If help information fails to assist users in trouble, it does not matter how easy the help system is to navigate through or how well users can paraphrase the information it gives. It is suggested therefore, that one should select the usability dimensions that are situationally most appropriate when planning and conducting usability studies.

1.5.2 USABILITY VERSUS USEFULNESS

Booth (1989) suggests that the notion of usefulness be incorporated into the definition of usability. He reasons that 'if the functions of the system do not match the users' goals in their everyday work environments, then the system will not be used' (p. 112). No-one could disagree with that, but it is argued here that usefulness differs from usability and should be assessed independently. A given system is useful to the extent that it covers adequately the range of tasks it is intended to support. Now, whereas usability should be quantified, it could be argued that it does not seem to make sense to define usefulness in the same terms. Would an organization really be satisfied with a system, for example, that covers '85% of the tasks it is required to support'? It seems doubtful. Coverage of tasks, identification of task boundaries and limits should be specified very precisely and agreed to before a project is commenced. Such coverage should not be measured in the same fashion as the attainment of usability criteria. Tasks intended to be supported by a new system should be covered 100% – nothing less! Attainment of this is measured by reference to the system specifications – not by testing user performance as is the case for usability tests.

Usability is related to human performance in the specific tasks supported by the computer system and to the user's attitude towards the system, but usefulness is judged by different criteria. These are related to performance in the wider sense that they take into account the entire job of the people whose tasks are incorporated into a computer system. Often, there are links between tasks that users perceive to be different, perhaps because they are performed at different times, by different people, or in various departments in the work place. This sometimes leads to duplication of data entry operations and redundancies in work practices. However, where two or more tasks carried out in a work environment rely on the same data, the tasks in which these data are handled should be linked in the computer system and require only a single data entry point. Users may not necessarily perceive the need for such links, especially when the data involved are entered and accessed or manipulated by different individuals. In order to achieve optimal system usefulness, it is therefore important to understand how the system fits into the entire organization. This level of understanding may well go beyond that of individual users or specifying isolated user tasks. Hence, if 'usefulness' were to be be assessed by asking users' opinions about the adequacy with which their tasks are supported, this may not give a complete picture of the situation. Even when users know that certain data are used elsewhere in the organization, or they think of two tasks performed by themselves as separate, independent entities, they rarely consider that these could be linked in a computer system. If such links are not made, users might rate the system very highly even though the technological capabilities to connect different tasks have not been exploited. Usefulness has, therefore, something to do with meeting users' needs by covering the tasks specified in specification documents, and facilitating work through linking tasks that share/depend upon the same data being handled by the same users, by other users who rely on outputs from the system in question, or by other systems employed in the same organization.

Usability is thus expressed in quantifiable, measurable terms by which to assess when a 'good' system is 'good enough'; usefulness is a separate entity which is defined in the requirements capture stage in terms of the tasks to be supported and explicit links between tasks, the attainment of which must be 100% unless renegotiated and modified during the system development process.

1.6 Why bother with usability testing?

Since 31 December 1992, European legislation requires hardware and software to meet certain standards with respect to systems usability and usefulness (Stewart, 1991b). Software and other IT (information technology) products which fail to meet the legislative requirements are thus unacceptable. Although it will be difficult to demonstrate that a particular system does not meet such requirements, some lawsuits will inevitably result. For anyone working in the IT industry and thinking of exporting their wares to Europe, usability should therefore be of concern. Indeed, Chapanis (1991a) describes several instances in which computer companies have been involved in – and have lost – court cases. In one such case, a company was awarded $US 286 000 in 'regular and consequential damages and $US 2 000 000 in punitive damages because a computer system didn't perform as expected' (Bigelow, R.P. 1981, cited in Chapanis, 1991a, p. 49). This is not an isolated case and, with the introduction of legislation, more such cases will emerge in which the IT industry will have raised false hopes among customers. Since the committee formulating the legislation is proceeding from recommendations of the ISO (International Standards Organisation), it is likely that the European model will soon become applicable to the whole world.

Legal requirements aside, usability evaluation ought to be of importance to designers, manufacturers, marketing departments, sales force and customers alike (Chapanis, 1991b). Designers/developers will not be able to find guidelines that cover every new technology and every type of system. Yet it is reasonable to assume that they want to produce good and usable systems. Even when guidelines can be found and they are applied, they do not guarantee that the resulting system is usable. Testing is therefore essential. Manufacturers should want to know that a product developed in their plant will be better than competing products and surpass the quality of its predecessors. They should also know and be able to describe how it will outperform existing products. Without usability test findings, they cannot substantiate claims of improvements in the usability arena. Marketing and sales are assisted by ensuring that products do live up to promises made in advertising which shape customer expectations. The notion of 'intuitive' systems that are 'easy to use' or 'user friendly' computers that 'require no training' is over-used, or even abused, as marketing catch-phrases (Jervell and Olson, 1985); in fact, systems rarely live up to these promises. A system that has undergone extensive testing and for which realistic promises can therefore be made with respect to usability could make life much more comfortable

for the marketing and sales force than one for which no test results exist
to support the sales talk. The ability to back up one's claims with genuine
data lends an air of respectability to one's words; it puts one in a
comfortable position of talking indisputable facts rather than nurturing
fictitious hopes. Customers should be interested in the outcomes of
usability evaluations, simply because they are the ones who will be paying
for the systems. They should want to make sure that their decision to buy

'Empty arm waving is not convincing in computer marketing'

one system or another is based on sound evidence supporting the claims made in advertisements.

1.6.1 PURPOSES OF USABILITY TESTS

Assessments of usability may serve a number of different purposes, and the purpose of a given evaluation determines the kinds of tasks, tests, performance measures and attitude scales, interviews or surveys one decides to apply. However, the purpose of any type of usability study must rest with those who perform them. Without a clear purpose and objective, a testing program has no focus, and it will not be certain exactly what, if anything, was gained by it.

One purpose might be to improve an existing product. Without knowing where in a system users run into problems or what kinds of problems they are likely to encounter in the existing product, one has little hope of improving anything. Or, if improvements result, one has little hope of understanding and demonstrating why the new system turned out to be better. This means that next time round, the project team starts from scratch again. Careful analysis of usability, using appropriate methods and asking relevant, answerable questions, should reveal usability defects and therefore give a good indication of what needs to be changed to make an existing system even better in the next version. Alternatively, a usability evaluation may be performed to compare two or more products. If you are in the business of buying systems, or if your next project is to be modelled on the best current system available, you would be interested to find out whether system A, B, C, or D is easiest to use, and perhaps whether system B is easier than system D, and so on. Examples in which two or more aspects of systems are compared may be found in many papers (Card *et al.*, 1990; Chapanis, 1991b; Ledgard *et al.*, 1981; Reisner, 1981; Roberts and Moran, 1983). Finally, the objective of a usability evaluation may be to measure a system against a standard or a set of guidelines. This requires that the standard itself be measurable and able to be applied. Whatever the reason for, or purpose of, a usability study or evaluation may be, it must be clear what is done, why it is done and what might be gained from it.

RDS, GUIDELINES, PRINCIPLES AND DESIGN RULES

eful if someone could produce an 'encyclopaedia of the and behaviour' in which one could find ready answers to stions that make it necessary to conduct usability studies. design standards are both widespread and useful in the sense give a clear indication of design requirements and constraints to be met, either via contracts or through legislation. Enforced in this way, they are prescriptive rather than descriptive and performative rather than informative (Smith, 1988). Even standards that are known to be less than optimal may be useful. Many types of keyboards have, for example, been designed, tested and found to be superior to the traditional Qwerty type, yet, it seems that the Qwerty keyboard layout is with us to stay despite its limitations, simply because it is so widespread and has been there for more than a century. Hardware standards tend to be related to human physiology. The optimal size of characters on a screen is determined by the limits to human vision; the best shape of keys on a keyboard, and the size and tilt of the keyboard are determined by the anatomy and muscles of fingers, hands, arms, and of human movement, and so on.

By contrast, software standards rely almost exclusively on psychology. Much more is known about physiology than about psychology, and it is very hard to translate what we know into something useful. Also, little is known about the limitations or boundaries of existing knowledge. It is not always clear when what one knows does not apply. This makes it very difficult to generate good, reliable standards for the design of software. Smith (1986; 1988) has drawn a number of comparisons between hardware and software design which show why it is difficult to establish software design standards because of this reliance on psychology. Hardware designers whose creativity is limited by technology and costs may ask 'can this be done?'; software designers would ask 'would it be most sensible to do it this way?', relying on their understanding of human behaviour. Important design features are usually observable and may be tried out by people quite easily on mockups, whereas many software features are hidden and their effect on the overall interactive process may be much more difficult to ascertain. Consequently, hardware design standards are clear and specific whereas software standards are vague and general. Yet, there is a clear trend towards establishing standards and even legislation for software requirements (Abermethy, 1984; McGregor, 1992).

If standards are difficult to establish, then what about guidelines and principles? Let us perhaps first distinguish between these concepts. Design principles are quite vague statements. For example, Gould's (1983) call for 'early focus on users', 'interactive design', 'early testing' and 'iterative design', are some of the design principles applied in user-centred design. These must be translated into something more concrete before they can be applied to a particular system because they are almost completely open to interpretation.

Design guidelines are generally stated recommendations with examples, added explanations and other commentary, selected, and perhaps modified, for any particular system application, and adopted by agreement among people concerned with interface design. Several sets of design guidelines exist (eg. Galitz, 1989; Hutchins *et al.*, 1985; Rubenstein and Hersch, 1984; Smith and Mosier, 1986). These are often based on authors' experiences, derived from 'a little common sense plus placing a value on serving the user well' (Newell and Card, 1985, p. 214). Others are purely conceptual discussions of display design in general (Cakir *et al.*, 1980; Miller and Thomas, 1977; Rosenthal, 1979). The lists of rules by which guidelines are generated are commonly too specific to a particular type of display or system to be applicable to other types of systems. Alternatively, they refer to details of a display without adequately addressing the display as a whole. Conceptual guidelines tend to be too general to be directly applicable to the design of a given display (Tullis, 1983a). For example, Smith and Mosier's (1984) guideline number 2.3.1 states with respect to consistency in format that designers should 'adopt a consistent organization for the location of various display features, insofar as possible, for all displays'. They provide examples, comments, exceptions, and cross-references to other guidelines to illustrate how it might apply. Software design standards are also generally stated requirements, but in contrast to guidelines, standards are imposed in some formal way such as by contract or legislation. For example, the US Department of Defense MIL-STD-1472, 5.15.3.2.1 states that (with respect to standardization) 'the content of displays within a system shall be presented in a consistent, standardized manner'. Design rules are a series of design specifications for a particular system application, stated specifically so that they do not require any further interpretation by designers. For example, the requirement to 'put frame !D at left in line 1' and to 'put body of display in lines 4–19' (Smith, 1988, p. 881) are typical design rules. Design rules are often captured in style guides, sometimes developed in-house, which specify how software should look and behave.

Like principles, guidelines must be translated in the process of describing specific design rules which would then be reviewed and approved to constitute detailed design specifications for a particular application. The role of guidelines is to highlight the issues concerning people which should be considered in the design, but they are not design rules. Sometimes, this distinction is not recognized, and designers may be disappointed to find general advice (Mosier and Smith, 1986) and consequently they reject guidelines. Another danger is that they may assume that designers know something which they do not. Smith (1986; 1988) argues that when you cannot rely on rules, the best you can do is to use your own judgment: 'where we cannot discover absolute truth by experimentation, we must try to establish a pragmatic vision of truth by informed judgment' (1988, p. 885). It would be better, then, to rely on the informed judgment contained in guidelines, incomplete, vague and often contradictory as they are, than on the less informed intuition of individual designers for achieving good usable computer systems. If applied sensibly, guidelines can be quite useful (Reisner, 1987).

Some people, who do not have a background in experimental design, tend to believe that usability evaluation is a waste of time ('useless'), that it does not provide useful information ('too little'), ('too expensive') (Belotti, 1988), that recommendations arising from usability evaluations cannot be accommodated within the project ('too late'), ('too cumbersome') (Melkus and Ferres, 1988), and that evaluation is what you do just before the product is released in the market place ('final gloss').

1.7 Myths about usability evaluation

Admittedly, some of these accusations are sometimes justified, much as one would like to dismiss them outright. At times, information does arrive when it would be too late to incorporate recommendations of a study into the current software version. However, this is often because testing is delayed and takes place too late in the development process to accommodate any findings that may require software modifications. In order to ensure that test results arrive in time to be included in the development process, tests must be conducted early enough in the process. When the accusation about lateness of usability test results is levelled, it is generally because insufficient time has been allowed for gathering data and analysing findings, or because the parameters of the system have already been determined so that changes would no longer be feasible regardless of the outcome of the usability evaluation. It is important to note that even when findings emerge too late to be included in a particular software version, it is still useful to know what will need to be improved in the next version, and so, information arriving late should not be dismissed or discarded.

The accusation that usability evaluations do not provide any useful information is usually an exaggeration, even if in some instances it might be the case that test findings have little to do directly with improving the design of a particular system. The value of information emerging from usability studies is dependent upon how well the purpose of the test, and the nature of the data it could generate, had been defined before testing took place. The thoroughness in defining data and evaluating possible outcomes of tests before they are performed is dependent on the skill, background and experience of the testers.

The belief that usability testing is the final layer of gloss a system is given just before it is released is a myth that will have to go. At that point in the development process, it is definitely too late to correct most usability defects, no matter how serious and glaring they might be. For tests to be effective, they must begin when the project starts and continue throughout the design/development process in test–modify–retest cycles. Changes made as a consequence of usability evaluations must be tested also, because it cannot be assumed that any change invariably is an

'Usability testing is not the final system-prerelease gloss'

improvement. Areas of the software other than the one changed might be affected, and even within the same area, a solution to one problem can inadvertently give rise to another.

Some authors distinguish between formative and summative evaluation (e.g. Hewett, 1986; Howard and Murray, 1987; Williges and Hartson, 1986), where 'formative' evaluation takes place at the early stages of system design, and 'summative' evaluation refers to assessments of the overall performance of the system. Although this distinction is important, because the type of evaluation to be conducted and the evaluative methods applied largely determine the issues to be investigated,

…ill not be used in this book.

…ensions along which usability can be defined, quantified and …made have been around for a number of years (e.g. ISO, …el 1986; 1991a), although there is still some confusion about … meaning and the exact boundaries of some of these. The …al Standards Organisation (ISO) considers 'effectiveness' and …as two separate usability dimensions. However, the definitions …r each of these are so similar that they are difficult to differentiate at an operational level. In particular, ISO identifies 'effectiveness' as 'measures of the accuracy and completeness of goals achieved', whereas 'efficiency' is defined as 'measures of the accuracy and completeness of goals accomplished relative to the resources (e.g. time, human effort) used to achieve the specific goals'. Conceptually, the notion of 'effectiveness' is straightforward; it is measured by how well tasks are performed. The concept of 'efficiency', however, appears to comprise 'effectiveness' as well as effort/speed. This description may be perfectly adequate for defining and keeping the meaning of the two concepts apart. However, when stated in operational terms, 'effectiveness' must entail some measurable aspect of human performance which is likely to include components of accuracy (= effort) as well as of speed (= time). The same is true for 'efficiency'; measuring how well a given task is performed requires an assessment of speed and/or accuracy. Operationally it is thus difficult to separate these two concepts and draw a clear distinction between them. Because it is so difficult to discriminate between the two terms, they would seem to be unsuited as a basis for formulating usability goals and criteria.

Taking a slightly different view, ETSI (European Telecommunications Standards Institute) considers two kinds of usability dimensions, namely those that are linked to performance and those related to attitudes, where performance is measured 'objectively' and attitude represents 'subjective' dimensions (ETSI, 1991). These two are relatively easy to distinguish at an operational level because performance measures are clearly separable from measures of attitude. However, they are also so general that it can be difficult to use them for guidance in defining quantifiable usability goals.

Shackel (1986; 1991a) maintains the distinction between performance and attitudinal dimensions, but he defines four distinguishable and quantifiable dimensions which may sensibly assume varying degrees of importance in different systems: effectiveness, learnability, flexibility and attitude. These dimensions are not mutually exclusive in the sense that measures of, for example, effectiveness can, at the same time, also give some indication of system learnability. However, they are a starting point.

Effectiveness refers to levels of user performance, measured in terms of speed and/or accuracy, in terms of proportion of task(s), proportion of users, or probability of completion of a given task. A typical performance criterion may require the average level of achievement across a given user population or sample of users to reach a certain cutoff point; for example, 'on average, users must be able to complete test tasks A and B in less than two minutes with a maximum of three errors'. Alternatively, it may require a specified proportion of users to succeed on the given task or suite of tasks, for example, '95% of users to complete all benchmark tasks correctly on their first trial'.

Flexibility refers to variations in task-completion strategies supported by a system. In many word processors certain effects may be achieved either by pointing and selecting options from a menu or by pressing specified combinations of keys simultaneously; some e-mail systems allow several operations to be performed using either one complex command or several single-step ones; these same systems also provide several different commands for achieving a particular operation. For example, to log off one may enter 'lo', 'bye', 'logoff', 'exit' or 'quit', depending on whether one wants to terminate the session, to exit the shell, or merely to exit from e-mail. The freedom to use a range of different commands with which to achieve similar goals adds to the system flexibility albeit not necessarily to the ease of learning for new users. Similarly, some menu-based systems allow shortcuts for users who know their way around the menu hierarchy; by keying in the ID of the particular screen they want to access, the screen-by-screen menu hierarchy is circumvented. Effects of flexibility may be measured by differences in performance as a function of absence or presence of added features; for example, providing five different ways to achieve a result may be an overkill, leading to confusion, errors, complex explanations in help and extra training, by comparison with providing one command only. Trade offs between flexibility and complexity may need to be measured to decide on the best solution for the users and their tasks.

Learnability refers to the ease with which new or occasional users may accomplish certain tasks. Learnability may relate to the amount of training provided, to time lapsed since training was completed or to the probability of committing one or more errors. It may be measured in the number of trials needed to complete particular tasks with no training or a controlled amount of training provided, to performance on two or more trials separated by a certain amount of time. Alternatively, it may be measured in terms of the number of times users look up the manual, consult help, ask questions of the observer, or go back to the opening screen whilst attempting to complete a certain task or tasks.

Attitude refers to user acceptability of the system in question. This is the only dimension of usability which explicitly seeks users' opinion. Attitudes are generally measured in interviews or surveys (Chapter 5), which also enables response categories to be quantified.

In summary, usability dimensions should be captured such that they can readily be translated into meaningful quantitative statements:

Effectiveness
- the required range of tasks, completed at a specified level of performance, within a certain time (i.e. speed, accuracy);
- by some required percentage of the specified target range of users;
- within some required proportion of the range of usage environments.

Learnability
- within a certain specified time, relative to the beginning of user training;
- based upon some specified amount of training and user support;
- within some specified relearning time each time for intermittent users.

Flexibility
- with flexibility allowing adaptation to some specified percentage variation in tasks and/or environments beyond those first specified.

Attitude
- within acceptable levels of human cost in terms of tiredness, discomfort, frustration and personal effort;
- so that satisfaction causes continued and enhanced usage of the system.

Adapted from Shackel (1991a, p. 25)

Despite the ease of translating relatively simple concepts into quantifiable measures, it is interesting to note that they are mentioned only fleetingly in the literature (Edmonds, 1987), and some authors note that relatively few studies are reported which discuss or seek to apply formal usability criteria (Butler, 1985; Eason and Harker, 1991; Olson, 1985; Whiteside and Wixon, 1987; Wixon and Whiteside, 1985). Since the level of interest in usability is rising, and given the immediate appeal of the ease with which these dimensions can be translated into meaningful quantitative statements, it is curious that they are not applied in more studies. Formal, iterative usability evaluation of emerging computer systems does not appear to be as common yet as one might wish (Eason and Harker, 1991; Gould and Lewis, 1985).

Usability defects tend to fall into the following categories:

1.9 Categories of typical usability defects

Navigation: the ease with which users move around the system, within and between modules – layout and understandability of menu options; an understanding of where the user currently is, where he came from and where he is going in a sequence of screens; attention to provision of short cuts and signals that such short cuts are available, and the removal of redundant screens, menu options, or steps. Also, error recovery assistance in the form of error messages, help information and hardcopy documentation which can assist or hinder smooth navigation.

Screen design and layout: the way information is presented on the screen (problems may arise when the screen is crammed, when there are too many alignment points to allow easy scanning, the logical flow of different fields, legibility of characters, identification of fields [distinguishing between mandatory and discretionary fields], nature of information to be entered, e.g. clearly YES or NO answers expected, date format, e.g. dd/mm/yy; organization of groupings, screen ID, title, etc.).

Terminology: words, sentences, and abbreviations (problems can occur when jargon is used inappropriately [i.e. for a population that does not know it] or not used where it should be, clarity of meaning of field captions, codes, prompts, commands, introduction of concepts, i.e. clarity and meaningfulness of vocabulary).

Feedback: the way the system communicates with users as a result of user actions or about the state of the system (error or warning messages, confirmation messages, highlighting, regularity of response times, e.g. if a system action takes a very long time to complete, is the user told somehow that the system is 'still working'?).

Consistency: the degree to which the system performs in a predictable, well organized and standard fashion (menu screens should be clearly distinguishable from database output screens; menu screens appearing in different areas of the system should be easily recognizable, mandatory fields should be distinguishable from discretionary ones, allocation of functions to F-keys, e.g. F1 is always HELP; F12 always EXIT, menu selection method should always be the same within a system).

Modality: the state of the system operation that the user selects to perform a particular function (e.g. in some systems, one must be in the INSERT mode to edit displayed text; how easy is it to move between modes; how many different modes must the user know; how easy is it to recognize where one is at any time?).

Redundancies: repetitions (do any unnecessary data, fields or screens get in the user's way; are there any fields or screens which are never used; are there any unnecessary prompts or messages that have no direct relevance to the user?).

User control: users' feeling of being in control (does the user feel in control of the system; are there any actions which are initiated, controlled or paced by the system; how well is the user kept informed about what is happening in the background; how much trust or confidence does the user have in the system and what it will do/has done what it has been ordered to do?).

Match with user tasks: the degree to which the system matches tasks as carried out in the current environment and as specified in the task analysis (how well does the software match the specifications outlined in the user needs analysis; how well does it map and reflect what users want and the way they want to do it; are any details left out; is every step in each task consistent with user expectations; is the flow of steps → subtasks → tasks → jobs logical; are all links between related tasks

'What do you think has happened to him lately? He is so – different'

established; that is, is data taken to all destinations where it is wanted when entered once?).

In summary, the categories of typical usability defects include:

- navigation;
- screen design and layout;
- terminology;
- feedback;
- consistency;
- modality;
- redundancies;
- user control;
- match with user tasks.

1.10 Iterative testing

It is impossible to produce a system that is completely right the first time round, so you must be prepared to change. Iterative testing refers to the simple fact that one keeps on repeating tests until one has achieved the usability level to which one aspires. Iterative testing is necessary because one does not always know for sure that modifications essentially improve the usability of a product. Through tests the changes required to any of the system components can be identified and the effect of these changes can be evaluated once they have been carried out. While it is tempting to assume that usability problems, once identified and dealt with, are definitely overcome by adjusting the particular system component, changes do not always have the desired effect. Even if they do, the changes can themselves, on occasion, introduce new problems which can only be detected by retesting the same trouble spot again. User interface management tools are emerging which make changes to the user interface easy to achieve (Alves *et al.*, 1991; Schulert *et al.*, 1985), but the effect of these must still be measured.

1.11 What this book will help you to do

A number of usability evaluation tools and techniques are introduced throughout this book which will hopefully help to clarify what human factors experts and usability testers mean when they talk about evaluation and tests. Some of the tools can readily be applied with a little experience but without special training; others are more complex and will require further reading, or will assume that you have access to a human factors expert with whom to discuss usability tests. In particular, experiments and quasi-experiments are tricky in the sense that it might look easy to design and conduct experiments, but it is even easier to introduce flaws into the design or analysis, or to ignore important variables that could have been included but were overlooked. When an experiment is flawed, results emerging from it are most likely to be invalid; conducting flawed experiments and tests is an extremely expensive way to gain nothing – other than perhaps the realization that the experiment was flawed. Even highly experienced experimentalists sometimes overlook important things in their first design of a new experiment, so this particular arena is very slippery. The detailed description of how to design and apply experiments to actual problems and issues (Chapter 6) is intended to help you realize when you should call in expert assistance, as well as to give you a flavour for the complexities, the time and effort involved in designing usability tests that yield the most useful information in different situations. Looking at the various tests and where they might fit into the process of designing, developing, installing and operating systems should also help you to assist in developing a usability test and evaluation plan (Chapter 8) as well as to calculate the costs associated with conducting a testing program.

After reading this book, you won't be a human factors expert, but you will be able to ask sensible and relevant questions about usability and user performance. Asking relevant questions, such that they are answerable by means of test findings, is perhaps the art of usability testing; good, crisp and relevant questions certainly stand a much better chance of being answered than vague, unclear ones.

The topics introduced in later chapters do not give a complete picture of all that usability testing entails, because that would be far beyond what could be achieved in a single book. So, certain assumptions have been made. It is, for example, assumed that definitions of, or access to, typical and representative users of a future computer system is achievable. In reality it is not always clear who the typical users will be, or what characteristics they might display, and it is often difficult to gain access to representative users for user profiling (Chapter 2) or testing purposes.

Organizational and/or political hindrances can be such that user participation in the design amounts to nothing more than wishful thinking. This is not to say that organizational issues, which have been left out here, are unimportant – they are extremely important, and they do influence projects and their progress, or lack of progress, a great deal (Clegg, 1984; Greif, 1991; Grudin, 1991; Hoerr *et al.*, 1989; Mackie and Wylie, 1988; Malone, 1985; 1987).

Summary

This chapter summarized a number of fundamental concepts in HCI, both practical and theoretical. The brief history of HCI was outlined first, followed by equally brief sketches of some of the theoretical models that have evolved over the past 15 or so years. Models focusing on performance such as GOMS, on learning and transfer, such as CCT, were discussed along with grammar models, CLGs and TAG, and cognitive resources as mapped in cognitive task analysis were dealt with. The notion of usability, reasons for conducting usability tests, and quantifiable usability dimensions were introduced together with a description of the most commonly encountered types of usability defects. A few notes on guidelines, design rules and principles were presented, and the notion of iterative testing was discussed briefly.

Questions

1. How can HCI help to improve interactive systems in the short term?
2. What are user models and why might HCI need them?
3. What do GOMS models aim to contribute to systems design?
4. How does CCT differ from GOMS in terms of its aims?
5. What is TAG's concern and what does it predict?
6. How does Barnard's CTA differ from MHPs in GOMS models?
7. How might PUMs be of value in systems design?
8. What do Gould and Lewis emphasize that differs from traditional design/development methods?
9. What is usability?
10. How does usefulness differ from usability?
11. Who should be interested in outcomes of usability tests?
12. Why must designers start paying attention to usability issues?
13. What are some of the purposes of usability testing?
14. Why is it more difficult to derive software than hardware standards?
15. Why is it necessary to translate guidelines before they can be applied?
16. When in the systems development process should usability testing ideally take place?

17. What is the danger in testing for usability too late in the development process?
18. Why is it useful to define particular usability dimensions?
19. What are usability defects?
20. What is iterative testing and why is it important?

Suggested further reading

The classic text in HCI (Card *et al.*, 1983). The authors present a family of GOMS models and show how to apply GOMS analyses. It is the first major text in which principles and laws used in psychology were applied in a modelling approach in HCI which seeks to predict expert performance and hence usability. The book is easy to read, but it is probably best if the reader has some basic knowledge of the underlying psychology.

Barnard (1987) discusses a model of human cognition based on 'interacting cognitive subsystems' such as the visual, object and the propositional subsystem, each of which is in charge of a particular aspect of human cognition.

Kieras and Polson (1985) propose a method for analysing cognitive complexity, which arose from the GOMS approach and seeks to predict transfer of learning from one system to another. Existing knowledge is mapped to a new system and analysed using Generalized Transition Networks. This paper is the beginning of a long series in which cognitive complexity theory is developed and tested, and is easy to read.

Moran's (1981) model is based on a description of the user interface from the point of view of the user. He shows how it can be used to generate a wide variety of command language system descriptions. The model has three structural components, the conceptual, communication and physical, which are further broken down into task, semantic, syntactic and interactional levels. This article is also easy to read and lays the foundation for a great deal of continuing work in the field of grammars.

Payne and Green's (1986) paper which needs to be read carefully to understand it, is an account of how we might map our conceptual model of a system onto actions. The model presented aims to formalize this mapping from task to action by certain simple rules. The number of rules applied to a given task is then used to predict the cognitive complexity of the task.

Shackel's (1991a) paper is very readable. It addresses the notion of usability in a wider framework that includes definition and criteria. Usability dimensions are discussed in some detail, and Shackel talks about different ways the assessment of usability may be approached at different stages of system development.

Smith (1988) shows why formal design standards cannot be applied to the user interface and calls for the development of flexible software design guidelines. He discusses why standards cannot yet be imposed on user interface design at some length, and argues that effective application of guidelines must rely on translation into system-specific design rules. This is also easy to read.

2 Designing useful systems: user needs analysis

What we have to learn to do, we learn by doing

Aristotle

No one could deny the importance of usability issues; if we want customers to commission or buy, and users to like, the systems we produce, a high level of usability is an absolute must. Yet usability alone cannot guarantee system usefulness as well, and if a computer system is not as useful as it is usable it will never offer real support nor be completely accepted by its end users. Many a well-designed and sophisticated system has been abandoned by the very people whose life it was intended to facilitate. A useful system is one that adequately meets the task requirements of its users and helps the customer to streamline certain procedures or organizational transactions, thereby saving effort, time and improving organizational efficiency. Therefore, in addition to ensuring that their systems are easy to use, developers should also ensure that the system does what the customer expects. Easily said! The task of specifying customer expectations is a very tricky business; people are not very good at telling analysts what they want, and analysts are not always very good at listening. Yet requirements capture is probably the most important activity of system design, because it guides the further system development.

When something goes wrong, the repercussions of inadequacies in requirements capture escalate in cost at a rate that should motivate us to pay much more and closer attention to the specification process. One author has estimated this cost of fixing problems that should have been detected during requirements capture, but which were present in delivered systems, to be more than 100 times greater than if they had been picked up before coding the system (Roman, 1985). It has also been estimated that more than 80% of all software malfunctions originate during this phase (Chapin, 1979). At the same time, it is claimed that more than one third of all requirements errors can be detected and solved by a thorough review of the system requirements specification document (SRS) before coding commences (Basili and Weiss, 1981). This observation suggests that a great deal can be done to improve the way user requirements are captured, documented and validated before the system development process progresses further and disasters occur.

Much research is still needed to understand precisely how, when and where requirements capture can be improved, methods be formalized and

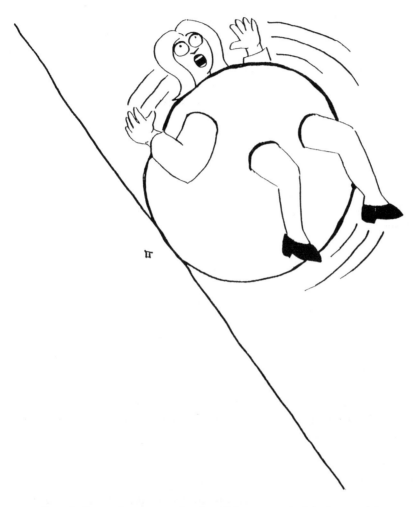

'Snowballs can become avalanches if they are not picked up early'

validated. Tools are emerging to assist design teams working through this process systematically. The HUFIT (human factors in information technology) project carried out at the HUSAT Research Institute, for example, has developed a number of tools and methods aiming to integrate human factors within design processes in an effort to produce more useful and usable products at a competitive cost (Catterall *et al.*, 1991). Similarly, the 'human factors guidelines for computer-based systems' (Gardner and McKenzie, 1990; HUSAT, 1988), also developed at HUSAT, devote one of the six volumes of guidelines to describing human factors in the requirements specification phase. Macaulay *et al.*

(1990) identify a set of elements that an SRS document should contain; Kirby *et al.* (1988) look at hurdles in the validation process; Harker (1991) reports a set of longitudinal studies in ongoing design activities and examines the potential contribution of early prototyping. The CORE (1989) methodology outlines in detail many different possible 'viewpoints', or perspectives, from which a system should be considered and describes how these can assist in capturing user requirements. Rather than repeating what has already been said elsewhere, the purpose of this chapter is to introduce you to the topics of importance in determining user needs.

2.1 Why are requirements capture and specification problematic?

Structured approaches to system requirements specification and analysis such as SSADM (structured system analysis and design methodology) (Downs *et al.*, 1988; Page-Jones, 1988), SDLC (systems development life cycle) (Burch, 1992) or JSD (Jackson structured design) (Jackson, 1983) tend to assume that the user requirements are already known (Macaulay *et al.*, 1990), or that they can readily be acquired through stereotypical descriptions of users' tasks (Harker, 1991). Unfortunately, this assumption amounts largely to wishful thinking, as evidenced by the numerous computer systems sitting idle or grossly under-used in many organizations. To overcome this gap between perception and reality and assist designers to gain a better understanding of user task behaviour, various task analysis methods have been developed or adapted from other areas of human activity in which task knowledge must be made explicit. One difference between traditional systems analysis and task analysis methods in HCI is that traditional systems analysis makes no claims about behaviour, whereas task analysis makes explicit assumptions about the knowledge users need to complete tasks successfully. Systems analysis tends to focus on external, non-psychological information about objects and data flows, and software engineering primarily decomposes systems hierarchically in terms of functions and data (Carter, 1991; Pressman, 1987), whereas task analysis concentrates on the user's perspective.

Misunderstandings between designers and users are frequent; communication is hindered because people speak different languages. People from different disciplinary backgrounds may well use the same words, but they often attach different meanings to them. For example, the computer scientist who talks about a given 'state' usually refers to a particular 'system condition'. A geographer on the other hand might well understand the 'state' to mean a 'nation' if that interpretation fits the context of the discussion. Systems designers tend to describe tasks in terms of logical data flows and system attributes. This is not how users think about their daily work. System attributes are generally too technical for describing what users do or what they should do, and they can be extremely difficult for users to translate into English. At the same time,

'I spent ten years of my life perfecting this, but people don't like it. What's wrong with people?'

users have difficulties articulating their needs and describing their models of the tasks to be supported by the computer system, and they are not very good at describing exactly how they expect their needs to be met (Murdic, 1980). In addition, we are all paradigm-bound, that is, we are heavily influenced in our thinking, perception, beliefs and world view by our respective backgrounds. Beliefs colour what we take to be 'truth' or 'reality'. System developers may believe that user needs are described at the right level of technical detail in the system specifications on the one hand, whilst on the other hand, users rely on the expertise of the designers to deliver what they expect, assuming that the 'experts' know best! Yet, while the experts know how to design a computer system, they are usually not expert at the user tasks to be supported by a new computer system.

Perhaps most importantly of all, developers often fail to realize that they themselves are not 'typical' end users; they believe that, because they are also computer users, they are so similar to end users that they do not need to verify this similarity through experiments, observations of users, or other types of interactions (Chapanis, 1992; Landauer, 1987). They therefore fail to realize that their often implicit understanding of users' needs reflect their own perspective which is not necessarily shared by the end users. Consequently, instead of helping users to build good, accurate models of their detailed needs, designers tend to get a few rough ideas from the users and then construct the system according to their own

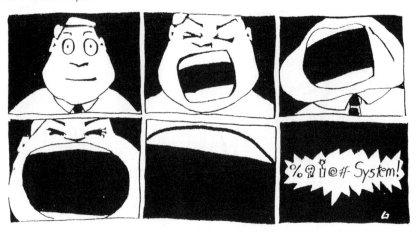

'Possible effects of user/designer misunderstandings'

understanding of these needs (Bostrom, 1989). This may happen because very little, if any, space is devoted to data collection methods, even in very recent software engineering texts (Diaper and Addison, 1992). Designers are thus rarely trained to master the level of communication and data collection skill that is essential to elicit user needs, or they do not have the resources to involve users in the requirements specification process. Even when designers do interview or observe end users with the intention of understanding their needs and task requirements, interviews and observations are, in themselves, insufficient unless they are followed up by clear descriptions of user tasks. These must be written in a language and presented in a format that users can understand: the users must be able to recognize these as descriptions of what they do to verify that they represent their tasks adequately.

The observation that users and designers differ from one another is no criticism of either population: developers are not inherently arrogant, and users are not stupid or ignorant, but both sides do make unfounded and unrealistic assumptions about themselves and each other. Users forget that they – not the designers – are experts at the tasks to be supported by the computer; they fail to realize that they must assist in conveying the relevant aspects of this expertise to enable the designers to deliver a good system. Even if users want to describe their tasks in detail, it is difficult to express the details in words; much of what is done as a routine cannot easily be verbalized. Designers commonly believe that, by virtue of being human, they understand what users need and say they need (Chapanis, 1991a), and their training does not help them to realize that what users tell them may not be consistent with what they want, need and expect due to cognitive mismatches and limitations on both sides. Systematic, careful data collection and analysis can assist in closing this gap.

A set of requirements may be defined as (1) a condition or capability needed by a user to solve a problem or achieve an objective or (2) a condition or capability that must be met or possessed by a system to satisfy a contract, standard specification or other formally imposed document (IEEE, 1983). Tenders for very large systems will normally specify the standards and formal criteria a system − or suite of systems − must meet to be acceptable. However, as was noted in the previous chapter, software standards are expressed in general terms which are open to interpretation. Hence, even where formality exists, it is still vague and uncertain. The purpose of defining user needs is to specify what a system should do and to enable comparative measurements to be made later of the extent to which these needs are being met successfully by the resulting system.

The level of generality of an SRS depends on whether it is written by a customer as a tender, open to competition among software companies, or by a developer as a first step in the software development process. The perspective from which the SRS is written also determines which aspects are emphasized. Developers are primarily interested in balancing costs against projected profits, in satisfying the market to retain (or gain) their market share, in the relationship of the emerging software to existing products and in the ability of their staff to do the required job. If developers want to sell copies of the product to many customers in a competitive market place, they will be motivated to keep costs as low as possible. By contrast, if competition between suppliers applies only in the pre-development phase when tenders are being called, keeping costs low may not be as important. If developers are contractually responsible for post-delivery maintenance, removal of bugs and repair of defects, the strongest motivation would be to build high quality, easily maintainable and modifiable products. When the customer bears the cost of post-delivery modifications, the opposite may be true. Hence, the SRS considers users' needs, customer needs, developer's perspective, technology risks, laws and standards to varying degrees, depending on the nature of the system (Davis, 1988; Gaver, 1991) and on the motivation and politics of the clients and system developers. This is one reason why it is impossible to detail categorically how an ideal SRS must be put together. However, the purpose an SRS aims to serve must be defined very clearly before it is written.

The SRS document is a means of communication between analysts, designers, users, customers, testers, management, and whoever has a stake in the system. It contains a complete description of all system inputs, outputs, attributes, and relationships between inputs and outputs. It defines both user and system behaviour to which designers must build, and testers must measure and evaluate, as well as being a means for controlling the evolution of a software system. It describes exactly what the software will do, but not the processes by which it will operate; that

2.2 Purposes of system requirements

is, the SRS document outlines what the computer system will do, not how this is achieved (Davis, 1988; 1990).

2.3 User needs analysis

Methods such as CORE (controlled requirements expression) encourage systems analysts, designers and developers to consider their systems from several perspectives, including that of the user. A user-needs analysis defines and describes who the users are and what they are required to do both in the current and in the projected future system. It specifies all tasks that are relevant to the new system, identifies tasks in users' job which are not incorporated in the present system, but that could be included in the future system, and considers the user's task or job demands in terms of physical characteristics and environment. The user-needs analysis is thus an analysis of what is currently done by users, a projection of what they will be doing, and a comparison of present and future tasks as well as a description of their equipment and the environment into which the new system will fit. It has two components: one specifies tasks and the other identifies user characteristics as documented in user profiles. The user needs analysis can be incorporated into a system analysis framework such as CORE by representing the users' viewpoint as well, but this does not replace the system analysis; rather, it adds an explicit user dimension. Requirements specifications form an integral part of the research phase in the process model followed in this book.

2.4 Developing a user profile

A user profile describes a number of characteristics of the users whose needs and requirements must be met in a new computer system. The purpose of a user profile is to ensure that the right level of terminology is employed, that potential user disabilities are taken into account, that the system suits their level of computer and task expertise, and so forth. Jargon used by, for example, pathologists communicating with colleagues should obviously differ from that used by patients filling in forms related to their medical history. People with poor vision should be given larger displays; people with poor hand-eye motor co-ordination or restricted movements of limbs may find the use of a mouse tiresome or impossible; people who know and use several different computer systems need no introduction to basic computer concepts in the help system, and task experts should not be exposed to unnecessary descriptions or coaching in task details, perhaps invented to suit the new technology.

End users are often regarded as an amorphous, stereotyped concept of 'people' with certain implicit 'human' characteristics, the relevant details of which remain undefined, vague and unspecified. End users may thus be regarded in the same way as in daily speech we refer to 'people', 'they', 'teachers', 'the elderly' or 'parents' without defining exactly who or what we mean. System designers are no different: they tend to have quite

'Know who your users are'

inaccurate and incomplete notions of whom exactly they are designing for and what the cognitive capabilities and limitations of these users are. In their concerted efforts to match system capabilities with users' task demands and their cognitive abilities, those characteristics that are of importance in the context of the computer system about to be designed must be defined.

In order to distinguish between different classes of users, some authors refer to 'direct' and 'indirect' users, where 'direct' users interact with the system and 'indirect' users receive outputs from the computer generated by someone else. Other authors distinguish between 'users' who are 'end users' and 'customers' who pay for the system and have the authority to commission changes to a product or project. 'Stakeholders' is another term used to identify anyone who has or will have a stake in the new system. Here, we will distinguish between three categories of users in a manner that reflects how close different people are to the target computer system, in line with a view put forward by Davis (1990). 'Primary users' are actual end users; 'secondary users' are the recipients of reports and the like which they have not generated themselves, and 'tertiary users' are the people who are responsible for the day-to-day maintenance of the system, the managers of other related systems, buyers of equipment, policy makers, and so on.

Checklists can be very convenient for defining relevant user characteristics. The objective in user-profile checklists is to identify and make explicit characteristics which particular user groups have in common and

USER PROFILE CHECK LIST

Date this list completed: ..../..../....

System: ....   Version: ....

User group: ....   Level of users
                                             (Primary/Secondary/Tertiary)

User Knowledge and Experience

Reading level language

☐ Less than Grade 5
☐ Grade 6-12
☐ Above Grade 12

Highest educational level

☐ High School not completed
☐ High School completed
☐ Diploma
☐ Degree

Native

☐ English
☐ Other

Computer literacy

☐ Low
☐ Moderate
☐ High

System experience

☐ Novice
☐ Moderate
☐ Expert

Application experience

☐ No similar systems
☐ One similar system
☐ Some similar systems

Use of other systems

☐ Little or none
☐ Frequent

Task experience

☐ Novices in the field
☐ Moderate experts
☐ Expert in the field

Typing skill

☐ Low
☐ Medium
☐ High

Physical Characteristics

Handedness

☐ Right handed
☐ Left handed
☐ Ambidextrous

Disabilities

☐ Speech impaired
☐ Hearing impaired
☐ Visually impaired
☐ Mobility impaired

which must be taken into account when making decisions about the user interface, the interactive dialogue and presentation style. It should be adjusted according to the type of system and users in question. More categories can be added where required; some of those listed in the 'user profile checklist' may be irrelevant or unnecessary in certain contexts and should be excluded accordingly. Since the primary users will be interacting with the system, their characteristics will tend to weigh most heavily in deciding how to structure the user interface, but other classes of users should not be ignored. Secondary users may need financial reports, product overviews, or personnel statistics presented in a specific format (taxation, legal) which must not be changed for, or by, primary users. If meeting these requirements means that the logic or the flow of the interactive dialogue, or the style of the user interface is not optimal from the primary users' point of view, possible compromises should be negotiated. Similarly, tertiary users such as system or LAN managers may well be far ahead of the present system in their strategic thinking and planning for the organisation's IT future; clearly, their views are important for ensuring that the proposed system fits into their long-term strategic thinking and the constraints they face with respect to integrating the proposed system with others in the organization.

The analyst should identify the lowest level of education of the people who will be interacting with a proposed system, to decide on the level of language complexity that should be employed. Similarly, users' levels of knowledge of computers in general should be made explicit to help decide how much device- and technology-independent information will need to be provided in tutorials, help and other forms of user support/documentation.

The level of task-expertise is important; experts hardly need coaching in the tasks they know perfectly well. If a public system is likely to be used by children, or by senior citizens, this should be noted along with characteristics of these populations who may have specific requirements. Any user disabilities should be taken into account in terms of how they may influence the physical and/or mental interaction with equipment. There are no hard and fast rules for selecting the information that should go into a user profile checklist, but any information that helps to specify the capability of users to handle systems, to understand information presented in diagrams/text/spoken output, perhaps in different languages, is beneficial. This information may be gathered from reading documentation, observing users of similar systems, or systems to be replaced, from interviews or surveys of users, or by using any of the data collection methods outlined in Chapters 4–6 here. The example shown below is not definitive or even complete; it is intended to give some hints for identifying the user groups one typically needs to specify; it shows how one might sort out who should be given user-profile checklists.

EXAMPLE: PHARMANET

Background (already known by the project team)

Imagine you are part of a hospital-based software development team. The team has just been given the task of designing a system streamlining all drug-related information in the hospital. The system will be connected to the outside world through the hospital pharmacy. The pharmacy orders all supplies directly from drug supply companies around the world. Within the hospital, drugs are ordered by the wards from the pharmacy. Some drugs are kept in store in the wards and the pharmacy at all times, and others are ordered for individual patients as needed. The system is intended to keep track of ward stock so that information about drug names, dosages, the quantity of various drugs and their location within the hospital, is available at all times. Similarly, use-by-dates and statistics related to usage/consumption rates are also monitored. Dangerous (addictive) drugs are monitored separately and controlled very closely, so that the pharmacist can trace the exact number of tablets, ampoules, etc., of each drug type at any time in any ward, emergency department or operating theatre in the hospital. In Australia this separate monitoring of dangerous drugs (DD) is required by law; the Drug Squad, a drug-policing body, may call at a hospital at any time, without prior notice, to audit all dangerous drugs and records.

The system is, at this very early stage, foreseen to contain the following components:

1. drug ordering module (from wards to pharmacy, from pharmacy to outside world);
2. drug dispensing module (what, how much is where, at pharmacy, ward, individual patient record level);
3. accounting module (balance sheets for tax purposes; hospital budget, individual patient bills);
4. statistical module (pattern of drug usage, hospital/ward level, day/week/month/year);
5. dangerous drugs (exact running account of usage and dispensing for Drug Squad);
6. MIMS information (detailed information about all drugs, listing chemical contents, possible side effects, desirable and undesirable combinations of different drugs, etc.).

The following user groups have been identified:

Primary users: 1.1 Pharmacists (pharmacy level);
                 1.2 Accountants (hospital administration level);
                 1.3 Nurses (ward level);
                 1.4 Doctors (ward level, authorize patient orders);
                 1.5 Ward administration (clerks);
Secondary users: 2.1 Hospital management;
                 2.2 Drug Squad;
                 2.3 Tax department;

Tertiary users: 3.1 System maintenance team;
                   3.2 Other (hospital) systems maintenance teams.

The user profile checklist will thus be administered to representatives of all of these ten user groups either as a survey or in interviews. A survey can be distributed and administered by users themselves (except for the tax department and the Drug Squad) as the project team is also part of the staff. Knowing who these users are, one already knows something about their educational background, their use of jargon, and by virtue of the project team's position in the hospital, assumptions may also be made of users' computer literacy and application experience. Verification will be necessary just to be certain that the assumptions made are correct.

In addition to generating profiles on current classes of users, we need information about projected future personnel planning and organizational policies for particular clients. It is, for example, important to know the level of staff turnover and whether staff are rotated regularly; if so, chances are that there will be novices on the system at all times, and this determines what and how much information goes into preparing tutorials, help system contents and structure and user manuals. These wider organizational issues are not addressed here, but more detail may be found elsewhere (Christie, 1985; Clegg *et al.*, 1988; Eason, 1989; Handy, 1985; Long, 1989; Malone, 1985; 1987).

A task analysis is a step-by-step comparison of the demands an operation makes on the user with user capabilities (Drury, 1983), described in terms of operational procedures and knowledge necessary to complete a task (Benyon, 1992a). A task is a purposeful, goal-oriented activity undertaken by one or more agents to bring about some change of state in a given domain (Johnson, 1992). The purpose of a task analysis is to contribute to design (Buckley and Johnson, 1987) by transferring some knowledge from one group of people to another (McGrew, 1991). Task analysis is used to gain an understanding of what people do in existing circumstances. A task analysis at some level of detail is required in all user-modelling approaches described in the previous chapter. Task analysis is a methodology which is supported by a large number of techniques to help the analyst collect and arrange data systematically, to make explicit the requirements to be fulfilled by people and systems, and to optimize the capabilities of both components. Task analysis is thus applied to make judgments about the best way to allocate human and machine resources for ensuring safety, productivity, performance and satisfaction in human–machine and human-human interactions. Task analyses can be done at any time during system development or operation and the choice of technique depends on the aim of the analysis. However,

2.5 Developing a task profile: task analysis

'Your system must fit the users' tasks to be useful'

it should ideally be done early in the design process. It can be done by designers, managers or evaluators, and the level of detail varies from one system to the next, between people, their roles and contexts.

Underlying the notion of task analysis is the belief that task knowledge can be analysed and modelled. In order to complete a task efficiently and systematically, people are assumed to store knowledge about the task in memory, and this knowledge is assumed to be represented by information about goals, methods, operators and selection rules – just the components underlying GOMS analyses discussed earlier (Ch. 1). So-called task-knowledge structures (TKS) (Johnson *et al.*, 1984) represent all the knowledge people have of tasks they are currently doing or have previously learned. TKS theory assumes that people develop knowledge structures based on previous task experiences and apply these to task performance as their knowledge increases. This knowledge is structured in a way that makes it relatively easy to be recalled and processed in a familiar or a novel situation. TKS provides a method for the analysis and modelling of tasks in terms of goals, procedures, actions and objects. The importance of task centrality and representativeness is stressed. Centrality is concerned with critical points in the task at which success or failure is determined; it is a measure of task importance. Representativeness refers to the typicality of a task component/subtask. It is assumed that knowledge deemed central to a given task is more likely to be transferred and used in carrying out similar tasks in different contexts. TKS is thus a summary representation of the different types of knowledge that have been acquired through learning particular tasks and that are applied in task behaviour.

Within each TKS, a goal substructure represents the plan for carrying out a task. A plan has a procedural substructure with alternative strategies. A procedure relies on knowledge of objects and actions which is represented in a taxonomy substructure. In producing a TKS the analyst is required to identify knowledge elements such as goals and plans; see Johnson's (1992) knowledge analysis of tasks (KAT).

2.5.1 TASK ANALYSIS TECHNIQUES

Whole families of task analysis techniques are currently available in ergonomics and other disciplines, all of which describe and analyse what people do at different levels of detail and with various emphases. These techniques may be grouped in many ways. Kirwan and Ainsworth (1992), in their detailed practical guide to task analysis which reviews some 25 different methods, divide these techniques into five categories:

- task data collection methods;
- task description methods;
- task simulation methods;
- task behaviour assessment methods;
- task requirements evaluation methods.

Task data collection methods focus on actual or proposed task performance and rely on the kinds of user modelling methods described in Chapter 1 as well as on interviews, surveys and related techniques. Task description methods structure the information into a systematic format, for example, flow charts or other kinds of graphical diagrams. These diagrams may then serve as reference material to enhance the understanding of the human-system interaction, or they can be used directly to identify training needs and content. Among the methods Kirwan and Ainsworth address in this category is hierarchical task analysis which will be described in more detail shortly. Task simulation methods aim to compile data on human involvement representing what actually happens during task execution in a dynamic fashion. Methods used at that level include computer modelling, runnable or dynamic prototypes and walkthroughs. Task behaviour assessment methods are concerned with the evaluation of system performance, usually to identify safety and risk aspects. Unfortunately, it is beyond the scope of this book to describe the relevant methods in this category as they are highly specialized and not among the first techniques that need to be mastered. Consult Kirwan and Ainsworth (1992, part 2) for a review of some of these, and Elkind *et al.* (1990) for examples of the complexity of problems encountered in the areas of risk, safety and task behaviour modelling. Task requirements evaluation is used to assess the adequacy of tools and facilities that are available to the operator to support task execution. Methods applied in this category include surveys, observations of operators and usability assessments via heuristic evaluation and confirmation studies. All the techniques described in this book may be applied in task analysis, but they do not represent all methods that are available – only enough to give you a flavour of the scope of task analysis, problems and issues in human factors.

2.5.2 EXEMPLARS OF TASK ANALYSIS TECHNIQUES (TAKD)

TAKD (task analysis for knowledge-based description) (Johnson *et al.*, 1984) is a technique that aims to identify and make explicit all the knowledge required for executing a particular task successfully in a systematic fashion. The objective of TAKD is to produce a specification of knowledge required to use a system, or the knowledge that a system would have to include to perform a task. The analysis progresses in four stages:

1. data collection about a task, leading to a task description;
2. identification of knowledge involved in the task, expressed in terms of objects and actions;
3. classification of these objects and actions to generate lists of generic objects and actions;
4. use of action or object association pairs in a knowledge representation grammar (KRG) to describe the task (Wilson *et al.*, 1988).

KRG allows for iteration, selection and sequencing to be represented in each task step observed. Each task step is redescribed in the KRG format in a primarily bottom-up process which begins with instances of behaviour. TAKD forces analysts to be aware of decisions they make about different aspects of the world by imposing an explicit way of thinking about tasks and their generic context (Diaper, 1989; Diaper and Addison, 1992). TAKD does not attempt to be a performance model of task execution or to capture aspects of task dynamics. Rather, the technique seeks to capture 'ideal' knowledge required to perform a task.

To do this, task descriptions are required from many different sources. For more detail on TAKD, see Diaper (1987; 1989) or Johnson (1992).

2.5.3 HIERARCHICAL TASK ANALYSIS (HTA)

HTA is a broad approach to task analysis that helps the analyst to establish when various subtasks should be carried out in order to meet a system's goals. It was originally developed in the context of training (Annett *et al.*, 1971). The authors attempted to identify where training was required for tasks and subtasks that were crucial for successful completion and attainment of goals. HTA is concerned with empirical analysis of existing task performance, but it provides no assessment metrics that can be used to address how well a person performs a given task. It is a top-down analysis in which tasks and goals are divided into a hierarchy of subtasks and subgoals. A goal is a desired state of the system. Goals are decomposed until some 'simple task' (Payne and Green, 1989) or 'unit-task' (Card *et al.*, 1983) is reached. An HTA produces a hierarchy of operations (the things people do in the system) and plans (statements of conditions which are necessary to undertake these operations). Indeed, operations and plans are its cornerstones. An operation is any unit of behaviour which can be defined in terms of its objective; a plan is assumed to be a particular collection of subgoals, subtasks and activities that are recognizable as achieving a specific goal. Implicit in the behaviour entailed in an operation is the capability of the task performer to carry out appropriate actions to attain the goal; the capability to locate and encode information necessary for selecting appropriate actions and the ability to locate and encode feedback to evaluate whether the goal has been attained (Kirwan and Ainsworth, 1992). This action-information-feedback loop is used within HTA to identify trouble spots in task execution.

Since the task description is hierarchical, the analysis can be developed to any level of detail required for a particular task. One strength of HTA is the empirical basis of the analysis. Analysts are required to study actual task performance to draw a detailed model of the task. One drawback of task analysis – and this is not exclusive to HTA – is that the nature of components is open and *ad hoc*, and this lack of formalism makes it difficult to use task analysis as the basis for task description in HCI (Brooks, 1991). One difficulty with task analysis is that it can be problematic to select the best level of detail at which to describe a given task (Benyon, 1992a). Diaper (1987) illustrates this in an example of a typical task requiring subjects to 'insert disk into disk drive'. This action can be represented as a single step. Alternatively, the action may be broken down into a sequence of steps:

1. remove disk from envelope;
2. slide disk into disk drive;
3. push button to lock disk drive.

In addition, simple tasks may be different for novices and experts (Benyon, 1992a) and task boundaries can be very difficult to establish. Despite its shortcomings, HTA provides an effective means of stating how work should be organized to meet a system's goals.

Plans state the conditions which specify when each of a set of subgoals should be carried out, that is, the sequence in which to do operations. Rules of thumb, called the P x C rules, are applied to decide when to stop subdividing tasks further: P refers to the probability of inadequate performance, C to the cost of inadequate performance. A stopping rule says that redescription of an operation/task is unnecessary if the probability of inadequate performance and consequences or costs is acceptable. Cost may be anything of value to the person, product or organization, such as safety, damage to equipment, or a degraded product. The formula is effective because it forces the analyst to consider both performance and consequences, but it is not an accurate, rigorous or reliable measure. When using HTA, the analyst adopts a numbering system to keep track of the work. Tasks, subtasks and operations may be numbered in any way that suits the analyst. An example is given in Fig. 2.1.

2.5.4 PRACTICAL HINTS FOR TASK ANALYSES

Regardless of which task analysis method has been decided upon for the situation a series of systematic steps will help you organize the data

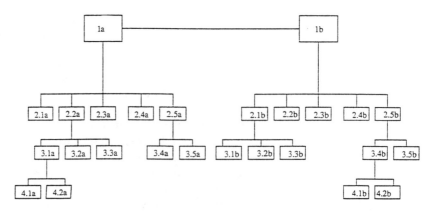

Figure 2.1: An example of a hierarchical layout of tasks, links between these, and sub-tasks.

collection analysis, and the selection of tasks to be analysed. First of all, establish the purpose of the task analysis. Why are you bothering at all? Then, identify a range of tasks to be analysed remembering to take into account their representativeness (typicality) and centrality (importance) for the users (primary, secondary, tertiary) and the users' organization. At this level, a list of tasks to be analysed is produced and verified with the respective task performers, and from the list, a task analysis plan can be set up. Involving users helps to stimulate their interest in the project, and also to ensure that they 'own' the product. This feeling of ownership is extremely important for the system to be accepted by users once it is implemented. System implementation is usually much smoother, simpler and faster when users have been involved from the outset than when a system is dumped on them with little or no warning.

For each task, identify its rationale, the criteria by which it is deemed to have been completed successfully by all classes of users who are involved in it, its products or outcomes. Identify its place in the job of the person or people who perform it or who need the outcomes, and its place in the establishment in which it is performed. If your system is intended to be used in a number of organizations, collect data from a range of these organizations to ensure it is relevant to all and not tailored to one that may differ in important ways from the others. For each task ask who performs it, who needs it or its output, which aspects are/should be/should not be technology dependent, and which ones are/should be/should not be technology independent. Map this in some form, for example, in diagrams or flowcharts, describe tasks in prose, or whatever is most sensible to the users with whom the maps or descriptions must be verified.

Then, focusing on the individual task performer, identify the person's goals, subgoals and subtasks to learn how the task is structured and perceived by the task performer. How are subtasks ordered into particular sequences? This is determined by the individual's task plan and task strategies, that is, how the person performs the task. Task strategies are evident from the procedure the person adopts. Finally, identify all objects and actions involved in the task. For each level of these task analysis procedures, there are thus four steps to be worked through:

- define the purpose (why is this done?);
- collect data (where does it fit, subtasks, strategies...);
- analyse data (what do these data do for the system, your understanding of tasks...);
- model task domain (prototype, represent steps diagramatically or in prose...).

Let us try to work through a high level view of the example introduced earlier (Pharmanet), concentrating on one class of primary users (pharmacists). The primary goal at this level is to select a range of suitable tasks for further analysis.

EXAMPLE: PHARMANET

Identify tasks to be analysed
1. Purpose: understand pharmacists' tasks to select those to be analysed.
2. Collect data: interview and observe users, read source documents, reports.
3. Analyse data: transcribe interviews, refine, distil, summarize until they can be represented at the required level.
4. Model task domain: produce a list with all pharmacist tasks that could be relevant to the system; select the most important to be analysed in consultation with pharmacists (task analysis plan).

Pharmanet: Task Analysis Plan, Pharmacists (Primary users)

Tasks to be analysed	*1.	2.	3.	4.	5.	6.
1. Take orders from ward	√			√		
2. Sign off when delivered to ward	√	√	√	√	√	
3. Order new drugs	√			√		√
4. Acknowledge unused drugs returned to pharmacy			√			
5. Set threshold for ordering		√			√	
6. Consumption reports			√			
7. MIMS						√

*1. drug ordering, 2. drug dispensing, 3. accounting, 4. statistics, 5. dangerous drugs, 6. MIMS

Note that this table shows which system modules will be activated by the pharmacists when they perform these tasks. Note also that all modules are represented more than once in these tasks. Next in this analysis determine, for each task, who needs it/its outcomes, format requirements, and then focus on task performers.

The four-step procedure is repeated for all types and classes of users, and the results may be summarized in a table showing which modules will be used by most users, and which ones will be used rarely. A summary table of this kind is shown below. Note that the number of users or user classes accessing various modules does not necessarily correlate positively with task importance. In Pharmanet, for example, the tax department needs information from a single module only once a year, but the amount of tax the hospital will be required to pay depends entirely on the accuracy of the contents of this one module. Also, the tax department will only accept reports in a single prescribed format that must be strictly adhered to.

EXAMPLE: PHARMANET

Users	Modules					
	*1.	2.	3.	4.	5.	6.
PRIMARY USERS						
Pharmacists	√		√	√	√	√
Ward administration		√	√			
Accountant		√	√	√		
Nurse	√			√	√	
Doctor		√			√	√
SECONDARY USERS						
Hospital management			√	√		√
Drug squad					√	
Tax department		√				
TERTIARY USERS						
System maintenance	√	√	√	√	√	√
Other systems	√	√	√	√	√	√

*1. drug ordering, 2. drug dispensing, 3. accounting, 4. statistics, 5. dangerous drugs, 6. MIMS

The table shows the pattern of usage of modules by all classes of users. Tertiary users are all system or computer experts. Their needs do not enter into user interface considerations, but relate more to the selection of technology, operating systems, etc. In the secondary users category, reports are prepared for the hospital management, the tax department and the drug squad. As the drug squad may conduct spot checks at any time they choose, it is important that system outputs correspond exactly with their requirements. In order to determine the format of system outputs for the tax department, it is necessary to consult with the hospital management to learn more about the other kinds of data they will need to enter into the overall tax statement. Drugs are only a small component in the entire hospital budget, so the format and other system entry requirements will need to be reviewed in the context of tax statements. From the point of view of supporting the human–computer interaction *per se*, the primary users will receive most attention when defining the user interface.

2.5.5 RATIONALE, CRITERIA FOR SUCCESS

The four-step procedure described earlier is applied repeatedly for each task entered into the task plan and at various levels of refinement. Still using Pharmanet as an example, let us consider a specific task, this time one carried out by nurses, administering a dangerous drug to a patient. The rationale for performing this task is first and foremost to keep the patient free of pain. Since a dangerous drug is requested, a number of subgoals related to legal requirements must be fulfilled. Similarly, removal of such drugs from the stock must be registered at ward level, at pharmacy level, in the patient's record and account; drug administration must be time-stamped to ensure that it is within prescribed limits, there must normally be at least a four-hour interval between dosages. Hence, criteria for successful completion of this task include availability of necessary equipment (sterile syringe and needle, gauze), up-to-date records (patient, ward, pharmacy), signed up-to-date drug order (permission to administer the drug to the patient in question), and availability of another authorized person to witness the drug administration. Knowledge of the outcome is thus required by the patient (pain relief, drug chart, record), the pharmacy (maintain stock and re-order when required), the accountant (bill to patient, hospital records), the drug squad (accurate record of consumption and usage), tax department (tax to be paid), statistician (drug record usage pattern in ward and hospital), ward and hospital management (reconcile different records from patient, ward, statistical tally, drug ordering schedule).

2.5.6 IDENTIFY GOALS, STRATEGIES, PROCEDURES

Now, we are ready to focus on the goals, strategies and procedures of the individual task performer. The overall goal at this level is to relieve the patient of pain, but to achieve that, a number of subgoals must be satisfied. These may be made explicit by observing what the nurse actually does and describing these steps.

EXAMPLE:

Goal	Strategy	Procedure
Patient record ok	1. Check record	*Drug order exists *Drug order has been signed *Time lapse since last dose ok
Get drug ready	2. Prepare drug	Count existing stock of required drug *Existing stock corresponds with entry in DD (dangerous drug) book Check contents of ampoule (drug and dose) Read this aloud to witness Witness checks tally in DD book and ampoule *Witness checks drug order and patient record Nurse draws up drug *Nurse enters time, dose, drug into patient record and drug chart *Nurse and witness sign DD book
Administer drug	3. Administer drug	
Complete task	4. Tidy up	throw needle, ampoule, syringe into correct disposal units clean injection tray and put away wash hands ready for next task

*Currently, these procedures are manual but they should be incorporated into Pharmanet

Finally, note the objects/data handled in each action

Action	Object/Data
1. Check record	Drug order in patient record Patient record/drug chart Patient name: Ward: Bed no.: *Patient ID #: *Drug ID: *Dose: *Mode of administration: *Quantity: *Signed by (physician) *Time (last) administered: *Date administered:
2. prepare drug	*Remaining stock:
etc.	etc.

* data also handled by other system modules

This task can now be verified with nurses, perhaps be rewritten in prose as shown below to ensure that the procedure tallies with the manner in which nurses perceive the task of administering dangerous drugs.

Administering dangerous drugs: Task scenario in prose
A patient has just requested an analgesic. Since she underwent major surgery yesterday, there must be a dangerous drug order. Having consulted the patient's drug chart to verify that an order exists and ensured that the order has been signed by the physician, check the time of the last dose. After obtaining the dangerous drug keys that open the cupboard, count the existing stock of the required drug (Pethidine 100 mg IM [intra-muscular]) and ensure that this corresponds with the entry in the DD book. Assuming that it does, remove an ampoule and read the label aloud to the witness who checks the tally in the book, remaining stock and the patient record. Having both signed the book, enter the details into the patient record before drawing up the Pethidine. Return the DD book, lock the cupboard, take the medication to the patient and administer it. That having been done, throw the needle, ampoule and syringe into the appropriate bins, clean the injection tray, put it and the patient record away, wash your hands, ready for the next task.

Clearly, it is a big job to gain the level of understanding of user tasks needed to design Pharmanet (or any system) such that it is consistent with user task requirements. Depending on the type of task to be analysed and therefore on the level of representational detail, steps may be decomposed further than in the above example. For example, time- or safety-critical tasks, or tasks in which the task performer's mental capacity is already stretched to the limit, would probably need to undergo a much more fine-grained analysis, perhaps at the keystroke level, expressed in a grammar (KRG, CLG), in terms of cognitive complexity (CTA) or task knowledge transfer and learning (CCT). Karat and Bennett (1991) describe a method for delineating tasks which they have found useful in analyses of large and complex tasks in which an entire team of analysts work together. In their method, they describe each task, identified by a specific name, in prose defining the function to be supported and the task to be carried out. At this level, the description is intended to provide a summary rather than a specific or complete definition of details. At the next level down, they define the necessary information that must be supplied by the system and the user. Each scenario has one set of generic steps, 'strategy', and specific steps, 'procedure', provide a description of the user actions involved.

It is also clear that co-operation is needed from the task performers to obtain all this information. It may not always be convenient to have analysts in the workplace, so it is necessary to convince the organization receiving the system of the importance of user involvement in task analysis, both from the point of view of transferring task knowledge to the analysts and to facilitate subsequent user acceptance during implementation and thereafter. One way to gain permission of organizations is to draft a component into the task analysis plan which identifies those people whose tasks are to be analysed, and the amount of their time required. One way to develop these details is outlined next.

2.5.7 DETAILS OF THE TASK ANALYSIS PLAN

The task analysis plan should specify the tasks to be analysed and the time commitment the analyst requires of users to construct a set of requirements. The reason for calculating the time requirements of participants is that clients might not realize that some time will have to be spent interviewing, observing and checking your understanding with the future system users. It is advisable therefore to get your task analysis plan approved and agreed to in writing before commencing the analysis.

It is necessary to estimate the resources needed to gather essential information about the tasks. 'Resources' refers to the amount of time users (client's employees) must spend assisting with identifying their needs. Using Pharmanet again, work through the list of users (primary, secondary, tertiary), determine how the requisite data will be collected and estimate how long their help will be needed. Preliminary analyses that are necessary to determine these details are assumed to have taken place during the feasibility phase, and the time spent so far to get to this level should be incorporated into the overall cost of the system.

EXAMPLE: PHARMANET

		User time (hours)	
		A	B
Users involved:	Pharmacists A, B		
Method:	Observations of users	20	20
	Interviews, pre-task analysis	4	4
	Walkthroughs, post task analysis	8	8
	Final check	4	4
	Total	36	36

Involvement by pharmacists amounts to a total of 72 hours during which two pharmacists will be observed, interviewed and asked to comment on the analysis which describes their system-related tasks. The 20 hours of observation will not take them away from their work, so this activity will not be very disruptive to their normal work even though the analyst will be asking lots of questions whilst collecting data. By contrast, the time allocated to interviews, walkthroughs and final checks will require users' complete attention. So, of the 72 hours allocated to define pharmacists' needs, 40 will be non-intrusive, and 32 are devoted entirely to assist the analyst.

By the time each of the relevant user groups has been included in the task analysis plan, the time which the client, in this case, the hospital management, will need to invest may be considerable from an employer's point of view. However, within the overall perspective of the total cost of developing of a new system, the time needed to conduct a thorough task analysis is low enough to be easily justifiable. Redesigning modules, or patching up flaws later, when the system has already been implemented, or when it is nearing completion, is far more expensive than committing the necessary resources to conducting a task analysis early in the project.

2.5.8 JOB ANALYSIS: SEEING TASKS IN CONTEXT

If tasks are identified and analysed in isolation, without gaining an overall appreciation of the job context within which they occur, chances are that an opportunity to connect tasks will be missed. When observing users in action, it is therefore a good idea to stay with them after they have finished the particular task that will be incorporated into the system. Have lunch or coffee with your users, ask questions about their work, the data they handle, time constraints, about what tends to be forgotten when things are busy, where and when they might want reminders about doing something, and so on. At the job analysis level, the task of the analyst is to learn how the tasks foreseen to be provided in a computer system fit into the overall job demands of system users. Indeed, by considering the user's entire job, opportunities for exploiting the technology may become obvious in ways and areas that were not foreseen in system planning.

Take Pharmanet as an example again, none of the nurses' tasks foreseen to be incorporated into Pharmanet have taken into account that nurses also write reports about each individual patient on every shift. Normally, the relevant information is entered into the running patient record when, for instance, a dangerous drug is given, to ensure that the right time of administration is recorded. Too frequent doses can be hazardous to the patient, so time is recorded accurately. However, things do get busy, and even important jobs can be forgotten. It would therefore be helpful if, at the end of a shift, each nurse could obtain a summary of all dangerous drugs administered by herself during her shift, to double check her memory and patient records. Also, when signing the patient's drug chart, the information should be dumped into the running patient report and ward report prepared for the next shift of nurses. The nurse should thus also be recognizable to the system by means of an individual

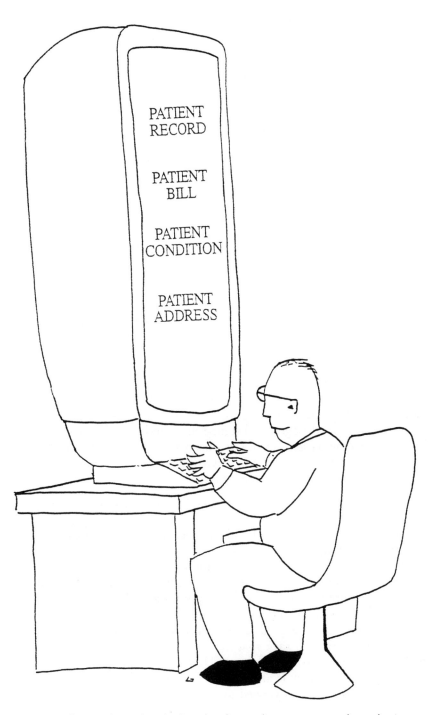

'Combine tasks so that the bits that fit together are presented together'

usercode or password, although the complete logon procedure should probably only be required once on a given shift, because nurses are likely to access the system many times during a single shift.

2.5.9 PHYSICAL AND ENVIRONMENTAL CONSTRAINTS

Consideration must be given to where the system will reside, in order to make the best judgments about input/output devices, interactive dialogue, and so on. A ticket dispenser, for example, which requires a lengthy question-answer dialogue is unlikely to be popular even though the progression of the dialogue may be logical, unambiguous and easy to follow. People rushing to reach their train will be annoyed at wasting time obtaining their ticket. Speed and flexibility are thus important. By contrast, a system erected in a city mall displaying 'what's on in town' information, is likely to be accessed by people who are not in such a hurry, and longer interactive dialogues may be more appropriate. In Pharmanet, it is intended that individual patients' drug records be stored. The way drugs are normally administered should thus be taken into account. The ward nurse who administers drugs on a shift normally pushes around a drug trolley which is an ugly metal monster, lockable, containing all drugs (except the dangerous ones which are locked up in a special cupboard) for every patient as well as providing just enough room for hardcopy patient records. The trolley is wheeled around to each patient, or at least to every ward, a minimum of six times every 24 hours. Patient records, kept in an A3 paper format, are opened, drugs prepared in the appropriate dosages, and signed there and then by the nurse as she gives them to the patient. Even this observation of one single task tells us a great deal about physical and environmental constraints to be taken into account, including the following:

- Whatever terminal is selected, it must be able to run on battery power intermittently.
- The terminal must be small and easily portable, and it must be able to withstand bumps and vibrations.
- Ideally, no keyboard should be required for this task, as it takes up too much space and makes the human-computer interaction clumsy.
- Whatever input device is selected, pointing with a mouse is out, as there is no space on the trolleys, and these will not be redesigned. If a keyboard must be used, then consider track ball inserted into the keyboard instead to save space.
- Beware of glare from the screen. Users are standing up for this task; the top of the trolley is at normal table height. This renders the angle at which the screen is viewed awkward.

This list is not yet complete, but it should underscore the point that a good understanding of the task and the environment in which it is completed eliminates certain possible hardware and software choices, input/output devices and types of interactive dialogues. It makes sense to enter all the constraints of each task investigated into a table which describes each constraint, allowing also for specifying solutions and possible compromise system solutions. Such a table may look something like Table 2.1.

Table 2.1   Physical/environmental constraints and solutions

Physical/environmental constraints

System: ....
Task: ....
Module: ....

Constraint description	System must fit/do	System must avoid	Ideal solution	Acceptable solution	Solution selected
1.					
2.					
3.					
:					
N.					

The purpose of this table is to document the physical and environmental constraints that must be considered and listing these, together with solutions, in a form that can easily be scanned when findings from all the task analyses are compiled. With a sheet filled in for every task under investigation, information can be taken from all of these and summarized for the entire system, module by module, on separate sheets. It is quite possible that constraints existing in one area are irrelevant in another context. In Pharmanet, for example, only the nurses have a requirement for terminal mobility. Therefore it might be appropriate to provide a laptop terminal for each ward as an additional feature, rather than adjusting the entire system to render it suitable for mobility in all user areas.

2.5.10 PROJECTING TASKS ONTO THE NEW SYSTEM

Task analysis has really been completed when tasks have been documented as they are being carried out, in their physical environment, and

'Think about the environment into which the system will go'

in the context of the users' particular jobs. With the understanding gained about tasks and the way they are linked within a job, between departments, and system modules, the pieces of the jigsaw puzzle can be put together and a projection can be made of how the tasks should be portrayed in the new system. As with the previous steps, the evolution of new tasks, or old tasks projected into a new environment, should involve users who need to 'own' the project and give their task-expert opinion on the relative feasibility of suggested solutions.

Summary

This chapter has outlined the major issues involved in defining, documenting and describing user needs within the framework of a user needs analysis. It discussed some of the problems associated with requirements capture and alluded to some of the misunderstandings that can drive both users and systems analysts or designers to make unwarranted assumptions about themselves and each other. The purpose of systems requirements specifications were outlined, and the various components of user needs analyses were discussed in some detail. Consideration about the users were mapped onto a user profile. The notion of task analysis was described and some approaches were discussed. The purpose of task analysis was exemplified and illustrated by reference to a drug administration system. In particular, the need for drafting a task analysis plan was emphasized. Steps involved in outlining tasks as currently done were described and these were captured in task scenarios, shown to be presentable in different ways. Tasks were then seen in an overall job perspective which, in turn, helped to establish the physical and environmental constraints.

Questions

1. Why do systems designers believe they know what users need and want?
2. How do designers normally arrive at their views of users?
3. How and why do users fail to deliver complete information in the requirements specifications phase?
4. What is the purpose of defining user needs?
5. What issues are considered in the SRS?
6. How are primary users distinguishable from secondary and tertiary users?
7. What is a task analysis?
8. What are the five groupings of task analyses described by Kirwan and Ainsworth?
9. What does TAKD aim to do?
10. What is the objective of TAKD?
11. Why might TAKD be an important tool for system analysts?
12. What is HTA?
13. What is the greatest weakness of HTA, or indeed any task analysis approach?
14. What are the four steps involved at every level of a task analysis?
15. Why is it essential to verify the outcomes of a task analysis with task performers?

16. How should task analysis outcomes be presented to task performers?
17. Why is it important to include the time and other resources the customer will need to invest in developing the task analysis plan?
18. Why should time commitments be agreed to beforehand with the client?
19. What is the point of a complete job analysis in the present context?
20. Why do you need to know about physical and environmental constraints in the context in which the system will be put?

Exercises

1. There are many different types and generations of automatic teller machines (ATM), some of which are quite difficult to use, and none of which are perfect. One of the major world banks has now decided to improve matters and develop the best ATM in the market place, and you, as the expert in user needs analysis, have been asked to conduct an analysis so that the bank can issue a realistic tender. Your contract requires that you outline step-by-step how you would go about gathering the necessary information. In particular, you will need to define who 'typical' users are, what range of tasks will need to be analysed, how you would analyse them. Consider any physical and environmental constraints, and design a set of suitable tasks for analysis.

2. The e-mail system used internally in a multi-national engineering company is to be updated, and you are involved in the systems requirements specification stage. So far, most users have been identified as computer experts, and user profiles have been drafted. Tasks as they are currently done have also been analysed, and the analysis shows that users access only a fraction of the options available in e-mail. In fact, their needs could be covered adequately by a set of features which allow them to create/edit, send, store-and-forward messages, reply to messages, store selected addresses, look up a directory of other users on the network, read and file away messages. Outline a series of task scenarios based on these facilities and design an ideal task-based solution to the problem, using any hardware or software you choose.

Suggested further reading

In his paper, Benyon (1992a) discusses the merits and disadvantages of task analysis methods. In particular, he defends the viewpoint that task analysis has not delivered, and will not be able to deliver, much to help systems analysts. It is an interesting critique which is easy to read. Diaper and Addison (1992) provide a counter attack, so to speak, to Benyon's views that task analysis does not have much to offer. Diaper and Addison focus on the merits of task analysis. The two papers, plus Benyon's final say (Benyon, 1992b), are an interesting and a nice example of the way academic debate should be exposed in the literature. All three papers are quite straightforward and provide additional references.

Johnson's (1992) very readable book is a nice way to be introduced to task analysis methods in theory and practice. It provides a good introduction to task analysis in the context of HCI, and many examples and summaries make it an easy text to understand.

Kirwan and Ainsworth (1992) provide a most comprehensive collection of task analysis methods and approaches, complete with full descriptions of each methodology. Their book can be used to select a particular task analysis method, to guide application of any one method, and it provides ready comparison of different approaches. It is probably not the sort of book one would read from cover to cover, but it is easy to read and to locate information.

Karat and Bennett (1991) present quite a simple method which can be readily used by HCI practitioners for separating and keeping apart a multitude of different, yet all relevant, aspects of user interface decisions and development. It is a great real-world example showing how practical techniques can get you very far, and is very easy to read.

3

Data, data collection, analysis and communication: background

A problem is a chance for you to do your best

Duke Ellington

How usable is your computer system? How easy is it to learn to use? Is it better than this or as good as that system? Questions such as these require some quantitative statement to be answered. But beware: taking measurements for the sake of generating numbers may not necessarily yield meaningful statements. What would it mean, for example, to say that 'system X is 15% more usable than system Y'?, or that 'our system is the most usable in the country'? – in isolation, without further qualification, such statements say absolutely nothing! So, when collecting data, careful thought must be given to what those data should demonstrate, and which measurements will allow us to produce meaningful and valid statements. This chapter introduces some of the most important background concepts that one should know a little about in order to make informed choices and sound judgments when planning and conducting usability studies as well as with interpreting and analysing outcomes of such studies and communicating the findings to different audiences. The material presented here is enough to get one started, but it does not discuss statistical methods in great detail, nor does it give any formulae for statistical manipulations, so do consult appropriate texts for more (Christensen and Stoap, 1986; Ferguson and Takane, 1989; Howell, 1985; Jackson, 1988; Lumsden, 1974; Moser and Kalton, 1975; Pfeiffer and Olson, 1981; Thorne, 1980; True, 1989; Winer, 1971).

3.1 Concepts in descriptive statistics

3.1.1 POPULATIONS AND SAMPLES

A population is an aggregate of people, objects or events. A population may be finite or infinite. In a finite population one knows, or can find out, exactly how many members belong to it, for example, the number of letters in the English alphabet, or the number of gold medallists at the Olympic games in Barcelona in 1992. With an infinite population one cannot be certain about the precise number of members belonging to it. The number of first-year computer science students in the world, or the number of Roman Catholics in Latin America would be examples of statistically infinite populations.

'And I'm telling you. Our system is absolutely intuitive, and for added value, it
comes with 10 342 smart features'

In most cases, one is unable to test every person who belongs to the
particular population whose performance, characteristics, needs, expertise or opinions one is trying to capture, analyse and understand. Even
if a highly specific computer system is being designed for a very small and
specialized user population, one is unlikely to consult with everyone who
will eventually be using it. Some ultimate end users may simply not be
available at the time they are needed, or it may be inconvenient or
unfruitful to invest the time that would be necessary to involve absolutely
everyone affected by the proposed system. Time and budgetary-con-
straints as well as considerations of efficiency force us to test samples. A
sample is thus any subgroup drawn by some appropriate method from
a particular population.

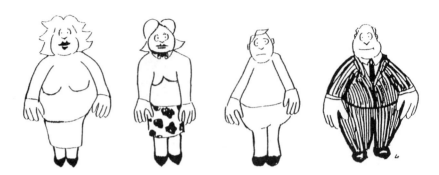

'In a finite population, every body counts'

3.1.2 PARAMETERS AND ESTIMATES

A parameter designates a measurable characteristic or property of a population. For example, one could measure the height, or the grade point average, of the undergraduate population at a particular university. The average height or grade point would then be said to be a parameter of that population. An estimate, also called a statistic, is any measurable characteristic of a sample. Information about properties of samples is of little intrinsic interest, because one is interested in estimating population parameters based on sample statistics. When testing usability, a small sample of subjects (test users) can be run, but the objective is really to generalize the findings to a wider population of people who were not included in the test.

Statistical procedures used in describing the properties of samples, or of a population where data are available from complete populations, are referred to as 'descriptive statistics'. The purpose of descriptive statistics is to summarize the information contained in the variable numbers obtained from measurements of sample or population properties to make it easier to manipulate, comprehend and apply that information. Measures of central tendency discussed below are examples of descriptive statistics. Inferential statistics is concerned with using the data to make predictions or inferences. For example, one might find that the performance of a group of potential users is superior to that of another using the same system and completing the same tasks. Inferential statistics could be used to estimate how likely it is that other samples would show similar superiority. Inferential statistics are not dealt with in this book, so a statistics text should be consulted to learn more about these procedures.

3.1.3 SAMPLING

Sampling methods occupy an important place in the social and behavioural sciences, because sampling is crucial to avoid biasing research
findings. Samples must be representative of the population whose
characteristics one is trying to measure, because the aim is to generalize
the research findings from the sample to the population in question.
Therefore, extreme care must be taken in selecting a suitable sample to
reduce the magnitude of sampling error. Sampling error is the difference
between a population value and a particular sample value. Even though
sample means may be very close to population means, they are almost
never identical. Say, for example, the IQ of every person in a given
population has been measured and the average IQ score has been found
to be exactly 100. If a small sample of that population is then taken, the
average IQ score of that sample would be highly unlikely to be exactly
100. This is because every person's score included in the sample affects
the arithmetic average much more than when scores from the overall
population are taken into account. Because sample scores will almost
invariably differ from population scores, sampling error cannot be
avoided. However, it can be reduced to a minimum by careful sampling.
Random sampling is a method by which every member of the population
under investigation has an equal chance of being included in the sample.
In practice, it is not always realistic or possible to sample completely at
random, in which case semi-random selection methods are often used.

One widespread source of sampling error is the tendency to collect
data about one population from another. For example, project leaders
might communicate with management to establish the user needs rather
than with those end users who will eventually be using the system
although this really does not make sense. It is just not possible adequately
to understand the needs of one group by sampling the opinion of another.
If someone wants to find out what students think about the level of
tertiary fees, for example, they do not ask the lecturers. If someone wants
to know how well, say, a new course in information management is being
received, they do not ask just any students on campus about it, but select
some who are actually doing the course. This is an example of
semi-random selection methods where 'students' are being tested, but
only those who belong to a certain group. If your interest is in the
performance of novices, don't observe experts in action, and vice versa.
Pitfalls and biases associated with sampling methods will not be dealt
with in this book. Suffice it to say that sampling is an area in which a
certain amount of error does occur which can easily lead to the wrong
conclusions about a given population.

'Samples must be representative of the relevant population'

3.1.4 TYPES OF VARIABLES

The purpose of an experiment is to establish cause–effect relationships between the phenomena under investigation. The data should show clearly how variations in one variable cause changes in another. The term 'variable' describes a property or characteristic that, obviously, can vary. That is, it can take different values or levels. In experiments using human subjects it is possible to distinguish between at least three types of variables: independent, dependent, and extraneous variables. Independent variables are the properties to be controlled and/or manipulated experimentally because the effect of these on the dependent variable is of specific interest. Tests might be carried out on different versions of the same system, user manuals varying in the amount of information, different levels of help, and so on. Performance measures such as reaction time, number of errors made, time to complete a task are examples of dependent variables. Extraneous variables are properties which may influence experimental data in ways not thought about in the planning phase. Suppose subjects performed very much better on system A than on system B in a particular study. Quite understandably, one is tempted to conclude that A is better than B. However, one then discovers that system B is placed such that the screen catches the sun in the afternoon and that this makes it almost unreadable. It is not surprising then, that it takes much longer to complete the tasks on system B than on A, especially in the afternoon. The reasons underlying this effect obviously had nothing to do with the design of the system, the tasks or subjects. Therefore, if one concludes that the design of system A is better because people performed better than in system B, the conclusion would certainly be questionable, if not wrong, because the findings from A were affected by something other than the design of the system. Glare, in this example, is an extraneous variable, referred to as an 'experimental error', which distorts, the experimental findings. In order to avoid glare, the terminal can be moved away from the window, experiments can be conducted in the morning only, or a curtain might be drawn across the sun-bathed window through which the sun caused the problem. Any of these measures serves to 'control' for glare, thereby eliminating the experimental error that biased the findings. In exerting control, something is being done to eliminate the effect of extraneous variables on the data. Control (Ch. 6) is thus a means by which to rule out possible threats to the validity of a piece of research.

In addition to independent, dependent and extraneous variables, there are continuous and discrete variables. A continuous variable is one whose measurement can take an infinite number of values. For example, time is a continuous variable. The passage of time may be broken down into an infinite number of units. Between one minute and the next we could subdivide the seconds into milliseconds (1/1000 of a second) or even microseconds (1/1 000 000 of a second). In the measurement of a continuous variable, gaps are introduced by the crudeness of the measurement. A variable is said to be discrete if it can take only certain fixed values. The number of people in a room, number of words spelled correctly, number of test items completed correctly, and so on, are examples of discrete variables. Discrete variables are mostly integers, that is, they consist of whole numbers.

3.1.5 VARIABILITY

Whenever quantitative information is sought about virtually anything, one is struck by the variability of the numbers found. Obviously, people come from different backgrounds, are better at some things than at others, enjoy some tasks more than others. When testing a computer system, performance scores will vary between individuals even when they are drawn from the same population. Once a comparison is made between the performance of members of different populations on the same system, of the same population on different systems, or of different versions of the same system, systematic variability can be detected between groups and/or events. The very point of testing a computer system iteratively is to demonstrate how modifications to the system improves user performance. One might expect the performance of samples drawn from the same population and performing the same tasks on different versions of a system to differ considerably. Hopefully, it will improve with each iteration! Variability within and between groups is thus the key to selecting measurements from which information can be inferred that gives substance to statements about usability, grade point averages, IQ, or whatever is being considered.

3.1.6 MEASURES OF CENTRAL TENDENCY

When some characteristic is being measured, the performance of a sample for instance, the actual scores represent the raw data. Before anything sensible can be done with these data, they should be arranged in some fashion, in some form of frequency distribution. In a frequency distribution the scores are arranged in order from the lowest to the highest, or highest to lowest, and it should be noted how many times each score occurs. Suppose, one wants to know how difficult it is for new users to complete a certain task or set of tasks in a particular computer system. One of the various performance measures, that one might decide to take, is to count the number of errors each test user makes in the task. For a sample of 22 users the initial datafile might look something like this:

13	13	11	10	8	12	10	10	9	8	6
11	6	5	12	7	10	9	11	14	10	12

Clearly, it is very difficult to see any patterns, relationships or characteristics in the raw, unorganized data, so the data is arranged into a frequency distribution:

No of errors	14	13	12	11	10	9	8	7	6	5
Frequency	1	2	3	3	5	2	2	1	2	1

This distribution shows the pattern of errors across test users, but one wants a single number to describe it and to convey as much information as possible about the distribution of scores. Which should it be? The highest, the lowest, or one somewhere in between? There are three measures of central tendency which are useful: the mean, mode and median. The mean, or the arithmetic average, is probably the one encountered most often. In the above example, the mean number of errors was 9.86. The mode is the most frequently occurring score in the frequency distribution and the easiest measure to determine, but it is also the least useful if data is to be manipulated further. It so happened in this distribution that most people made ten errors; the mode was very close to the mean. This is not always the case. The median is the measure least commonly encountered, but it is sometimes the most important one. Formally, it is the point above which half the scores, and below which half the scores lie. It is not as useful for further statistical procedures as the mean, but it is at times the best descriptive measure of central tendency. For example, if you read in the paper that the average income in your town is $250 000, this sounds like a good place to live. If you then learn that the three millionaires living on the outskirts of town were included in the sample, and that it comprised 100 families, together with the fact that the median income is $28 000 in that sample, which measure would you say is more representative of the population, the mean or the median? Whenever there is a sample in which a small proportion of the scores contribute disproportionately to the mean, it is useful also to calculate and report the median. For example, if you had a mean of 9.83 errors but a median of 3.5, what would you say about the distribution? Well, apparently, there were a few users who made a substantial number of errors, but most made very few or even none.

Descriptive statistics can be used (or abused) to reveal different stories about the distribution of scores or events which they represent (Huff, 1954). Care should be taken to report measures that are both meaningful and fair. Reporting a mean score without mention of the sample size, the population from which the sample was drawn, the task from which scores were generated or the instructions subjects were given does not give readers enough detail to form their own judgment about the representativeness of the score. Learn to be critical of what you read, and make sure that your reports enable the reader to get a clear and accurate picture of your study.

Measures of central tendency help to describe some characteristics of a distribution in economical summary statements, but, as mentioned previously, variability is very important. Variability refers to the spread

'It's all a bit of a balancing act'

of scores, and an area of particular interest is the spread of scores around the mean.

3.1.7 VARIANCE

The most commonly used measure of dispersion is the standard deviation. If one wants to know how much each score in a distribution differs from the mean, it is first necessary to calculate the mean and then subtract it from every single score. Obviously, those scores that lie below the mean would result in a negative figure, and those above it would be positive. If one wants to know the average deviation from the mean in the distribution, it does not help to add up all the individual-score deviations, because one important property of the mean is that the sum of deviations around it is zero. So, in order to use deviation scores, some other procedure is needed. The mean is therefore subtracted from each individual score and the result squared. The sum of squares of deviations about the mean is called the variance. The standard deviation is the square root of the variance and is probably the single most useful measure of variability in a distribution. Standard deviations are used to compare means and the dispersion of scores on different sampling distributions in order to determine the likelihood that two or more sets of observations were drawn from the same population. Space does not allow us here to discuss variance or standard deviation in more detail, but if you are planning to run experiments, you should familiarize yourself with the procedures for calculating them.

3.1.8 CORRELATIONS

Correlation is the degree of relationship between two or more variables. Take, for example, height and weight. In general, the taller you are, the more you weigh; height and weight are therefore highly correlated. Similarly, the number of hours one devotes to studying for an exam in, say mathematics, is mostly related to the score one obtains in the exam. It is customary to speak of three classes of correlation: positive, negative and zero. The relationship between height and weight is an illustration of a positive correlation. A positive correlation exists when a high score on one variable is associated with a high score on the other, or a low score on one is associated with a low score on the other. Hence, in a positive correlation there is a direct relationship between the variables; knowing the value of one variable can provide information that would allow us to predict the value of the other.

A negative correlation is one in which a high score on one variable is associated with a low score on another. In other words, there is an inverse

'Is hyperactivity related to computers in the workplace?'

relationship between the two variables. One would expect, for example, to find a negative correlation between the amount of destruction to a given area of the brain and the amount of retention on certain previously learned tasks. That is, the more tissue is destroyed, the poorer we expect the resulting task-performance to be. As with positive correlations, knowledge of the value of one variable can help us to predict the value of the other, but, in contrast to the relationship between two variables in a positive correlation, variables in a negative correlation are inversely related. In a zero correlation there is no relationship between the variables; a high score on one is just as likely to be associated with a low as it is with a high or even with a medium score on the other. In other words, knowing a value for one variable would provide absolutely no information that would allow us to predict a value for the other.

One way to study the relationship between the two variables is to look at the scatter plot of the data. The scatter plot is a graph that plots pairs of scores on one of the variables along the abscissa (x-axis) and the scores on the other variable on the ordinate (y-axis). In general, if the pattern of points on the scatter plot of some data falls close around a straight line slanting upwards to the right, there is a positive correlation. Conversely, if the data falls close around a straight line slanting downwards to the right, a negative correlation can be expected. Where there is zero correlation, the scores are 'scattered' and do not seem to be well described by a straight line. A point that is often overlooked is that high correlations do not imply causality. That is, even though two sets of data are highly correlated, it does not necessarily mean that one causes the other.

Correlation coefficients are applied to determine the degree of relationship between variables. One of the most useful functions of the correlation coefficient is that it helps to predict a value of one variable if the other is known. That is, one can predict how someone will score on variable Y if one knows how they scored on variable X. It was stated earlier that there would be a high correlation between the amount of time spent studying and the score a person achieved on an exam over the material. Given this information and an equation for prediction, someone's performance in exams could be estimated from knowledge of the time that person spent studying. Now, the correlation is the degree of linear relationship between the variables – the degree to which the relationship can be described by a straight line. The instrument developed for prediction, the regression equation, is the equation for the straight line that best describes the relationship between the variables. It makes little sense to determine a regression equation from some data just to predict scores already known. Rather, the equation is used to predict the performance of individuals who have not yet been assessed on both variables (Edwards, 1976).

3.1.9 FACTOR ANALYSIS

Factor analysis is an extension of correlations. The purpose of a factor analysis is to find a limited set of factors (dimensions, attributes, underlying abilities) which permit an economical description of sets of relationships. Suppose one puts together a set of 100 user tasks and one is interested in the relationships between performance on these varied tasks. Then a large sample of potential users, say 40, can be arranged to do these tests, providing $40 \times 100 = 4000$ entries. This amount of information can hardly be comprehended or sensibly used to estimate the relationship between tasks. Factor analysis aims to reduce the problem space to a manageable size by reducing the outcome to the factors which exerted the major influence on the original findings.

3.2 The notion of reliability

The term reliability used in this context means stability or replicability. A set of test scores or other research findings is reliable to the extent that repeat measurements would yield the same results when everything else is kept constant. Human behaviour is notoriously unreliable; performance of any one person varies from one occasion to the next, even when the tasks on which performance is being measured are precisely the same,

administered in exactly the same manner, in the same laboratory by the
same people and under the same conditions as before. Reasons for this
human unreliability include fluctuations in alertness, fatigue, motivation,
mood and level of concentration. Because human performance is known
to vary both between people and within individuals when tested on
several occasions, this variability should be taken into account when
designing, measuring, analysing and interpreting research findings including results from usability tests. One way to deal with the variability
between people when assessing system usability, is to record the
performance of a sample of subjects where each person is tested
individually, but all are doing the same tasks. If one carries out a trial-run
of a computer system on a single person, that person may or may not
perform the way a 'typical' user would. Without comparing that person's
performance to that of several others, one does not know whether he/she
was more or less error prone, was much faster, slower, more or less
interested in the tasks and the system than the fictitious 'typical' user.
Therefore, if crucial decisions about interface design, layout, structure or
contents are based on one set of observations obtained from a single
person on a given occasion, the resulting system may be unusable for
most people.

In addition to testing several people doing the same tasks, the same set
of tasks can also be run through on several different occasions to
compare performance. Whether the same people are used on both
occasions or different samples of subjects are recruited from the same
population, will depend on the purpose of the tests, that is, on the
research question. If, on the one hand, one wants to monitor learning
rate, as evident through changes in performance with increasing experience, one would obviously need to compare the performance of
people to their own results from earlier trials. If, on the other hand, a
system is being modified iteratively to improve its usability, the performance of different people should be compared before and after the
modifications were made precisely because people who have already done
the tasks once have learned something. This 'something' will interfere
with, and be indistinguishable from, effects of the modifications. Since an
assessment is wanted of the effects on system usability of modifications
made to it, a new sample of subjects would be needed who are
uncontaminated by their previous experience on the system. This would
be the 'after modifications group'. Using the first set of results obtained
from an independent group of subjects as a baseline measure (the 'before
modifications group'), one would naturally expect performance of the
'after group' to be better than that of the 'before group'.

A number of different tools can be used to test reliability. Outlined
here are only those that are most relevant to usability tests, but you are
encouraged to consult other sources for further detail (eg. Anastasi,
1976; Carmines and Zeller, 1979; Fisher, 1982; True, 1989). In order to

measure reliability at all, you basically need two sets of data which are comparable in some fashion.

3.2.1 TEST–RETEST RELIABILITY

Establishing a baseline measure against which to compare subsequent data is one method with which one can assess reliability using a test–retest formula. Strictly speaking, the reliability coefficient is the correlation between scores obtained by the same persons on two different variables or occasions. However, testing different groups, or samples, on two occasions but under the same conditions also gives an indication of baseline reliability. For example, usability test scores obtained before and after system modifications respectively could be expressed as a correlation and would require the matching and pairing of subjects from the two tests. Retest reliability shows the extent to which scores can be generalized over different occasions.

3.2.2 SPLIT-HALF RELIABILITY

The split-half reliability is calculated by dividing the test into two comparable halves and then comparing individuals' performances on the two test halves. Designing tasks so that subjects are required to perform the same operation at different stages of the test will reveal whether they actually master the procedure, or whether someone got it right (or wrong) first time because of the particular task context. Obviously, the entire set of user tasks could be built around two comparable test halves if the decision was taken to apply a split-half reliability test to the results. One advantage over test–retest reliability is that reliability tests are built into one experiment or test, saving repetition later. The choice of one method over the other, however, depends on the purpose of the test and the nature, length and complexity of the material being tested. A detailed discussion of these considerations is beyond the scope of this book, but may be found in texts such as Anastasi (1976), Carmines and Zeller (1979), or True (1989).

3.2.3 SCORER RELIABILITY

The final type of reliability test is the so-called scorer reliability. Scorer reliability refers to the stability, or the level of agreement, between observations made on a single occasion by two individual observers. Imagine, for example, that you are conducting a usability test in the field where you cannot readily videotape the test session, or in which it is not always clear how performance should be scored. Suppose you are observing how system experts use a particular piece of new software, the usability of which you are trying to assess. It will probably be difficult to determine exactly when such a user is committing an error based on a misunderstanding of how the system works, and when he is playing to explore the system. Whether or not the session is videotaped, it might be useful for two observers to note and score the user's performance to assess the level of agreement between them on the problems observed. Scorer reliability provides a degree of control to the observations as such, thereby reducing the risk of scorer bias entering into the data.

Validity concerns what a test measures and how well it does so. That is, **3.3 Validity** it is an assessment of the success of a test in measuring what it sets out to measure. If in a particular computer program under the usability microscope, one concludes that there are 20 major flaws based on observations of experts' error rates, one wants to be reasonably sure that the definition of 'error' is accurate. The criteria used to define a particular kind of observation an 'error' may themselves be flawed. If the criteria for labelling an event an 'error' were too conservative, it would be possible to over-correct the system by modifying areas in which modifications were not required because some explorative user behaviour would be incorrectly identified as 'erroneous'. By contrast, if a too liberal approach was used in setting the criteria for defining user errors, the test might well have missed several important system areas that should have been looked at more closely. Either way, the validity of the usability test results aiming to expose 'user errors' would be lower than ideal. As was true for the concept of reliability, there are several kinds of validity which should be considered in different circumstances. Only three kinds that are most relevant to usability tests are discussed here. These are content validity, face validity and ecological validity.

Content validity refers to the content of a test, a set of questions in a questionnaire or an interview. Content validity focuses on the actual content of the tasks or questions under consideration, and it is built into tests or tasks from the outset through the choice of appropriate test items, questions, or task requirements. Objectives to be covered in a test should be determined first. From explicit statements of objectives, one can then specify the areas of skill, knowledge of methods or principles, navigation and comprehension that would help to achieve these objectives. Next, lists of items, subtasks or questions designed to test each objective should be drawn up. For each item, one would then determine which of the areas it covers to ensure that all areas are represented in the final array of subtasks or questions in the test. Answers can then be obtained to two questions central to content validity:

'Does your test measure what it says it measures?'

- Does the test cover a representative sample of the specified areas?
- Will test performance be reasonably free from the influence of extraneous variables?

The way content validity 'works' is perhaps best illustrated by an example:

EXAMPLE:
Staff in a university department in Australia recently expressed concern with the quality of the contents of some of its courses. To get a feeling for the students' perception of course content quality, the staff devised a questionnaire which was administered to the students. On closer scrutiny of this questionnaire, it was evident that the term 'quality' had been translated into 'communication efficiency' in the sense that students were asked to rate things like the speed of getting feedback from lecturers (exam marks, project marks), and the adequacy of their comments on the students' work. The questionnaire therefore really measured the students' perception of the efficacy of course delivery rather than yielding data about actual course contents. Yet, the original concern was with quality of course content, not with course delivery. The questionnaire clearly failed to measure what it set out to, and the findings were correspondingly low in validity: the department knew no more about students' perception of course-content quality after the data had been gathered than it did before.

In this example, inadequate thought had apparently been given to identifying the areas that represent 'course-content quality'. Consequently, the selection of questions directed to the students was not guided by their relationship to the representative areas, and the objective of the questionnaire was not met.

Content validity should not be confused with face validity. Face validity is not validity in the technical sense; it does not refer to what the test measures, but to what it appears superficially to measure. Face validity pertains to whether the test 'looks valid' to the people who will be completing it. To the extent that a test situation attempts to capture 'typical' usage of a computer system, face validity is both an important and desirable feature. Usability tests that appear irrelevant, inappropriate, silly or childish are likely to be treated rather less formally by the test users than one would prefer. Consequently, the resulting data may not give an indication of how users would behave naturally in the kind of situation observed. It is not enough to ensure that a test is objectively valid; it also needs face validity to secure the co-operation of test users. This is not saying that artificial, esoteric tasks are always out of place – far from it! Most formal laboratory experiments strip reality away from the tasks, thereby removing any resemblance to 'real' work, to allow better control of the variables being tested. This will be discussed in Chapter 6. Yet, even when tasks are not 'real' or 'natural', one simply needs to set the scene by instructing subjects appropriately, thereby lending some degree of face validity to the situation.

The notion of ecological validity originated in the work of Egon Brunswik (1955) whose philosophy of 'probabilistic functionalism' led him to study the successes and failures in an uncertain environment (Slovic and Lichtenstein, 1971). Brunswik realized that behaviour is not only about people who emit it, but also about the tasks that elicit observable behaviour. Brunswik's theoretical orientation was committed to an analysis of the interrelation between an organism and its environment. He was the first to make explicit the fact that modelling tasks is different from modelling people, and he sought to devise tools for modelling tasks that would provide linkages between models of tasks and models of people (Edwards, 1971). The important message to researchers and evaluators in the usability arena is that it is not enough to evaluate usability in a laboratory setting; one must also observe how well the system functions in its environment by observing what real users do in their environment and the context in which the computer supports their tasks. (Holtzblatt and Jones, 1992; Whiteside and Wixon, 1987)

Having talked about some of the background concepts one needs to know about in order to design usability tests, let us now turn to the actual data. Before one sets out to gather data, the problems to be pursued must be identified and, to identify reasonable problems, it is necessary to know about some of the traps one can fall into that can lead to spurious, invalid results and conclusions. These are discussed next.

3.4 Where people often go wrong: problem formulation

The strategy people employ in solving a particular problem is determined by the manner in which they perceive and interpret the nature and cause of that problem. People's perception of a problem is, in turn, determined at least in part by what they already know from their experience and background. Taking an everyday example, suppose you are baking a loaf of bread and find it has not risen during the baking process as you would expect. There could be several reasons for this, including:

1. the oven was too hot from the outset – this killed the yeast cells, thereby preventing them from completing their job of making the bread rise;
2. the ingredients may not have been mixed well enough for the yeast to have the desired effect;
3. the amount of yeast may have been insufficient relative to the amount of dough to be baked;
4. the dough had not been left long enough to mature before being placed in the oven.

Now, if you believe the oven was too hot, your problem solving strategy would be to lower the oven temperature next time you bake a loaf of bread. If you have more faith in cause 2., you would naturally mix the dough more thoroughly next time; if 3. seems to explain the cause of the problem, then you would add more yeast next time you bake bread – and so on.

Whichever you choose as the most likely explanation for your dilemma will depend on your experience as a bread baker. An experienced baker will look for further evidence to strengthen the case in support of one, eliminating other possible causes by disconfirmation, before deciding which of the alternatives is most likely to apply. An expert bread maker will judge the loaf by its appearance, colour, the extent to which the bread is baked through, how well it cuts, its inside looks, and so forth. All of these pieces of information are sources of evidence of which the novice baker may be ignorant. Therefore, the reasoning underlying a particular choice of possible cause will vary substantially between experts and novices simply because their level of experience dictates the questions they are able to ask when examining a certain outcome.

In computing, it is also true that novices and experts differ in their approach to problem solving which, in turn, gives rise to a variety of potential solutions. Evidence for novice and expert differences come from other areas as well. In distinguishing between different degrees of expertise conceptually, Kolodner (1983) has, for example, argued that the 'expert is more knowledgeable about his domain and uses his knowledge more effectively than does a novice' (p. 497). This implies that expert knowledge differs from that of novices in both kind and degree (Ehrlich and Soloway, 1983; Larkin *et al.*, 1980). Studies in the expert and novice differences area include investigations of the way knowledge structures develop (Kolodner, 1983; Wagner *et al.*, 1985), and attempts to analyse the relationship between users' prior knowledge and their performance on a computer in a similar task (Waern, 1985). Experts are found to use fewer, but more powerful, commands for completing certain computing tasks than novices (Elkerton and Williges, 1985), and in contrast to novices, they tend to chunk information as well as to remember the rules which string chunks together in areas such as programming (Barfield, 1986). Similar examples of distinct differences are found in areas as diverse as studies of skill in algebra (Lewis, 1981), reasoning skills and misconceptions of motion (McCloskey, 1983), space and motion (Forbes, 1983), or students' theories of temperature and heat flow (Williams *et al.*, 1983; Wiser and Carey, 1983).

It is sometimes suggested that insight gained through training can be instrumental for students to see problems in new perspectives. Wagner *et al.*, (1985) conducted an experiment in which subjects made ratings of similarity for pairs of commands taken from two commercial word processing systems. The authors found that, after training, the basis for perceiving commands to be similar shifted from natural language to functions in the system. For example <FIND> and <GET> were seen to be highly similar prior to training, but were perceived to be quite dissimilar after training. This, the authors assert, reflects the fact that <GET> refers to a function in the file to recover a stored document, while <FIND> refers to a function within a document to locate specified text. Hence, appreciation of specificity appears to develop as a function of training, of exposure to, and understanding of, the functions available in a given system. It is perhaps not surprising, therefore, that novices and experts differ in the way they formulate problems, and that they select different frames of reference for solving problems.

It has been found that students with extensive computer training tackle problem-solving tasks unrelated to computing in a different manner to students without such training (Waern *et al.*, 1986). One may speculate whether computer training helps students to approach problems in new ways, or whether students who tend to view problems in ways that suit the computer environment are more likely than others to take up computer studies. It is an open question whether computer experts are also better general problem solvers *a priori*, or whether they acquire more analytic skill through computer training that can then be applied to other areas. Both sides of the argument have received support in the literature, that is, effect of training (Mayer, 1975; 1979; 1980; 1981; 1988; Mayer *et al.*, 1984) and inherent differences in cognitive style (Ash and Loeb, 1984; Braune and Wickens, 1986; Egan, 1988; Kak and Ambardan, 1984).

All this amounts to saying is that it cannot be assumed that people will formulate problems in a particular fashion, and that training may not necessarily enhance the users' ability to formulate problems exactly as foreseen by designers. Always keep this in mind and take it into account both when designing and testing systems.

3.4.1 FLAWED HYPOTHESIS TESTING APPROACHES

The ability to formulate problems is intimately intertwined with hypothesis-testing strategies which, in turn, are closely related to data-sampling strategies. Returning for a moment to the example of the bread loaf that refused to rise, say, you hypothesize that the oven was too hot at the outset. As an expert, you know that too hot an oven will make the outside of the bread very dark, with a very thick crust, especially at the bottom. At the same time, the bread will be doughy in the middle, not quite baked through. If you hypothesize that the mixing was at fault, you will cut your loaf through in the middle looking for lumps of flour, pockets of fat, or places in which a few air bubbles indicate the presence of yeast that did its job – and so on for any other possible causes. In other words, the evidence to look for (the data to sample) depends on the hypothesis to be tested.

Differences in hypothesis-testing strategies have also been noted in various areas in which human problem solving has been studied. Chi *et al.* (1981), for example, required novices and experts to sort physics textbook problems in any way they liked. Novices sorted these according to the type of apparatus involved (lever, inclined plane, balance beam), the words used in the problem statement, or the visual features of the diagram presented with the problem. Experts sorted the problems according to the underlying physics principle that was required to solve the problem (energy laws, Newton's second law, etc.). Hence, novices were affected more by the way the problem was presented: experts brought their knowledge of important principles to bear in a way that enabled different hypotheses to be tested, thereby reshaping the problem, usually into a more soluble form. In this kind of task, novices apparently translated the given information directly into formulae (Resnick, 1985). They then spent the bulk of the remaining time working on these formulae using rules of algebra. In other words, novices sought to massage the problem into a particular solution which seemed, at a first glance, to 'fit' the conditions. By contrast, experts worked for a while on reinterpreting the problem and specifying the various objects and relations in the situation described and testing various hypotheses. Their point of departure for solving the problem was a consideration of the general underlying principles; focusing on the problem itself was a second step in the problem solving procedure. By the time they were ready to write equations, the experts had virtually solved the problem. This suggests that experts tend to take a global view of the problem, such that a new version of it accords with the information given, but one that is reformulated in terms of general principles, testable hypotheses and laws that make the solutions more apparent.

In order to test an hypothesis systematically, one must understand the testing principles. People have a tendency to seek evidence confirming the hypothesis they have in mind; this is the so-called 'confirmation bias' (Klayman and Ha, 1984; Mynatt *et al.*, 1977; Nisbett and Ross, 1980; Snyder and Swann, 1978; Wason, 1960; 1968). However, confirmatory evidence does not test anything, and nor does it 'prove' that the prevalent hypothesis is 'correct'. In fact, it can never be 'proven' that something is 'right' or 'correct' at all, although confirmatory evidence can lend support to a hypothesis. The only way to test the truth of a statement is to expose it to a situation in which it is possible to falsify it (Popper, 1980). Falsification is achievable by changing one variable at a time, and then retesting before another one is changed. This need to eliminate different competing explanations of a phenomenon is the basis for effective learning and for increased understanding.

When one conducts usability studies, trouble-shooting a particular product, the immediate goal is first to identify, and then to fix, usability defects. It may be satisfactory to show that a given problem which occurred in an early version of the product has been successfully removed. However, the more interesting questions to ask are 'why' did this problem occur at that point, and 'what' motivated the user to do what he did? The investigative methods outlined in this book are as well suited to answering such questions as they are to identifying usability defects. If you are interested, and you are fortunate enough to have the time and resources to pursue deeper issues, you might find the areas of problem formulation and hypothesis generation/testing rewarding places to look for research ideas. Even if you are not interested in developing a greater depth of understanding of user behaviour, it is still worth the effort to consider what might underlie user responses that turned out to be 'incorrect'. The search for possible reasons can help widen your own reasoning base and open up new avenues for generating and testing hypotheses. Besides, it is also much more fun trying to reason through different possibilities. Because we are paradigm-bound, we tend to limit ourselves to explanations within reach from our immediate knowledge base. Asking why something happens, exploring new possibilities may help us move beyond our limited horizon, create new challenges to widen our understanding of how people interact with computers. That's what HCI is all about.

3.5 Data generation and collection: vehicles and mechanisms

3.5.1 PROTOTYPES, PHYSICAL MODELS AND MOCKUPS

Apart from the concept of user models which were addressed in Chapter 1, the notion of (physical) models and mockups has been applied in ergonomics/human factors since these became fields in their own right, that is, since the end of the First World War (Shackel, 1991b). Models and mockups have traditionally occupied an important place in conceptualizing ideas in the physical sphere, simulating the size and layout of equipment, control panels and consoles in the design and development of large systems. According to Meister (1986), a mockup is a full scale simulation of a system which can be either two- or three-dimensional. A two-dimensional mockup may consist of a complete set of engineering drawings pinned up on a wall and representing the entire system proposed, in its full, natural scale. A three-dimensional mockup may be static or dynamic. A static mockup has no moving or functioning parts, whereas a dynamic mockup does include a range of functionalities. Functionality may be as simple as a switch that can be flicked but which controls nothing, or it may be so sophisticated that it can function in a quasi-operational manner which utilizes microcomputers to simulate actual operation. Physical models, by contrast, are reduced-scale mockups which cannot be used for conducting human performance tests that require the user to interact directly with the system. As with mockups, models can be two- or three-dimensional. The distinguishing factor between models and mockups is the scale: mockups are full scale, and models reduced-scale representations of systems. A good discussion of advantages of mockups and models in systems development may be found in Seminara (1985).

The notion of prototypes tends to be confined to computers and matters to do with the development of computer systems. The purpose of a prototype is to demonstrate a set of abstract ideas about a computer system in a concrete form. Prototypes aim to show that the proposed system is, in principle, realizable. They are, much like models and mockups, early versions of a particular system or type of system. Exactly when an abstract idea qualifies as a prototype is unclear. The boundary between a prototype and a fully fledged system is also somewhat blurred, as some prototypes are operational and quite sophisticated. Indeed, some authors distinguish between functional, design and implementation prototypes which differ in their degree of completeness and similarity to the final system. However, one useful distinction is drawn between 'dynamic' and 'static' prototypes (Harker, 1991), where 'dynamic' prototypes allow hands-on experience and 'static' ones are for demonstration purposes only. A similar distinction is made by Johnson (1992) between 'runnable' and 'non-runnable' prototypes where the former is a 'dynamic' simulation of an evolving system and the latter a 'static' representation of what the system might look like. There are many testimonies to the value of early prototyping (Gould, 1988); some arise from cases in which early prototyping did not take place (Woodmansee, 1985), and others describe benefits, for example, facilitating communication between users and designers (Alavi, 1984) and as vehicles for testing user performance (Wasserman and Shewmake, 1990). Models, mockups and prototypes are all representations of system concepts which, in themselves, are incomplete, but which vary in completeness and sophistication and which can be useful for conducting certain types of usability tests early in the design and development process. Models and mockups are good for trying out physical dimensions and relations. As the concern here is with usability in the cognitive sense, the following comments will be confined to prototypes only. No further mention is made of physical models or mockups.

3.5.2 THE ROLE OF PROTOTYPES IN USABILITY TESTING PROGRAMS

Computer system prototypes can be useful for conducting system-specific usability tests early in the development process. In order to tie test and evaluation findings to a particular system, one needs prototypes at some level so that at least the system concepts can be portrayed in a concrete form. The central role of prototypes in usability testing is to demonstrate and test aspects of HCI that might be difficult or more time-consuming to produce in another medium. One important disadvantage is that prototypes are examples of 'trial-and-error' design, and they may lock a project team into a particular way of thinking about a proposed interface early on rather than encourage the team to explore several possibilities. This may be especially true for a dynamic prototype presented on a computer: even with rapid prototyping tools available, they require considerably more effort than producing series of sketches on paper.

At the most primitive level, a (static/non-runnable) prototype may be a mere façade capable only of demonstrating the system concept but unable to respond to user input. At the other extreme, the (dynamic/runnable) prototype might be sufficiently advanced to perform certain interactions, perhaps lacking only access to a live database. Whether a prototype belongs to the primitive, the supremely adv or somewhere in between at the time one employs it in a set of us tasks, would depend on the questions one wants to answer and form the basis for further decisions about the development of the s In terms of programming productivity, prototyping has been com with specifying design approaches. Boehm *et al.* (1984), foun students undergoing a one-semester design course wrote 40% les and required 45% less time to complete their systems than specification students, and that their systems were judged easier to and use. Design specification students, by contrast, designed systems that had more functions, were more robust and more coherently designed.

Considering the power even of pen and paper experiments, it is often advantageous to produce two or more prototypes portraying the same concepts in different modes. Consider, for example, a geographical information system that stores information about land packages. A land package may be a vacant building block, a park, or an occupied building block. Each land package has a title which is owned by someone (e.g. a private person, a business or the government). A database can show the exact position of any land package, its relationship to roads, gas and water pipes, electricity and telephone cables, drains, and whatever is dug into the ground; it has information about the exact size of each land package, the ID number/lot number, perhaps information about soil composition, about the person/department who owns the land, how long they have held the title, about existing dwellings and date the building permits were issued, and so on. Now database queries may be performed via interactive form filling dialogues with text outputs. This will probably be the easiest and quickest method to adopt for answering certain queries such as locating title holders, lot numbers, land size, and so on. Alternatively, one could design such a system in a windows-type, graphics-based environment which is likely to be much better for answering queries about relationships between roads, gas pipes, water drains, etc. by people who want to build an extension or a new house on a vacant block of land. Such relational information may be most easily perceived when presented in graphical form. The form of interaction chosen should depend on the nature of the information users need to retrieve, the relative frequency of different types of enquiries, the tools they prefer to use and whether they answer more queries over the counter or on the telephone. Given the level of user expertise, it could actually be quicker to retrieve the information needed to answer any query using simple commands, perhaps using F-keys. A geographical information system could be one in which it might be wise to produce two prototypes to demonstrate the different concepts to the users, and then rely on their judgment as well as on the user-needs analysis and a measure of the frequency with which different tasks are performed.

3.5.3 HOW TO COMPENSATE FOR THE INCOMPLETENESS OF PROTOTYPES

When designing usability tests for incomplete systems, one basically needs to invent ways to add missing information that users must have available to complete typical work-related tasks. Test conditions must thus be compatible with the task requirements and the system philosophy. Now, since test design is under the control of the tester, as is the selection of data types, methods of data logging and analysis, it really is up to you to work out how to get the most mileage from prototype testing. A few suggestions are given next.

3.5.4 PEN AND PAPER SIMULATIONS

The value of pen and paper studies is often overlooked. Yet, pen and paper studies can save a great deal of time, effort and money by enabling different ideas to be shown and user tested before a particular approach is settled upon. Some authors doubt that pen and paper studies are of much, if any, value in a systems design/development context (e.g. Williges and Hartson, 1986). However, many studies fail to simulate very accurately the situation that would have existed if the variables investigated had been presented online. It is therefore not surprising that authors are sometimes disappointed in the degree to which they were able to predict user performance on the system from their pen and paper observations. When planning a pen and paper simulation study it is important to ensure a high level of correspondence between conditions and responses in the simulation representing the proposed system. A pen and paper study that investigates specific issues which have been removed from the system context in order to arrive at a generic answer that can be applied to several different types of systems is naturally not subject to the same requirements of fidelity.

Four types of situation suitable for investigation in a pen and paper format are given next to illustrate how, with a bit of imagination and application of the principles underlying experimental designs (Chapter 6), they can be useful. The list is not exhaustive, but intended to give a few ideas for how to think about and test a problem.

EXAMPLE: NON-INTERACTIVE PEN AND PAPER SIMULATION

Testing electronic message headers
When you create and send e-mail messages, you need to activate a number of options available in the system. Many options could be phrased as questions and presented in a form displayed on the screen, which could also be custom-tailored to assume certain default setups. The form itself (e.g. layout, caption-clarity, sequence of items, responses required from the user and so on) might as well be given to a group of subjects on pieces of paper, together with typical data to be entered against the captions. In a pen and paper format, you are able to test several people simultaneously; on a system this must be done one at a time unless you are using a network of computers.

```
┌─────────────────────────────────────────────────────────┐
│                                                         │
│   Sender's name: ............................................  │
│                                                         │
│   Sent on behalf of: .........................................  │
│                                                         │
│   Message description: ........................................  │
│                                                         │
│   Replying to previous message: ..............................  │
│                                                         │
│   Related messages: ..........................................  │
│                                                         │
│   Forwarded message: .........................................  │
│                                                         │
│   Multiple recipients: ........................................  │
│                                                         │
│   List of other recipients: ....................................  │
│                                                         │
│   Primary recipients: ........................................  │
│                                                         │
│   Copy recipients: ...........................................  │
│                                                         │
│   Reply requested: ...........................................  │
│                                                         │
│   Speed of delivery                                     │
│   (express, normal or low priority): ...........................  │
│                                                         │
│   Delivery confirmation: ......................................  │
│                                                         │
└─────────────────────────────────────────────────────────┘
```

The instructions from which subjects are required to enter information on the 'screen' might be presented in the following manner:

- include a brief outline of what the message is about (pneumatic valves);
- include the sender's name on the envelope (Mr Edwards);
- indicate that this message is a direct response to a previous message with identification number 8823;
- this message is to be sent to more than one person (Answer Y*);
- request that the message be delivered at the fastest possible rate;
- notify the recipients that this message includes another message which is being passed on (Answer Y*);
- indicate that the message requires a response (Answer Y*);
- each recipient of this message is to be informed as to who else will also be receiving the message (Answer Y*);
- indicate that the contents of this message are relevant to previous messages 5436, 7692, 3881;
- Mr Wright is the main recipient of the message. Mr Young and Mr Elder are to receive copies;
- inform the recipients that the sender is writing for his boss Mr Bell;
- request that the sender be informed when the message has been successfully delivered (Answer Y*).

*this information is not given to subjects, but is presented here for the convenience of the reader.

(Adapted from Lindgaard and Perry, 1988)

Evidently, form length, captions, appearance, sequence of items, and so on, can be simulated quite accurately in a pen and paper format. The findings arising from the study should then be readily transferable to the system being designed or improved. A pen and paper study of this kind would normally be done before programming commences.

The second type of pen and paper study is a variation of the so-called Wizard-of-Oz technique (Good *et al.*, 1984). In this approach, an assistant 'simulates' the computer by responding in the fashion one might expect a computer to respond, except that the software tested is only a façade. Two computers are connected such that, whatever the user enters is shown on the experimenters' screen as well. The experimenter, who is hidden from the subject's view, types a suitable response displayed on the user's screen which makes it appear as if the computer was implemented and fully operational. Gould *et al.*, (1983) and Kelley (1984) give examples of similar techniques.

The experimenter must know exactly how the computer, which does not yet exist, is intended to respond to every entry a subject might submit. Tasks are presented on cards, paper or audiotape. The subject is given a piece of paper with the legal 'system prompt', which looks like the computer screen, and he writes his first entry on the paper, just like he would be typing it into the computer. At the end of the entry, the subject writes a RETURN or other agreed upon symbol to indicate an ENTER action. The experimenter then looks at the entry and, with her knowledge of the task the subject is trying to complete as well as of the system, she is able to respond verbally in the same fashion that the computer would provide written output on the screen. In contrast to the original Wizard-of-Oz method, the experimenter is not hidden from the subject's view. The experimenter's responses are strictly confined to 'computer outputs' in the sense that she 'responds' to entries made on the paper screen yielding only the kinds of messages the computer would emit if it were operational.

Whilst this method is less elegant than an online display, it can be a most enlightening and easy way to gather data very quickly. The method has been used profitably in our laboratory to test a wide range of issues and systems, including auditory prompts, as a means of comparing the performance of subjects online with those doing the same tasks offline. In one study, findings from the pen and paper condition were very similar to those obtained from the live system; results from the auditory prompts tests led to modifications to the system which subsequently were shown to have improved the comprehensibility of the prompts considerably.

The third type of pen and paper studies referred to is the so-called 'hybrid' studies which comprise a mixture of computer displays and paper simulated aspects of systems or system parts. Hybrid studies are combinations of several different conditions, where perhaps parts of a system have been implemented and others, yet to be provided online, are undergoing systematic testing. Hybrid studies are appropriate, for example, when designing help for an existing system, or when ways are being sought to modify certain system responses. In the case of providing help, one would design the system and present it screen-by-screen as if it were available online. When requested by the subject, one would simply show him/her the screen or prompt he/she would have been given if the system had been implemented. If the interaction traverses several screens, the necessary information must be provided to enable navigation; that is, present relevant and appropriate commands on the screen allowing access to 'previous page', 'next page', and so on. From each screen, the subject can then make appropriate requests by implementing a command verbally. The experimenter will respond as the computer would. So if the user requests an invalid option, the experimenter would respond with the appropriate error message, ready for the next action. When the simulated interaction is finished, for instance when the user wants to 'exit help' or has received the information he/she was after, the task is continued on the computer system.

The final pen and paper simulation is the 'storyboarding' method. Storyboarding is a means for prototyping aspects of a system that allows users to experience the system concept in a concrete fashion (Andriole, 1987). Storyboards are interactive screen displays of system functions. The prototype system models may include a variety of flowcharts, e.g. pictorial, serial presentation of the flow of information; work flowcharts which are visual presentations of the flow of paper or manual work. These can be presented on a computer system or as a wall display. Storyboarding is used as a means for the project team to keep abreast of the possible solutions rather than as a vehicle for testing usability.

3.6 The when, where and how of data collection

Having considered some of the mechanisms (or vehicles) that may be employed in data collection, let us now discuss some other aspects, the when, where and how of data collection. There are many ways to divide up these fields, and none is more 'correct' or 'logical' than others; how the jigsaw puzzle is broken up really depends on what one proposes to do with the bits. Here, an overview is presented that gives a number of choices that can be made. With respect to the 'when' of data collection, it is easy: data will be gathered either during task performance or at some other time. Methods for collecting data during task performance include experiments, quasi-experiments, confirmation studies, contextual in-quiries and protocol analysis. The 'where' of data collection is either in the field or in the laboratory. Data gathering in the laboratory is discussed in Chapter 6, and field studies are described briefly in this chapter. 'How' data are collected may be through observation, inspection, or retrospective. Observations are usually made of one or more persons, or of a system. In either case, data are likely to be recorded on videotape, audiotape, electronically, or manually. Techniques for inspecting a system, simulation or partial system such as a prototype, include heuristic evaluations and walkthroughs. Retrospective methods include a variety of knowledge elicitation techniques. In summary, the picture presented in this book is like in Table 3.1 below.

Table 3.1 The when, where and how of data collection: methods presented in this book

When	Where	How
during task performance	laboratory	experiments (Ch. 6)
		quasi-experiments (Ch. 6)
		confirmation studies (Ch. 4)
		contextual inquiries (Ch. 4)
		protocol analysis (Ch. 4)
		question-asking protocols (Ch. 4)
any other time	laboratory	heuristic evaluation (Ch. 4)
		cognitive walkthroughs (Ch. 4)
		source documentation (Ch. 4)
		repertory grids (Ch. 4)
	field	knowledge elicitation methods (Ch. 4)
		interviews (Ch. 5)
		surveys (Ch. 5)
		multi-dimensional scaling/card sorting (Ch. 4)
		content analysis (Ch. 4)

3.6.1 OBSERVATIONS IN THE FIELD

Data collection takes place in the laboratory or in the field. Observations in the field are conducted either in an effort to describe what is going on in a given environment or situation, or as field experiments. Descriptive field studies aim to understand procedures or interactions between people as they normally occur when researchers are not present to record events. In these kinds of studies the researcher behaves unobtrusively, trying to 'blend in' with the background so that his/her presence does not distort or hide the patterns of human communication he/she is trying to elucidate and understand. However, the very presence of an observer is likely to change the behaviour of those being observed. For example, when trying to understand how people interact with a particular computer system which is to be replaced, the researcher needs to be so close to the user and the screen and keyboard that he/she can see exactly what the user does at all times. When sitting right beside or behind an active user, taking notes and asking questions, the researcher could hardly pass as just another person on the shop floor. Indeed, it would be a gross invasion of privacy openly to spy on people without telling them what is being done and why, so normally a researcher would explain the purpose of the study and obtain the users' consent to participate before starting observations.

In other situations, it would be more appropriate for the researcher to pretend he/she is a new member of the team. Suppose, for example, one wants to investigate different strategies people might employ in doing the same set of tasks. The purpose of such a study could be to explain large differences in productivity or in product quality between different shifts in a manufacturing environment. Alternatively, one could try to elucidate the merits associated with different procedures adopted in the care of patients in several hospitals or a number of wards in a particular hospital, to identify an optimal one in order to specify how the tasks involved in the procedure could best be supported by a computer system. Because it is very difficult for people to describe exactly what they do and how much time they spend on various activities, the best way to find out is to become part of the procedures using the so-called 'participant observation' method. If the people concerned know they are being studied, they are likely to put forward their best behaviour, work faster, be more accurate, co-operative and conscientious than under normal circumstances. Impressions thus gained would then be unrepresentative and quite distorted when compared with normal work practices. A computer support system designed on the strength of such incorrect impressions would probably fail to meet the users' needs. Field studies are discussed in more detail in Fisher (1982), Shaugnessy and Zechmeister (1985), or True (1989).

Several ethical considerations must be taken into account when conducting field studies. Among these are invasion of privacy and the issue of deception. Methods of covert observation, for example, videotaping people without first obtaining their consent, would be regarded as a questionable activity because it violates people's rights to confidentiality and anonymity. However, even more controversial is the issue of deception. People might well be aware that they are participating in a research project, and they may give a degree of informed consent, but the true nature of the research is often withheld; in fact, subjects are often actively misled about the true nature of the research. Deception is most often associated with experiments in which the researcher wants the subject to be unaware of the causal relationships being studied because awareness of these may result in unnatural behaviour and hence invalid findings. As a researcher, your obligation is to avoid practices that cause your subjects any mental or physical stress, but rigid rules by which to ensure that people's rights are not being invaded or overridden by research purposes do not exist. If deception is unavoidable, one must at least inform participants after the event about the nature of the study and about the reasons for the failure to disclose this before the experiment was completed. A debriefing session is always conducted after a session to fulfil this obligation.

Field experiments differ from field observations in the sense that the researchers intervene in a real-world setting by introducing or manipulating particular variables and assessing the effect of their manipulations on certain aspects of people's behaviour. This requires a before–after design in which different samples of subjects are observed before and after the manipulation. Subjects do not know they are in a study, because the object of a typical field experiment is to observe people's reactions to the phenomenon at the centre of the study. It is a method favoured by social psychologists exploring different types of behaviour, for example, helping behaviour. They might stage an 'accident' to observe how passers-by will respond or, indeed, who will respond. Field experiments are not often used in connection with usability studies and are not discussed further in this book. The method is described in virtually any textbook on social psychology.

3.6.2 REAL-TIME OBSERVATIONS AND NOTE-TAKING

Real-time observations refer to situations in which the test user is being watched whilst completing the test tasks. Observations of what actually happens are one of the most powerful investigative tools for describing, understanding and asking questions about what users are doing. Observations help to elucidate the order, or sequence in which users perform different tasks and how tasks can be decomposed into subtasks in a suitable manner. Observations may be made by one or several people, as discussed earlier (section 3.2.3). Once you start recording user behaviour, you will very quickly realize just how difficult it is to observe, take notes and record data at the same time; while you are writing, you are likely to miss at least some of what is going on. Depending on the speed with which different events of importance occur, it might be necessary to supplement one's observations with further evidence supporting the data, perhaps by logging data electronically (section 3.6.4) or by videotaping (section 3.6.3). An example of how to generate a datafile from real-time observations is given in Chapter 6.

When trying to establish the user's goals, actions, feedback, objects and data dealt with, there is a number of questions to be answered:

- **What** is being done here? The answer is probably some high level goal statement like 'a new customer is entered into the database', or 'the patient's drug record form is updated'.
- What went **before** the current task? This refers to relationships in time between the current task or task component and some process completed before this task, for example, 'the customer rang up to be registered in the database' or 'the patient requested tablets for a headache'.
- What follows **next**? This refers to processes that occur after the current task in time and which affect the system, for example 'when patient record X has been found, sign for drugs administered', or 'does process A or B apply here?' Here, one process is chosen as appropriate, and according to predetermined control conditions, for example, 'if drug to be administered is addictive, use form A. If drug is not addictive, use form B'.
- What **data** are required to complete the process? Identify source and destination(s) of all data elements. This includes finding out who else needs the data both within the organization and elsewhere (taxation department, legal office, accountants).
- What is the **product** or outcome of a particular process? How does the user know that the process has been completed? What tools are being used to carry out the task? Depending on the system, its purpose and level of complexity, other questions might be added to this list. A more complete list can be found in the HUSAT human factors guidelines (1988).

3.6.3 VIDEOTAPING

Videotaping test sessions is excellent when a given situation is too complex to record data manually. Complexity, in this sense, refers to situations in which too much of importance is happening simultaneously for observers to be able to write it all down, to note everything, and to record the events in the correct sequence. Similarly, if events occur in too rapid a sequence to observe it all, or if timing is critical and/or cannot be measured by using a stopwatch, videotapes are very useful. Videotape recordings allow accurate time stamps to be made so that events from the screen could be taped and the observer could take notes about behavioural events at the same time. Using a coded recording method, these behavioural observations could be correlated with screen events to reconstruct a complete picture of the entire session.

Videotape recordings are ideal for demonstrating that users are experiencing difficulties and pinpointing when during a given task, and where in the system, rare problems occur. Showing users who are 'stuck', in 'frozen' images, is a very convincing way to illustrate a point a tester wants to make and to support an argument he/she wishes to propose concerning the need to change a particular aspect of the user interface. A single, concrete example of this nature can weigh more heavily than the most impressive statistical statement based on hundreds of observations.

In the field, videotape recordings can be most useful for capturing rarely occurring events, for example in situations in which safety is dependent upon the correct diagnosis of these events. Being able to see, show and analyse behaviour from a videotaped replay of reality will often eliminate the need for multiple recordings of the same type of event. In particular, when analysing dangerous situations that one would not wish to re-create in the laboratory, videotape recordings are most fruitful. Of course, one cannot easily predict when a dangerous situation is likely to arise, so it is sometimes necessary to let the cameras roll for many hours before one such situation will occur and can be captured. Indeed, even with many hours of videotape recordings on file, there is no guarantee that rare or dangerous events will occur at all.

One needs to assess carefully when videotaping is required. If videotape recordings are not giving value over and above what one can record manually, or in a combination of manual and electronic data logging, forget about them: videotapes are extremely time-consuming to process and analyse. It is sometimes believed that videotapes can replace the need for the experimenter to be present during an experimental session. Do not be fooled – analysis of the tapes will still need to be done, and this usually takes longer than observing subjects in real time. Also, the video camera might not capture every element of the session that might be particularly important, revealing, interesting or thought-provoking.

3.6.4 ELECTRONIC DATA LOGGING

Electronic data logging methods are the most accurate tools with which to measure aspects of time during task performance. Typically, the measures of interest might be

- RT (reaction time);
- time spent in a given field within a screen;
- time spent on a given screen;
- time spent completing a particular task;
- time from committing an error to recovering from it;
- amount of progress during a fixed period of time, and so on.

Time stamps are generally adjusted according to the type of measurement one wants. It may be measured in continuous, incremental steps throughout a particular task, or the timer, if RT is measured, may be triggered by a certain event, starting the timer at '0' each time a new task is commenced. Examples of time-stamped outputs are given in Chapter 6.

Because it is very time-consuming to program an electronic data logging device, great care should be exercised in the planning and design of such programs. Their value increases to the extent that they are transferable between experimental programs and systems. Flexibility is thus a prime consideration when designing electronic time and data logging devices. Ideally, the testers should be able to select the time units in which they want the data measured (millisecond, second, minutes) and to specify what, how and when time stamps are to be applied.

Once a good time-logging tool exists, it is tempting to run parallel sessions on multiple systems, enabling data recording to take place from many test users simultaneously, instead of running them one at a time. In principle, it sounds attractive to gather data quickly. In practice, however, the approach is normally not advisable. Electronic time and data logging should not be assumed to replace manual data logging or even observation of subjects. Even when certain important aspects of the session are recorded electronically, the subject should, more often than not, be observed and notes be taken as well. In the absence of observations, much of the data generated electronically may be uninterpretable, as some researchers have experienced (Moll and Sauter, 1987). The electronic datafile may, for example, show that a particular subject spent several minutes entering a certain character string into a field, the completion of which should take 1 second. Unless the test user makes entry errors, or consults help, both of which activities should be clear from the datafile, that datafile alone cannot tell the researcher exactly what was happening. What was the user actually doing? Was he/she searching for the to-be-entered characters on the keyboard? Was he/she reviewing the task or task instructions? Was he/she looking up the manual? If so, what information did she look at and what was she after? Was he/she daydreaming? The important point to note is that behaviour will occur for which electronic data logging cannot account. In order to understand the nature and richness of such unaccounted-for behaviour, it is essential that the tester be there to fill in the gaps in the electronic datafile. In usability evaluations, it is generally wise to use electronic data logging for obtaining additional data that supplements one's own observations instead of assuming it to represent an observer replacement mechanism!

How will the results affect the computer system about to be designed, redesigned, or evaluated? If diligence and careful thought has gone into planning, the data analysis will be easy. The choice of data analysis depends on the research question and the way it is framed, as well as on the nature of the data and the way they are going to be used. Analytic methods may range from simple descriptive statistics discussing percentages of responses falling into different categories, group means, medians or the mode (section 3.1.6) to elaborate statistical analyses of trends, multiple regressions, complex comparisons, factor analysis and various correlations. The point to note is that data analysis is very important and must be taken into account when planning a usability study.

It is always a good idea to think through, and perhaps to plot, the possible outcomes of the data before conducting a usability study. This forces one to think about the data a given study is capable of yielding, the analysis and interpretation, as well as the extent to which the data might be able to answer a specific question. Main data analyses are the so-called planned analyses which are supposed to give an answer to the research question. In addition, one might have observed some unexpected aspects of behaviour which should now be analysed and which offer additional insight into the data. However, make sure that interpretation of the outcomes from the analysis is conservative. It is sometimes tempting to move beyond what the data says, but do resist that temptation and make sure that every statement made is substantiated by the data. Data analysis and interpretation is one aspect of research where one is likely to need help from an expert.

Data, once they have been collected and analysed, are passed on to someone. Exactly what and how the findings are communicated depends on who the target audiences are. The communication format is also dependent on the audience and the situation. In the following sections three types of typical audiences are considered: the project team, management, and a scientific audience. Two presentation formats are described: written and oral. Different audiences will need to be informed about the findings in different ways, so one needs to think carefully about what is communicated to whom by what means and at what level of detail. Essentially, one must define

1. who one is communicating with;
2. what that audience will be interested to know;
3. how they are best informed;
4. how much they will want to know.

3.7 Data analysis and interpretation

3.8 Communicating your findings: presenting the results of your efforts

3.8.1 CONVEYING FINDINGS TO THE PROJECT TEAM

Since the goal of the project team is to produce a good system within a certain time frame, the purpose of communicating test results is to rectify usability problems through appropriate action. The team will need a detailed list specifying what problems have been identified, how badly they affect the user, where in the system they occur, and how they could be overcome (Chapter 8). A list of problems identified could be presented in the form of checklists that should be handed out and used when determining who will be looking after which problems, and the data by when they should be overcome. A typical check list might look like Table 3.2.

Table 3.2   List of usability defects, cause/solution, severity and who takes responsibility

Problem	Cause	Solution	*Defect classification	Solved by Name	Date
1. Cannot login	System accepts password only when usercode has been accepted	Allow usercode and password to be entered together	critical	F Jones	6.7.93
2. Length of usercode uncertain	System does not show length of usercode required	Prompt user by '.......'	high	T Morgan	6.7.93
3. Timeout during data entry	Timeout is too short (1 min)	Extend timeout (2 min)	medium	T Morgan	6.7.93
4. Entry deleted from database	'Delete' action completed as soon as command issued	Confirm action with user before completing	high	F Jones	13.7.93

*see Ch. 8 for details

Of course, more complex problems will occur for which the solution may not be as obvious as in the examples shown here. If further testing is required, or testing of different solutions is to be done, put this in the 'solution' column and enter the name of the person responsible in the 'solved by' column, together with a future date.

Checklists are revised at review meetings and actions taken are noted. As problems are identified and solved through further usability tests, they are removed from the active list. New problems arising from further tests are entered on the list, so that all team members know exactly what they are responsible for and by when action is required. The checklist is thus a dynamic document that changes as problems are dealt with and as new ones emerge so that it always contains 'current' problems.

The project team is normally not particularly interested in test design methodology or in statistical outcomes of analyses, so concentrate on making the problems explicit and focus on action to be taken. Be prepared, however, to back up statements by test data in case someone does want more detail. For some types of problems, it can be helpful to show video clips of subjects being 'stuck' to support the arguments, so do keep the evidence handy when presenting test findings.

3.8.2 INFORMING MANAGEMENT

Although one can expect the project team to be interested in defining the actions they need to take to overcome usability problems, the management of both the receiving and the project organisation is not interested in gory detail. Management will want to be reassured that

1. the project is progressing on schedule;
2. budgets are not exceeded or, if they are, a brief explanation of how much, why and where in the project this has happened;
3. possible problems are overcome.

If managers do come to at least some of the project meetings, fine! They will receive the same problem summary sheet and checklist as handed out to the project team. The checklist does, however, say nothing about how well the project is faring with respect to timing and keeping within the budget. This information, together with a summary of usability problems, should be conveyed regularly through whatever formal communication channels exist. Writing a minute or a memo to each of the senior managers involved with, or responsible for, the project, will ensure that communications go down on file. This can be extremely useful, especially if the project runs a little behind schedule at any time. A minute of this nature should contain a broad summary stating

1. the stage the system is at (e.g. prototype testing);

2. the system status in the light of targets and deadlines;
3. usability tests done since last communication;
4. problems revealed in these;
5. how problems are dealt with;
6. whether they are all under control.

At the end of a project, a full report is usually required. The format of such a report is discussed in Section 3.9.

3.8.3 COMMUNICATING WITH A SCIENTIFIC AUDIENCE

The purpose of communicating with scientific audiences is primarily to share new ideas and findings by exposing one's work to the criticism of peers. Scientists employed in systems design and development teams often work in isolation from like-minded colleagues with whom interaction is absolutely essential for a prospering community and one's own development. When one is very closely involved with a project, it is easy to become locked into a certain framework. The danger of becoming too narrowly focused is that it is so easy to overlook flaws in one's own

'Management tends to listen more than challenge your arguments'

arguments, in one's test designs, analyses of test results or in the interpretation of these. It is easy to pull other people's work apart; flaws are much more 'obvious' in others' than in one's own work. Similarly, other people will find it easy to pull your work to pieces, and you must be prepared to let this happen in an effort to refine your tools and to see your results with different eyes, thereby widening your mental horizon.

Peers who proceed from the same disciplinary background as oneself are the best qualified critics to evaluate one's work, so use them as much as possible. Communications with peers can take place at different levels of formality, ranging from submitting papers to journals, to holding weekly seminars that act as a forum for immediate feedback on research ideas, arguments and findings. In between these two extremes are conferences, symposia and panel meetings in which the level of research detail provided is lower than in formal journal papers, but which are nevertheless run by people qualified and experienced in judging the quality of research.

Journals communicate details, and a scientific audience will want statistical evidence supporting the claims made on the basis of your findings. Unlike management, the scientific audience cares little about the budget, time frames and deadlines. Instead, the focus is on the arguments, methodology, selection of subjects and tasks; scientists want to know

'Your scientific colleagues will challenge you and be critical'

how the data was analysed, what the analyses yielded and how these findings were interpreted. A fully fledged scientific paper should be written so that anyone from the relevant scientific community is able to replicate exactly what was done and, to the extent that the data and analyses are sound, the results should also be replicable. Whenever findings cannot be replicated, their validity must be seriously questioned. Particular care must be taken when describing the details of the testing in order to facilitate such replication. Normally, a scientific journal paper contains the following sections: abstract, introduction, method, results, discussion, conclusion, references and acknowledgments. Conference papers are shorter and do not allow as much detail as formal papers, but if they address the same audience as journal papers do, descriptions of what was done and what was found, as well as justifications for the arguments and conclusion are expected even in short papers.

3.9 Written communication

This section describes in more detail the various parts that, taken together, constitute a certain type of report. Although the length of any communication varies widely, one should always start broadly and gradually work into increasing detail. Always start with the most important points to give the paper a distinct focus, and also in case the readers get bored before they reach the end.

The **executive summary** is intended for senior management. Most managers read only this section, so make sure that the most important points are included. An executive summary should, ideally, be no more than one page long although, sometimes, it can extend to cover two pages. Never go beyond two pages – they will not be read! Choose a font that is easy to read and print the summary in large letters, preferably in double spacing as this is easier for the eyes to read than single spacing. **Recommendations** summarize the actions that should be taken as a consequence of the findings listed in the report. An **abstract** is a summary of what was done, how it was done, what the data revealed and how it was interpreted. Abstracts are generally 100–200 words long, so select the vocabulary with care and be parsimonious. Only the main points are emphasized in the abstract, but note that abstracts generally motivate people to read on. A boring abstract will put many people off who might otherwise have proceeded to read the paper. **Keywords** are a list of, normally, up to five words by which the contents of the bulk of the work reported in an article can be described. Keywords are mostly used for indexing and to give the reader a quick idea of the issues addressed. The **table of contents** lists the various sections and subsections contained in the paper or report. The main body of the report starts with an **introduction** which sets the scene for the argument(s) to be put forward. In a scientific paper, it would state the theoretical, or at least opposing, viewpoints that were tested in the research. It points to the basis of the line pursued. It ends with a hypothesis which the research is designed to test or with a summary of the issues to be explored. In an internal report, theoretical views may not be relevant, so the introduction states why the research was done, and how it is relevant to, and captures, the issues addressed.

The **method** states exactly what one did. In a scientific publication, the descriptions given in this section should enable others to replicate the work. Typical subsections within the method section include apparatus used in the investigation reported, such as computer systems, data logging and recording tools, or video recorders. The materials subsection describes the task and tools given to the subjects, how these looked, how they were presented and selected, what subjects were required to do, and perhaps the nature of their responses. The subjects subsection describes the sample of subjects; it details how they were selected, characteristics relevant to the sampling procedure, and other aspects of the participants themselves. The design subsection refers to the experimental conditions, showing how the research was assembled into a complete study and how the various parts interlock. The procedure describes how sessions were run, instructions given to the subjects, constraints such as time or accuracy, the sequence in which tasks were presented, practice items included, debriefing given, and time taken to complete the tasks. The data analysis subsection describes the planned data analyses, analytical and descriptive or inferential statistical tools used, and so on.

The **results** section reports the outcome of the analyses. Main points addressing the hypothesis directly are reported first, followed by an increasingly detailed exposure of relevant findings and analyses performed which were not necessarily planned before obtaining the data. The **discussion** sets the results in the framework of the argument stating the degree to which the hypothesis was supported or could be rejected by the data. It discusses the findings in the light of the arguments set in the introduction and considers alternative ways in which the data could be explained.

In internal reports to management, the body of the report contains the introduction, method, results and discussion, all of which are summarized in less detail than is necessary for a formal scientific paper. Managers are not interested in the details of what was done or what was found; they will not want to replicate the work, and they are generally less interested in the scientific soundness or in the statistical or theoretical justification underpinning the research. They need the broad brush approach in which a suitably short and coherent story is presented without detailed distractions from the main theme.

The **conclusion** is based on all the preceding sections. A conclusion states what the research has established and where it points to, that is, what should be done next, hopefully lending further support to the available evidence. Conclusions should be brief and should be justified by the approach, the data, analysis and arguments from which they arise. **References** are presented as a list of papers and books mentioned in the report and, in many internal reports, of papers taken into consideration without necessarily being mentioned in the body of the report. Different publications have their own rules, and many companies have their own style guides setting out the way in which references should be presented; these should be consulted before completing and submitting a paper. **Appendices** provide details that are of relevance but which do not belong in the report itself. Statistical summary tables, task instructions, detailed screen displays, arrangement of equipment during the study, and so on, may be reported. Few scientific journals allow extensive appendices to be submitted, whereas internal reports generally encourage reporting of all relevant details. **Acknowledgments** state the names of people and/or organizations who have contributed to the study, perhaps by building the system tested, by recruiting subjects, or by forwarding ideas pursued in the study or through funding. It is a matter of courtesy to mention those who were involved in some way.

3.10 Oral presentations

As is true for written communication, one must know whom one is addressing and adjust the level of detail as well as the emphasis of what is reported accordingly. Know exactly how much time you are expected to speak and keep within the time limit. Be aware that the audience will only take away a few explicit messages, as they are not as involved in the project as you are. Think clearly about the messages to be put across and shape the presentation accordingly. The most important aspect is to define the main message.

A presentation to senior management should show that

1. the project is progressing according to plan;
2. usability problems have been found, but that these have been overcome or are being dealt with;
3. the budget is on schedule;
4. the entire project management is under control.

By contrast, when reporting to the project team, the problems found should be stated, how and where they were found, together with suggestions for overcoming them. A scientific audience will want to know much the same as would be presented in a written paper.

Prepare the visual support well. Slides and overhead transparencies must be kept simple, conveying one, or at the most, two messages, written in large, legible letters. Graphs must have clearly labelled axes and values and must support the argument unambiguously and in a manner that can easily be grasped by the audience. Tables must be labelled. If they are too busy, reduce their contents by summarizing, presenting only averages, or whatever can be done to make the contents easy to read and interpret.

Videotape clips may be used to the extent that they support or help to emphasize what is being said.

Compile a list of main points to be made as each slide is presented but do not read from notes. Maintain eye contact with the audience, use different tones of voice to bring out different points, and try to concentrate on what is being said instead of being nervous about how it is coming across. With a bit of experience, you will soon feel quite comfortable when giving oral presentations.

Summary

This chapter provided a mosaic of background knowledge of data collection, analysis and communication methods needed to conduct good usability tests. Some basic statistical concepts were introduced first, including the notion of sampling, a description of different types of variables, measures of variability, measures of central tendency and correlation. The importance of reliability and validity was then discussed and different types of each were addressed. Flaws often arising in problem formulation and hypothesis testing were outlined, followed by a discussion of models, mockups and prototypes. Pen and paper prototypes were discussed in some detail and four types of these were introduced. Observations in the field were described followed by a brief discussion of data logging methods in real time, videotaping and electronic data collection methods. Data analysis and interpretation were dealt with briefly and finally some hints on written and oral communication of findings to different audiences were given.

Questions

1. Why should samples be representative of the population from which they are drawn?
2. What is the best sampling method? Why?
3. What are the three main types of variables encountered in usability tests and experiments? What role do they play?
4. Name three measures of central tendency. Which is the least useful of these?
5. When is the median the best, most representative measure of central tendency?
6. Why is the standard deviation useful?
7. Why are correlations useful?
8. What does it mean to say that a set of scores is reliable?
9. Why is it necessary to assess reliability?
10. When would you use repeated performance scores from the same people to assess reliability?
11. What is validity?
12. Why is confirmatory evidence not very useful?
13. Why are prototypes useful?

14. What is the difference between static and dynamic prototypes?
15. What four types of pen and paper studies might be useful and which ones can be applied in usability tests?
16. What are some advantages of field studies over laboratory studies? What are some of the dangers?
17. How do field experiments differ from field studies?
18. Why do you still need to be present when logging data electronically?
19. What is the main purpose when communicating results of usability tests to a project team?
20. Why is it important to convey details of method, analysis and interpretation to a scientific audience?

Suggested further reading

Fisher (1982) covers all those aspects of social psychology that are of relevance to researchers wishing to do field studies or field experiments. This book summarizes a great deal of research, provides theoretical foundations and discusses advantages and disadvantages of observing human behaviour in its natural context. Readers can select chapters to fit needs and interests; it is both easy and entertaining reading.

Holtzblatt and Jones (1992) discuss the method they use to generate ideas for design by observing and interacting with system users in some detail. The method is easy to learn and use, and it is a very practical tool which can be applied to many situations and systems. Holtzblatt and Jones explain how to use the technique, and their chapter is very easy to read.

Meister's book (1986) is a very thorough and systematic account of the methods used in physical, environmental, and cognitive ergonomics. He discusses testing processes, use of models, development of text plans, problem and pitfalls associated with all of these, and gives many examples based both on the literature and his own extensive experience as a human factors expert; it is somewhat dry, but invaluable if you are developing very large systems.

True (1989) takes the reader through all aspects of designing, conducting, analysing and interpreting social research. In particular, the chapters on interviews, questionnaires and survey design are of relevance both to trained social researchers and others. Topics addressed here are discussed in much greater detail, and numerous examples are provided – very easy to read.

Data collection techniques I: knowledge elicitation and inspection methods

4

Let our teaching be full of ideas.
Hitherto it has been stuffed only with
facts.

Anatole France

This chapter introduces a number of methods for knowledge elicitation and inspection that may be applied in evaluating usability. These methods are all diagnostic without being performance-based. Elicitation methods are devised to learn more about how users perceive their tasks and what they encounter during task performance, or how they judge task similarities. Inspection methods are investigative tools designed to uncover inconsistency, controversy, and other user stumbling blocks, where the project team or a team of evaluators work through typical tasks or deliberately seek to crash the system by performing unexpected actions and testing the system to its limits. Most of the methods introduced in this chapter are subjective, that is, they are informal and their outcomes as well as the value of the data depends on the craft, skill and knowledge of the analyst. Even so, benefit can be gained from most of these methods even by relatively inexperienced usability testers. Only the confirmation study is an exception to this diagnostic approach in the sense that it is performance-based. User performance is measured in tasks which are designed to test the severity of potential usability defects identified, for example, in heuristic evaluations. Confirmation studies tend to be experimental or quasi-experimental, so Chapter 6 might need to be read as well.

4.1.1 PROTOCOL ANALYSIS

4.1 Knowledge elicitation methods: describing what is going on

A protocol is a verbal account given by the people who perform tasks. This method requires people whose task performance is to be analysed to 'think aloud' whilst completing the relevant task or set of tasks. That is, users (who may be task experts or novices) are asked spontaneously to verbalize thoughts, ideas, facts, plans, beliefs, expectations, doubts, and so forth, that come to mind during the observation period (Jorgensen, 1990) and sessions are audio- or videotaped for later coding and analysis. Protocols may be concurrent or retrospective. In a concurrent report, the person talks whilst doing, trying to tell the observer what they are doing or going to do, why, what response they expect from the system and so forth. Retrospective reports are accounts given of behaviour and reasoning by the task performer after the event. The performer is either asked to memorize why and how certain acts were carried out, or to review and comment on the videotaped performance. The method yields a large amount of qualitative data concerning the manner in which users perceive, interpret and understand the task demands (Kato, 1986). It is one method with which to gain an appreciation of the users' perspective. Introduced into the context of user interface research by Lewis (1982), it has been dealt with extensively in a variety of contexts (Ericsson and Simon, 1980; 1984), and applied in many studies (e.g. Gould *et al.*, 1987; Jorgensen, 1990; Mack *et al.*, 1983; Wright and Monk, 1989; 1991).

It is easy enough to collect protocol data, and one usually gets masses of data this way, but the value gained from such data is highly dependent on the insight and skill of the analyst whose role it is to abstract interesting and salient issues from the reports (Barnard, 1991a; 1991b; Barnard *et al.*, 1986). Neither concurrent nor retrospective reporting is without problems. Concurrent reports are dangerous because the requirement to talk while doing something is likely to interfere with task performance (Bainbridge, 1986; Ericsson and Simon, 1980). Retrospective reports are particularly subject to error when they require the performer to report implicit behaviour or thought processes because our ability to reconstruct the past accurately is quite limited, and insight into our own thought processes is also known to be fraught with error (Ericsson and Simon, 1980; 1984; Nisbett and Ross, 1980; Nisbett and Wilson, 1977; Salter, 1988). Protocols are also quite difficult to code and analyse, but if used together with other methods, they can be very useful.

Advantages of protocol analysis
- easy to generate data;
- generates a wealth of data;
- data collection is very quick.

Disadvantages of protocol analysis
- coding and analysis is difficult and time consuming;
- value depends on analyst's skill and knowledge;
- may not provide accurate descriptions of what is happening.

4.1.2 QUESTION-ASKING PROTOCOLS

In this family of methods, the analyst asks questions of the user. Typical questions include, 'what are you doing now?', 'why did you do that?',

'Well, ehm. . . oh, I just do it'

and so forth (Holtzblatt and Jones, 1992; Kato, 1986). The method can be applied during task completion, or it may be applied retrospectively. It is useful for understanding what is happening, but, as for protocol analysis, it should be supplemented by other methods because the knowledge elicited is likely to be distorted. For example, reporting one's knowledge about an issue or task involves self-presentation and can therefore be influenced by social factors. Similarly, reports that require translation of movements or spatial relations into words, may be distorted. Try, for example, to explain to someone how to mount and ride a bicycle without doing it at the same time. It is almost impossible. Retrospective accounts may be influenced by distortions in memory in the sense that decisions made under time constraints may not be represented in the reports. Bainbridge (1986) elaborates on these and other relevant points. Also, the perspective of the systems designer most probably differs from that of the user. This difference in 'framing' can give rise to misunderstandings in the transfer of knowledge between people (Bostrom, 1989). Despite their limitations, question-asking protocols are sometimes effective as a means of learning what users are doing.

One example of question-asking is the on-line comment analysis in which completion of the task is purposely slowed down. To ask questions well requires a good deal of task expertise of the performer, and also careful selection of suitable tasks for analysis. Some tasks cannot easily be interrupted, especially those we do almost automatically (e.g. mounting a bicycle). Also, as with concurrent protocols, it is unclear how much interruptions change natural behaviour. Interruption analysis is similar to on-line comment analysis except that the task-completion process is interrupted at various points instead of merely being slowed down (Salter, 1988).

One method of observation used very successfully in the field is the 'contextual inquiry' (Holtzblatt and Jones, 1992). Contextual inquiries aim to discover design opportunities by understanding the client's work, tools, job demands and use of current tools. The researcher conducts ongoing interviews while the interviewee is working. The user leads the discussion and the researcher converses, keeping the conversation directed at the task being performed. Questions such as 'what are you doing?', 'why are you doing that?', 'is that system response what you expected?', are asked frequently during a session. The researcher's understanding of the situation is shared with the user so as to identify 'holes', misunderstandings and misinterpretations. Sessions are taped and transcribed, and from these records, concrete design ideas emerge as the team, which includes the user, reads through the transcripts. Content analysis may be applied depending on the purpose of the inquiry. As ideas are generated, they are each written on a sticker. The stickers are then grouped into logical concepts and swapped around on a board until the team agrees that all ideas are placed in sensible categories. The labelled categories are then arranged in a hierarchical order. This way, ideas take on a concrete form which can then be used directly as design inputs. Holtzblatt and Jones (1992) provide more detail on this method.

Advantages of question-asking protocols
- questions are unconstrained and relevant to the situation as it occurs;
- context is preserved;
- much can be clarified while it is happening;
- it is easy to ask questions and generate data.

Disadvantages of question-asking protocols
- reports may be inaccurate;
- performance may not reflect how the task is normally done;
- tasks may be unsuitable for this analysis.

4.2.1 REPERTORY GRIDS, MULTI-DIMENSIONAL SCALING AND CARD SORTING

4.2 Judging task similarity

To use repertory grids, the analyst must already know most, if not all, components of a task or set of tasks. The analyst selects task components in groups of three, and the respondent is asked to judge similarities and differences between the components. This process is repeated until all components have been evaluated. It results in groupings of similar items that are assumed to share certain attributes. It should be noted that selecting the sets of three components can have a very strong influence on any comparison or grouping, and that the method may enforce arbitrary classifications which may not be representative of actual relationships between components (Johnson, 1992). The method is efficient for eliciting attributes that are important in distinguishing outcomes, especially if the distinctions are fine or not normally verbalized. Repertory grids are limited to classification problems and cannot elicit problem-solving strategies.

A similar method is multi-dimensional scaling in which experts are asked to judge the similarity of items in the domain. The judgments may be used to generate the minimal set of dimensions that would explain them (Gammack, 1987), or the experts may be asked to name the relationships between them. In contrast to using repertory grids, the analyst does not select subsets of task components but presents the entire array to the expert.

Card sorting is another example of a technique in which the analyst is interested in similarities between task components. These may be actions, procedures or objects. Each component is presented on a card, and the task is to group items from the domain into categories, explaining

'What's the similarity between papers on a desk and files in a computer?'

why they belong in categories and how each item differs from the others in the category. Card sorting is a good way to elicit conceptual structure of the domain. One advantage of this over the repertory grid is that it is less likely to be subject to analyst bias.

Advantages of task similarity judgment methods
- establish relationships between tasks and task components;
- add a different dimension (expert judges tasks rather than performing them).

Disadvantages of task similarity judgment methods
- task selection is *ad hoc*;
- task selection may result in artificial groupings;
- selected groupings may distort or hide real task relationships;
- expert's representation of task knowledge may be inaccurate and incomplete.

4.2.2 CONTENT ANALYSIS

Content analysis (Berelson, 1952) was first applied in communication research. It consists of techniques with which to code or categorize written or spoken information into a set of descriptive categories in a selective, systematic and reliable fashion. Content analysis reduces verbatim data records into a manageable and quantitative form for more precise description or for testing specific hypotheses. Some researchers prefer to group material for content analysis into three categories, namely:

1. words and mentions;
2. pictures and appearances;
3. space   (True, 1989).

The whole idea behind a content analysis is to examine how much attention is being paid to an idea or topic of concern by counting the number of occurrences of certain words, phrases, events, actions and/or objects. According to True, words and mentions include single words, references to a subject, or whole discussions. Pictures and appearances are mostly sampled from publications or appearances on radio or TV and are therefore of little relevance to most usability studies of computer systems. Similarly, measuring the amount of space devoted to a topic in a publication by counting lines, pages, or by measuring square centimetres gives an indication of prominence of the topic which may be important for analysing user documentation and help systems. Frequency of occurrence of words and mentions are the most commonly used techniques for analysing usability data, for example interview data.

Advantages of content analysis
- reduces size of data records;
- enables generation or testing of hypotheses;
- can deal with data from different sources and media;
- requires no specific skill to analyse data.

Disadvantages of content analysis
- reduction of data incurs a loss;
- selection of topics is subjective which may give a distorted view of the contents.

There are other techniques which are useful for eliciting task knowledge, task components, or relationships between tasks. It is useful, for example, to go carefully through all relevant and available source documentation to gain a better appreciation of user tasks and task demands. Documentation includes instruction manuals, forms filled in by users, reports, and other items that are relevant to the tasks and jobs of all classes of users. For more detail, see Johnson (1992), Salter (1988) or Welbank (1990).

4.3 Inspection methods

4.3.1 HEURISTIC EVALUATION

A heuristic evaluation is an informal, subjective usability analysis, conducted from the perspective of intended, typical end users. Its purpose is to isolate potential usability defects and through these identify areas or aspects of the user interface which might need improvements to enhance usability. The heuristic evaluation is a trouble-shooting tool used to flag potential stumbling blocks in the user interface. A heuristic evaluation is probably the best method with which to achieve a quick and relatively coarse usability input into a project because it tends to uncover many potential user problems in a reasonably short period of time and with comparatively little effort.

The term 'heuristic' is used in a similar fashion as in computer science in which it refers to short cuts, or simplification strategies which serve to reduce a large 'problem space' (Newell and Simon, 1972) to a manageable size. It is also used in the judgment and decision-making literature to denote informal 'rules of thumb' strategies which people have been shown to employ in many varied judgment tasks (Kahneman *et al.*, 1982; Nisbett and Ross, 1980; Wallsten, 1980). In the present context, the term is used to mark the informality of the evaluative approach adopted in heuristic evaluations. It does not prescribe a specific set of methods, rules or procedures to be followed by the evaluator. Instead, it relies on a set of general statements which represent vague guidelines such as 'speak the user's language'. The number and types of problems identified in an evaluation therefore depend very much on the background and experience of the evaluator. To the extent that an evaluator is unable to assess the usefulness of the computer system, he/she will also be unable to evaluate usability accurately. Knowledge and understanding of users' tasks, their task environment and the organizational as well as the social context in which users may perform the kinds of tasks supported by the system, will also affect the outcome of the heuristic evaluation. Heuristic evaluations may be performed by groups or individuals. User-interface have been found to uncover more potential problems than Karat *et al.*, 1992; Nielsen, 1992), but they can certainly experts. The number of evaluators employed in a ds on the time frame for testing, on the size, ystem, its users, the tasks the system is intended udgetary constraints. Any interactive system can, able candidate for a heuristic evaluation. This emit voice prompts, systems that contain textual systems, systems based on animation, pictures, or es of all of these – in short, any type of system tive use involving people, regardless of whether it is ata entry or data retrieval system.

One limitation of heuristic evaluations is that many of the potential trouble spots identified may be red herrings in the sense that they may say more about the personal taste and stylistic preferences of the evaluator than about actual usability defects. Because there are no systematic, rigorous rules attached to the method, it is totally open to idiosyncratic whims of the evaluator(s). To the extent that such complete freedom from methodological constraints can encourage more creative exploratory behaviour on behalf of evaluators, this freedom can be advantageous; it might lead to detection of a larger number and more varied potential usability defects than are likely to be uncovered using more formal methods. However, because many of the problems un-covered are also likely to be quite trivial, the effort associated with weeding out trivia from the more serious problems may, on occasion, be more substantial than the work done by the evaluator to uncover problems. It is therefore recommended that heuristic evaluations be combined with other usability assessment tools, applied at least in the form of follow-up usability tests.

The more specialized the user tasks are that are to be supported by a system, the more specialized at least some of the evaluators need to be. How would you yourself, for example, fare if you were asked to evaluate a decision support system (DSS) for, say pathologists, lawyers or account managers? In terms of understanding the tasks to be supported, people

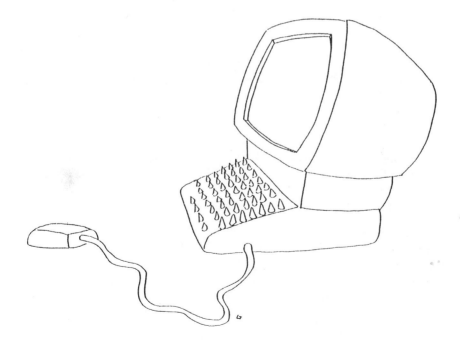

'Some usability defects are easier to find than others'

who are not specialists in the area of application are unlikely to have enough task-related background to make sound judgments in the evaluation. They cannot judge the usefulness of the system adequately. In specialist systems it is particularly important to include representative end users on the evaluation team. These experts are unlikely also to possess the necessary understanding of human factors issues, of the technology, of conformance to standards and so on. A team of evaluators from a range of different disciplines working together is therefore most effectively employed in the evaluation of large and complex systems. By contrast, publicly accessible, general information systems, can be evaluated by people experienced in conducting heuristic evaluations, and by designers or software engineers who are not directly involved in the particular system being assessed. However, it is preferable if at least some user-interface experts can be involved (Desurvire et al., 1991; Desurvire et al., 1992; Karat et al., 1992). Software engineers who have been directly involved with developing the system should preferably not be asked to conduct a heuristic analysis because they will want to verify and confirm system behaviour rather than challenging it. Besides, the designers have presumably already eliminated as many potential sources of user problems as they could identify – so they are unlikely to imagine many more strange situations that users could get themselves into.

4.3.2 WHEN IS A HEURISTIC EVALUATION FEASIBLE?

In general a heuristic evaluation is done when the system or system-part is capable of responding to user entries, although, in principle, it could be carried out at the development stage when series of screens exist on paper only, consisting of a few screens, prompts, drawings or icons. As soon as a system, or parts of a system, have been defined in sufficient detail to determine 'what happens when..', and this can be tried on the system itself or a dynamic prototype, heuristic evaluations can be conducted profitably. Hence, they are most appropriate during development and operation.

EXAMPLE: EWP (electronic white pages)

Aim of the heuristic evaluation:
To determine the exact nature of all potential usability defects so as to provide appropriate help information.

THE SYSTEM:
The database underlying the Electronic White Pages (EWP) contains details of name, address and telephone number of every registered telephone subscriber in Australia. The EWP is updated every 24 hours, and 3.5 million changes are carried out to the database annually. The

EWP consists of a single screen comprising 26 lines and 80 columns. The topmost 20 lines are reserved for data output upon successful retrieval of targets from the database. Lines 24 and 25 display six fields into three of which the user can enter data, namely the NAME, the STRT (= street, road, court, etc.), and the LOC (LOCality = town or suburb) fields respectively. The AREA field displays the STATE (e.g. Victoria), and the TYPE field shows the section of the database in which the last search was issued. The database is divided into several sections: RES(idential), BUS(iness), GOV(ernment) and EMeR(gency) to limit the search for a given target. The bottom line of the EWP screen displays the functions of F-keys ranging from F1 to F10. This screen is shown in Fig. 4.1 below:

OUTCOMES FROM THE HEURISTIC EVALUATION

The problems uncovered fell into two logically and functionally distinct categories, namely:

1. problems with entries in the various fields, in particular the NAME field;
2. problems with geographical locations.

NAME field problems were mainly related to the fact that certain EWP-specific rules were in conflict with one another. For example, the EWP requires entry of at least three characters in the NAME field to conduct a search, but, at the same time, the full stop is used as a wild card. When searching for companies such as 'I.B.M.', this must be entered as 'IBM' without the full stops. Yet, when successfully retrieved, the entry is displayed as I.B.M. on the screen. Hence, screen output is at times incompatible with user entry requirements and with user expectations. Other problems were that the EWP is unable to recognize or

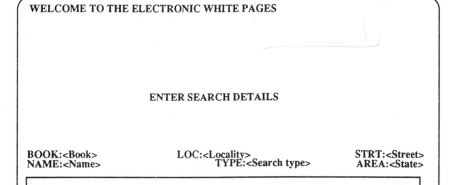

```
WELCOME TO THE ELECTRONIC WHITE PAGES




                    ENTER SEARCH DETAILS




BOOK:<Book>              LOC:<Locality>                   STRT:<Street>
NAME:<Name>                    TYPE:<Search type>         AREA:<State>
F1:HELP F2:SEC F3:RLS F4:CLR F5:LOC F7:GOV F8:EMR F9:BUS F10:RES
```

Figure 4.1: The EWP screen as presented online.

ignore words such as 'and', 'of', and 'for' and to recognize characters such as and, *, $, %, and so on. In order to locate a company 'X and Co.', the user must enter 'X Co.'. Finally, there is no relational database enabling translation of aliases; that is, the EWP does not 'know' that Municipal Offices = City Offices = Shire Offices = Civic Centre, and so on. Since any Government department is entered in the database under a single name, it can be very time-consuming to locate one if the user does not know exactly how it is entered into the database.

Geographical problems were due to idiosyncratic rules also, but not because they were in conflict with one another. Geographical locations are stored in a pre-programmed sequence which the EWP searches through in a top-down fashion to locate a town. The name of the town is typed into the LOC field. F5 must then be pressed to change the phone book (displayed in the BOOK field) accordingly. When searching for a town such as 'Sale', the name 'Springvale' is displayed when the user first presses F5. Pressing F5 again brings up the name 'Seaholme', then 'Scarsdale', and so on. In fact, it is necessary to press F5 eleven times to locate 'Sale'. Another problem is that a search for a country town must commence from the correct state. If searching for a town in Queensland, such as 'Toowoomba' while the BOOK field shows 'Melbourne 03' the search will be unsuccessful (the correct BOOK is 'Brisbane 07'). Unfortunately, the EWP is not smart enough to tell the user why or what to do about it.

4.3.3 WHAT TO DO WITH THE OUTCOMES OF HEURISTIC EVALUATIONS?

The potential usability defects likely to emerge from a heuristic evaluation will tend to cover the full range of problems, from the highly serious to the most trivial. Having identified a large number of problems, one might want to group these in various ways to decide how to proceed. For example, if you want to ensure that all the most (or least) serious problems be eliminated in the new version of the system, you would probably rank the problems uncovered in terms of seriousness, where 'seriousness' refers to the degree to which a problem might hamper usability.

If a problem-fixing priority is imposed, you would rank the problems identified in terms of these priorities. Compare, for example the extracts from two lists presented below. Both deal with the same set of problems uncovered in an evaluation of a fictitious electronic mail system. List 1 was designed to categorize the severity of usability defects in typical mailing tasks and rank these; the purpose of list 2 was to rank the same problems in terms of cost, from least to most expensive, in order to eliminate as many as possible, spending no more than $10 000 in total.

EXAMPLE: E-MAIL

List 1: Most to least serious problems

1. There is no confirmation before actions are carried out (e.g. delete).
2. There is no indication of how to send messages.
3. No clear or obvious exit-system method is shown.
4. Error messages are non-specific and do not help users to recover.
5. The system does not allow users to commence a new message whilst another one is unfinished and in progress.
6. No help is offered with commands or command syntax.
7. Timeout (two minutes) is too brief.
8. There is no indication of whether copies of own messages can be kept and filed.
9. No feedback is given concerning the status of messages sent (e.g. delivered OK; undeliverable because addressee cannot be found, etc.).
10. The system does not offer a directory of addressees.

List 2: Least to most expensive problems

1. Timeout (two minutes) is too brief.
2. There is no indication of how to send messages.
3. No clear or obvious exit-system method is shown.
4. There is no indication of whether copies of own messages can be kept and filed.
5. There is no confirmation before actions are carried out (e.g. delete).
6. Error messages are non-specific and do not help users to recover.
7. The system does not allow users to commence a new message whilst another one is unfinished and in progress.
8. No help is offered with commands or command syntax.
9. The system does not offer a directory of addressees.
10. No feedback is given concerning the status of messages sent (e.g. delivered OK; undeliverable because addressee cannot be found, etc).

The sequence in which you decide to fix problems is dependent upon the priorities of your project. This issue is discussed in detail in Chapter 8.

Advantages of heuristic evaluations
- quick to perform;
- relatively inexpensive;
- uncover lots of potential usability defects.

Disadvantages of heuristic evaluations
- several evaluations must usually be performed for maximum benefit;
- ideally done by experts;
- high probability of 'false alarms';
- not always easy to distinguish between trivial and serious problems.

'Heuristic evaluations yield masses of data in a short time'

4.4 Follow-on from heuristic evaluations: confirmation studies

Confirmation studies are usually conducted to ensure that the usability goals are being met, and also to confirm findings arising from other studies, for example, heuristic evaluations. In this sense, the purpose of confirmation studies is to confirm that problems uncovered actually are sources of trouble; if they do not constitute stumbling blocks for users, there is little point spending time and effort fixing them. Some of the problems identified in a heuristic evaluation will be difficult to classify in terms of how badly they will affect usability. These might need to be tested further to ensure that they do exist and that they do cause user problems. Some problems detected may turn out not to bother users at all. Hence, it is necessary to conduct one or more confirmation studies to be sure time is not wasted in fixing purely cosmetic issues whilst leaving more serious problems in the system which could be overcome within the present stage of the project. When designing confirmation studies

- decide which problems to investigate, and
- design tasks that expose the problems to be verified.

'But too much of a good thing can be destructive too'

Once one is certain that every problem to be exposed is represented in typical tasks, decide how to order these tasks into experiments, how many experiments to run, and which measures to take to assess user performance. Issues in experimental design are discussed later (Ch. 6).

Now, let us re-visit the EWP to outline some of the typical tasks that were designed to expose problems identified in the heuristic evaluation. Since the aim was to design a help system, the measures should also be able to capture improvements in user performance once a help system was in place. Hence, it was not enough to ensure that the problems isolated actually existed and that the measures selected would reflect this. Something had to be measured that would be expected to change, by increasing or decreasing, as user performance changed.

EXAMPLE: EWP

Problems to investigate: NAME field and geographical problems.

TYPICAL TASKS:

1. find I.B.M. in Melbourne (Enter IBM);
2. find K&B Automotive Electrical Engineers (Enter KB Auto.);
3. find Department of Education (Enter Dep.Education);
4. find Berwick Municipal Offices (Enter Berwick Civic Centre);
5. find Wagga Wagga Hospital (Start search in Sydney 02).

PROBLEMS EXPOSED IN THESE TASKS:

1. full stop used as a wild card plus requirement of three-character entry clash; user input requirements do not match system output;
2. cannot interpret or ignore '&' plus character string exceeds size of NAME field, requiring use of wild card;
3. cannot interpret or ignore 'of';
4. actual entry does not match input string plus does not know aliases;
5. change book *before* issuing search plus press F5 several times.

During the heuristic evaluation it was noted that GOVernment departments were far more time-consuming to locate than RESidential targets; many more searches had to be issued per target for successful retrieval. It therefore seemed reasonable to assume that the number of searches issued per target would be useful for measuring differences in user performance in the various database sections. To the extent that the EWP-specific rules do affect performance, the retrieval of GOVernment targets would require more searches than RESidential targets, with BUSiness targets falling somewhere in between. This is because GOVernment searches potentially violate the most system-specific rules, and RESidential searches the least. By contrast, if these rules do not affect user performance, there should be no differences between the number of searches conducted, on average, in the three database sections. Now, assuming that violation of system-specific rules would cause user problems, it follows that a future help system which does its job and assists users in trouble should lead to improvements in user performance when compared with that of users who were given no help. Fewer searches should then be required to retrieve the same targets successfully for a new group of users. Graphically, these predictions would resemble those shown in Figs 4.2–4.4:

Geographical problems were separated from field problems, as the number of targets included in an experiment would be too high and because the issues would be too complex to explore systematically in a single experiment. Experiment 1 therefore concentrated exclusively on field problems and Experiment 2 on geographical locations. A brief outline of Experiment 1 is given below to give you an idea of the design considerations and the data obtained:

EXPERIMENT 1, DESIGN
18 targets were included (6 BUSiness, 6 RESidential; 6 GOVernment departments).

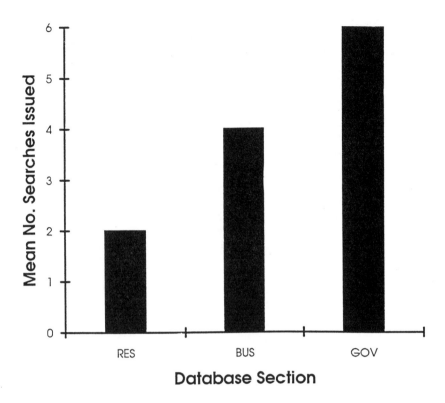

Figure 4.2: Expected outcome if the violation of EWP-specific rules affect performance, given that more rules are likely to be violated in the GOV than in the RES database section, with BUS falling somewhere in between the two. Note that only a single subject-group has been considered in this and the following data plots.

Measures: Number of searches issued per target and number of errors committed, where an error was defined as a search issued with incorrect information in the NAME field.

Subjects: Two groups, none of whom had any previous EWP experience but who were distinguishable by their relative amount of computer expertise: one group comprised computer experts (CE) – computer scientists or engineers who had all been employed full-time for several years in the field of computer research/design/development; the other group comprised computer novices (CN), and were undergraduates, including computer science students who, by comparison with the experts, could still be regarded as novices.

Data: Copy manually what the subject enters in the NAME field when a search is issued as well as system output. Write LOC and STRT details only when they differ from those given on the target card.

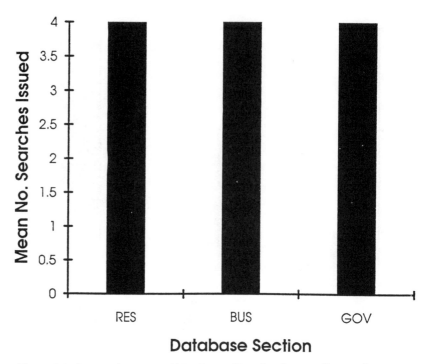

Figure 4.3: Expected outcome if EWP-specific rules do not affect performance.

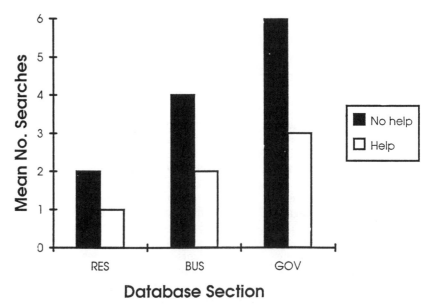

Figure 4.4: Expected outcome if performance is affected by EWP-specific rules (no help) and it is improved with availability of help (help).

Typical extract of datafile:
Target (presented on card): FESTO Pty. Ltd.
179 Browns Road
Noble Park

Subject's responses:

> FESTO.   + LOC + RES → List of names
> FESTO PTY LTD + LOC + RES → NG
> FESTO PTY.LTD. + LOC + BUS → OK

'>' = search issued; FESTO (etc.) = entry in NAME field; LOC = entry
in LOC field (as per card, i.e. Noble Park); RES/BUS = area of database
searched; → = leading to system output. (NG = No Good)

In the first search issued, the subject entered FESTO plus the name of
the suburb plus issued a search in the RESidential database. This
retrieved a list of irrelevant surnames, commencing with the character
string 'FESTO'. No entry was made in STRT field which is acceptable
by the EWP. In the second search, the entry in the NAME field was
extended, but because the RESidential database section was searched
again, no targets were retrieved due to the 'PTY LTD' typed in the
NAME field. Finally, in the third search, the target was successfully
retrieved.

Design: All targets given in the same order to all subjects to keep the
amount of EWP experience constant. However, the order in which items
were presented was randomized first.

Procedure: No practice items were included, as the EWP should be
usable by everyone, including computer novices, without training. Tasks
were carried out online with the experimenter sitting behind the subject
taking notes.

Results: The mean number of searches issued for targets correctly
located in the three sections of the EWP database by each of the two
subject-groups is plotted in Fig. 4.5 below.

The figure shows that novices (CN) issued more searches, on average,
than experts (CE) in two of the three database sections. Most searches
were issued in the GOVernment and least in the RESidential database
section. Both these findings were statistically reliable ($p < 0.001$),
indicating that computer expertise helped even when exploring a new
system, and that EWP-specific rules did give rise to user problems. The
usability defects identified in the heuristic evaluation were actual
stumbling blocks. For the purposes of designing EWP help, the results
clearly supported the hypothesis that the more EWP rules could be
violated when searching for a particular target, the more likely it was
that the user would experience trouble.

4.5 Conceptual walkthroughs

A conceptual walkthrough, or 'talk-through' as it is sometimes referred
to (Meister, 1986, Ch. 2) is a thinking exercise which is normally done
before a concrete system exists, although some argue that it can be

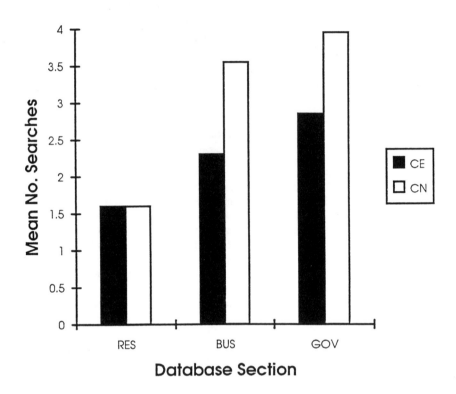

Figure 4.5: Mean number of searches issued by novices (CN) and experts (CE) in all three areas of the database (RES, BUS, GOV).

applied profitably throughout the entire systems design and development process (Lewis and Polson, 1992; Rieman *et al.*, 1991). The purpose of conceptual walkthroughs is to identify spots in the user interface which might be ambiguous with respect to user goals/actions, and to make specific design decisions. The method is similar to techniques used by the software community (Yourdon, 1989); it is a theory-driven technique which aims to support exploratory learning (Polson and Lewis, 1990) and to link the development of cognitive theory with 'state of the art' case projects (Lewis, 1991). No experimental verification is carried out during the conceptual walkthrough – all work is done on paper forms or on a black or white board. Critical issues include: (a) task selection, coverage and evaluation; (b) the actual evaluation process; (c) requisite knowledge; (d) interpretation of results. (Wharton *et al.*, 1992).

Task selection is absolutely critical. Wharton *et al.* recommend that evaluators start with simple tasks and then work through the more complex ones. This gives the team the 'hang' of doing walkthroughs, so that they are reasonably efficient at it by the time they tackle more difficult tasks. The evaluation should include at least one task that mirrors the complexity of that which a user will typically encounter during interaction. The task selection should also balance with the system's range of functionality. Realistic tasks should be selected, preferably some that cover several core functions, to evaluate the connection between different subtasks. Although task selection is critical, there are as yet no guidelines on granularity or on how to achieve an optimal number of tasks within time and budget constraints.

The evaluation process progresses through three phases, namely preparation, evaluation, and interpretation of the results. Paper forms guide the evaluators through the preparation and evaluation phases with detailed instructions, but the interpretation is *ad hoc* and, like so many other evaluation tools, the value of the analysis depends critically on the skill and knowledge of the analysts. Steps required to accomplish a task are evaluated by examining the behaviour of the proposed interface and its effects on users. Both successful and unsuccessful steps are recorded.

The flow and consideration of different ideas is particularly important in a multi-disciplinary project team. Whilst working together in multi-disciplinary teams can be trying, because members are constantly challenged to give reasons for their points of view and because different philosophical perspectives often clash, it can also be a most fruitful and enriching experience. Some of the best systems seen and tested by the author have invariably been designed by multi-disciplinary teams. The contribution of people from many backgrounds has brought out numerous issues affecting usability to which a representative from any single discipline would most likely have been blind.

The walkthrough method presupposes some knowledge of cognitive science terms, concepts and skills. For example, it can be difficult to distinguish between 'goal' and 'activity' which makes the evaluation more complex than it ought to be (Wharton *et al.*, 1992).

Interpretation of results: walkthroughs identify mismatches between system affordances and user goals. This can lead to suboptimal solutions especially if the links between tasks and subtasks are not exposed in the sense that a good solution to one task may be problematic for another. This is especially dangerous because the interpretation is *ad hoc*.

4.5.1 'JOGTHROUGHS'

Using a similar approach, Rowley and Rhoades (1992) found walkthroughs too restrictive in the sense that many a good design solution raised was not taken up because the evaluators concentrated on the highly structured walkthrough. These authors skipped many of the atomic actions and combined several where the group deemed it appropriate. This 'jogthrough' method saved quite some time compared with more formal walkthroughs, and the relaxed method allowed freer discussion in which developers became much more involved. The jogthrough method could thus be seen as a method for collaborative design. In our laboratory, it has been found worthwhile to conduct relaxed walkthroughs, much in the line suggested by the jogthrough method, in teams of up to ten people representing a range of different disciplines. One person, often the project leader, chairs the discussion, albeit informally, and writes questions, answers, and possible solutions on the white board as the discussion progresses. That person also takes responsibility for summarizing the outcomes of meetings and for ensuring that the discussion stays 'on track'. Depending on the purpose of the exercise, a typical user task or set of tasks that the system is intended to support is selected to walk (or talk) through. Starting at logon, the team then works through this task in great detail considering all user actions, one by one, in the sequence they would occur in the task under consideration. The effect of these actions on the system, and changes in system states, are considered as well. All along the way, the team imagines as many 'what if the user does X right now?' situations as it can in an effort to think through the task and its implications. Having followed through a task or set of tasks in this fashion, the team may then decide to set the same problem in a different framework, for example use an alternative technology, or a different dialogue modality. The user task is then worked through in the same fashion, and all imaginable cognitive stumbling blocks are turned, highlighted, different solutions applied, until agreement is reached by the team that solution X is the best way to proceed.

EXAMPLE: PROBLEM SOLVING BY CONCEPTUAL WALKTHROUGH

During the development of an electronic mail system (EMS) in our own research team, the provision of a RESUME key was considered very attractive. However, we were not quite certain how to handle it, so we conducted a conceptual walkthrough using the following task scenario:

Suppose Janice W. wants to arrange a meeting with Fred S. in Sydney, so she writes to Fred setting out a list of the topics she needs to discuss with him. She then realizes that she has forgotten the date of her Sydney trip. Rather than interrupting her e-mail session to look up the relevant date, Janice chooses to leave the message to Fred unfinished for the moment while creating a few other messages and scanning her incoming mail. At some later stage which may either be during the present, or in a subsequent session, Janice can pick up her message to Fred by pressing RESUME to insert the correct date before sending it off.

So far, so good. Now, consider the following scenario: Janice has exited the unfinished message to Fred, has scanned through four of the seven new messages that have arrived in her mailbox since the last session. She has also commenced another message to Myra on a different topic. Now, when Janice presses RESUME, what happens? Considering the chronological order in which Janice progressed through the session (Fred/scanning mail/Myra), there are at least three possible ways in which RESUME might function in this single session.

1. PRESSING RESUME DISPLAYS THE MOST RECENT TASK FIRST

    RESUME could take us back to the most recent task and work area, thereby reversing the chronological order in which the unfinished tasks will be displayed. That is, Myra's message will appear first on the screen upon pressing RESUME. How does Janice access Fred's message in this scenario? She could press RESUME several times until Fred's message is displayed. However, that requires displaying successive screens and deciding for each whether it is the one intended. Where multiple tasks have been left unfinished, this is clearly not a desirable situation: the effort of locating the desired message by pressing RESUME successively and correctly rejecting every unwanted message exceeds that of calling up a file from a directory.

2. PRESSING RESUME DISPLAYS THE FIRST TASK LEFT UN-FINISHED

    Now, if Janice wants to display the message to Fred first, this is fine. However, if she wants the message to Myra first, this leads to precisely the same problem as described above, only in reverse order. Hence, the task of locating a given message increases with the number of unfinished messages stored: this reduces the perceived advantages of providing access to multiple unfinished messages in some linear, chronological fashion by means of a RESUME function.

3. LET THE USER SELECT THE MESSAGE HE/SHE WANTS FROM A MENU

    If the system is a conventional one using a Qwerty keyboard and a 24 × 80 screen display, pressing RESUME could, if multiple unfinished tasks are stored, show a menu of these from which the user can select the one desired. The effort of this would seem to be equivalent to calling up a file from a file directory, as the user must first press RESUME and then select an option from a menu.

In a windows environment, one could provide a pull-down RESUME menu in which unfinished messages are stored and automatically removed upon completion. This would require the user to tell the computer explicitly when a task is finished. However, it is equally smart to allow the user to mark unfinished tasks in some fashion so that these 'stick out' when listing the directory containing all files, both completed and unfinished ones. Either of these solutions would be fine, but because they use the menu structure which is part of the system anyway, the benefit of the RESUME function has thus been entirely eliminated!

The magnitude of these problems increases when we consider whether the RESUME function would be available across multiple systems where the PC is used as a gateway, or across multiple sessions with a given system. The walkthrough led to the decision not to include a RESUME function at all in the EMS. The simple tasks were fine, but it was the complex ones that uncovered this problem (from Lindgaard, 1988).

Conceptual walkthroughs can be conducted by using forms – see sample – adapted from Lewis *et al.*, (1990). Using a standard design of such a form helps to focus on the task and consider all the essential issues, some of which might otherwise be overlooked or forgotten. Alternatively, forms might be adapted to suit different systems or types of systems. You might consider devising your own form for tasks in your system – the one presented here gives you something to start on.

4.5.2 WHAT TO MEASURE?

Conceptual walkthroughs are not a user performance measuring tool, although one is trying to expose troublesome spots in the software. The statements made as a result of a conceptual walkthrough are thus not statistical either. Instead, a conceptual walkthrough is an ideal tool with which to work out best solutions very early in the design and development of systems from a number of perspectives and technological possibilities. As it is not a performance evaluation tool, the conceptual walkthrough cannot strictly be said to 'measure' anything, in the sense that it does not lead to quantifiable variables and findings, but it gives us a level of insight that would be difficult to gain otherwise. In an attempt to illustrate the value of conceptual walkthroughs, let us look at two examples of cases that could have profited from this kind of scrutiny, if someone had invented the tool at the time these systems were designed. It should be noted that both the systems are reasonably old; they have been included here because they do help to illustrate a number of important and pertinent points about conceptual walkthroughs.

CONCEPTUAL WALKTHROUGH

Evaluator's name: .... date: ..../..../....

System/version evaluated: ....

Task evaluated: .... Step #: ....

---

1. Is the user's immediate goal clear?   Yes/No

2. First/next action user should take
   (a) Is it obvious that the action is available?   Yes/No

       State why/why not: ....

   (b) Is it obvious that the action is appropriate to 1. above?
                                                               Yes/No

       State why/why not: ....

3. How is a description of the action accessed? ....

   (a) List access problems: ....

4. Is it clear how the description is linked to the action?   Yes/No

   (a) List linking problems: ....

5. How will the user execute the action? ....

   (a) List any problems associated with execution: ....

6. If timeouts apply, is there sufficient time for the user to make
   necessary decisions before timeout: Yes/No

7. Execute the action and describe the system response: ....

   (a) Is it obvious that progress has been made towards the goal
   stated in 1. above?

       State why/why not: ....

8. Describe appropriately modified goal, if any: ....

   (a) Is it obvious that the goal should change?   Yes/No

State why/why not: ....

(b) If the task is completed, is this obvious?   Yes/No

State why/why not: ....

9. At every point of the interaction, are exits clearly marked?
                                                                                Yes/No

Note where they are not: ....

10. Is there a clear distinction between 'exit from the current task/environment' and 'quit from the system' at all times?
                                                                                Yes/No

Note where it is not clear: ....

11. Is help clearly accessible at all times?   Yes/No

Note where it is not: ....

12. At every point of the interaction, list every error that you can imagine a user could commit:

1. ....   7. ....

2. ....   8. ....

3. ....   9. ....

4. ....   10. ....

5. ....   11. ....

6. ....   12. ....

(a) Is there a relevant error message for every error noted?

1. Yes/No 2. Yes/No 3. Yes/No 4. Yes/No 5. Yes/No 6. Yes/No
7. Yes/No 8. Yes/No 9. Yes/No 10. Yes/No 11. Yes/No 12. Yes/No

(b) Does each error message clearly indicate to the user where the error occurred, what is wrong, and how to recover from it?

1. Yes/No 2. Yes/No 3. Yes/No 4. Yes/No 5. Yes/No 6. Yes/No
7. Yes/No 8. Yes/No 9. Yes/No 10. Yes/No 11. Yes/No 12. Yes/No

EXAMPLE: AUSTRALIAN VIATEL

The following is the main menu of an Australian videotex-type system which has now been superseded. However, it still makes a nice example so, even if you cannot find it in a working system any more, have a look at Fig. 4.6 below.

Even if this system were presented on paper screens, a large number of potential usability problems are readily identifiable even before deciding on a typical task to be walked-through relying on heuristics instead. For example, from this single screen it is not clear what the user is supposed to do here (how to select items from the menu); there is no marked exit if the user should want to quit; it is unclear why some options are presented in capitals and others in mixed case; the numbering of menu items does not seem to make much sense, and the fact that some menu lines contain several options and others only one is confusing; wording is meaningless to newcomers (e.g. what is SPI? what does 2@25c mean?); the abbreviations do not follow any rules that are easy to grasp and recognize, and so on.

VIATEL BUSINESS

1 HEADLINES 1.40pm
11 $A recovers overnight losses 3@15c
12 SPI encouraged by Tokyo 6@15c
13 Surprise as mrkt holds up 2@25c
2 BUSINESS WHAT'S NEW & FEATURES
21 Tax Office on the attack
22 Bain & Co share chart. commentaries
23 Product liability legislat. dangers

3 Info for commercial prpty investors

4 BANKING & FINANCE 42 Telebanking
5 STOCKMARKETS 59 MONEY WATCH
6 BUSINESS NEWS & INFORMATION
7 TRAVEL 71 News & What's New
8 MAILBOX, TELEX & TELESERVICES
9 HELP 91 How to use 92 A to Z Guide

0 MAGAZINE   #WHERE IS THAT INFO?

Figure 4.6: The opening screen in the Australian VIATEL system.

iNET

iNET is a gateway to several hundred databases. For each of these, there is a tutorial complete with a set of instructions which explain what type of data may be found and how to interrogate the particular database. These tutorials are several pages long (up to 24) and contain a great deal of information which need not be recalled later. Database-specific commands are generally given on the last page of these instructions which is annoying to the user who wants only to refresh his/her memory for the commands. Once inside the database, these commands are no longer accessible, and nor is it possible to skip through the initial pages of the tutorial and access the command page directly. Hence, unless commands are written down on a piece of paper before accessing the database, the user must exit to obtain the commands and then re-enter the database. This means that no task can be completed from the information provided on the screen – the user has to recall and enter a certain command to get anywhere at all.

Most of the potential usability problems alluded to in these examples could readily have been identified if a conceptual walkthrough and/or a heuristic evaluation had been conducted before the system was released. The same is true of many existing systems.

In summary, a conceptual walkthrough is a diagnostic decision tool, and a walkthrough may be carried out before any coding has been commenced, but at a time when system functions usually have been laid down in sufficient detail to work through a typical user task or set of tasks on a white board or paper forms. Conceptual walkthroughs are quite time-consuming and tedious to conduct because they force the team to work through the selected tasks in great detail. However, they can provide extremely profitable information which may save many, many working days further along in the development process. For that reason, it is a very valuable tool when applied early enough in the system development process, at a time when aspects of the system are quite easily altered in an effort better to suit user needs.

Advantages of conceptual walkthroughs
- allow detailed usability insight early in the process;
- tasks can be set up quite quickly;
- allow evaluation of competing solutions before coding commences.

Disadvantages of conceptual walkthroughs
- data analysis and interpretation is difficult and *ad hoc*;
- do not match current software engineering practice;
- pay attention to detail when designers might want only the most important interface problems;
- task suite is best selected by usability experts.

'Conceptual walkthroughs are, well, time-consuming'

A global usability analysis yields an overall impression of system usability. The method was derived by a number of researchers working together in two major projects within ESPRIT (European strategic programme for research and development into information technology) who developed a comprehensive checklist for evaluators. This checklist is presented in Ravden and Johnson (1989) together with the underlying rationale, examples of test cases and a full description of how to apply it and analyse the outcomes. The checklist addresses ten areas, or aspects, of usability, including visual clarity, consistency, error prevention and control, and user guidance. Each aspect is evaluated on a number of relevant questions which evaluators work through, and a summary section is provided for each aspect as well as an overall summary section which also shows how the various aspects are related to one another.

In order to perform such an analysis, evaluators must first familiarize themselves with the entire system to be able to comment on system strengths and weaknesses. The first step in the global usability analysis is to perform a heuristic evaluation as was described earlier (section 4.3.1). Once evaluators have completed this first phase, they are asked to work through a number of set tasks, designed by the human factors specialists or the entire project team. These tasks are selected to cover or highlight those areas of the system in which users are likely to experience problems, and they also represent typical tasks.

4.6 Global usability analyses

Each evaluator fills in a complete checklist, and all findings are then collated by the project team to form the basis for usability defect fixing strategies (Chapter 8). One great strength of this approach is that evaluators from different disciplines can and should perform the evaluation, simply because different people are likely to uncover different usability defects. Typically, one would include users with task knowledge, software engineers who are not directly involved in the project, human factors experts, as well as members of the project team in the evaluation. As with conceptual walkthroughs and heuristic evaluations, outcomes are generally not statistical but rather practical usability statements.

Advantages of global usability analyses
- can be done in evaluator's own time;
- allow input from a range of different disciplines (tend to uncover different usability defects);
- quick to administer because checklists already exist.

Disadvantages of global usability analyses
- tend to give a rough overview of usability defects rather than identify specific usability defects;

'It's all in the eye of the beholder'

- evaluators must be thoroughly familiar with both system and tasks;
- task selection best done by expert;
- difficult to generate fixing strategies from generic usability defects.

Summary

This chapter was intended as a kaleidoscope, or a broad smorgasbord, showing a number of different knowledge elicitation and inspection methods. The first group of knowledge elicitation methods dealt with different kinds of protocols, where a task performer reports what is going on during or after performing the task. The next group introduced a number of methods in which task performers, usually experts, judge the similarity of different tasks or task components. These judgments are not carried out during task performance. Next, a discussion followed of some more inspection methods. In particular, heuristic evaluation and conceptual walkthroughs were dealt with in some detail. Confirmation studies, which differ from the other methods introduced in this chapter by virtue of being performance-based, were introduced to show how one might submit potential usability defects uncovered in studies such as heuristic evaluations, to more rigorous testing in order to separate trivial from serious problems. Global usability analysis was introduced as an alternative method in which people from different disciplines may fruitfully take part; it is a hybrid of heuristic evaluations and pre-designed tasks, although task performance is not measured, but the evaluators integrate task experience into the usability analysis as part of the overall impression.

Questions

1. Why do you think protocol analyses are very popular in usability evaluations?
2. What are some of the drawbacks of protocols?
3. What might some of the advantages of contextual inquiries be?
4. What might the task-similarity judgment methods add that observation of user performance or protocols cannot yield?
5. What is a heuristic evaluation?
6. Why is the outcome of such an evaluation dependent upon the experience and background of an evaluator?
7. What are the advantages of heuristic evaluations?
8. What are some of the disadvantages?
9. Why are tests which seek to verify and confirm that the system is running properly not applied in a heuristic evaluation?
10. Why is it important to identify and fix as many usability problems as time and budget permit before a system is released?
11. What is the advantage of involving a group of evaluators representing a range of disciplines, compared to asking a single person to evaluate a given system?

12. Why are the software engineers who designed and developed a certain product likely to be your worst choice when asking someone to conduct a heuristic evaluation?

13. Why should you identify the relative seriousness and frequency of occurrence of 'fuzzy' usability problems?

14. Why do you need to conduct confirmation studies?

15. What purpose are the user tasks in confirmation studies intended to serve?

16. What is a conceptual walkthrough?

17. What are the critical issues in conceptual walkthroughs?

18. Why is it a good idea to include people from a variety of relevant disciplines to perform a conceptual walkthrough?

19. How would you categorize conceptual walkthroughs as an investigative tool?

20. What role do the structured tasks play in global usability analyses?

Exercises

In this exercise you are asked to evaluate two very sketchy and very early versions of an emerging system intended for use in local councils for access to land information, title information, and so on. All you have are a few paper screens drawn by the project team to illustrate their ideas. The two proposed versions are competing in the sense that they are both reasonably attractive. So far, they exist only in paper form, and coding has not yet commenced, not even for the prototypes. Primary users require quick and easy access to information, as they often need to answer telephone enquiries. The philosophy of System A is Windows (GUI), and that of System B is form-based although it has graphics capabilities. In terms of hardware, both solutions are possible and cost is not even considered at this early stage in which an optimal solution is to be found. Your task is to ascertain which of the two systems is likely best to suit its users, their tasks, and the environment into which the system must fit. How would you go about making the best decision, and how would you justify it?

Note: System A is shown first (pp. 145–6) in terms of the progressive steps to be taken to achieve retrieval of a particular land title, and then a view of the block of land in question. For System B (pp. 147–8) five screens are displayed, including the follow-up 'Help' screen.

Land Type Database File Layout Lines

Land Type	Database File Layout Lines
Commercial Crown Residential	

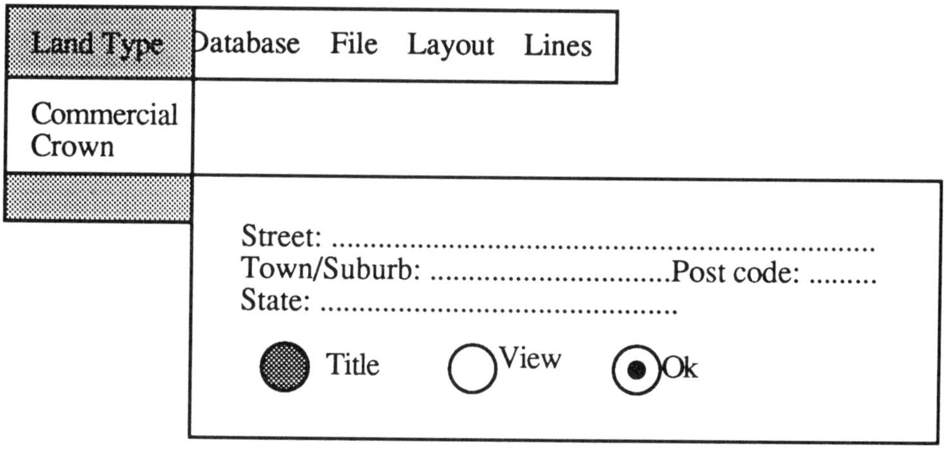

Land Type	Database File Layout Lines
Commercial Crown	

Street: ....
Town/Suburb: ....Post code: ....
State: ....

⬤ Title   ◯View   ◉Ok

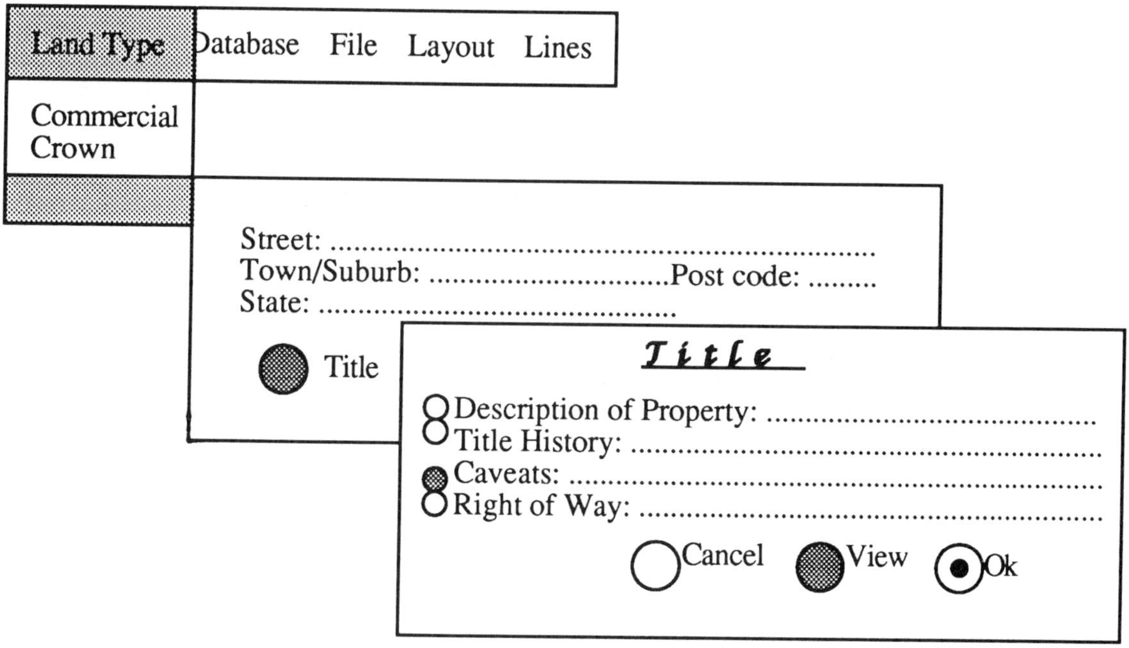

Land Type	Database File Layout Lines
Commercial Crown	

Street: ....
Town/Suburb: ....Post code: ....
State: ....

⬤ Title

Title

◦ Description of Property: ....
◦ Title History: ....
⬤ Caveats: ....
◦ Right of Way: ....

◯Cancel   ⬤View   ◉Ok

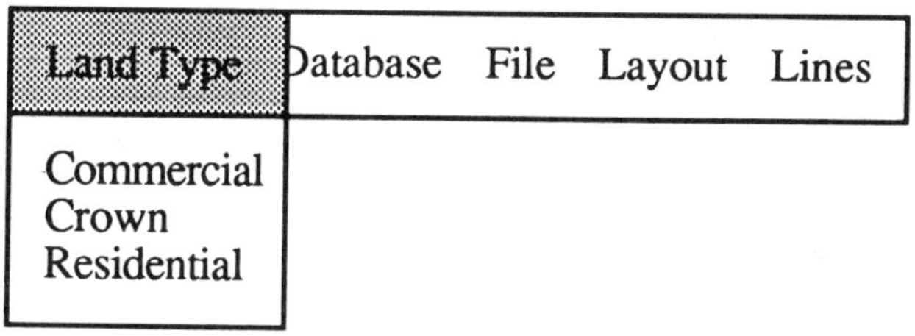

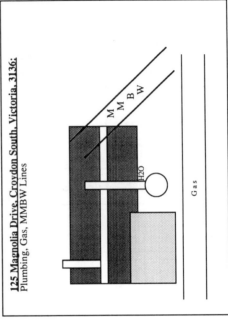

125 Magnolia Drive, Croydon South, Victoria, 3136:
Plumbing, Gas, MMBW Lines

Title

○ Description of Property: ....
○ Title History: ....
● Caveats: .125 Magnolia Drive...........
○ Right of Way: ....

○ Cancel

Belmont Rd

125

Magnolia Drive

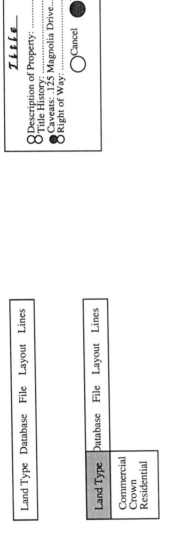

Land Type   Database   File   Layout   Lines

Land Type
Commercial
Crown
Residential

Land Type   Database   File   Layout   Lines

Land Type
Commercial
Crown

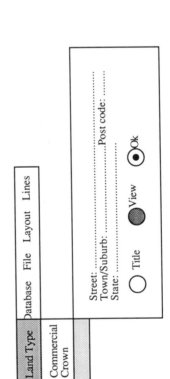

Land Type   Database   File   Layout   Lines

Street: ....
Town/Suburb: ....   Post code: ....
State: ....

○ Title   ● View   ● Ok

Lbase III
Land View Screen, Level 1

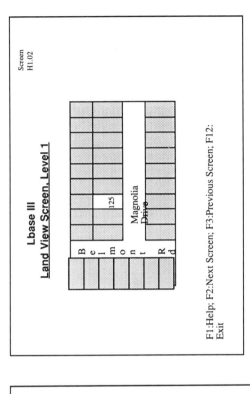

B
e
l
m
o
n
t
R
d

125

Magnolia
Drive

F1:Help; F2:Next Screen; F3:Previous Screen; F12:
Exit

Lbase III
Land View Screen, Level 2

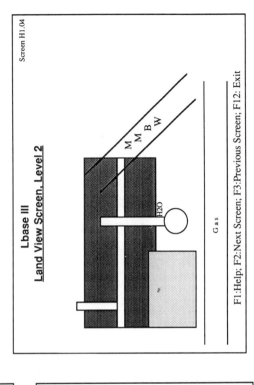

M
M
B
W

H2O

Gas

F1:Help; F2:Next Screen; F3:Previous Screen; F12: Exit

Lbase III
Land Query
Screen

*Database:

* Land Type:

*Street:

Town/Suburb:

State:

Title:

View:

When form completed, press <ENTER> for next screen

F1:Help; F12: Exit

Lbase III
Title Display Screen

Title

Description of Property

Title History:

Caveats:

Right of Way:

F1:Help; F2:Next Screen; F3:Previous Screen; F12: Exit

```
┌─────────────────────────────────────────────────────────────────┐
│                          Help Information                         │
│                                                                   │
│  Database: Need not be specified for TITLe/VIEw search            │
│  Land Type: Available types or COMmercial/CROwn/RESidential       │
│  Street: Refers to address at which search is to be issued        │
│  Town/Suburb:                                                     │
│  State:                                                           │
│  Title: Requires a Y/N response                                   │
│  View: Requires a Y/N response                                    │
│                                                                   │
│                                                                   │
│  F12: Exit                                                        │
│                                                                   │
└─────────────────────────────────────────────────────────────────┘
```

Suggested further reading

Karat, Campbell and Fiegel investigated the relative effectiveness of different usability assessment methods in two graphical office systems (Karat *et al.*, 1992). They found that empirical methods were able to highlight more usability defects than walkthroughs, and that walkthroughs conducted by a team achieved better results than when conducted by individuals. This is a nice comparison and can help you to decide when to use which method. Their paper is short and very easy to read.

Lewis, Polson, Wharton and Reiman (1990) give a nice example of the way a walkthrough method may be applied and the results it is capable of achieving. Their paper is very readable and should be read to learn more about walkthrough methods.

Ravden and Johnson (1989) include a very comprehensive checklist for global usability evaluations in their book which can almost be used as it is. Some ten aspects of usability are addressed, and the authors show how the checklist should be used and how to integrate and interpret findings into an overall assessment of system usability. It is a very practical book, easy to learn and use.

Data collection techniques II: 5
interviews and surveys

Our so-called limitations, I believe.
Apply to faculties we don't apply.
We don't discover what we can't
achieve
Until we make an effort not to try.

Piet Hein

Anyone can design a questionnaire – anyone can conduct an interview! Certainly, but there are a lot of traps one can fall into, blunders that one can overlook, and pitfalls that can only be avoided if the person doing the planning, conducting and data analysis knows what he/she is doing. Recall the example of the university staff who wanted to assess students' perceptions of course quality. Nothing was gained from that survey because it had not been planned carefully enough; sadly, it is often the case that investigators find only too late that they cannot interpret the data they have collected, that the analysis yields no new information, or that the data are so ambiguous that their efforts were largely wasted. In an attempt to help you bypass many of the common traps, this chapter discusses considerations underlying the planning, designing, conducting and analysing of interviews and surveys. Three types of interviews are discussed; hints are given for ways in which the success of a well-planned interview can be ensured. Steps and points to consider are gone through sequentially so that you should be able to design and conduct a fruitful interview at the end of reading the relevant sections. Much the same treatment is then given to questionnaires used in surveys; an outline is presented showing how a good questionnaire is designed, planned, administered and used to obtain information relevant to making decisions in the systems design and development cycle.

An interview involves at least two, but may involve an entire group of, people. In a typical interview one person may be trying to help or educate another, or one person may be trying to extract knowledge or information from another. The interview as a research method is defined by Cannell and Kahn (1968) as a 'two-person conversation, initiated by the interviewer for the specific purpose of obtaining research-relevant information, and focused by him on contents specified by research objectives of systematic description, prediction, or explanation' (p. 527). The research interview is thus a directive, information-gathering process in which the interviewer controls the situation, sets the purpose of the

5.1 Interviews

interview, and controls the pacing (Fisher, 1982; Stewart and Cash, 1978). In the present context, the kind of interview described is one in which the interviewer aims to extract knowledge from the interviewee that is relevant to designing, evaluating, or exploring the possibility for creating a new computer system.

When planning and conducting an interview, four issues must be taken into account to ensure its success. First, the interviewee must have access to the information the interviewer wants. If he/she does not have the information, the questions cannot be answered correctly. This simple point is often ignored when specifications are being developed for a new or a replacement computer system. Too often information about end users' needs and details of their tasks is specified and communicated to the project team by managers who tend to have only a rough idea of what exactly end users are required to do. In order to design a system that is useful for the very people for whom it is intended, it is absolutely essential to communicate directly with those people to ensure that the nature and details of their tasks are taken into account early in the systems design and development process. Contacting the right people is also fundamental to conducting a successful interview.

The second requirement for a successful interview is that the interviewee understands what is required from him/her. He/she must, for example, know what information is relevant, how completely, in how much detail, questions should be answered, and in what terms of reference the answers should be expressed. The interviewer must clarify the interviewee's role, both in the initial explanation of the purpose of the interview and in the amount of probing for further details in the answers offered.

Third, it is necessary to ensure that respondents are motivated to give accurate answers. An interview that, in the respondent's view, takes too long becomes tedious for people who want to get on with other things which for them are much more important than answering questions. Similarly, if the content of the interview is boring, too personal or potentially embarrassing, unclear, convoluted, or if the interviewee simply does not like the situation or the interviewer, the resultant information may be inaccurate and the interview may be terminated abruptly.

Finally, one has a responsibility towards the people who give their time to participate in an interview, and also towards future researchers. People want to know how their data is going to be used, how their contribution fits into the overall scheme of things, and they want to be assured of anonymity, privacy and confidentiality. Most of these details are not revealed before the interview takes place, so allowance must be made for debriefing after the data have been collected. Take time to explain the wider framework, allow interviewees to ask questions until they are satisfied that they know all they want and that their time was worth it.

'Well, Mr Average, what do you think about enterprise bargaining in the light of
forthcoming legislative requirements to register pecuniary interests
blah. . .blah. . .blah?'

Thorough debriefing also makes it more likely that interviewees will agree
to participate in future research, whether this be conducted by oneself or
by someone else. Debriefing thus achieves two objectives: it keeps
participants happy about their involvement, and it establishes a positive
attitude towards future research.

An interview is a social process in which both the interviewer and the
interviewee size up the other party. Their inferences about each other are
likely to affect the way questions are being answered. The interviewer is
not a passive ingredient that extracts information and records it.

Interviewer bias, or interviewer effect, is a reality which must be carefully guarded against. Interviewer effect exists when interviewees respond in a manner that reflects what they think the interviewer wants, rather than answers being an expression of the interviewee's own opinion. It can be difficult to detect when interviewees are trying to please instead of offering honest answers to the interviewer's questions, but certain steps can be taken to avoid interviewer biases. One way to prevent it is to train interviewers to avoid stating their own views and to ensure that they remain courteous and interested in the respondent's answers. Interviewers must, at all times, refrain from showing any signs of disapproval, disagreement or disappointment in the respondent's opinions. Techniques can also be employed encouraging the interviewee to expand and elaborate on his/her answers, depending on the purpose and format of the interview. One such technique, probing, is discussed later (section 5.1.1). So, the essential ingredients for a successful interview are ensuring that one interviews the right people who have access to the information one wants, that the aim of the interview is clearly stated and that respondents are kept interested and motivated by the display of appropriate behaviour. The skilled interviewer fulfils his/her role in a fashion that increases interviewee participation (Fisher, 1982; Richardson *et al.*, 1965).

'An interviewer who dominates the conversation is unlikely to get much information at all'

The golden rules for interview success are as follows:

- The interviewee has access to the right information.
- The aim of the interview is clear to the interviewee.
- The interviewer is interested but neutral during the interview.
- A debriefing session is offered at the end of the interview.

When one plans, conducts and analyses the outcome of interviews, one should allow approximately one-third of the total time allocation for the actual interview. The remainder is spent planning it, locating respondents, making, and physically getting oneself to, appointments, analysing and interpreting the research data. By the time one has gone thoroughly through the data, taken out the most important details, sifted through them to ensure nothing has been missed, summarized and written up the findings, more time will have passed than inexperienced researchers would believe; even highly experienced researchers often underestimate how long interviews really take from beginning to end. Provided the interview has been thoroughly planned, it is well worthwhile to analyse in detail the fruits of one's labour. If the time available for exploratory data gathering does not permit proper planning, conduction and analysis of interviews, it might be more appropriate to conduct a survey, observe users in action, or apply some other research tool for obtaining the information required. Sloppy research is a waste of time, and is likely to lead to conclusions and decisions that will prove inefficient, if not downright wrong and probably very expensive later in the system design and development process. Successful research is a combination of knowledge, skill, tactics and ability to adapt to the constraints of the situation and environment within which the researcher operates without sacrificing the discipline of research. Part of the research skill lies in selecting the right tool and adjusting it for the task at hand to maximize the benefits and accuracy of the research outcome.

If consideration is given as to where in the various phases of the system development cycle interviews fit, one finds that they can be slotted in at almost any point except perhaps during development. In the feasibility and research phases, one would define what, whom and how the proposed computer system should serve. Using interviews as a means of obtaining data concerning users' knowledge and opinions of a system is an obvious tool to apply. At the development stage, usability tests would be concerned with assessing ease of use of the emerging system rather than with collecting further background material. For that reason, interviews are not suitable during the systems development phase. At the prototype and operation stage, it might again be necessary to sample future users' opinion of the new system to direct its further development and evolution.

5.1.1 TYPES OF INTERVIEWS

Unstructured interviews

An unstructured interview is often conducted in the exploratory feasibility phase. The interview aims to accomplish a certain goal and with this in mind, the interviewer guides the direction of the remarks during the interview. In the unstructured interview, the research goal includes discovering relevant issues to be explored through further research, perhaps in follow-up, structured interviews in the first instance. The interviewee is allowed to suggest related topics, and no restrictions are placed on his/her answers, on how issues are tackled, or on what issues are discussed. Questions do not follow a rigid schedule but are flexible and open-ended. Some researchers always use a tape recorder during an interview to make sure they capture all that is being said. Tapes are then transcribed, and coding, analysis and interpretation follows from these records. Others prefer to take notes, either because the tape recorder is perceived to be too intrusive and therefore to inhibit interviewees, or because they are certain they will get enough ideas down on paper to work from later.

Semi-structured interviews

The semi-structured interview is more focused than the unstructured, and less rigid than the completely structured one. Generally, the interviewer would be clear about what he/she wants to know but, at the same time, room would be left for exploring additional issues as the interview progresses. A set of questions should be prepared to be used as a guide but, in contrast to the structured interview, one would not necessarily be concerned about administering the questions in precisely the same way and in the same order to all respondents. Data capture techniques are the same as for unstructured interviews.

In order to stimulate exploration of undefined territory during the interview, probe whenever it is relevant. A probe is a word, phrase, sentence or utterance made by the interviewer in response to something the interviewee mentions. The purpose of a probe is to encourage the interviewee to clarify an answer or expand it. Sometimes, an encouraging nod or an 'uh-huh' is all that is needed to encourage the interviewee to keep talking. At other times, it may be necessary to add remarks like: 'Really! That's very interesting. Do you remember anything else about it?'

Some researchers distinguish between two types of probe, the 'echo' which is a repetition of what the interviewee said, and the 'extension' in which the interviewer asks for more in some way. Take the following examples, drawn from interviews in a troubled workplace in which something was obviously affecting people's productivity. A research team was called in to investigate what was going on, what, where and who was creating problems. Interviewing one person, the conversation progressed something like:

EXAMPLE:

Interviewee:	'I could easily have solved that problem, but they wouldn't let me.'
Interviewer:	'Ah, they wouldn't let you?' (echo)
or	
Interviewer:	'What did they actually say to you?' (extension)

Either of these responses would encourage the interviewee to elaborate on his initial statement. By contrast, statements such as:

Interviewee:	'I could easily have solved that problem, but they wouldn't let me.'
Interviewer:	'They are really objectionable in their attitudes towards you!'

would be quite destructive because the interviewer is closing the subject by drawing a conclusion after which it is difficult to open up the topic again. The aim of this interview was to expose and understand the practices, the culture, if you like, of this particular workplace in order to identify the reasons for the declining level of productivity. Reaching such an understanding included disentangling the various informal groups that exist in a workplace. Questions such as who makes up which 'groups'; what makes a person belong to, or be excluded from, a certain 'group'; the between-group fights, jealousies and problems which form part of the culture and communication norms had to be dealt with. Identifying these patterns helped to highlight the workers' perception of the way power is distributed within and between the various groups. It was thus necessary to create opportunities for people to talk.

The semi-structured interview permits flexibility in how information is obtained and in how much is obtained. In order to maximize such flexibility, the interviewer must know and understand the role and impact of 'facilitators' as well as 'inhibitors' in the interviewing process (Gorden, 1980). 'Facilitators' are statements or actions that enhance communication such as the 'echo' and 'extension' discussed above. 'Inhibitors' are statements or actions that cause communication to decrease. An interviewer who states his own opinion, disapproves of the interviewee's answers or draws conclusions from what the interviewee has said will discourage the interviewee from disclosing much information. An interviewer who dominates the conversation in an inappropriate and undesirable manner will not be a very successful information gatherer. Asking 'leading' questions (ones that indicate to the interviewee how he/she should answer it) is another one of the many pitfalls to be avoided.

Questions such as 'Don't you think that...' or 'Wouldn't you agree that...' must not be allowed to enter into the interview at all.

Structured interviews

In the structured interview the questions asked are fixed and inflexible. The situation does not really allow for probing, and questions are mostly asked to yield codeable answers. For example, in asking about an interviewee's amount of computer experience, the responses might be divided into pre-defined categories such as 'none / < 6 months / 6–12 months / 1–3 years / > 3 years'. Every person will fit into one, and only one, of the categories, and the amount of work in subsequently coding the data is reduced by using this method. The structured interview can obviously take place only when one knows exactly what information is sought; when the critical variables, topics and categories can be defined and delineated.

Questions are often read aloud to the interviewee as are the instructions and introduction of the interview to ensure uniformity in its administration across all participants. Uniformity is important in so far as it helps to reduce bias and error. The interviewer should behave in exactly the same manner towards all respondents.

The structured interview is very similar to a questionnaire. It is conducted at a time when the researcher knows precisely what issues are to be dealt with, when their boundaries have been clearly defined, and he/she is seeking quantifiable answers to well-defined questions.

5.1.2 PLANNING AN INTERVIEW

Where are you going to conduct the interview? If you will be interviewing end users for a new system, there might be some merit in conducting interviews in the work place. This gives you a feeling for the atmosphere and for how things are done there. However, unless the interviewee can be taken to a quiet place where you can work uninterrupted, without telephones, working machines or other equipment such as computers that must be monitored, those benefits may quickly be overshadowed by negative, unwanted influences. If you cannot find a quiet place in the respondent's work environment, consider interviewing after work, perhaps in your office, or in some other neutral spot that is reasonably quiet and pleasant to be in, where there are no distractions.

Apart from knowing where you are going to work, and whom you will include in your sample, you need to think about the structure of the interview. As stated previously, this depends on the stage you are at in the investigations. The earlier in the systems design and development phase you are, the more you will want to explore people's needs, habits, preferences or opinions unhindered by the restrictions of printed questions and pre-coded answers. Yet, even if you conduct an unstructured interview at this very early stage, you will need to prepare a list of questions which you can use as a guide, or at least you will need a list of topics to address.

If your interview is to be completely structured, or semi-structured, think ahead of how you are going to analyse your data. Open-ended questions are asked when encouraging respondents to expand on a given topic. They therefore belong predominantly in the unstructured arena, when topics and issues of relevance are still being defined and explored. In an open-ended question there are no pre-defined answers; rather, the interviewee is free to interpret the question and answer it in any way he/she likes. One limitation to this type of question is that answers cannot easily be coded or grouped for analysis. Therefore, when the interview is structured and the emphasis is on the quantitative aspects of the answers, pre-coding into discrete categories certainly makes life a lot easier at the data analysis stage. In order to allow such pre-coding of answers, pose close-end questions in which the responses are constrained by the pre-defined categories. More will be said about scoring responses in section 5.1.4.

5.1.3 DEFINING QUESTIONS

To help decide whether or not to include a particular question in an interview, consider its length, clarity and relevance to the information being sought. Every question included must have a clear, well-defined purpose, and no unnecessary question should be included at all. It takes quite a lot of effort to print, ask, answer and analyse each question, so you must be completely objective, even harsh, in your judgment of whether or not to include certain questions. Questions should be brief and to the point. Ambiguous, uninterpretable waffle has no place in an interview; double-barrelled questions should not be asked. For example, the question 'Are you still of the opinion that touchscreen technology is unsuitable for these tasks?' is making the assumption that the interviewee is not keen on touchscreen technology and that he/she believes it is not suited to the tasks in question. It is really asking two questions, namely:

1. What kinds of tasks do you think touchscreen technology is suited for?
2. Do you think touchscreen technology is suitable for the tasks in question?

Divide any double-barrelled questions so that each can be answered independently of the other(s).

5.1.4 SEQUENCE OF QUESTIONS

An interview should be divided such as to have a distinct beginning, middle and end. Begin the interview with a few 'warm-up' questions. These are very brief questions that are easy to answer and are designed to put the interviewee at ease. An interview tends to feel a bit like an exam for the interviewee at first, so these easy, routine questions serve to break the ice. Then, as the interview progresses, more difficult or delicate questions. If you were to start with the delicate ones before the interviewee has sized you up, you might never succed in breaking the ice or in obtaining any useful information. Towards the end of the session ask a few more easy, routine questions so that the interviewee is at ease and feeling good about the interview and its outcome. When conducting an interview, try to match the interviewee in mode of dress. Jeans might

'Begin with a few easy-to-answer questions'

be fine if you are talking to, say, farmers on the job, people in the store or in the back room, but they are unsuitable if you are interviewing the senior executives of a bank. Aim to present yourself as being neat, clean, courteous, low-key and avoid mimicry – you don't want to look, sound or act like some character actor!

5.1.5 DATA RECORDING

Some researchers prefer to audiotape interviews because it is quite difficult to take sufficient notes and conduct a successful interview at the same time. If all the answers are coded, there is the problem of remembering the codes and deciding how to note down information of importance but for which no codes exist. Keeping the flow of the

'Else you might not get the information you want'

interview going whilst taking notes means that you have to juggle between being a bit behind what is being said with your writing whilst asking the next question or listening to an answer. At the same time you are supposed to look and sound interested which is best done by maintaining eye contact whenever possible. Also, you should probe for more at appropriate points using the techniques described earlier. This is not an easy task! However, if you think your problems are all solved by audiotaping interviews instead, think again! You will either have to transcribe the tapes yourself or hire a typist to do it for you. Not only is transcribing a very time-consuming task, the reams of paper it produces will have to be proofread and analysed just the same as the notes you would be taking if you were not using tapes. The analysis will also take longer from tapes than from notes because you have so much more data to sift through when every utterance is included. No matter what data recording method is used, it will cause some problems in the analysis phase.

In addition to recording data during the interview, it is generally a good idea to write a post interview summary recording those details, impressions and relevant items that were not noted down earlier. Read notes taken during the interview, transcribe shorthand, abbreviations, and fill in any gaps. Include explanatory material that may help in the later interpretation of the responses. It is important to write up the post interview summary straight after an interview when it is still fresh in your mind. It is surprising how quickly memory fades and some things will already have been forgotten if writing the interview summary is delayed by a day or even a few hours. Indeed, give it a try it for yourself right now. Take a pencil and summarize all you can remember you have read in this chapter so far – without looking back, of course. Then, tomorrow or the day after, write another summary without first refreshing your mind by looking at the chapter or your first summary. Now, simply count the number of points made in both summaries and compare them. If you did not forget any vital points, you must be a genius!

5.1.6 INTERPRETING THE DATA

The unstructured interview identifies mainly those areas one wants to explore further and other topics one might want to pursue. It may take time to extract these topics from the data, but most often it is not too difficult to sift through the available data in search for the valuable parts. The unstructured data are often processed and interpreted anecdotally, partly because their purpose is to give us new ideas, and partly because they do not generally lend themselves to more formal data analyses. Finding statistical differences between phenomena is, at times, irrelevant;

it is often the observation that a phenomenon exists at all, or an event occurs, that is important and captures your interest.

By virtue of its stringent design, the structured interview yields quantitative, or at least quantifiable, data that are generally analysed statistically. Tools and techniques are also available with which even unstructured data may be analysed in a more quantitative fashion (contextual inquiry, section 4.1.2; content analysis, section 4.2.2).

5.1.7 SUMMARY OF THE MAIN POINTS

Here is briefly what has been stated about interviews:

- identify what you want to find out;
- identify who has the information you want;
- select a sample of interviewees that is representative of the relevant population;
- choose the kind and format of interview that is most appropriate for obtaining the information you are after;
- define an outline, or formulate the precise questions you will be asking;
- if the interview is structured, design codes and categories for answers;
- consider how you are going to analyse the data;
- consider how each question helps you to achieve your research goal and exclude any that do not contribute anything;
- ensure that there are no double-barrelled or ambiguous questions;
- consider which reliability coefficient you will apply to the data;
- dress appropriately for the interview;
- make interviewees feel at ease by asking warm-up questions first, then the more delicate ones and finally, a few routine questions at the end;
- remember the debriefing session, giving the interviewee a chance to ask questions;
- after each interview, write up a summary and fill in gaps in your notes immediately.

5.2 Surveys and questionnaires

A questionnaire is a tool that is generally employed when carrying out a survey. A survey may serve a single or several purposes, and it is simply a method for systematically collecting information on a given topic or topics from a number of people. The questionnaire, designed to ask a series of structured and uniform questions, is essentially a written interview which can easily be administered to a large number of respondents. Questionnaires mostly guarantee anonymity and allow respondents to work at their own pace. Researchers do not always have the opportunity to check that respondents interpret the questions the way they were intended; in these cases findings must be taken at face value.

It is tempting to believe that, because one can gather a lot of data very quickly by administering questionnaires to many people simultaneously, surveys are a neat and 'easy' data collection option. Not so! A great deal of time and work goes into planning, designing and pilot testing a questionnaire to get it right. Avoid redundancy and ask unambiguous questions, phrased to trigger the intended interpretation by respondents, placed in a logical structure. Design a questionnaire of the right length to ensure respondents do fill it in, establish a coding scheme and, finally do the actual administration, data entry of responses, analysis and interpretation. If you are going to do a survey, do it properly. Any job worth doing is worth doing well; preparing good surveys to secure maximum benefit is very time consuming. So, think about what type of responses you need before starting to design a questionnaire. Ask yourself whether they are worth the effort of a survey, or whether it might be better to observe a number of users, read more documentation first, interview experts, or apply any other data capture method that could yield the same answers better, faster, or cheaper. Unless the research gains additional information from a large number of responses, do not bother conducting surveys.

Two kinds of information come out of surveys: objective and subjective. Objective information is factual, answering questions like 'what is your gender/nationality/religion'; 'how many siblings are in your immediate family'; 'how many different software packages do you use daily'; and so forth. Subjective information expresses people's opinion, perceptions, beliefs, subjective estimates of events, probabilities, what people think, feel or believe is being sampled. In general, objective data is best arranged in mutually exclusive categories where responses fit into one and only one category per question. Subjective information is usually better suited for some kind of continuous scale. These are discussed later in this chapter. Surveys are usually conducted throughout the systems design and development process, except perhaps during the actual development, when users' needs should be well and truly settled. This is the same as for interviews; the two tools are very similar, and the information gleaned from applying either type concerns factual data or opinions, knowledge, feelings and predictions of a particular population.

5.2.1 INTERVIEWS OR SURVEYS?

Let us quickly review the reasons for conducting an interview or a survey.

Interviews

- provide access to people who cannot complete questionnaires;
- encourage exploration of ideas and suggestions;
- offer room for flexibility;
- direct interaction with interviewees;
- permit deeper questioning;
- allow clarification on both sides;
- include background and context.

Surveys

- are easier to administer and process;
- are less likely to embarrass respondents;
- are faster to analyse as the major effort is in preparation.

Given that interviews and questionnaires serve pretty much the same purpose, the decision to do one or the other will depend on resources and goals. Resources are time, money and access to respondents. Interviews tend to take much longer than questionnaires to administer, code and analyse, because quite a bit of time is spent with each interviewee. Also, interviews often contain open-ended questions as well as side remarks that must be analysed. Because the processing of uncoded, unstructured data is extremely time consuming and much more difficult than collating coded material, the decision to conduct an interview rather than designing a questionnaire is often guided by the number of unstructured questions: the more unstructured questions are included, the better it is to conduct interviews than surveys.

In terms of access to respondents, one's choice is usually guided by who and where they are. If people are being sampled whose native, or first, language is not English, or who represent another culture, one might have to conduct interviews rather than administer questionnaires. If the respondents speak little English, it could even be necessary to translate the questionnaire or conduct the interview in their native language. It might also be necessary to hire someone from the same cultural, religious and language background to carry out the interviews; people are more likely to provide honest answers to someone who is obviously familiar with their own customs than to a foreigner whose attempts to match them in dress, mode of speech and conduct may be perceived as clumsy, arrogant or rude intrusions. Surveys *do* invade respondents' time and privacy, perhaps their territory and feelings, so it is better to acknowledge this and keep it in mind during research planning. It is easy to get carried away by a project and one can lose track of the fact that respondents' time is just as valuable to them as ours is to us.

5.2.2 PLANNING A QUESTIONNAIRE

Having decided to design and administer a questionnaire, the research question must then be reviewed. Precisely what information is required and how is it going to be applied once it is obtained? In the context of designing and developing a computer system, budgets generally do not allow one to undertake research that merely satisfies one's curiosity but adds nothing to assist the project team. Therefore, for every topic explored and each question asked, think about how the possible answers will affect the future system in terms of its design, presentation, implementation or the context in which it is to be introduced. Every question included in a questionnaire must be there for a reason that is directly related to the research question which, in turn, depends on the aspect of the system the survey is intended to explore. If necessary, partition the research question into several components as illustrated in the example below.

EXAMPLE:

Imagine you are involved in a project which aims to to design a data retrieval system for a large multinational company with workers in many countries, from different backgrounds, cultures and languages. Among the many issues raised and decisions to be made, user interface presentation is most important. Should it be mono- or multi-lingual? Certainly the decision rests partly on the cost and the willingness of the receiving organization to pay, but cost is also related to product usefulness and usability. In order to provide a reasonable basis for making the best decision you will need to pursue a number of questions.

English
- What proportion of end users speak English?
- How adequately do they master the English language?
- How much of their daily interaction with other people, written material, formal and informal, communication takes place in English?

Other languages
- What other languages are represented among the workers?
- What proportion of workers speak each of the other languages?

Typical users
- Who will be using the system?
- How often will the typical end user access the system?
- How much computer experience do typical users have?

User groups
- For how many and which specific tasks will the typical user access the system?

- What groupings do workers fall into with respect to tasks to be done on the system?
- How much computer experience do the various worker groups have?

Now, if only a few select tasks are to be supported, one way to overcome language barriers is to apply icons and colour coding instead of English expressions as navigation aids. This means that task complexity and navigation steps must be investigated; even occasional users could be expected to find their way through a system with 10–15 colour-coded icons, but if the number of icons required exceeds, say 40, alternative communication languages should be considered. As you can see, even a relatively simple question can be subdivided into several categories, each of which impacts on the decision to go one way or another.

While any issue tends to expand as one thinks more about the details it involves, care must also be taken to keep questionnaires short. People do not want to spend hours filling in questionnaires, and, especially when they are mailed out to respondents, response rates tend to be quite low. A questionnaire that is easy and quick to complete is more likely to be properly filled out than a complex and long one. The way to proceed in the planning of a questionnaire is thus to write out the research question explicitly and clearly, then to list the categories of issues that must be addressed in order adequately to answer the research question. Finally, formulate the necessary questions for each category. At this level, work out precisely what each question achieves, how it will be used and analysed.

Different methods may be considered for administering the questionnaire, and here are some rules of thumb for the maximum number of questions that should be included in each:

- individual   20   questions
- group   100   questions
- mail   60   questions
- phone   20   questions

Experience shows that if you exceed those limits, the quality (accuracy) of answers drops; people get tired and their patience wears thin!

Individual administration   is one step removed from the structured interview. The researcher is present when the respondent fills in the questionnaire and may be consulted for clarification. This method gives the researcher the opportunity to scan through the completed questionnaire to ensure that all questions have been answered.

'Above all, think about how people might respond to your questions'

Group administration is done with large groups of respondents in one room filling in the questionnaire simultaneously. It may be done by several researchers because, typically, many respondents finish at the same time and wait to leave the room immediately they are ready. Questionnaires must be scanned very quickly for omissions and to ensure that they have been completed before respondents leave.

Mailed questionnaires are sent out to respondents who are asked to fill them in and return them in the mail. If this method is being used, be sure to include a stamped self-addressed envelope and a covering letter explaining who is doing the study, why, how respondents were selected, and why their assistance is required. If anonymity is promised, respondents' names and addresses are recorded on individual index cards together with the ID code of their particular questionnaire. As each questionnaire is returned, it is checked for completeness, and the index card is destroyed.

In an attempt to increase the response rate, potential respondents could be contacted by phone first to explain the purpose of the study and to emphasise the importance of their co-operation and value of their opinion. People who expect to receive a questionnaire following a personal conversation might be more likely to respond and return their completed questionnaires than people who have not been contacted first. However, direct mailing is a costly affair and, if working with reasonably small specified samples, one is probably better off establishing personal contact, administering the questionnaire individually or in groups to ensure a high return rate. If you contact potential respondents by phone before the questionnaire is sent out, write down exactly what is going to be said and how much is going to be revealed about the study. This is one way to ensure that all respondents are given the same type and amount of information. If this level of control is not exerted, one might inadvertently influence respondents, thus introducing unwanted and unnecessary variance in the findings.

Phone surveys are used for quick feedback from a large number of people; they are rarely employed in the context of designing or evaluating computer systems. Rather, they tend to be used in market research in which people's buying habits or consumer differences are investigated. If you are about to conduct a phone survey, however, make sure the questions are short and simply worded. Remember also to offer very few response options, three at the most; otherwise, the respondents will be tired out in no time. After all, you intended to sample their tastes and opinions – not to test their capacity to memorize, store and retrieve response categories!

Before designing the content of a questionnaire, the following activities should have been completed during the planning phase:

- define the research question;
- divide it into categories and sub-categories;
- select the best method for administering the questionnaire.

5.2.3 ADMINISTERING A QUESTIONNAIRE

Before administering a questionnaire to a large sample of potential respondents trial-run (pilot test) it on a few people. This will reveal whether the instructions are adequate, unambiguous, or whether something has been missed or expressed poorly. It will also show very clearly any weaknesses, incomplete or ambiguous questions or response categories. Correct the weak areas a trial-run exposes, and give the questionnaire to another small sample of people to ensure that the problems have been overcome. It is a good idea to give it to colleagues and invite their comments and criticisms as well as asking them to fill it in; it is amazing just how many inconsistencies and small problems are detected in trials. Just think of how annoying and expensive it would be if a questionnaire was administered to 500 people only to find one had overlooked, left out, or contaminated something important. Regardless of which method of administration is selected, prepare a set of written instructions which tell respondents about the study, about the researchers, the purpose of it all, how and why they were asked to participate. Instructions must also explain how the questionnaire should be filled in, approximately how long it will take to complete, and what should be done with it once it is filled in. Above all, do not forget to thank respondents for their time, and tell them also how the data will be used in the research project and beyond. Ensure response anonymity where appropriate. This is especially important if the data are in any way sensitive; people will not talk about their innermost relationships, feelings, beliefs, political or sexual preferences if they cannot be sure their record will be completely unrecognizable once the data have been collated.

I tend also to provide respondents with feedback on the findings of the study if they wish. Respondents' names and addresses must obviously be retained if you do offer feedback, at least of those indicating they would be interested in knowing the outcome of the study. Generally, I summarize the early findings before they are analysed formally. I include information about the number of people approached, the response rate, research question and its wider context – such as, explaining why we bother even to ask that particular question – and so forth, in the first feedback. At that time, I can generally give some indication of when a full report will be available, and invite respondents to request this if they want. The advantage of this approach is that people who have received feedback are likely to be positive towards assisting with future research. This might help fellow researchers or myself sometime in the future. Also, it keeps me on my toes in terms of getting the data analysed, interpreted and written up within a reasonable period of time. In other words, promising a report delivery date really acts as a bit of healthy self-imposed discipline.

Above all, do remember to keep promises; if feedback is promised by a certain date, provide it by that date. Respondents out there are waiting for it. Even if, for some very good reason, all the information cannot be provided by the target date, give something, perhaps an explanation of why one is running behind schedule and when the promised information can now be expected. Failure to keep promises is much worse than making no promises, and one has an ethical responsibility towards one's respondents as well as towards all those future researchers who could be wanting information from the same people at later dates.

5.2.4 ANALYSING AND INTERPRETING THE DATA

It has been recommended all along that consideration should be given as to how the data will be analysed, what the questions included measure, and how the results are to affect the computer system about to be designed, redesigned, or evaluated. With diligence and careful preparation the data analysis will be easy. The choice of data analysis depends on the research question and the way it is framed, as well as on the way the data is going to be used. If the respondents' preferences are being measured, say, for dialogue style or language type, comparison of the percentage of respondents who fall into the various categories will give the answer. By contrast, if an understanding is being sought of complex, implicit relationships between several variables investigated in the study, more elaborate analyses will be required.

Systematic coding of responses suggested earlier provides a basis for obtaining frequency distributions for each question, each option, and every concept dealt with; this is the absolute minimum one would expect to get from a questionnaire. You are advised to consult relevant sources for further details on coding (Anastasi, 1976; de Vaus, 1985; Dillman, 1978; Fisher, 1982; Jackson, 1988; Labaw, 1980; Miller and Thomas, 1977; Moser and Kalton, 1975; Richardson *et al.*, 1965).

5.2.5 DESIGNING A QUESTIONNAIRE

Five issues are dealt with when designing questionnaires, namely:

- the format and content of questions;
- response categories and scales;
- coding of responses;
- layout of questionnaire;
- structure of questionnaire.

Format and content of questions

All questions must be brief, clear and relevant to ensure that the meaning of each is interpreted in the sense it was intended. The wording must be simple; using positive sentences phrased in the present tense and active voice is the most effective way to avoid misinterpretations. Questions should be phrased to yield the answers you need. Questions may be formatted in a number of ways, but the format naturally depends on the nature of the responses you are trying to analyse.

Single choice, pre-coded questions   require the respondent to identify one of several categories in which he/she belongs.

> **EXAMPLE:**
> Religion
> ☐ Roman Catholic   ☐ Muslim
> ☐ Church of England ☐ Buddhist
> ☐ Lutheran   ☐ Jewish
> ☐ Greek Orthodox   ☐ Other (please specify): ....

Present/absent questions   allow a single choice from two options.

> **EXAMPLE:**
> Do you have your own personal computer?   YES/NO
> Have you ever sold livestock through the CALM System?   YES/NO

Rank ordering questions   require respondents to rank order a number of statements from, say, the 'most important' to the 'least important'. However, note that people prefer to select 'the three most important' or 'the most and the least important' categories than to rank order long lists of variables or statements.

> **EXAMPLE:**
> Please indicate three (3) systems from the following list which you access most frequently from your DISNET terminal (write a '1' against the most frequently used, a '2' against the second most, and a '3' against the third most frequently used system):
>
> ☐ DCRIS   ☐ PERKINS
> ☐ CABS   ☐ FAMAD
> ☐ LEOPARD   ☐ DEMON
> ☐ FACS   ☐ KEYLINK
> ☐ FINAC   ☐ CONTRACTS
> ☐ STOCKAID   ☐ POCUS

Semantic differential questions   require people to assign values or characteristics to a person or an object by selecting one of two extremes that best describes it.

EXAMPLE:
How would you best describe your present work environment?
(Please tick one in each category):

(a) ☐ quiet   ☐ noisy
(b) ☐ relaxed   ☐ tense
(c) ☐ pleasant   ☐ frustrating

Magnitude estimate questions   require respondents to provide numeric statements, or to draw lines varying in length against a standard line. This type of question is generally used only when questionnaires are administered individually to ensure that respondents understand clearly what is required of them.

EXAMPLE:
The line drawn below indicates the average level of satisfaction with the ULTRAX software in terms of communication speed. Please draw a line underneath and parallel with the standard line to your level of satisfaction. The more satisfied you are, the longer you should draw your line, and the less satisfied you are, the shorter your line should be.

Standard line: _____

Response line: _____

Probably the most popular type is the **Likert scale question** in which the respondent is asked to indicate his level of agreement with a particular statement. The number of choices is up to the researcher, but a five-point scale is commonly used. Scales are arranged horizontally, with the 'strongly agree' option in the far right, and the 'strongly disagree' option placed in the far left position, with the 'indifferent' option in the middle of the scale.

EXAMPLE:
All employees should be offered a training course on the new computer system, regardless of how much or how little they will be using it to do their job.

Please circle the answer that best represents your opinion

strongly
disagree   disagree   undecided   agree

Numerous variants exist on the Likert scale, and several othe scales have been developed which allow for expressions of opi which are easy to code.

EXAMPLE:
Please indicate your satisfaction with the ULTRAX software in terms of communication speed, by circling the appropriate number below:

completely dissatisfied								completely satisfied	
1	2	3	4	5	6	7	8	9	10

Response categories and scales

The way questions are phrased is related to the types of response categories offered. Whether respondents are required to circle answers, draw lines, tick boxes, number options in order or preference, or to write longhand responses will depend on the nature of the information being sought. Questions requiring longhand answers fall into the category of open-ended questions discussed earlier, and if several of these are included, one should perhaps reconsider using interviews instead of questionnaires. Note that, in general, longhand answers are much more difficult to code than pre-defined categories. One exception to this is the case in which several categories are provided and some respondents do not fit into any of those given. In such instances add a category labelled 'other (please specify)'.

EXAMPLE:
Religion
☐ Roman Catholic   ☐ Muslim
☐ Church of England   ☐ Buddhist
☐ Lutheran   ☐ Jewish
☐ Greek Orthodox   ☐ Other (please specify): ....

Here, the religions in which the researcher is interested in are specified, and the 'other' category might simply be assigned a code exactly like the rest. By allowing respondents to specify their religion in the 'other' category, the researcher avoids offending anyone whose religion is not categorized. Also, by encouraging people to provide accurate information, he/she does leave the door open for extra, unexpected details that go beyond statements such as '9% of the 490 respondents labelled their religion as 'other'. The observation, for example, that '24 different religions were mentioned by the 37 people who ticked the 'other' box to this question' could be of interest for further exploration, as could the statement that 'of the 37 people who ticked the 'other' box in this question, 24 labelled themselves Jehovah's Witnesses'.

Coding of responses

This book constantly encourages researchers to think ahead and plan their data analysis at the same time as designing the questions to be included in the questionnaire. This is most important in the coding of responses also. Once the decision has been taken to administer a questionnaire rather than conduct interviews, one is likely to expect quite a large number of responses. Life will be made a lot easier if responses are coded so that they can be entered into the computer and analysed with the least amount of transformation. The more the data must be re-arranged before they can be entered, the more time and effort is required to conduct the analysis. This should motivate the researcher to do two things, namely

1. be consistent with response categories;
2. assign numbers to response categories.

In other words, use as few different response formats as possible. If you settle for Likert-scale type questions, try to phrase most questions to fit that layout; assigning consistent numbers to response categories throughout the questionnaire, e.g. yes = 1; no = 2, reduces confusion. If 'yes' is sometimes 1 and sometimes 2, this will only cause confusion later and increase the probability of making errors while entering the data into the computer and also during the data analysis phase. Similarly, once codes have been assigned to multiple categories such as 'strongly disagree = 1; disagree = 2; undecided = 3; agree = 4; strongly agree = 5' the same is true. If 'strongly agree' is sometimes = 5 and =1 at other times, problems will occur later.

Layout of a questionnaire

Make sure respondents can find their way easily through the question-naire, by numbering them sequentially. Give plenty of sign posts and do not cram too much information onto every page. If different formats of questions must be included, give each format a different look, either by using colour coding or by providing instructions that clearly indicate how the respondent is expected to fill in the new categories.

EXAMPLE:

For each of questions 19–27, please circle one option to indicate your response.

26. Have you logged on to BIGGS.WS in the last week?   YES/NO
(Please circle the relevant answer)'

26. Have you logged on to BIGGS.WS in the last week?
(Please tick the relevant answer)

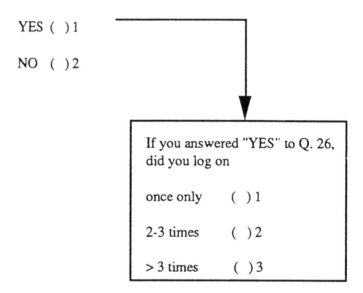

YES ( ) 1

NO ( ) 2

If you answered "YES" to Q. 26, did you log on

once only   ( ) 1

2-3 times   ( ) 2

> 3 times   ( ) 3

or

26. Have you logged on to BIGGS.WS in the last week?
(If your answer is 'YES', go to Question 27. If your answer is 'NO', skip Questions 27–32 and go directly to Question 33 overleaf)

The relative position of question and answer should also be consistent throughout the questionnaire. For example, if the response follows the category in some questions like this:

YES ... ( ) 1
NO ... ( ) 2

make sure there are no questions in which this is reversed as in:

1 ( ) YES
2 ( ) NO

Structure of the questionnaire

If you are dealing with several issues in a single questionnaire, separate these from one another and indicate clearly to the respondents what each section is about.

EXAMPLE:
Section 1 (questions 1–10) are about your personal details. Please fill in each question by circling the appropriate category.

Questions 1–10 follow
Then:
   Section 2 (questions 11–23) addresses your computer experience. Just follow the instructions and fill in the questions that are appropriate to you.

Questions 11–23 follow

Questions that address the same topic should be presented together, and questions phrased and presented in the same format should also be presented together. Number the pages as well as the questions sequentially, and indicate how many pages are involved, e.g. 'Page 2 of 4' to ensure that respondents do not miss a page.

Response codes should also be printed on the questionnaire itself, saving the need to transcribe the data onto data sheets before entering them onto the computer. However, if there are only one or two response formats, it is probably not necessary to list the codes in the questionnaire.

EXAMPLE:

24. Religion		For office use only
☐ Roman Catholic	☐ Muslim	01 05
☐ Church of England	☐ Buddhist	02 06
☐ Lutheran	☐ Jewish	03 07
☐ Greek Orthodox	☐ Other	04 08
	(please specify):	

In this example, the codes are all presented in the right-hand margin labelled 'For office use only'. That way, coding can be done directly on the questionnaire itself and requires no additional data files or transformations. Even though there are only eight different categories in the question above, there could be others with more than ten categories in the questionnaire. Hence, keeping the data entry requirements and the format of the online data file consistent by requiring two digits per data point regardless of the number of possible categories per question reduces the likelihood of data entry operators committing format errors. The code could be placed next to each category instead of in the right-hand margin, but that makes it more time-consuming to read and enter the data into the computer later. However, if a questionnaire contains several different question formats, it might be necessary to keep separate data files all together. In that case, one would probably not place the category codes on the questionnaire but rather keep a scoring sheet with the codes for each question.

As was said about interviews, the questions in a questionnaire should be arranged such that a few short, routine, easy-to-answer questions are presented first. This eases respondents into the swing of it, and it also gives the impression that the questionnaire will not take too long to complete. The longer and more tedious a questionnaire seems, the less likely it is that respondents will be motivated to fill it in. The easy-to-answer questions are followed by those that request the most important information – the delicate, tricky ones. At the end of the questionnaire, again administer a few routine questions. The delicate ones should appear approximately at the one-third point, when respondents have 'warmed up' and before they become tired or bored with the task.

When all the questions have been formulated, write each one on a separate card and lay out the cards in different conceptual stacks. Try out different ways of arranging the cards until the best arrangement is found. The fewer categories needed, the better, and the more coherent the entire questionnaire will appear to the respondents. Then, go through the questions again. Revise what exactly each one measures and check for redundancy. If two or even more questions measure the same issue in the same fashion, include only one, unless a split-half reliability check is being used. In that case, all the important questions are repeated within the questionnaire. Questions that are repeated should be presented far enough apart that respondents are likely to have forgotten exactly how they answered the first time and will not bother to look back. Obviously, the split-half reliability coefficient demands a long questionnaire. However, these are not popular, and the response rate is normally quite low. Of course, there are circumstances in which it is appropriate, or even necessary, to design and administer extensive questionnaires, but this is rarely the case in connection with designing or evaluating computer systems.

Once a decision has been made on the number of categories to be included, place questions within each concept in a logical order and arrange concepts themselves in a logical order.

EXAMPLE:

Category	Concept	Questions
Personal details:	Education, general	(highest level attained, institution, when ...)
	Education, specific	(specify programming courses, ...)
	System experience	(no. years, which systems, ...)
	System preferences	system A versus B, for certain operations/tasks, ...)
Current job:	System access	(which systems, mandatory/ discretionary, frequency of access, ...)

Manual tasks   (list, which could be computerized, ...)

Likert scale-type questions should be arranged so as to avoid a certain response-set. People might agree with all the questions if they are all phrased in a similar fashion. The danger exists that respondents fail to read the content of all questions carefully but simply circle the answer they think should be appropriate. Response-sets can become problematic when a long list of similar questions are presented together. To guard against the effect, present a few questions for which agreement reflects a certain attitude. Alternate these with some where disagreement reflects that same attitude. When coding the responses, one will quickly detect whether respondents are assuming that all questions are arranged in the same way, or whether they are reading carefully and giving semantically consistent answers. If they are not, the questionnaire might have to be shortened and the method revised for the research questions.

5.3 Some notes on scales

Sometimes survey data are processed and analysed by methods such as correlations (Ch. 3), but these are not the only techniques within the regression paradigm that are of interest. Analysis of variance (ANOVA) is one method that establishes the extent to which two or more sets of data differ from one another statistically. ANOVAs are generally applied to analyse data from experiments in which one seeks to uncover cause and effect relationships, but they can, on occasion, also be used in analysing survey data. In order to identify differences between samples of data, reasonably fine-grained data are required. Scales using distinct categories such as Likert scales usually allow only a limited number of responses, ranging from, say 1–5 or 1–10. This is often too coarse grained for detecting statistical differences. It can also be problematic to compare responses made on different scales (Anderson, 1982) because the unit of a response scale is 'not a fixed quantity but depends (amongst other factors) on the given range of stimuli (categories)' (p. 21). Unless the category range is the same on all occasions included in a comparison, the validity of comparisons is questionable. In an effort to overcome this limitation, one can employ a continuous scale rather than restrict responses to certain categories, for example, by using an unmarked line. The line is anchored at one end with 'very unfavourable' at one end and with 'very favourable' at the other end. Respondents mark the line at the point that most accurately corresponds to their estimate or judgment. It is easy to use and advantageous because it eliminates the need for respondents to confine themselves to an explicit category or to translate their estimate into a numerical statement. It is also advantageous for the analyst because it enables him/her to treat the judgement as a continuous variable. Responses may be measured in millimetres from the 'very unfavourable' end of the scale to the point where the respondent's mark intersects with the standard line (Godden, 1976). Provided the standard line is exactly 100 mm long, this measure yields a percentage. The unmarked line is appealing because it has been validated (Levin, 1975) and used in a number of studies (Bennett, 1980; Levin, 1976; Levin *et al.*, 1977).

Summary

Interviews and surveys were discussed in some detail in this chapter, with specific emphasis on the considerations that go into planning, conducting and analysing research data emerging from these. In both methods, a great deal of planning and careful attention to detail of what is asked goes into the preparation. How questions are asked and the structure of an interview or questionnaire were discussed in some detail, as well as the pitfalls associated with conducting either type of investigation. The need to consider how the data should be analysed, what the information gleaned could mean and how the results will affect decisions about the emerging computer system, was emphasized very strongly.

Questions

1. What four issues must be considered to ensure a successful interview?
2. How can you avoid interviewer bias?
3. What are the characteristics of an semi-structured interview?
4. Describe what a probe is and its purpose in the interview.
5. What two kinds of probe are frequently used in interviews?
6. What characterizes an open ended question?
7. How do you partition your interview in terms of the types of questions you ask and when they will be asked?
8. When should you write your post interview summary?
9. What are the most important differences between interviews and questionnaires?
10. Which activities are carried out during the planning phase of a survey?
11. How can you reduce the amount of data transformation that will be needed to enter the raw, unprocessed data onto the computer?
12. How do you best structure the sequence in which questions are presented in a questionnaire?
13. Why is a split-half reliability test rarely applied in questionnaires?
14. What is a 'response-set', and how can you guard against it?
15. What are the four most used methods for administering questionnaires?
16. Why should you keep the number of response options to a maximum of three in a telephone survey?

17. Why would you write out instructions to participants in a survey even if it is administered over the phone?
18. Why should you provide respondents with feedback?
19. Why is this important to you, the researcher?
20. List some of the advantages of continuous scales.

The following is an extract from a questionnaire designed by the suppliers of a system called 'POSNET'. The system is a gateway which allows simultaneous access to several databases residing on a mainframe system used in all telephone districts in Australia. A district is the point of customer interface; that is, when you call Telecom in Australia, the people in the district are the ones you talk to. The nature, scope, distribution and usage of the system is immaterial for the present exercise. However, the questionnaire was mailed, after several iterations revising the contents layout and structure.

1. Your first task is first to pull the questionnaire apart to identify weaknesses and flaws it might possess. Write out each flaw in point form. Be as critical as you like, but remember that only constructive criticism is acceptable. That is, for every point you make, think about how the flaws/weakness could be overcome. You should at least comment on the following:

    • the format and content of questions (Are the questions clear and unambiguous? Are they as brief as they could be? Does each relate to the purpose stated under 'objectives'?);
    • response categories (How many different kinds of response categories are there? Is the format of response categories consistent throughout the questionnaire? Could we reduce the number of categories? How? Are all questions framed in the best, most sensible way?);
    • coding of responses (Is it clear how the researchers are going to analyse the data?);
    • layout of questionnaire;
    • structure of questionnaire.

2. Now, taking into account your criticism and what was said about designing questionnaires in this chapter, redesign the questionnaire to be consistent with the principles outlined earlier. You will find a sample solution at the back of the book.

Suggested further reading

Cannell and Kahn's (1968) book tells you all you might ever want to know about interviews and interviewing. It is both comprehensive and readable.

POSNET SURVEY

OBJECTIVES

The purpose of this survey is to identify the general level of user satisfaction with POSNET, in particular with the original installation.

QUESTIONNAIRE

About You

What is your position in the District office? Select and mark ($\sqrt{}$) the most appropriate description of your position.

District manager ☐
Internal plant manager ☐
LAN administrator ☐
Sales staff ☐
Other ☐ Please indicate _____

How frequently do you use the LAN?

Select and mark ($\sqrt{}$) the most appropriate description of your position.

Never ☐
Rarely ☐
Once a week (approximately) ☐
Several times per day ☐
Continually ☐

How frequently do you access systems such as DCRIS, CABS or LEOPARD?

Select and mark ($\sqrt{}$) the most appropriate description of your position.

Never ☐
Rarely ☐
Once a week (approximately) ☐
Several times per day ☐
Continually ☐

About your District or Section

The District or Section Name is _____

What size is your District?
How many telephone lines? _____

How many terminals connected to your POSNET LAN(s)? ___

How many terminals not connected to your POSNET LAN(s)?

How many sales staff? _____

Your District is in the state of
Select and mark (√) the state your District is in.

☐ New South Wales   ☐ South Australia
☐ Queensland   ☐ Victoria
☐ Tasmania   ☐ Western Australia

Do you have POSNET installed at this District/Section?   YES NO
Circle 'Yes' or 'No' whichever applies

Do you have any dumb terminals (not PCs) operating in your
District?
If so, how many? _____

About POSNET and your District

Is POSNET doing what you expected it to?   YES NO
Circle 'Yes' or 'No' whichever applies

If not, how is it failing?

_____

_____

How would you measure your level of satisfaction with POSNET as
a whole?
Select and mark (√) the one that most closely matches your level
of satisfaction.

very high   ☐
high   ☐
moderate   ☐
low   ☐
very low   ☐

Are any of your business processes inhibited by constraints imposed
by the POSNET LAN?

If so, what are the business processes that are constrained?

Comment: _____

_____

_____

Use an additional sheet of paper if necessary.

What additional capabilities would you require within POSNET to overcome these constraints? _____

_____

_____

Use an additional sheet of paper if necessary.

This question is only for the IPM and LAN administrator, if you hold another position go to the next question.

Does your District use pooled LIDs on POSNET?   YES NO

Now thinking about response time to mainframe systems such as DCRIS, the way users interface with customers and the likely rise in cost to you of response time reductions below two to three seconds.

What are your current average response time for users accessing mainframe systems such as DCRIS?

_____ seconds

What do you consider to be the optimum response time for access to mainframe systems such as DCRIS?

_____ seconds

How was this response time measured?   RTM   Stop-watch
Circle response time monitor (RTM) or stop-watch.

Are the people who use the systems on a daily basis satisfied with:

the speed of logging on to the POSNET LAN   YES NO
the response time of the system they access   YES NO

In the last month what are the longest response times your DISTRICT has experienced accessing mainframe systems such as DCRIS? _____ seconds

For what consecutive period of time did you experience this worst case response time? Give a period during the day

_____ seconds

Planning and Information

Now thinking about pre-implementation planning, discussions of your needs and the advice and information that was provided to you and your staff.

Were you or your staff involved in pre-implementation planning for the POSNET LAN?
Circle 'Yes' or 'No' whichever applies.

YES NO

Are you satisfied with the level of involvement your staff have had in the planning of your POSNET LAN?

YES NO

If no above, was there sufficient planning:
for the installation of your POSNET LAN?   YES NO
to meet your business communications needs   YES NO

other _____
          Please specify

Installation

Now thinking about the installation of POSNET are you satisfied with:

the programming of the installation	YES NO
the staff who installed POSNET	YES NO
the way they went about their work	YES NO
the amount of time it took to install POSNET	YES NO
the state of the POSNET LAN when it was handed over to the District	YES NO

Circle 'Yes' or 'No' whichever applies.

Moser and Kalton's (1975) book is a classic used in courses on social science methodologies. It gives a rather lengthy and very detailed account of all aspects of surveys. Is likely to be easy to get hold of and it is certainly easy to read.

Dillman (1978) discusses the merits and problems of telephone surveys. His book provides a most comprehensive account of all considerations underlying the planning, designing, conducting and analyzing of survey data. It is readable but may give too much detail if your purpose of reading it is to learn about, rather than actually to run telephone surveys.

Gorden's (1980) book is similar to Dillman mentioned above, except that it is newer and perhaps more accessible for you. It is comprehensive and easy to read.

Two books mentioned in Chapter 3 as well, worthy of reading, are (Fisher, 1982; True, 1989).

Data collection techniques III: introduction to experimental design 6

Every erroneous inference, though originating in moral causes, involves the intellectual operation of admitting insufficient evidence as sufficient.

John Stuart Mill

In this chapter the concept of formal laboratory experiments is introduced. Traditionally, laboratory experiments have been employed by psychologists to investigate theoretical issues. In this tradition an experiment commonly pitches two competing, theoretical viewpoints against one another, and the experiment is designed in such a way that the experimental findings are likely to support one and disconfirm the other of these. Experimental design is thus firmly embedded within a theoretical framework, and the experimental question is generally phrased in the form of a testable hypothesis. In a computer environment and other applied contexts, it is not always possible or even appropriate to propose a hypothesis, at least in the first instance. Instead, much of the work in this arena is exploratory, with initial findings yielding information from which hypotheses might later be generated.

Laboratory experiments are thought by many to be of little or no value in computer system design and evaluation. Proponents of this view argue that experiments yield little if any system-relevant information, and that it generally takes so long to generate valid results that they cannot be incorporated into the design cycle. Often, perhaps too often, the sceptics are absolutely right; human behaviour is full of surprises because people rarely behave in the manner we expect and so, it often does take longer than anticipated to produce experimentally based solutions to system design problems. Even when the same type of behaviour of a single person completing a certain task is sampled on more than one occasion, the performance of that person will differ from one occasion to the next. This variation makes it very difficult to predict experimental results accurately. Consequently, researchers often produce findings that are inconclusive and which require further research to resolve the problem originally addressed. Despite the difficulties associated with designing, conducting and interpreting the outcomes of laboratory experiments, it is important to note that experimentation as such is not always to blame if experimental results fall somewhat short of expectations. Rather, expectations can themselves often, on closer examination, be shown to be unjustifiable for a number of reasons.

The problem that the researcher decides to address may not be suited to rigorous laboratory experimentation at all, or at least not before it has been refined and reduced to a very clear question that can be answered experimentally. If one is asked, for example, whether the 'cognitive demands on operators are too great' in a certain system, one will need to understand a great deal about the operators' tasks and re-phrase the question to make it 'fit' into an experiment; as it stands, it is un-answerable because it is far too broad to be tied into a laboratory experiment. Even if the problem to be addressed is appropriate for experimentation, the specific research question which the researcher wants an experiment to answer may be ambiguous or poorly defined. Asking, for example, whether 'system A is better than system B' is meaningless without clearly defining what is meant by 'better', or without

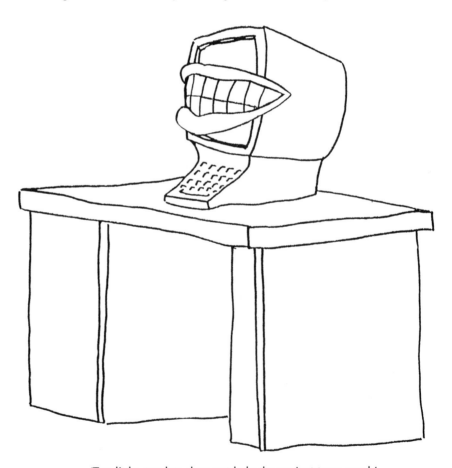

'Too little, too late does not help the project team much'

clarifying which characteristics are to be measured and how they are to be quantified.

In addition to the risk of addressing problems that are too broad, or asking questions that are poorly defined, ambiguous, irrelevant or wrong, numerous other sources of potential problems exist. Sampling problems might, for example, occur which may lead to experimental error and, in turn, could lead to wrong or questionable conclusions. The sample of subjects recruited may not be representative of the population it is intended to characterize, or too few subjects may have been tested to yield sufficient data to warrant a clear and well-supported conclusion. Alternatively, the sample of subjects selected might be biased in some fashion that influenced the data in ways not foreseen. Experimental tasks are other possible sources of error; they might fail to capture the problem, or the level of task difficulty may be too high or too low to yield meaningful performance data. Furthermore, the kinds of statistical analyses applied may be inappropriate for the types or the amounts of data generated, and finally, the interpretation of findings may be unjustifiable on the basis of the data obtained.

All of this should make the point clearly that it is difficult to design, conduct, analyse and interpret laboratory experiments. It is probably always better to call upon the assistance of an experienced experimenter who will, at least, go over the details of the proposed experiment. Although even highly experienced researchers do not always succeed in avoiding all possible flaws, much can be done to avoid many pitfalls and experimental blunders by planning carefully and thinking through the experiment and its possible outcomes before data collection commences. This chapter illustrates some of the considerations which can help us to reduce the number of problems we might otherwise inadvertently encounter and which could invalidate many inferences made from experimental data.

Before describing the details that must be thought through when planning an experiment, let us consider what a laboratory experiment is, what it is not, and when or where in the systems design process it could be most appropriate.

What a laboratory experiment is:
A tool which allows a thorough and systematic investigation of a well-defined, highly specified and detailed research question, pursued in a rigorous fashion under well-controlled conditions. (This will become clear later in this chapter.)

What a laboratory experiment is not:
A data-gathering tool for addressing global and general issues in broad terms. Nor is it a means by which to 'prove' that something is 'right' or 'best'.

Many examples are found in newspapers and magazines of claims along the lines of 'research has proven that vitamin C taken in large doses can cure common colds', or 'experiments have proven that rose-coloured glasses can cure dyslexia'. Such statements are misleading because experiments can never 'prove' anything to be 'correct'; results might fail to support an argument or disprove an hypothesis, but they cannot prove that confirmatory, or supportive, evidence is 'right' (Reichmann, 1970). Experimental tools can suggest how or where one might look for further evidence in uncovering a fundamental problem, or they can demonstrate that a certain line of thought might not be fruitfully pursued in the particular paradigm followed in a set of experiments. By disproving one hypothesis, the experiment can lend support to another, but such support does not constitute 'proof' that the reasoning underlying the hypothesis supported is 'right'. Laboratory experiments can be appropriate throughout the design and development cycle, except perhaps in the feasibility phase when very specific questions are likely to be asked that may be resolved in the laboratory.

6.1 Structuring observations systematically

In many usability laboratories it is commonplace to collect vast quantities of data on a routine basis with the uncritical and misguided belief that analysis can get something useful out of it all. Indeed, many people, who have shelves, or even cupboards, full of unanalysed video- or audio tapes, generally have the best of intentions of 'submitting them to analysis some day' (Moroney, 1960, p. 120). Let it be clear that mere intentions to analyse occasional, unstructured data are of little value. Unless a particular model of certain behaviours is being developed or tested that requires large amounts of data, it is usually true that data which are not worth analysing at a suitably near date are rarely worth the labour of collection. The same is true within the framework of laboratory experiments: if proper consideration has not been given to what will happen to data before it is collected, time could be wasted and the result will be masses of uninterpretable data. Less time collecting, and more time planning and analysing data, would be a valuable resolution in many laboratories, even though the temptation to gather lots of data is difficult to resist with the availability of videotapes, audiotapes and electronic data logging devices. When planning, designing and conducting formal laboratory experiments, keep in mind that all data should be collected for a clear purpose. Even exploratory experiments are not totally unstructured, unconstrained, or undisciplined collections of data; samples of behaviour serve to test ideas and tighten the research question, revealing whether the design, the tasks, or the data are likely to resolve the problems addressed. Good exploratory laboratory experiments should allow more insight into facets of the research question from which experimental hypotheses can be tested in follow-on experiments.

Throughout this chapter reference will be made to two examples of experiments which illustrate each step along the experimental design path. The first of these, adapted from Bednall (1992), is a set of true, traditional, formal laboratory experiments in which the research question and the selection of variables to be investigated are not tied to a particular computer system. In such experiments, the experimenter has complete, unconstrained control of the design and the experimental variables (section 6.2). By contrast, the second example, the ticket dispenser prototype, adapted from Felix and Kruger (1989), is an example of a quasi-experiment. These are characterized by less than complete control, and are generally performed on particular systems. The ticket dispenser prototype is included here to show that quasi-experiments (section 6.11) should be planned and conducted with the same amount of care as a formal, traditional laboratory experiment.

EXAMPLE 1: VISUAL LIST SEARCH:

THE PROBLEM:
Imagine you are reviewing a data retrieval system which is used by operators in a customer services area in a telecommunications company. Specifically, the system supports operators who answer calls online in directory services. Their main task is to take calls from customers, find the phone number requested, and then take the next call. One problem in this area is that customers often have to wait for service in a queue for up to ten minutes. One of the key management objectives aimed at with the system review is therefore to reduce the customer waiting time, without employing more operators. In your heuristic evaluation (Ch. 4), you noted that the search algorithm could be improved by allowing searches to be issued on several attributes currently not allowed. Also, it is appropriate that wider use of wild cards should be allowed to make searches more flexible and the system more usable. The system response time (SRT) seems to be acceptable, especially given the technology currently employed, so there is no need to seek to reduce this further. In your observation of users, you noted that operators seem to take a long time, once the relevant screen is displayed, before they locate the target. The screen appears untidy, with a staggered left margin, and lines that are so close together that the text, which is shown in capitals, is difficult to read. From your observations it would seem that the screen display could be improved to facilitate visual scanning.

Your calculations show that each operator takes approximately 40 calls per hour. Roughly half of these require operators to view two successive screens, and the other half present the entire listing on a single screen. With a working week of 38 hours, this adds up to 1520 calls (2280 screens) per week per operator. Over one year, consisting of 46 weeks, each operator thus consults some 104 880 screens. Now, a saving of just one second per screen works out roughly to some 29 hours per operator per annum (1740 screens, or 1160 calls). Considering that there are 120 of these operators in the company, the total saving would amount to some 3480 hours, or 92 weeks per annum.

Now, while the project team is investigating ways to improve the search algorithm, your task is to find ways to optimize the visual display, and you decide that a set of experiments is the best method for investigating the problem. Hence, your objective is to find out how long lists of items shown sequentially over one or several screens should be displayed to minimize visual list search time.

EXAMPLE 2: TICKET DISPENSER PROTOTYPE:

THE PROBLEM:

The Public Transport Authorities (PTA) have decided to erect automatic ticket dispensers on railway, bus and tram stations in the city of Zurich (Switzerland) in the first instance and eventually all around the country. You have been called in as an expert human factors consultant. The PTA is responsible for transport using train, tram, bus and boat, and the city is divided into several districts, or zones, by a set of concentric circles. Special tickets, weekend tickets, combined tickets (for boat plus train, tram plus bus plus train, etc.), as well as local and regional tickets are to be made available from the ticket dispensers. The general public is not particularly computer literate, but zone tickets for trams and boats have been available on tram stops from automatic dispensers in Zurich for some years already. These dispensers are, however, much simpler in scope than the prototypes here, and they have been used by city dwellers who are also regular tram commuters. The machines being tested here will be erected in country stations as well, thereby being exposed to a much wider population. The PTA is keen to encourage usage of the automatic ticket dispensers in order, eventually, to move staff who issue tickets manually at present onto other duties. The PTA system development team has produced two prototypes which both enable the operations necessary for making available the full set of different combinations of ticket requirements. Both prototypes have been developed according to international ergonomics standards and guidelines, but the PTA is uncertain as to which of the two should be developed into a system.

As the chief human factors consultant, your task is to find out which of prototypes A or B should be developed into an operational system. Your decision must be supported by objective data.

6.1.1 DEFINE THE RESEARCH QUESTION

Once the purpose of a laboratory experiment has been defined, the research question should be stated explicitly. The nature and scope of this question can help one decide whether a formal laboratory experiment really is the most appropriate investigative tool to apply. The more poorly defined the research question, the more disappointing the data generated experimentally will be either because the question will not have addressed the problem at hand, or because limitations to the experimental method and its underlying assumptions were not taken into account in the planning phase. In order to design good experiments, the research question must be defined clearly, explicitly and unambiguously before going any further. So, with respect to our two examples, the research questions might look like this:

EXAMPLE 1: VISUAL LIST SEARCH:
1. Is it easier to locate a target in a list typed in mixed case letters rather than in a list typed in capitals?
2. Is it easier to locate a target when redundant information is suppressed than when it is not?

EXAMPLE 2: TICKET DISPENSER PROTOTYPE:
1. Is it faster to obtain tickets in System A or in System B?
2. Are people more accurate in their ticket selections in System A or B?

6.1.2 MAKE YOUR RESEARCH QUESTION OPERATIONAL

Once the research question is defined explicitly, ways must be found to make it operational. That is, it will need to be restated in such a way that it can be quantified. By quantifying the behaviour to be measured, the data obtained in the experiment can be submitted to statistical analysis. The outcome of the analysis, in turn, enables us to make a statistical statement, and such a statement is the evidence needed to settle the experimental question. As was discussed in Chapter 3, statistics enable us to determine the extent to which, say, two systems, differ in degree of usability along the dimensions (Chapter 1) tested. Although statistical statements are probabilistic, they are much more accurate than an untested and unsupported belief that, for instance, our two prototypes differ in usability, or unstructured observations suggesting that one type of screen 'seems' to lead to faster target search times than another. In terms of our examples, the operational research questions for visual list search would translate 'easier' into 'faster', as would the first of the two ticket dispenser questions. Some measure of task-completion time would thus be called for. 'Accuracy' in the second ticket dispenser question may be translated into '% correct key presses', 'number of errors', or some such measure.

'Know your question before you attempt to answer it'

6.1.3 DEFINE TASK DIFFICULTY

When the research question has been defined operationally, the experimental tasks must be specified. The point of an experiment is that it should enable us to distinguish between different levels of human performance. This can be achieved by variations in certain aspects of the design, the instructions, the subjects selected to carry out the experiment, and by the experimental tasks designed and administered to subjects. If the tasks are all very easy and quick to complete and give rise to no errors or very few, they will not allow us to distinguish between, say, experts and novices, because all participants will be performing at a level that is close to perfection. This effect is referred to as a 'ceiling effect'. Since experts are are assumed to be tangibly better at some tasks than novices, the experiment is not sensitive enough to separate the two types of users if the tasks are too easy. In order to overcome the ceiling effect, the experiment would need to be revised and redesigned, allowing experts to demonstrate their superior performance.

At the other end of the continuum, the tasks may be so difficult that it is impossible for any subjects to complete them. In such cases, interesting data are unlikely to be generated either, because performance is equally poor in the two subject-groups. This is a 'floor effect' which

'The level of task difficulty should match the capabilities of your subjects'

also makes it impossible to distinguish between experts and novices from the performance data. The aim is to avoid either of these effects by designing tasks that allow us to discriminate between 'good' and 'poor' performance. In other words, tasks should be difficult enough to allow 'good', 'fast', 'accurate' performers to be distinguished from 'poor', 'slow', or 'sloppy' ones from their performance data. Ideally, tasks should therefore be just a little too difficult for people to perform perfectly, or equally well at all of them, and easy enough for us to obtain some data with which to answer the research question. In terms of our two examples, the following tasks might be chosen:

EXAMPLE 1: VISUAL LIST SEARCH:
Find a target amongst non-targets in many screens which vary in a systematic fashion along the dimensions specified in the research question. That is, pitch CAPITAL against mixed case letters, and spaced (i.e. redundant information is suppressed) against non-spaced (i.e. redundant information is not suppressed) screens as shown in Fig. 6.1:

Spaced capitals (SC)

```
BEECHAM B...62
        D...57
        F...90
BORLAND E...61
        H...41
        J...50
        M...43
BRISTOW B...29
        G...22
        J...95
```

Non-spaced capitals (NC)

```
BEAMISH A...61
BEAMISH C...56
BEAMISH G...98
BIRRELL D...60
BIRRELL G...40
BIRRELL I...59
BIRRELL L...42
BOLITHO A...28
BOLITHO E...20
BOLITHO G...94
```

Spaced mixed (SM)

```
Bellamy D...64
        G...59
        I...92
Blewett G...63
        J...43
        K...52
        M...46
Bradley D...21
        G...24
        J...97
```

Non-spaced mixed (NM)

```
Beasley C...63
Beasley E...58
Beasley H...91
Bittman F...62
Bittman J...42
Bittman K...51
Bittman N...45
Boulton C...20
Boulton F...23
Boulton H...96
```

Figure 6.1: Four types of screens used to compare the effect of CAPITALS (SC, NC) versus mixed case (SM, NM), and suppressing redundant information (SC, SM) versus non-suppression (NC, NM).

mixed case (SM, NM), and suppressing redundant information (SC, SM) versus non-suppression (NC, NM).

EXAMPLE 2: TICKET DISPENSER PROTOTYPE:
Obtain tickets that vary in degree of complexity, i.e. (a) simple tickets and (b) complex tickets.

Simple tickets consist of the elements 'ticket type (single or return fare) plus destination plus mode of transport (train, tram, bus, boat)', and complex tickets 'ticket type plus destination plus mode of transport plus at least two of the following: special-event tickets (show, exhibition), ticket class (first, second), fare (child, adult), combined tickets (boat plus bus, train plus tram plus boat, etc.), special discount tickets (family, day, weekend, season).'

Examples:
Simple ticket
'Select a one-way ticket to zone 3 going by tram.'
Complex ticket:
'Buy a first class, return ticket to Basel for a family of two adults and two children going to the Basler Fassnacht (Basle annual carnival) by train and tram'.
The two prototypes are shown in Fig. 6.2.

6.1.4 DEFINE MEASURES

Having defined what the experimental tasks are and what they require subjects to do, decide upon the types of data which might best serve as units of measurement. Your selection must be guided by what is most meaningful with respect to the research question. If you concentrate on some aspect of task-completion times, you might consider 'duration' of some target activity (minutes, seconds, milliseconds). Alternatively, you might look at 'errors' (number/types) committed. You could consider the number of certain 'events' occurring during a particular period of time, or you could, amongst several other possibilities, count the number of attempts test users make before a certain task is completed.

It is not enough to identify the 'best' measures to ensure that you will get something useful out of your experiment. If you settle on counting errors, for example, you might find it necessary to distinguish between two or more types of error to help you decide when one has occurred. For example, a 'slip' is generally defined as a situation in which the test user knows what he/she should have done but does something different, such as pressing a wrong key or looking for an item in the wrong place. Characteristic of a 'slip' is that, although the user commits an error, the slip is generally corrected immediately, because the user knows what should have been done. By contrast, when making a 'mistake', the test user is uncertain about what to do and runs into a real problem from which it will take time and effort to recover, and where it may take several attempts for recovery to succeed (Norman, 1981; 1984).

Superficially, it seems easy to keep these two concepts of 'mistakes' and 'slips' apart. Yet, consider the possibility that test users might be 'doing the wrong thing' to discover something about the system by playing and exploring. How do you, the observer, know whether they are playing or making genuine mistakes? Instances in which users play with the system and which are inferred by you to be mistakes could contaminate your data so that you end up drawing incorrect conclusions. So, you will probably need to observe a number of subjects in a pilot study (section

TICKETS

(a)   **Destination**

(b)

(c) **Select your ticket type**

(d)

(e)

(g) city
c   c
a   a

(h)

(i)

(j)

(a) geographical area by
     post code
(b) map. city of Zurich
(c) special ticket
     selection area
(d) visual display
(e) money slot (coins)
(f) credit card slot
(g) city tickets/child or
     adult selection
(h) numeric keypad
(i) regional ticket
     selection
(j) money slot (notes)

TICKETS

(a)   1. Select

(c)

(d)

(h)

(g) city

(b)

(e)

(f)

(j)

(a) geographical area
     by post code
(b) map. city of Zurich
(c) special ticket
     selection area
(d) visual display
(e) money slot (coins)
(f) credit card slot
(g) city/special
     tickets/child or adult
(h) numeric keypad
(j) money slot (notes)

Figure 6.2: The two ticker dispenser prototypes referred to in example 2.

6.8) first to define when an error is a genuine instance of a mistake, and where errors and instances of 'playing' are likely to occur. You might also, for the purposes of the experiment, discourage your subjects from playing to avoid the occurrence of play instances by adjusting your instructions accordingly. When deciding upon the measures you will take and the data you will be using, you must therefore also ensure that you define and apply explicit rules for identifying the 'events' that make up your data. Now, returning to our two examples, the following measures might be decided upon:

EXAMPLE 1: VISUAL LIST SEARCH:

We decided to test which is easier to locate, targets written in CAPITALS or in mixed case letters, and spaced or non-spaced entries. Now, we translate 'easier' into 'faster' and measure the time it takes to find a target on a screen and enter the number associated with that target. This is called reaction time (RT). We program the timer to start the moment a screen is displayed, and stop it as soon as the first digit is entered from the keyboard. In order to ensure that the search times are as 'clean' as possible, we alternate between search screens (with targets) and another screen saying 'Read the next target, and when you are ready to continue, press the ENTER key'. Targets are presented in a deck of cards, with one target per card. Subjects thus inspect a card long enough to memorize the target, then press ENTER which brings up the display and triggers the timer. The timer starts at zero each time a new screen is displayed, thereby yielding an RT for each screen.

EXAMPLE 2: TICKET DISPENSER PROTOTYPES:

As in the visual list search example, we rely on some measure of time to compare the speed with which the correct tickets are obtained in the two prototypes. However, the contract does not permit you to program an electronic timer, so time must be measured manually with a stopwatch. The most unambiguous measure to take is the time it takes to complete each task, but one could consider measuring the time between each step within tasks. One could also count the number of attempts made before a ticket is successfully obtained; one could count the number of keys pressed per task. A comparison of actual key presses with the number of necessary key presses gives a measure of accuracy. This measure gives us the number of wrong keys pressed, and we should also take note of which keys are pressed incorrectly in the various tasks.

Note that, in the ticket dispenser example, the measures are somewhat vaguely defined, and we are not entirely sure whether we should take one measure or another. This is because we do not know how long subjects will take to decide what to to before pressing the keys, nor do we know how long each task will take, whether, where or when subjects might experience difficulties operating the ticket dispensers, or what problems we might observe. Furthermore, we do not know how easy it will be for observers to measure the various components accurately; subjects might be pressing lots of keys in very rapid succession, in which case we will probably need to videotape the sessions because no datalogging facilities are built into the prototypes. Alternatively, the subjects might look long and carefully at the various keys before they start a task, or they could take a long time to decide what to do from one step to another within tasks. These uncertainties are some of the reasons for us to conduct pilot studies (section 6.8).

6.2 The notion of experimental control

6.2.1 DEPENDENT AND INDEPENDENT VARIABLES

The purpose of any laboratory experiment is to establish cause–effect relationships between the phenomena under investigation. The data should show clearly how variations in one variable (Ch. 3) cause changes in another. Recall that independent variables are the properties which are to be controlled and/or manipulated experimentally because of the effect of these on the dependent variable. In our visual list search experiment, for example, capitals and mixed case letters, spaced and non-spaced screens are the independent variables manipulated. In the ticket dispenser experiment, the most important independent variable is the two prototypes as such and also variations in task complexity. The dependent variable is the characteristic or property measured and which cannot be manipulated without changing the independent variable. Reaction time is the dependent variable in visual list search; in the ticket dispenser experiment, it is task-completion time as well as the number of errors subjects commit or some other measure of accuracy which will be decided when pilot studies have been conducted.

6.2.2 APPLICATIONS OF THE NOTION OF CONTROL

In psychology the notion of control is used in two ways. First, it is seen as providing a standard against which to compare the effect of a particular independent variable. If two sets of findings emerging from a given experiment differ only on one independent variable, then any difference between the two sets of data may be attributed to that variable which is then said to have an effect on performance.

Imagine, for example, that you suspect you could improve user performance on the two prototypes by adding a set of instructions on the panel. To test this, you might give one subject-group a set of instructions for operating the machine, whilst giving nothing to another subject-group. Given that both subject-groups can be assumed to come from the same population and are completing the same set of tasks, the only difference between them is, as far as we know, the availability or non-availability of instructions. The extent to which the instruction-group outperforms the non-instruction group (assuming that it does!) can be attributed to the effect of instructions, provided there were no relevant characteristics by which the two subject-groups could be distinguished before the experiment. In this instance, the non-instruction group is the so-called control group, the performance of which provides a baseline measure of user performance. The instruction-group, by contrast, is the so-called treatment group, the performance of which is measured against the baseline (control group) data to determine the size of the effect of instructions.

The second meaning of the notion of control refers to our ability to restrain the sources of variability in research. The higher the level of experimental control, the more likely it is that differences in the behaviour measured are due to the effect of the independent variable. That is, experimental control is maximized when the sources of variability have been limited to such an extent that user behaviour may be explained in one way only. The more stringently the variables associated with an experiment are controlled, the smaller the probability becomes that the findings may be explained in several different, yet equally plausible, ways. Experimental control, then, is one way to rule out as many alternative explanations of the results as possible, thereby increasing the likelihood of uncovering actual cause–effect relationships. Control 'cleans up' data by reducing the variance and the 'experimental error' rate, thereby tightening the data distribution. Let us see how sources of variance could be reduced in our two examples:

EXAMPLE 1: VISUAL LIST SEARCH:

SUBJECTS:
Select university undergraduates (control for level of education), who are native English speakers (control for first language), aged between 20 and 30 years (control for age), who have normal or corrected vision (control for visual ability to detect the targets).

TASKS:
Present an equal number of each of the four types of screen (section 6.1.3). Randomize the line numbers associated with the targets (preventing subjects from predicting the line number of any target) (control for guessing line numbers).

Ensure that each digit (0–9) is placed first in the two-digit line number an equal number of times (in case some digits are inherently typed faster than others) (control for typing speed that might vary systematically).

Present targets the same number of times in every position on the screen (20 lines per screen, 160 screens, hence targets are placed eight times in every possible position throughout the experiment – twice in every position for every type of screen) (control for serial position of the target).

Divide the targets in eight blocks of 20 screens in each. Randomize the order in which these are presented between subjects so that no two subjects receive them in the same order, in case some blocks happen to be easier than others (control for order effect of blocks).

Make sure that each block of 20 screens is presented first an equal number of times, as performance is likely to improve with experience (control for practice).

Match items for word length, the pattern of repetition of surnames, and for first letter (controls for high variance that could be caused by presenting completely unmatched items in the different condition).

Provide practice items to allow subjects to get a feel for the tasks (control for task novelty).

KEYBOARD:
Modify to contain one numeric keypad only (the Qwerty keyboard has two). Remove all keys which are not used in the experiment to avoid confusion about which keys to use.

EXAMPLE 2: TICKET DISPENSER PROTOTYPE

SUBJECTS:
As for the visual list search experiment.

TASKS:
Design two sets of tasks, each containing an equal number of simple (say, six) and complex (six) tasks. Make sure tasks in the two sets are comparable in terms of degree of complexity, number of steps required, and features accessed to ensure that tasks in Set 1 do not differ systematically from those in Set 2.

Give tasks in the order simple → complex for one half of subjects, and reverse this order for the other half (i.e. complex → simple).

Give tasks in the order Set 1 → Set 2 for one half of subjects, and reverse for the other half (i.e. Set 2 → Set 1).

Let one half of the subjects use the prototypes in the order A → B, and the other half in the order B → A, as subjects are likely to improve with experience.

The design now looks as follows.

Group 1	Prototype A →	Prototype B
S 1-5	Task Set 1 (simple → complex)	Task Set 2 (complex → simple)
6-10	Task Set 2 (simple → complex)	Task Set 1 (complex → simple)
11-15	Task Set 1 (complex → simple)	Task Set 2 (simple → complex)
16-20	Task Set 2 (complex → simple)	Task Set 1 (simple → complex)

Group 2	Prototype B →	Prototype A
S 1-5	Task Set 1 (simple → complex)	Task Set 2 (complex → simple)
6-10	Task Set 2 (simple → complex)	Task Set 1 (complex → simple)
11-15	Task Set 1 (complex → simple)	Task Set 2 (simple → complex)
16-20	Task Set 2 (complex → simple)	Task Set 1 (simple → complex)

(S = [experimental] 'subject', or test user)

It is not always easy to ask the 'right' question, particularly when we are uncertain about the causes of particular effects and therefore investigate the 'wrong' variables. Early efforts in HCI, for example, attributed the difficulty people have in learning a new system to poor command names. This learning appeared very similar to a classic laboratory paradigm, paired associate learning, which has been pursued vigorously and which has generated a large literature by psychologists. HCI laboratory findings seemed to say that command names should be 'highly available', that is, learners should be able to associate the terms with concepts already known to them. This should make it easier to learn such terms than others which were unrelated to existing meaningful concepts. A great deal of research was generated to investigate the reasons underlying difficulties in learning command names, but the results varied widely from one study to the next so that, taken together, they were equivalent. Apparently, the difficulty with learning new systems was more complex and lay elsewhere (Landauer, 1987). So, although some researchers found support for the hypothesis that 'natural' command names were easier to learn than more esoteric ones, these did not appear to contribute much to the difficulty of learning to use computer systems. The point is that there is no guarantee that a research question addresses the 'right' or the 'central' issue, even though the question might be clearly formulated and enable good experimentation and possibly robust effects.

Since laboratory experiments are designed to uncover cause–effect relationships, they are normally very tightly controlled. In our efforts to achieve this, experimental tasks tend to be quite remote from anything people might actually do whilst interacting with their computer system. In the visual list search experiment, for example, the screens do not resemble actual lists of surnames as they would appear in white pages entries, and nor does one expect operators to have their job performance measured in reaction time. However, recall that the objective was to optimize the screen display in an effort to save operator time, and that way to improve customer services. Hence, even though the tasks employed in the experiment do not resemble exactly what operators do, the results are relevant to the problem. That is, although surnames are viewed as they might appear in online white pages listings, the principles of visual scanning uncovered through this and further experiments are likely to be true for other listings of item codes displayed vertically in columns on computer screens. Of course, this claim would need to be tested for other types of listings to confirm the generality of the principles.

Now, although the tasks employed in a laboratory experiment typically differ substantially from what people might do in an interactive session, this is not invariably true. The ticket dispenser experiment does, for example, represent tasks that actual users might do once the system has become operational. Yet, in contrast to the visual list search experiment, the experimental findings are tied more closely to the particular prototypes tested and are unlikely to be generalizable to many different types of complex vending machines. One major difference in the underlying philosophy between the two experiments lies in the problem and the research question under investigation. In the visual list search experiment, we were looking for an optimal display solution without any constraints other than sequential presentation of items on one or more successive screens. In the ticket dispenser experiment, the question was specifically to determine which of designs A or B is better. If the task had been to optimize ticket dispensers in the same fashion as the screen design in visual list search, an entirely different design might have been produced to tackle the issue of optimality.

In general, clear answers may be expected to explicit, well-defined and narrow experimental questions although, admittedly, a clear and unambiguous answer is rarely arrived at in a single experiment. It is often necessary to conduct quite a few experiments to do this, as only a limited range of issues can be addressed in any one experiment. It is this kind of narrowness which sometimes leads people to claim that laboratory experiments are useless in a systems design context.

6.4 Data recording in the laboratory

It was stated in Section 6.1 that the researcher should decide upon the kinds of data that would provide the most meaningful answer to their research question. In principle, there are four types of quantitative measures which represent most of the types of human behaviours one might observe in the laboratory. These include:

- counting events (for example number of errors, number of trials, number of trials to success, number of moves made to reach the

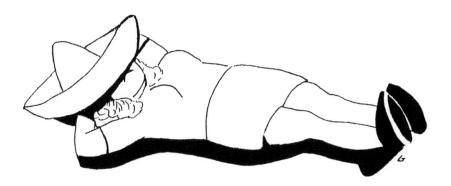

'Think carefully about the experimental design, data analysis and how the data might answer your research question before you rush into action'

target(s), certain utterances, eye blinks, occurrence of certain words, body movements, gestures);
- measuring time (duration of task, of looking up manual, time to complete certain tasks, interval between events, reaction time);
- noting the presence or absence of a phenomenon;
- measuring the level or amount of a phenomenon (e.g. physical measures might include amounts of certain fluids, amount of oxygen consumed, etc.).

Often these measures are combined in a way that describes several aspects of behaviour under observation and, at the same time, also gives us some statistical data for later analysis. One may, for example, count the number of moves made in a system navigation task, or the number of errors as well as measuring the task-completion time and checking whether the subject is choosing a colour or a monochrome display during the task. This may be combined with a measure of the amount of pressure with which different keys are pressed, muscle tension, amount of adrenalin in the blood, and so on.

The methods employed to focus on different aspects of behaviour vary according to the research question. If one wants to understand the operators' job and task demands, one might go into the workplace and observe them for long periods of time (field studies, Ch. 3); if one wants to find ways to reduce viewing time on screens, experiments could be conducted in the laboratory. Laboratory experiments concentrate predominantly on quantifiable elements of behaviour that form the basis for statistical analysis, rather than on a global overview of all the subject might do during the experimental session. Hence, decide in advance on which aspects of performance to record and which ones are irrelevant for the purpose of the experiment. Additional comments might be made in one's notes about utterances subjects make or about anything special that happens which is not part of the experiment but which might be relevant to the system and to further experimentation. Experimental data can be recorded in several ways and a number of data recording techniques are reviewed in the following sections.

6.4.1 LOGGING DATA MANUALLY

Because it is physically impossible to record everything that happens, it takes quite some skill to concentrate and to record only the data required for further analysis. One reason for conducting pilot studies (section 6.8) is to refine that skill within the proposed experiment. It also helps data recording efforts if some short cut, or coding, system can be invented, or some means by which observations are hampered only slightly by the need to write down what is seen. It is necessary to devise a method for generating a raw data file that is uniform across all subjects in terms of the types of events being noted.

Take the ticket dispenser experiment as an example. The subjects are likely to press some keys in rapid succession so that you cannot afford to take your eyes away from these activities for too long. To improve the speed of recording, you could replace the various areas in the prototypes by numbers:

EXAMPLE: TICKET DISPENSER PROTOTYPE
1 = geographical area plus postcode
2 = special ticket selection
3 = region selection
4 = (visual) display
5 = keypad, etc.

Now, using the complex task mentioned earlier ('Buy a first class, return ticket to Basel for a family of two adults and two children going to the Basler Fassnacht (Basel annual carnival) by train and tram'), your data file might look like in Fig. 6.3.

In the header of this raw data file, S3 refers to subject number three in subject-group 1 (G1), completing tasks in ticket dispenser A, Task Set 2, the third of the complex tasks (3c). This information, together with your explicit experimental design, enables you to identify precisely where in the experiment these data belong. It is advisable to use a new sheet for each task the subject completes, and perhaps to label your task sheets before the experiment commences. The data in the body of the data file tells you that the subject first looked in the geographical region (1) to locate the postcode for Basel. Then he entered the postcode via the keypad (5), verified it in the display (4), looked in the regional section for 1st. class (3), (this is an error!), found it in the ticket selection area (2) and selected it, followed by selection of a family ticket in the same area (2). Note how you can trace what the subject did, the sequence in which he did it, where he went wrong, and so on. At the same time, you

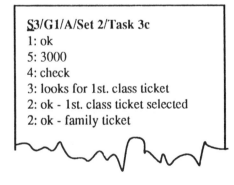

Figure 6.3: Manual datafile recording behaviour in the ticket dispenser.

S3/G1/A/Set 2/Task 3c
0   1: ok
11   5: 3000
16   4: check
39   3: looks for 1st. class ticket
44   2: ok - 1st. class ticket selected
52   2: ok - family ticket

Figure 6.4: Datafile as in Figure 6.3, with time measured in seconds/task step.

are measuring the task-completion time with a stopwatch and entering it into your data file either at the end of the task, or cumulatively, with each step as shown in Fig. 6.4.

The names of subjects are not normally used, because people's right to anonymity should be respected. That is, the data from a certain person should not be traceable by name through the data files once the sample of observations has been completed, although, of course, it is necessary to know where in the experimental design the subject 'belongs'. There might, however, be circumstances in which one wants to compare the performance of people on several different occasions. It does make it easier to be absolutely certain that a person is compared with his/her own performance if their name and contact phone number are used. Just make sure to get the subject's permission to do so before you start. Given an explanation as to why one needs to recognize people's datafiles on later occasions, subjects generally do not mind having their name associated with their data as long as they receive assurance that their name will not be published.

6.4.2 EXAMPLES OF ELECTRONIC DATA FILES

Time stamps are generally adjusted according to the type of measurement one wants. It may be measured in continuous, incremental steps throughout a particular task, or the timer, if RT is measured, may be triggered by a certain event, starting the timer at '0' each time a new task is commenced. Three examples of time-stamped output are shown below, in which the timer started at '0' each time a new task and sub-task was commenced:

'Volume does not assume quality: masses of data might not help you to a better understanding of the research domain'

EXAMPLE:

1. Visual list search

Screen	Time	Ans.	Result
2NM511	2.491	65	Correct
2NC517	1.485	78	Correct
2NC509	2.230	89	Correct
2NC501	1.972	91	Incorrect
2SM507	1.511	58	Correct
2NM503	1.836	68	Correct
2NM519	1.690	54	Correct
2SC521	3.169	90	Correct
2SC537	2.547	69	Correct...

Screen = Screen ID; Time = time spent on that screen (in seconds); Ans. = the number keyed in by the subject; Result = whether the number in the Ans. column is correct or incorrect.

2. Interactive Electronic Mail System
DIR/T1

MM	SM	State	Time	Entry
3	0	1	32	
3	7	0	7	
3	7	1	18	LEWIS
3	6	1	39	
3	0	3	88	
3	6	1	5	
3	6	1	29...	

DIR/T1 = Directory/Task 1; MM = main menu selection; SM = sub-menu selection; State = system prompts; Time = time spent (in seconds); Entry = what the subject entered from the keyboard.

3. Message Handling System

SENDER TEST#1

Field	Answer	Time
1	Mr White	24
2	Mr Donald	73
3	WHAMOO... super	54
4	y	74
5	349, 605, 871	37...
11	urgent	...13
12	y	10

Total task time: 392 seconds

Keystrokes
Mr White ← * Mr Donald ← * WHAMOO... super ← ! ← * y ←
* (etc.)

Sender Test#1 = first of several tasks in which the subject acts as
sender; Field = specified area on the sender screen; Answer = what the
subject typed into that field; Time = time spent (in seconds); Total task
time = the sum of entries in the Time column which = total time for
Sender Test#1; keystrokes = a reproduction of all keys pressed during
the task (e.g. '← *' = Enter, and so on).

Note how, in all of these examples, it is possible to determine
exactly

- where in the program/screen/field the user currently is (task/field/screen
  ID);
- what he/she is doing (data entered/deleted/retrieved);
- how long he/she spends in each field/screen/area.

Fulfilling these three criteria is a prime requirement of most, if not all,
datafiles. Although these extracts do not show it, each datafile also gives
an indication of whose data are being recorded, but of course, without
revealing the subject's name. This is similar to the example of the manual
ticket dispenser datafile (section 6.4.1), in which the header showed
which subject, task, etc. the data belonged to. Information in the header
enables the researcher to place the data in the framework of the
experimental design, and that way to reconstruct an entire experimental
session; the data in the body of the datafile show what was done, how
long it took, and so forth.

6.5 Planning a laboratory experiment

As was stated in the beginning of this chapter (section 6.1), one must first
decide upon the question to be answered experimentally. Only when this
has been clarified, made operational and defined in detail, can a decision
be taken as to whether the research question is best answered in an
experiment or whether it would be better to apply another investigative
tool. In general, it is true to say that the narrower the operational issue
or question is, the more precisely it can be formulated or reformulated
quantitatively, and the more likely it is that it is suitable for formal
experimentation. Yet, even if the question falls into this precise, quantifiable category of events, other constraints may be at work, preventing you
from doing what would be best. Maybe it is impossible to get hold of an
electronic timer/data logging tool for tasks in which accurate timing in
milliseconds is crucial; maybe an answer is required before sufficient data
could be generated. Sometimes budgets do not allow for experimentation,
or the necessary experimental control cannot be exerted over the system,

the tasks, the subjects or the experimental conditions to warrant experimentation. When too many factors mitigate against one to venture into formal experimentation, use other methods for answering the research question, such as quasi-experiments, heuristic evaluations, or global usability analyses.

Assuming that a decision has been taken to perform a formal laboratory experiment, it will then be necessary to define what type of data should be used, decide on suitable tasks, and so on, as has already been discussed. Planning should start with the general aspects of the research question, gradually refining them in increasing detail. In most cases try to limit each experimental session to roughly one hour. Sometimes an experiment might take longer, perhaps up to two, or even three, hours. If it requires constant and hard concentration from the subjects, as is mostly the case with interactive computing, limit the length of the session, or conduct it over several sessions, perhaps one per day for as many days as needed. Attention and concentration does wane over time, and unless one is investigating the effect of fatigue upon performance in certain tasks, it is best to avoid wearing out the subjects.

6.5.1 SELECTING SUBJECTS

When comparing the performance of different groups of subjects, strive for a 'balanced' design in which each group comprises the same number of subjects. This makes it easier to analyse the data statistically. However, there are no hard and fast rules for predicting the optimal number of subjects to include in a given experiment; groups may range anywhere from four to 50 or even 100 in a particular subject-group. Once some data is at hand, calculate how many subjects would be needed, assuming that performance observed so far is typical, to achieve statistically significant differences between groups. Some recent usability studies, conducted on different kinds of systems, have found that 80% of previously identified usability defects were found after five subjects had been tested and that important usability defects were more likely to be found with fewer subjects than less important ones (Virzi, 1992). Anecdotal evidence exists also which suggests that, using heuristic evaluation methods, roughly three times as many novice than expert evaluators may be needed to uncover 75% of pre-defined usability defects (Nielsen, 1992). In formal experiments, however, the only rule is that more subjects yield more robust findings.

6.5.2 THE ROLE OF PRE-EXPERIMENTAL TRAINING

Next, consider whether pre-experimental training is desirable or even necessary. Given that some aspect of user performance is going to be measured, one must take into consideration that subjects will not perform at their best at first, before they are acquainted with the system, the task requirements, or with other aspects of the experiment. Subjects are also likely to be quite anxious at first, which will influence their performance. If the experiment is not designed to measure learning in some sense, or observing how complete novices differ from experts in their approach to the experimental tasks, some kind of pre-experimental training should be included in the session. It is customary to exclude training data from the statistical analysis of experimental findings, as the training is not part of the formal data set and because they are likely to differ dramatically from the experimental findings.

Pre-experimental training may consist of a small number of practice items. Recall that in the visual list search experiment, all subjects completed a number of tasks (practice items) before going on to the experiment, to get them into the swing of it. Pre-experimental training may be conducted in sessions that are so long that they are separated in time from the experimental session. When only few practice items are given, these precede the experiment and are intended to give the subject an indication of what he/she is expected to do in the experiment. Subjects are generally allowed to ask questions after they have completed the pre-experimental training, and are mostly discouraged from doing so once the experiment is in progress.

In experiments that presume prior knowledge either of the system or the tasks, it may be necessary to design a comprehensive training program. If this extends over, say, 1–2 hours, the experiment may be launched after a short break, or after an interval of a day, or even a week. At times, if the effect of the training as such is being measured, one might make it part of the experiment as shown in the design outlined below.

> Group 1: Training   → (no delay) →   Experiment
> Group 2: No training   Experiment

Assuming one finds an effect of training, the next step could be to measure retention/ effects of delay between training and task performance (different subjects, same tasks, same instructions, same training as above to allow comparison of results later):

> Group 3: Training   → (delay 1 day) →   Experiment
> Group 4: Training   → (delay 1 week) → Experiment

Group 1 gives us a 'baseline' measure, that is, a measure of how people perform in these tasks without any training, but otherwise with everything kept constant.

Alternatively, one could design different types of pre-experimental training by varying the amount of information given, or the way in which the information is presented in the training session; it might be necessary to include exercises and control the amount of feedback subjects receive on their performance during training. Regardless of the level of task complexity, duration, feedback etc. decided upon, just remember that pre-experimental training will affect the performance of the subjects. For that reason, consider very carefully the effects to encourage and those to avoid. The pre-experimental tasks may expose the subject to all, to only some, or to none of the conditions included in the experiment, depending on the purpose it is intended to fulfil. Therefore, the pre-experimental training program/tasks must be planned with as much care as the experimental tasks.

Occasionally, the provision of pre-experimental training is not wanted because the researcher wants to know how subjects might behave when they are first completing a new task. For instance, the performance of novices using a new computer system might be under investigation. In the ticket dispenser prototype discussed earlier, no practice tasks were given, precisely because it was necessary to find out how well subjects would fare using the two prototypes without any priming or training. This would have been more difficult to detect if pre-experimental training had been given because, once subjects know how to use each ticket dispenser, the tasks themselves would be unlikely to reveal usability differences. Also, since the population for whom the prototypes are intended would not undergo any training once a system is fully operational, it was desirable in this case to measure system usability without any pre-experimental training. Hence, in usability evaluations we often choose not to administer pre-experimental training.

6.5.3 THE EXPERIMENTAL ENVIRONMENT

In addition to pre-experimental training, look carefully at the experimental environment. This too, may be entered as an independent variable, depending on the focus of the experiment. Consider varying the level of noise or light systematically between subject-groups, if these are elements of interest. If one is not interested in effects of the environment on performance, control it by holding it constant between all subject-groups. Consider the time of day the experiment is conducted. For example, straight after a meal one is less able to concentrate than before a meal, and in the late afternoon people might be more tired, hence less alert and less able to concentrate, than in the morning. If there is no particular interest in measuring the effect of time of day, control for this by avoiding those periods known to result in poor performance.

Finally, thought must be given to when and how to recruit experimental subjects. Is age, sex, native language, professional background, level of education, amount of computer or task experience important, either as an independent variable which might be varied systematically, or as an element to be controlled? A good rule of thumb is that any element that is of no interest should be controlled for, because remember – the aim is to reduce variability as much as possible, enabling a clear link to be exposed between cause and effect. Every variable one leaves free to vary is likely to add 'noise' to the data. In summary, when planning an experiment, decide

- where to conduct it;
- whom to include;
- how many subjects to include;
- when to conduct it;
- what to test;
- what to control for;
- how to test and log the data;
- what and how much to include in pre-experimental training.

6.6 Designing experimental conditions

The values of the independent variable are generally referred to as experimental conditions. Two conditions are the minimum number that can be dealt with in an experiment, because the performance of subjects is always compared on at least two distinguishable variables. Sometimes, comparisons may focus on performance of a treatment group with a control group. In such cases, the treatment group is the focus of an experimental hypothesis, and the performance of the control group serves as a baseline measure against which the effect of the treatment is assessed. Imagine, for example, that you are in charge of designing the next generation of ATMs (automatic teller machines). Much like our ticket dispenser, an ATM should be so readily accessible and usable that people are encouraged to use the convenience of 24-hour banking, thereby reducing the queues inside the bank. Despite efforts to make bank transactions self-explanatory in the ATM, you suspect that a set of step-by-step instructions will need to be imprinted on the ATM panel with the user interface. So, you decide to test this and recruit two subject-groups of people with similar educational background, same number of females and males of similar age group, perhaps new customers, and whatever characteristics you feel you need to control for. The design might look as follows:

Group 1:   Instructions
Group 2:   No instructions

Given that all subjects complete the same set of tasks, the data should indicate the extent to which the instructions facilitate performance. You can, of course, expand the design to include as many conditions, or differential treatment groups, as you like. You might, for example, suspect that elderly people are likely to experience more difficulties with using the ATM than young ones, so you decide to test it by controlling for age and testing certain age groups. This could lead to the following design:

Group 1: (old) Instructions   Group 3: (young) Instructions
Group 2: (old) No instructions   Group 4: (young) No instructions

Now, you have a classical 2×2 design – two cells along the horizontal and two along the vertical dimension. With this design, you will be able to make statements about the effect of instructions as a function of age, so you really have two baseline groups, the two 'no-instruction' groups serving as control for age and for instructions. A 2×2 design was also adopted in our visual list search experiment.

6.7 Planning the data analysis

It was stated in section 6.1 that the kinds of data to be collected must be thought about early. When the research question is defined operationally, one is really asking what measurements could generate suitable data to give you a meaningful answer. The data types to be gathered go hand in hand with the design of experimental conditions and data analysis. Which statistical tool is applied will depend upon the kinds of data generated and on the experimental design. In terms of design distinguish between within-subject and between-subject designs. In a between-subject design each subject is tested in only one experimental condition. This was the design used in the ATM example. By contrast, in a repeated measures, or within-subject, design, the same subject completes tasks in several conditions, on one or on several different occasions separated in time. Both the visual list search and the ticket dispenser experiments employed a within-subject design, since all subjects completed all the experimental tasks in both cases and, in the latter experiment, they also used both prototypes.

The range of statistical tools applicable to data analysis is very wide, and underlying each tool are sets of assumptions or criteria that must be met for that particular tool to produce valid outcomes. The details of such assumptions and the mechanics of applying a given tool as well as the analytical procedure are discussed extensively in statistics books and are not dealt with here, but you must familiarize yourself with them if you want to conduct experiments (Ferguson and Takane, 1989; Hays, 1988; Keppel, 1991; Lumsden, 1974; Thorne, 1980; Winer, 1971).

6.8 The role of pilot studies

When planning an experiment it is always advisable to carry out one or several pilot studies before launching into fully fledged experimentation. Even highly experienced researchers put their design to the test before commencing the formal experiment because they know there will be some aspects to refine or modify before everything is running smoothly. The time allowed for the task completion part of the exercise may have been miscalculated, or the instructions given to subjects may need clarification, more information may need to be included, or another example. It may be necessary to include more practice items, or one could discover that the experimental method breaks down at some point where it might be unclear to subjects what to do next.

The purpose of pilot studies is to eliminate as many ambiguities as possible. These are potential sources of error, which, if they were left in, could contaminate the experimental findings enough to render them questionable at best – or invalid at worst. One reason for conducting pilot studies is that researchers cannot predict accurately how people will behave or where they might have difficulties in meeting the task requirements. Another is that pilot studies provide a way of refining the experiment, checking that every aspect of it has been covered adequately and that the experimental session progresses in a planned manner. Furthermore, pilot studies give us, the experimenters, a chance to practise our data recording methods. Pilot studies allow us to detect flaws in the design before it is too late, that is, before a full set of data has been collected only to discover that something went amiss, was forgotten, or should have been considered or have been dealt with in a different fashion.

It is sometimes necessary to conduct several pilot studies before one can be satisfied that the experiment will provide the information required. That is fine – the important point is that pilot studies help to ensure that, once time and resources are committed to an experiment, no extraneous variable, or experimental error that could be controlled for is interfering with the experiment. It is much easier and cheaper to modify the instructions, tasks, conditions or data logging methods before running an experiment than trying to squeeze information from the data after the event that was not foreseen at the outset.

When conducting a pilot study, one is thus ensuring that the

- instructions are right;
- procedure is under control (described at the right level of detail);
- timing of tasks is right;
- data logging tools are adequate;

'Time your pilot studies to make sure you are not wearing out your subjects'

● data are collected such that all that one is interested in is there.

Even the data generated in the pilot study are not enough for a formal data analysis, it is a good idea to check the averages and plot the pilot data graphically to ensure that it looks like giving one what is expected. You get some feeling for whether or not the data appear to go in the predicted direction. Line graphs, histograms and scatter plots are most commonly used to make it easier to inspect data visually. To convince yourself, compare the two data sets presented in Fig. 6.5 which, in fact, are identical except for the way they are presented. They represent training data from a hypothetical experiment in which two groups of subjects (experts and novices) completed a particular set of tasks on a computer system for three days.

Mean time on training schedule (in seconds)

	Day 1	Day 2	Day 3
Novices	455	374	287
Experts	255	249	244

Figure 6.5: Training data for two subject-groups over three days.

The message from these data is that novices take longer than experts, especially on day 1, and that they improve their performance more than experts during the three training days sampled. These relationships stand out much more readily from the line graph than from the table, probably because it is more 'natural' to think about these types of relationships as some 'distance'; this information is not easy to grasp from a series of digits.

If the data do not seem to conform to one's predictions, one might want to reduce the amount of 'noise' by increasing the sensitivity of the experiment. This may be achieved by altering the level of difficulty of certain tasks to avoid a ceiling or floor effect, by including more data points, by excluding or changing certain tasks which appear to add noise to the data, or by reviewing the criteria on the basis of which subjects are selected. Pilot studies are in many ways similar to the ticket dispenser testing in the sense that we are checking and exposing to scrutiny a number of aspects of the experiment we are designing before running it using a large number of subjects. Similarly, ticket dispenser testing gives us a chance to modify the design and retest it before the complete system is programmed. Do make it a habit to run pilot tests – they will save considerable work, expense and embarrassment later.

Once enough pilot studies have been conducted to satisfy oneself that everything about the experiment is going smoothly, then the formal experiment can commence. When running it, ensure that every participant gets the same amount of information to set the experimental context and start the experimental tasks. It is a good idea to type the experimental instructions and either read these instructions aloud to the subjects or let them read these themselves. This ensures that some people are not given hints about the experiment which could influence their performance. Always allow subjects to ask questions before they commence the experiment, but be sure to set certain criteria and limits beforehand to the kinds of questions you are prepared to answer. As a general rule, it is not advisable to allow subjects to ask questions once the experiment is in progress – tell them so before the formal experiment begins and be prepared to remind them if they do ask questions during the experiment.

When conducting the experiment, be sure that everything needed is at hand before the subject arrives, so that you can get going straight away. Stay in the background and be as unobtrusive as possible during the experiment. Take notes and do the data logging discretely. Do not comment on what the subject is doing or not doing, or on what he/she is saying, and make certain there are no interruptions or random disturbances and distractions. Put a sign on the laboratory door informing people that an experiment is in progress and divert, or even unplug, telephones to prevent random error from being introduced.

Subjects will need to be briefed about the purpose of the experiment beforehand, but be careful with the wording. Instructions can strongly influence human performance (Kantowitz, 1992), and people will normally try to behave in accordance with what they expect the researcher wants. Such guarded behaviour may give no indication of how they would behave if they had been briefed differently. It is fine to stress speed or accuracy if that is an element of the experimental design, but do not discuss how the data are going to be treated, and do not reveal the hypothesis or any of those aspects or elements to be tested before the experiment. People are very keen to help and in their quest to do so, they will try hard to deliver what they think one is after. The less they know about the reasons for the particular experimental design (tasks, hypothesis, instructions), the smaller the likelihood is that the data will be contaminated by their goodwill and well-intended assistance.

Once the experimental tasks have been completed, the subjects should be debriefed. Now they can be told about the real aim and the design, and so on. But do make sure that this happens only when the data logging has been completed. As was argued when talking about interviews (Chapter 5), it is very important that the subjects leave with a feeling of having assisted in some useful and purposeful manner, and that they feel good about their involvement, contribution and performance. If an experiment

6.9 Conducting the experiment

is being conducted in which subjects are likely to commit many errors, reassure them that this is part of what is being investigated, that other subjects do the same, and that you are trying to expose the weaknesses of the system. Above all, make sure subjects do not believe that their intelligence is being tested. Unless subjects are told that the researcher stacked the odds against them by making the tasks so difficult that perfect performance would be impossible (avoiding a ceiling effect), they will tend to believe that their level of intelligence leaves something to be

'You are responsible for how your subjects feel after the experiment'

desired. Explain therefore why it was necessary to design and run the experiment in the manner you did and what weaknesses you hoped to expose. Remember, the researcher is responsible for how the subject feels when leaving after a completed session.

It is a good idea to plot the possible outcomes of the data before starting the experiment. This forces one to think about the data, the analysis and interpretation, as well as the extent to which the data might be able to answer the research question. The main data analyses are the planned analyses which are supposed to provide an answer to the question. In addition, some unexpected aspects of behaviour might have been observed which one now wishes to analyse and which offer additional insight into the data. Also, the error rate might be found to be so high that errors warrant a separate data analysis all together.

6.10 Analysing and interpreting the data

Statistical data analyses are conducted to help decide how likely it is that these same differences would be found if the experiment was repeated using different subjects. Repeatability and replication of findings given the same conditions, lends robustness to the experimental data and to the interpretation thereof. As with the application of analytic tools and procedures of analysis, the interpretation of the outcomes from the analysis should be conservative. Take the visual list search experiment as an example. The results obtained, plotted in terms of the average time taken, across all experimental subjects, in each of the experimental conditions, are shown in Fig. 6.6. Recall, we were comparing the effect of capital letters versus mixed case letters and spacing versus non-spacing.

As is clear from the data plot, it took longer to locate the target on non-spaced than on spaced screens, regardless of whether these were presented in capitals or they were in mixed case letters. By contrast, there was no evidence to suggest that mixed case letters facilitated visual list search as compared with capitals. Statistically, the difference between capitals and mixed case letters was not significant, whereas the difference between spaced and non-spaced screens was significant (Bednall, 1992). That is, we can be reasonably certain that spacing does have a reliable effect on visual list search, and that, if we were to repeat the experiment, we would find similar differences in search times between the two types of screen. This is the kind of statement that lends meaning to our data.

6.10.1 SOME COMMON EXPERIMENTAL DESIGN TRAPS

Care must be taken when drawing inferences from experimental findings: support for a given hypothesis does not necessarily imply that the hypothesis was valid, that the test was fair, that the results were not

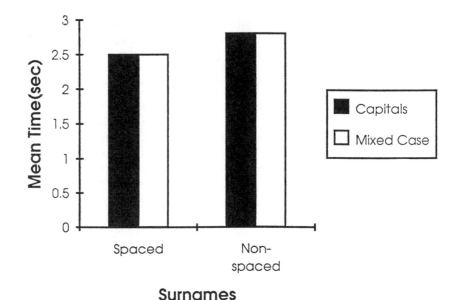

Figure 6.6: Results from the visual list search experiment comparing the effect of capitals versus mixed case and spaced versus non-spaced items.

influenced by extraneous variables, or that the variables' measures were relevant to the research question. Beware, in particular, of confirmatory evidence; as stated earlier confirmation of hypotheses does not 'prove' it is right! Let us look at some problematic examples.

EXAMPLE

TESTING INVALID HYPOTHESES:
'Breathing causes death'. Everyone breathes, everyone dies, but since there is no way you can falsify this hypothesis, it cannot be tested. Remember, confirmation does not constitute 'proof'.

FAIR TESTS:
Hypothesis: 'Sugar pills cure depression'. You take a sample of, say, 20 depressed elderly males living alone and caring for themselves. Ten are controls (for baseline measures); they receive no treatment whatsoever and are left alone for the duration of the experiment (eight weeks). The remaining ten, the treatment group, receive two pills three times daily, and the experimenter visits them twice weekly to replenish the pill supply and ensure they are taken. After eight weeks, tests show that the treatment group has improved dramatically, whereas the control group is slightly worse than before. So, do sugar pills cure depression? Probably not, but we cannot say from these results because, in addition to receiving pills, the men in the treatment group also received regular

visits by the experimenter which the control group did not. This is likely to have had some impact on people who, living alone, are probably not normally the focus of anybody's attention. If we were to be fair, the control group should have received some different substance, the same amount of attention during the testing period, and the regular visits by the experimenter. As it stands, nothing was really tested.

EXTRANEOUS VARIABLES:
Suppose that you want to know whether rats can localize the source of sound accurately. You place a test animal in a box located in the centre of a circle comprising 12 identical food boxes. You place a food pellet in one food box, sound a bell above the box with the food, open the trapdoor to let the rat out into the circle, and what happens? The rat runs straight to the correct food box. This happens repeatedly when food is placed in a different box. So, you now know that rats can localize sound accurately. But you are not satisfied yet. You have a hunch that auditory localization in the rat resides in its legs, so to test this, you amputate the rat's legs and repeat the experiment. Surprise, surprise – the rat no longer runs to the food box at the sound of the bell, so what have you demonstrated? This is perhaps a grotesque example, but it makes the point that extraneous variables may not only remain uncontrolled – they may be introduced by experimental manipulations if we are not careful.

IRRELEVANT VARIABLES:
We described earlier how HCI studies sought to establish that meaningless command names were responsible for difficulties in learning them. It turned out that the issue was more complex and that the effect had to be looked for elsewhere (Landauer, 1987).

6.11 Quasi-experimental design

A quasi-experiment is one in which the experimenter does not have the same level of control over the variables entering into the experiment as in a formal laboratory experiment. According to some authors, procedures in which subjects are selected for the different experimental conditions from pre-existing groups, rather than by random assignment, would qualify as quasi-experiments (Campbell and Stanley, 1963; McBurney, 1990, Ch. 7; True, 1989). Other authors label procedures in which the experimenter has less than full control over the selection of subjects 'non-experiments' (Spector, 1981), although both groups expect experiments to fall along a continuum rather than into absolute and discrete categories. A valuable discussion of the issue concerning experiments, non-experiments and quasi-experiments may be found in Campbell and Stanley (1963).

Here, we use the term quasi-experiment to describe experiments in which the level of control over the independent and the extraneous variables is incomplete. The fact that certain variables cannot be controlled by the experimenter limits the scope of experimental design and the types of data that can be readily gathered. The train ticket dispenser prototype experiment was said to be a quasi-experiment because of this incomplete level of control of variables. However, one can still design neat studies that address the problems one is seeking to expose. Regardless of what one chooses to call a certain type of study, the considerations underlying good experimental design should not be relaxed, because every variable that is left to influence the data also renders the findings subject to at least some degree of ambiguity which makes clear interpretation difficult and results possibly invalid.

Summary

Laboratory experiments are believed to offer little, or nothing, of value in the system design process, often because researchers neglect to consider carefully what the data arising from a particular experiment are likely to tell them. This chapter aimed to highlight several ways in which many potential problems arising through experiments may be avoided. The need to structure observations of behaviour made in the laboratory systematically was discussed, and it was shown why data need to be collected for a particular purpose. It was shown how research questions, once they are defined explicitly, can and should be made operational enabling the researcher to quantify the target behaviour he intends to measure experimentally. The operational questions, it was argued, form the basis for designing the experimental tasks and the data analysis. The need to define the type of data to be generated was discussed, and the notion of experimental control was dealt with in some detail. Tasks, research questions and control together give rise to the experimental design, which was illustrated by means of two examples referred to throughout the chapter. Issues to be considered when planning a laboratory experiment were outlined and the importance of pre-experimental training and of running pilot studies was highlighted. The planning of data analyses and the importance of plotting possible experimental outcomes were discussed and hints given on issues to consider whilst running an experiment. Data analysis was mentioned and the need to consult statistical texts for details was stressed. Finally, the notion of quasi-experiments was introduced.

Questions

1. Why are laboratory experiments assumed to yield little information of value to systems design?
2. State some of the reasons that experimental results may fail to meet the expectations of the experimenter.
3. Why is it important to define the research question explicitly?
4. What is meant by saying that a research question is operational?
5. Describe a ceiling effect and contrast this with a floor effect.
6. How does a control group differ from a treatment group?

7. What is the function of experimental control?
8. List the most common types of quantitative measures of behaviour that are generally employed in laboratory experiments.
9. What is the purpose of the header in a datafile?
10. What should be recorded in the datafile header? Why?
11. Why might it not be enough to log data electronically?
12. Why do you need to consider pre-experimental training?
13. What are the kinds of decisions you need to make when planning an experiment?
14. What are experimental conditions?
15. What is a pilot study?
16. Why should you bother to conduct pilot studies?
17. What do you need to be careful of when briefing experimental subjects?
18. What is your main responsibility when debriefing subjects?
19. What are some of the traps you might fall into when interpreting results and inferring what they mean?
20. How do quasi-experiments differ from formal laboratory experiments?

Exercises

1. The visual list search experiment showed that spacing facilitated target location compared with non-spacing. Now, you suspect that it might be easier for the eyes to travel horizontally across the screen if it is aided by, say lines of dots or perhaps dots and dashes alternated. Also, you have read that an increase in the amount of 'white', that is 'vacant', space on screens improves search performance (Tullis, 1983a; 1983b; 1990). Design one or more experiments to test these assumptions. Plot the expected outcomes for each predicted effect.
2. You are designing a graphics-based computer system which gives the user access to a large number of different databases. You have the option of portraying each database by an icon or by a verbal label describing it. Some members of your project team claim that icons are better than verbal labels because, they say, 'a picture is worth a thousand words' (Lindgaard *et al.*, 1987), but you are not convinced that this is correct. Design a suitable experiment to test this claim.
3. You have inspected a very large and complex computer system which is causing problems for its users who are relatively inexperienced and who do not use any other system in their jobs. Among the issues you uncover in your investigations, you suspect that the error messages shown on the screen are not very helpful, so you decide to re-write them. Design an experiment that allows you to test the extent to which your messages might be more interpretable than the standard ones.

4. What would need to be done to support the claim that 'advanced features in UNIX mail (the so-called tilde-escape functions) should be eliminated because they are useless?'
5. You are designing a hierarchical menu system storing information about all available drugs, when to give them, quantities in which they should be administered, side effects, and so on, to be used by medical personnel. You have compiled all the information, divided up into sensible categories that are suitable for the hierarchical menu structure. You find that two of your solutions seem equally attractive, but they differ so much from each other that they cannot be combined. You decide to test both to help you decide which of the solutions is likely to be more successful in a complete system. Design the necessary tests and describe how you could conduct them.

Suggested further reading

McBurney (1990) provides a thorough introduction to experimental psychology, including a comprehensive discussion of all aspects of experimental design and data analysis. This book is intended for psychology students, and is therefore very detailed. It is recommended particularly for readers who want to take up the challenge of designing and conducting formal experiments. This book is easy to read, but the contents are, by their very nature, quite heavy.

Robson (1990) outlines how experimentation fits into the HCI framework in a very clear description of the steps a researcher must go through to design good experiments. The chapter is easy to read and very informative.

Integrating usability evaluation into the design process 7

Only the hurried, the stupid, and the
strong close a reference book upon
satisfactory completion of the original
search.

F. Gordie

The career of any human factors specialist is generously dotted with cases in which, by the time his/her expertise is sought, the system to be evaluated is already 'cast in concrete', so to speak. In these cases, the system design has progressed so far that, no matter what problems a usability evaluation would uncover, the chances of getting them fixed are very slim indeed. Human factors band-aid treatment is in nobody's interests, and the few changes which may be made often amount to little more than superficial adjustments to cosmetic appearance. Repairing real design flaws which are likely to cause serious problems is often too time-consuming and expensive once a system has advanced beyond a certain point, because every problem detected tends to affect it in several different areas. Problems which could have been fixed at the outset by changing a few lines of code, by an additional option in a menu or by restructuring the menu hierarchy tend to snowball and become insurmountable when detected too late in the process. If the benefits to be gained from a usability testing program are to be maximized, such a program must be well planned and must commence when the project commences.

This chapter shows that human engineering principles can and should be incorporated into the entire systems design and development cycle in an effort to ensure that necessary adjustments which affect usability can be made progressively rather than be added on at the end. The same is true for usability: pretty screens or a friendly, persuasive dialogue will not hide serious blemishes well enough to make users believe they are not there.

It may be recalled that feasibility studies focus on assessing users and the tasks one may wish to support in an as yet non-existing computer system. Empirical measurement may be done at this stage, but because neither the project team nor the organization's management is committed to the system until the end of the feasibility phase, one tends to rely on more informal investigative tools at this very preliminary phase. However, at every other stage of the process, empirical testing is central to usability testing and evaluation. Iterative design means that problems detected through usability testing must be overcome and, once they have been fixed, the solution must be tested also, just to make sure that it actually eliminated the original problem. It is often the case that solutions themselves introduce new, unforeseen problems which must then be fixed and retested. So, the iterative cycle of system development is one of design, testing, redesign, retesting until usability goals have been reached.

7.1 The feasibility phase

7.1.1 DEVELOPING THE PRODUCT CONCEPT

A product concept is developed during the feasibility phase. Even though the process by which the necessary background information is gathered can be specified and reduced to a number of points to be satisfied, the process itself varies according to the system in question. For a follow-on system, the crucial issue to investigate may not be its market position among possible competitive systems, even if it is a fully commercial venture. If the older version is well placed and already widespread, an update will not need to prove itself to the same degree as an entirely new system would; it is likely to survive on its good name and reputation. This is, by some authors' descriptions, what happens to successful companies (Peters and Waterman, 1981) as well as to proven software! Feasibility studies must thus be adjusted according to the system and the issues involved in the individual case and the kind of decision to be made on the basis of information gathered during this phase.

Let us consider the hypothetical development of two types of systems, namely:

1. a specialist system for dentists in private practice;
2. a system which integrates a customer records and a billing system into one.

The dental support system will be designed from scratch imagining that you have total freedom to select hardware and software platforms, technology, user interface style, and so on. The customer records and billing integration replaces the two present systems residing in a telecommunications environment.

EXAMPLE 1: DEVELOP A PRODUCT CONCEPT: DENTAL SUPPORT SYSTEM

Who is the target audience?
Imagine that uncle Leo is a dentist. When he visited for dinner yesterday he complained about having to go home early to type up his monthly statement. Every cheque he has issued over the past month to pay bills at the clinic has to be entered into the statement, along with every dollar he has received from patients paying their accounts. Uncle Leo thus spends a few hours every month balancing his books, taking details from

cheque butts and receipt books. These are all amounts of money that have already been entered elsewhere.

It should be easy to streamline the accounting side of a dental practice so that a computer system could

1. generate the patients' accounts;
2. send out monthly reminders to people who owe money but who have not yet paid;
3. enter the amounts into a ledger;
4. keep track of outgoing money.

A list of item numbers, describing each kind of treatment offered for which the patient can get a health care rebate could be stored in macros along with the price uncle Leo currently charges for each item in the list, enabling him to generate his patient bills by simple macro selections. Dentists use X-rays which are stored along with patient records. These could probably be integrated with the records in an interactive system. Yes, you have just found a sensible use for integrating images into text files. You know also that, when uncle Leo makes a cap or a crown to fit on top of a sick tooth, it can be difficult to match the colour, or shading, to the rest of the patient's teeth accurately. If you could project a live picture of the patient's teeth onto a screen, then it should also be possible to show the patient what his mouth would look like with differently shaded caps and, that way, to select the best shading that satisfies the patient before treatment is commenced. As a cap costs quite a bit of money, it could be reassuring for patients to see how they will look if they decide to have the treatment done. Congratulations! You have just made use of live video images in your system. It looks as if you may have found a viable solution to sensible use of multimedia.

The main emphasis of the feasibility study following on from this brain wave will be on assessing the usefulness of the tasks you want to support in the light of the cost of producing the system and buying the necessary hardware as well as assessing the probability of its success in the market place.

EXAMPLE 2: INTEGRATION OF CUSTOMER RECORDS AND BILLING SYSTEMS

The purpose of this assignment is to integrate two systems residing in a telecommunications service company. One of these contains all customer records showing who is connected to what phone number, the address, occupation, contact number, type of equipment hired from the company, and other customer details necessary for the organization's service records. The other system contains all information about customers' bills, like the itemization and cost of equipment hired, the running cost of phone calls made from the registered number, the customer's paying history, date when the last bill was issued, credit information, and so on. In order to allow operators to take all types of enquiry calls from customers concerning information about bills as well as requests to change customer record information, the systems need to be integrated. At present, operators use only one of these systems. When taking a customer query that requires access to the other database, the customer is passed on to another operator who uses that database. This is both time-consuming and annoying for the customer, and it also results in inefficient use of the organization's own communications network. Both existing systems rely on outdated technology, although they do allow a full range of customer activities to be performed. The systems differ in the terminology they employ as well as in the amount of coded and abbreviated information; abbreviations are inconsistent both within and between systems. In addition, the systems differ in the types of transactions they support, in query language, command language and in the display formats. The product your team is employed to develop will not be marketed, as it is very specific to the company and its practices; potential competitiveness in the market place is thus irrelevant to this project, so, you need not bother about its attractiveness relative to other, possibly already existing systems.

Your main challenge in developing the product concept is to determine the best possible technology, the time frame for strategy and implementation, and an assessment of the degree to which different possible technologies may be successfully integrated into the existing environment. The goal of the feasibility study in this project is to develop a viable plan for the design and development, as well as for graceful integration and implementation of the new system.

'Select technology with care. Voice interaction is, for example, not everyone's idea of good computing'

In addition to developing a product concept, the potential success of a proposed system is investigated during the feasibility phase. To do this you should

- identify the target audience;
- identify the target environment;
- identify a suitable technology;
- develop a business case.

In order to develop a business case, you should obtain rough estimates of

- who your users are;
- the general environment into which the system should fit;
- tasks that your system could support;
- task links;
- current task-completion times;
- a cost/benefit analysis;
- the importance of calculated savings;
- the usefulness and usability of other competing systems;
- the advantages your system offers over current task completion methods;
- the system development costs.

Finally, you present the business case to management.

7.1.2 DEVELOPING A BUSINESS CASE

Once you have established the kind of system you want to produce, and you have determined who your target audience is as well as the tasks you would aim to support with the system, you should prepare a business case. The purpose of a business case is twofold. First, it is used to assess the potential success of your system in the market place in the light of the size of your target audience and the system development costs. Second, the business case is the tool with which you attempt to persuade your management to form a project team and allow your system to proceed. Naturally, the business case will vary, depending on whether you want to produce a commercially viable system such as the dental support system referred to here, or whether you are assigned the task of producing a follow-on system in line with the telecommunications integration system.

In a commercial system, its survival depends on how well you have identified a niche and are filling a realistic gap in the market place. In a follow-on system, its position in the market place is likely already to have been determined by preceding versions of it or, as in the case of the telecommunications integration system, marketability may be irrelevant.

In such cases, the purpose of a business case is to project which tasks and functions the new version will improve and how much will be saved in terms of time, money and effort on behalf of all classes of users. Compared with the present version, time savings should include estimates of reduced learning time for new system operators, of reduced task-completion times for experts as well as for novice users, and of savings due to improved efficiency in task-completion methods. You might, for example, find that certain user activities currently performed outside the system could well be accommodated within it. With respect to saving money, you should estimate how your system would contribute to reductions in the need for operators to seek information outside the system. For example, in the integration of the two systems mentioned here, substantial sums of money are spent on internal telephone communication when an operator needs to pass on a customer with queries relevant to the other database to someone using that database. With respect to operator effort, application of a more recent and more appropriate technology to the tasks supported should result in reductions in the amount of effort it takes to complete these, perhaps by relying on direct manipulation interfaces rather than on operator-typed entries. With respect to the two examples used in this chapter, the following considerations could exemplify typical business cases:

EXAMPLE 1: DENTAL SUPPORT SYSTEM

Developing the business case to support your dental support system will give you a basis for the arguments you will need to furnish to sell the idea of the system to the management of the large software development firm in which you work. Management will be interested in the viability of your system in the sense that they will want to be reasonably certain that it would do well in the market place. In order to ascertain where your system could improve the efficiency and attractiveness of dentists' present work habits, you will need to work through the areas and/or tasks that your proposed product could support. The point of this would be to elucidate how the system would change the way these tasks are currently done, and work out exactly where and how it would benefit users in terms of time and/or labour savings.

Once you have a feel for how your system would improve matters for users, you should then compare it with other available systems in terms of software cost to users, system capabilities, effort in learning and using these, in interactive dialogues, user support materials, and so on. Forcing yourself to make explicit the ways in which you believe your system would be advantageous to practitioners, you would also need to relate these advantages to actual dental practice. In particular, you must find out whether the assumptions you make are consistent with practice, and determine the degree to which the features you consider advantageous would be welcomed by your intended target audience. After all, you are expecting dentists to pay for the software, so the features you are trying to sell better be attractive to them! Consequently, your system will be favoured over others to the extent that the features you propose can readily be integrated into dental practice and result in a more useful and usable system. Fancy gimmicks that look good or interesting but which are impracticable, too expensive for what they offer, or that pose problems with hygiene, flexibility, system reliability or cost, are not going to give your product much advantage in the market place in the long run. So, be careful – it is easy to get carried away wanting to develop imaginative technological capabilities, but unless they are perceived by your future customers to be useful, your efforts and expenses might be wasted.

1. Define the general environment into which the system should fit.
At this early stage of your system conceptualization, you will be 'shooting from the hip', at least a little bit, because you will be unlikely to get permission to devote many months preparing your business case. However, if you are lucky enough to have ample time in which to conduct your preliminary investigations, you should consider using questionnaires, surveys and interviews (Ch. 5) thereby learning enough about dental practice to define your most promising market, the best functions to include into your system, and the most practical, usable method and technology for presenting these functions.

Most likely, you will need to gather some data in a hurry, so start by questioning your uncle Leo – perhaps get his permission to observe what goes on in his practice for a couple of days. This will give you a fair idea about what data are handled by the dentist, by nurses, receptionists, and so on. On-site observations will give you some preliminary insight into who needs access to what information when in the work flow, how this information is currently obtained and stored; that is, being there will give you a good feel for the patterns of communication within a small dental practice. However, you cannot know the extent to which your uncle Leo is representative of dentists, or whether his practice is run in a way that exemplifies the majority of dental practices in your country. To establish a credible business case, you will therefore need additional information. You should, for example, find out about the distribution and size of dental clinics, about how many dentists are employed in an 'average-sized' clinic. There are no hard and fast rules on how or where to obtain information you might consider important or necessary, but in this instance, you should get on the telephone, call the professional Dental Association and ask for relevant literature and statistics. They are likely to have much of what you need at their fingertips, and if they do not, it is at least a good starting point in the sense that they are likely to help you get access to better resources.

In pursuing general information you could, for example, find that there are only 20 clinics with ten or more dentists in the whole country, all of which are found to be connected with universities. Obviously, these would not be the first places to visit, as they are not 'typical' representatives of most dental clinics. The Dental Association is likely also to tell you what proportion of dentists already have computers in their practice, possibly give you an indication of what systems are available so that you know how big your proposed target audience is likely to be. It is hard to imagine that dental practice has changed so radically in the past few years, so unless your system really offers some crucial elements that have been missing, and are being missed, in existing systems, you will be unlikely to attract those dentists who already have computerized their practice to convert to your system. If a sizeable proportion of dental clinics already have computers, this diminishes the chance of your system succeeding, at least in the short term.

In addition, you could think about writing an article in the *Dental Bulletin* telling dentists about your proposal and inviting them to offer their views on the proposal, to forward their needs and ideas to you. Or you could arrange to give a talk at a local branch meeting, addressing the professional audience to gauge their feelings about computers in general, and about the particular features you intend to offer. Use census data to find out where dental clinics are located; use the phone book to check dental advertisements and listings. Talk to the dental suppliers and depots; talk to the schools of dentistry linked to universities to find out how many students graduate every year and how long it takes them to establish their own practice; talk to dental technicians about possible expansions to your system to explore the possibility of catering to their needs as well. Contact the schools that train dental nurses to find out whether they would like to be given tuition in computing during the basic, or in post-graduate courses. The more you talk to different people, and the more up-to-date statistical data you can gather, the better your picture of dental practices will be, and the more accurate your decisions about your system will be as well as the predictions about market opportunities; the more finely tuned your system is towards targeting the market, the more likely it is that it will be successful and remain so for a long time once it is released.

2. Define tasks that your system could support.

In the dental support system, you would first define the broad areas to cover. Let us say hypothetically that we will divide our system into the modules shown in Fig. 7.1:

Functions that would be required to complete typical user tasks include:

Appointment module: word processing (WP) capabilities;
Treatment module: WP capabilities, image generation plus storage (X-rays), graphics (dental charts), live image (video);
Accounting module: spreadsheets, calculator, knowledge of tax (% of gross staff salary to deduct, sales tax on equipment, cost of item numbers);
Administration module: WP plus spreadsheet capabilities.

In total, we need WP, spreadsheets, calculator, image generation, graphics and live video capabilities.

Now, let us assume that this first rough approximation summarizes your ideas about those aspects of dental practice that may be of relevance in a support system. These will naturally need to be verified by

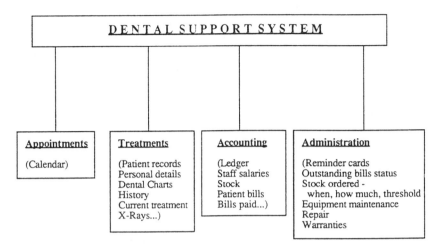

Figure 7.1: Modules forseen to comprise the dental support system.

practitioners. If you did not have access to a dentist whom you could visit and observe in action, you would need to walkthrough typical, yet hypothetical, tasks to work out how the system will cope with them. From your own experience with dentists, you know that you, for example:

1. receive a reminder notice every six months (administration module);
2. make an appointment (appointment module);
3. have your treatment (treatment module);
4. receive an account (accounting module);
5. pay it and receive a receipt (accounting module).

So, it appears that your partition of the system could cover most of the activities that interactions with patients might demand.

3. Define task links.
Now, let us define how the discrete tasks and steps involved in fulfilling these tasks could be automated and linked in the system.

1. Reminder card is generated. Data taken from date of end of last treatment plus six months (administration module takes data from treatment module, verifies date with appointment module ... last appointment = 01/06/93 plus six months = 01/12/93).
2. You make an appointment: entered into appointment module.
3. Treatment: history is retrieved. Treatment entered into card according to:
   a. what is done on this visit, description plus item numbers;
   b. what further treatment is proposed plus time frame.

4. Accounting module is activated from the appointment module plus takes other data from treatment module. Generates account, makes a note of this (amount plus date) in treatment module plus administration module (bills outstanding).
5. Administration module notes 'plus 30 days' to generate reminder.
6. If bill is paid before 30 days have lapsed, reminder in administration module is cancelled. Amount paid is entered into accounting module and cancelled from administration → administration generates receipt.

4. Estimate current task-completion times.
Assuming that uncle Leo has no computer and uses completely manual processes. After observing the following tasks on a number of occasions, you might work out the average time taken to complete them is as follows:

Task	Time
1. Generate reminder card	∼ 2 min
2. Enter appointment	∼ 3 min
3. Enter data in treatment card	∼ 2 min
4. Write account	∼ 2 min
5. Write reminder at date = + 30 days	∼ 2 min
6. Cancel reminder; write receipt	∼ 2 min.
Total task-completion time	∼ 13 min.

5. Do a cost/benefit analysis.
An examination of the manual tasks and their automated equivalents suggests that we might save:

Task	Status	Time
1.	automated	2 min
2.	No change	0 min
3.	No change	0 min
4.	Automated	2 min
5.	Automated	2 min
6.	Automated	2 min
Total savings		8

Now, these are the projected savings in administration per patient. If we assume that dentists see roughly 20 patients per day, we could construe an argument to suggest that a saving of 160 min (= 2 hrs. 40 min) could be made per day.

6. Define the importance of calculated savings.
The next issue to address is: whose 2 hours 40 minutes savings are we talking about, and how might that time be better spent. Your observations in uncle Leo's practice showed that all tasks 1–6 outlined above

were completed by the dental nurse or the receptionist. Now, if a receptionist is employed, her job will be to greet patients and technicians, to answer the phone etc. as well as entering appointments, perhaps administering the writing of reminder cards and writing receipts. Most likely, these activities are well run-in, and in uncle Leo's clinic, you also noticed that the receptionist does not work overtime. Hence, the workload associated with administration is distributed across the whole day, and there is no backlog.

The receptionist belongs at the front desk, regardless of any time savings achieved by a computer system. In fact, introducing the system may simply mean that the receptionist will have more time during which he/she could pursue other administrative duties which currently do not fall inside his/her domain. If you would want to encourage your target audience to buy your system, you must therefore identify which additional jobs could be taken on by the receptionist. This could pose a problem at this stage, as you will need a much more detailed understanding of the day to day running of a clinic. Such knowledge should emerge during the user needs analysis. Since dentists in small clinics with a single receptionist would not be motivated to save enough time to make that job redundant because the receptionist fulfils many human-human interaction tasks that your system neither could nor should replace, the savings estimated in tasks 1–6 above would be important particularly in clinics with more than one receptionist. In such large clinics they could possibly add up to saving a person without affecting the customer service adversely.

In clinics which do not employ a receptionist, the tasks outlined above are mainly completed by dental nurses. The dentist generally needs to have two nurses at his/her disposal; the nurses' duties go well beyond writing out accounts and making appointments, and they must be available during working hours, even if a certain number of minutes can be saved by installing the system; these cannot replace a dental nurse.

At this point it should be clear why you need to know something about the distribution and size of dental clinics. If there are only a few clinics with two or more receptionists, your administrative time-saving argument will not be a useful marketing tool with which to sell the system to small clinics. Assuming that the majority of dental clinics are small, with one receptionist or none at all, you will need to isolate other administrative tasks in which time-savings and increased efficiency will be meaningful.

You might, for example, look at the value of the accounting and administration modules. Whereas, when tasks are completed manually, there is quite an amount of administration associated with book work, keeping all in/out entries accurate and up-to-date, ready for auditing at the end of the year, you could offer substantial savings. Treatment items need only be entered once; thereafter they are selected from the list already residing in the system as needed. Since payments are entered automatically into the accounting module when they are made and numbered receipts are generated, these accounts need not be touched further. Equipment, stock, maintenance, repairs, etc. are, similarly, entered only once. All the dentist has to do is to check bank statements against computer entries once a month. Apart from having ready access to all figures (amounts paid, received, dates when paid/received), up-to-date records are available at all times at the stroke of a key. This means that the dentist has no additional bookwork to worry about when the time comes for annual auditing and tax purposes. It means also that he/she is able to monitor how the clinic is going compared with last year and the year before, as well as being able to project expenses ahead of time. Savings may also be valuable in terms of placing orders for supplies in a timely fashion, in terms of sending out reminder cards on time and for other administrative purposes as well as increasing efficiency by reducing the risk of running out of stock. In the accounting module, we are thus talking about dentist's own time, and in the administration module, we can increase efficiency by helping the dentist to remember and anticipate events in a timely fashion.

7. Investigate the usefulness and usability of other competing systems.

Find out what systems already exist which fulfil all or part of what you propose to do with this one. To what extent do these facilitate the dentists' job? Where do they fall down? How well do they meet the needs of the target audience? Could any tasks be linked which are now separate entities? What could current technology provide to improve interaction with a system? What usability defects exist in the current systems? How could these be overcome in a new system? In other words, you should investigate the market to learn about existing, possibly competing, systems, their advantages and disadvantages, merits and shortcomings, cost and so on. Doing your market research thoroughly, you should also investigate how widespread the existing systems are; if 90% of dentists recently installed computers, they are unlikely to spend a lot on updating their systems within a couple of years.

8. State the advantages your system offers over current task completion methods.

Knowing which other dental support systems exist, you should also be able to make explicit how potential buyers would gain from installing yours. If available systems are particularly attractive for larger practices, perhaps you might aim to serve the single dentist practice. Alternatively, advantages of your system might lie in the interactive dialogue, perhaps being the first system to be speech activated or GUI (graphical user interface) oriented offering colour or video integration. Perhaps yours integrates more tasks than existing systems, or does so in a more elegant fashion. Working out precisely how and where your system offers real advantages to the practitioner gives your marketing efforts an automatic boost later in the sense that you can make precise and justifiable statements about the advantages of your system rather than the normal vague 'faster to learn' or 'easier to use' statements one finds in the popular press.

9. Estimate the system development costs.
The advantage of thinking through your proposed system as a collection of specific modules is that you can estimate your development costs more accurately, even at this sketchy stage, than if you imagine your system as a monolith. We said earlier that we would integrate:

- word processing
- spreadsheets
- graphics
- video
- images
- calculator.

Many of these capabilities exist already in a form that is sufficiently advanced so that re-development of capabilities as such is unnecessary. Apart from the integration and ability to manipulate images, the other modules are likely to be adaptable from existing software, thereby reducing the overall development time substantially.

10. Present the business case to management.
The information gathered will enable you to put together a credible business case and present this to your management (sections 3.8.2; 3.9).

'How will you sell your idea? Efficient storage mechanisms look tidy but this may not be enough to impress your target audience'

EXAMPLE 2: INTEGRATION OF CUSTOMER RECORDS AND BILLING SYSTEMS

Compared with the dental support system, our task here is somewhat easier because there is no doubt about whether or not the system will be developed. Let us quickly review the ten points made earlier:

1. define the general environment into which the system should fit;
2. define tasks that your system could support;
3. define task links;
4. estimate current task-completion times;
5. do a cost/benefit analysis;
6. define the importance of calculated savings;
7. investigate the usefulness and usability of competing systems;
8. state the advantages your system offers over current task completion methods;
9. estimate the system development costs;
10. present the business case to management.

Going through these for the present system, it is evident that you need not waste time identifying other competitive systems (7) or the general environment into which the new system would fit (1). Similarly, the exact time needed to carry out each of the possible transactions needs not be measured at the feasibility stage (4), and nor do the advantages of your system need to be spelled out in great detail as yet (8). The cost/benefit analysis will not need to be detailed to the same degree as if your feasibility study aimed to convince management that the system would be a worthwhile investment (5)(6). Tasks (2), task links (3) and transactions are reasonably well-defined and will only need to be analysed in more detail at the time you conduct your user needs analysis. In the light of the ten points guiding a feasibility study, it means that your main task in the feasibility phase is to estimate the system development costs (9) and present this as a business case to management (10). The focus of your business case is the selection of hardware and software platforms; your main job is to find the best technology for the tasks at hand, to estimate the development time frame and costs, and to present these findings to the management. You will need to look at the tasks to be performed, even in rough terms, and estimate how much of the data currently entered and handled by operators could be handled by the integrated system using different technologies. However, you may do these analyses from screen dumps at this stage rather than basing your calculations on observations of operator behaviour. All you need is a reasonable estimate of relative efficiency of different technologies for the tasks as they stand to prepare your business case. This could be done in the following manner:

System response time (SRT) is eight seconds, on average, in the current customer records system and 14 seconds in the billing system. It is likely to be even shorter in the command-driven user interface (CUI) update, but figures are not available. SRT is not relevant to a graphics environment, as dialogue boxes, menus, and other necessary objects pop up instantly.

Transaction	Current System	~Task-time	*CUI update	**GUI update
New customer	13 screens/118 data	15 min	6 screens/72 data	4 screens/72 data
Reconnect	5 screens/76 data	7 min	3 screens/50 data	3 screens/50 data
Disconnect	4 screens/28 data	4 min	1 screen/24 data	1 screen/21 data
Billing enq. etc.	3 screens/3 queries	3 min	2 screens/3 queries	2 screens/3 queries

*CUI = Command-driven user interface;
**GUI = Graphical user interface; data = data points

Comparing the data points and screens to be handled by operators in the current systems and in the two possible enhancements suggests that either of the two solutions would be more efficient than the present ones. Differences between CUI and GUI appear negligible, except that no SRT is associated with the GUI. In addition, one could calculate learning time reductions, amount of jargon that is eliminated, number of redundancies that can be removed, incomprehensible abbreviations and codes that will be translated into English. We will not go into further detail with this case; you probably get the general idea of what could be done reasonably quickly and using readily available data. For the purpose of estimating your development time, you might want to proceed on a task-by-task and transaction basis.

7.2 Usability in the research phase

Assuming that the decision to let the system go ahead has been made, now is the time for performing the user needs analysis to understand in detail what users require and how these requirements can best be met by the technology available, the style of the user interface and the way the system components will be put together. From the results of the user needs analysis (Ch. 2) it is possible to define the usability goals and put together a usability test and evaluation plan (Ch. 8). During the research phase the features the system will contain are defined together with the functions the system must be able to perform. Individual tasks that users will want to carry out are described in detail, and the sequence in which different tasks and sub-tasks will need to be linked will become clear from the user needs analysis.

Issues that must be investigated independently of, but parallel with, the development of the system, will emerge, and a research plan outlining how these should be pursued can be drawn up. Experimentation on these issues commences here. Data flow diagrams will be drawn from the perspective of the user tasks and goals as well as from the perspective of programming efficiency. The end result of the research phase is a set of specifications. These include at least functional specifications which state the functional and data requirements for the system. The usability test and evaluation plan states what is to be tested when, during the

'Work together with your users to define their needs – otherwise they might not recognize their job in your system'

system development, as well as the usability goals that should be achieved and how test results will be fed back into the design process. The research plan outlines the issues that will be pursued independently of the specific design plan. Finally, a time line should be drawn up stating what should be done and what should be completed by when on the basis of the details entered into the other documents. During the research phase one would:

- perform a user needs analysis (user profiling/task analysis; Ch. 2);
- define usability goals (Ch. 8);
- develop usability test and evaluation plan (Ch. 8);
- isolate and investigate specific issues;
- develop research plan;
- develop SRS documents.

Let us now outline what could be done in the research phase for the two examples presented in this chapter. Only usability issues are considered; data flow diagrams, functional specifications and other documents are not discussed here.

EXAMPLE 1: DENTAL SUPPORT SYSTEM

DETAILED USER NEEDS ANALYSIS: widen the sample of dentists (N = 8–10) to understand work practises of different-sized clinics and task support requirements.

HEURISTIC EVALUATION: (Ch. 4) assess existing competing systems for merits and disadvantages and discuss these with dentists who are

'A research plan includes different methods for detecting usability defects'

using them, remembering that the use of any of these systems is discretionary.

OBSERVATION OF USERS IN ACTION: (Ch. 4) informal pen and paper notes for own use.

CONFIRMATION STUDIES: (Ch. 4) review the outcomes of observations with the dentists you observed to ensure you understood and interpreted correctly what you saw.

INTERVIEW (Ch. 5) dentists and, if possible, offer a reward for their time. Rewards could be access to cheap (or free) software once it is completed, or use of a computer system with the developing software before it is completed. Find out how dentists describe the elements of their tasks, that is, determine the right jargon. Dentists have their own way of describing treatments, treatment items and item numbers; they are accustomed to describing different types of fillings, crowns, caps, bridges, dentures, and referring to materials used (amalgam, gold, porcelain), and so forth, in their own language. Test the vocabulary you arrive at in independent studies (Ch. 6) to make sure you have established a vocabulary that is common to all, or at least to most, dentists, and to be certain that you have interpreted the meaning of the words you have picked up from reading and observing dental practise in a manner that is consistent with the way dentists are accustomed to speaking.

Translate your observations into system presentation matter. Draw up paper screens (Ch. 4) to construct and present complete task scenarios. Conduct **conceptual walkthroughs** (Ch. 4) using these paper screens and scenarios. Participants in these conceptual walkthroughs should ideally be a sample of dentists and the project team.

SPEECH RECOGNITION: find out which tasks must be given to speech recognition. That is, what tasks are completed in a hands-free mode, for example while wearing sterile rubber gloves. Review speech recognition systems to find the most suitable one; indeed, assess whether speech recognition systems are sufficiently developed to use them in a system such as this, considering also the cost of alternatives. If the cost turns out to be prohibitive and the performance of a speech recognition system is not sufficiently reliable, decide whether to invest in exploring ways to improve these or to consider alternative input modes.

STERILIZING CAPABILITY: find out which components must be sterilizable in the autoclave and review materials you intend to use. Explore the possibility of producing certain elements in sterilizable materials, for example, the casing for the video camera to be inserted in the patient's mouth might need to be removable and made either of throw-away or sterilizable material.

SELECTION MECHANISMS: find out how dentists want to utilise, and inspect, X-rays. What mechanisms should be used, which selection methods would be best, how do dentists want to manipulate the X-rays, how do they want to store them, and so forth.

ICONS: the user needs analysis should tell you if you must allow several areas and sub-areas of the system to be viewed on the screen simultaneously. If so, test different presentation modes. If, for example, you want to design system specific icons, establish a set of rules for the generation of these to ensure consistency (see Fairchild *et al.*, 1989; Lindgaard *et al.*, 1987). Test different alternative sets of icons and perhaps also icons versus words for clarity, comprehensibility and acceptability (Bewley *et al.*, 1990).

EXAMPLE 2: INTEGRATION OF CUSTOMER RECORDS AND BILLING SYSTEM

HEURISTIC EVALUATION of both systems to be integrated to locate trouble spots and shortcomings.

CONFIRMATION STUDIES: after translating the current tasks and transactions completed in the two systems and reviewing the user needs analysis, establish task scenarios and design screens to fulfil these. Test the scenarios on experienced users and verify data handling from screen dumps.

CONCEPTUAL WALKTHROUGHS of new tasks to ensure consistency, availability of help and identification of where users might get stuck.

OBSERVATION OF USERS IN ACTION to define what information should be online that currently is not. For this system, **surveys** are not as relevant as observations and **interviews** with operators.

VOCABULARY used in the present system is highly technical. Translate to English and test on both experienced users, some of whom will be using the new system, and novices, who will need to learn the system in a hurry. Verbal clarity is most important because there is a very high turnover of staff in this area of the organization. Clear, English vocabulary will make it faster and easier for new users to learn tasks and the system.

CHECK TASK SCENARIOS against existing data to ensure that all that is needed is there and that whatever can be done by the system has been considered. If **abbreviations** are used, devise and rely on explicit rules for generating these for consistency, and test them for comprehensibility.

INPUT MECHANISMS: users do not have much work space, so it might be cumbersome or impossible to use a mouse. Test the feasibility of different input tools such as joysticks, track balls, light pens, and so forth. Speech is obviously out of the question, as the operator works while the customer is on the other end of the phone and can hear everything. Consider that evaluations of input tools generally focus on speed of learning to use them and relative speed of input capability (Card *et al.*, 1990; Goodwin, 1975). Your study must take into account the fact that operators will be using the computer system all day every day (see Bewley *et al*, 1990 for relevant details).

GEOGRAPHICAL EXCHANGE BOUNDARIES: exchange boundaries define the geographical areas within which the ranges of telephone numbers belonging to that exchange may be allocated. When customers contact the company to apply for installation of a new telephone, the operator must assign a phone number to that service and submit the number together with the installation details of the customer's name and address to the technician doing the installation. The operator takes a number from the list of currently vacant numbers and, before allocating it, he must make sure that the number belongs to the exchange that covers the customer's address. The address must thus be matched with the correct exchange and the number must be within the range of that exchange. To facilitate this matching, maps should be displayed which show exchange boundaries and number ranges clearly, perhaps super-imposed on an accurate street map. Research could establish the optimal scale of such maps; it could determine the optimal way to query the system either by entering the address or the phone number the operator wants to allocate to the customer, or both. Entering the address could, for example, result in a display of the relevant section of the map with the legal number ranges; entering the phone number could result in the section of the map covered by the range to which the given number belongs, highlighting the exchange boundaries in a colour that differs from areas not covered. In exploring various possible solutions, you would thus be playing with map sizes (e.g. the section on pictorial interfaces in Diaper and Winder, 1987), the amount of detail, colour, shading (Travis, 1991), and with query languages (Maguire, 1990).

Note that issues isolated for research may be continued into the development phase.

7.3 Usability in the development phase

In terms of usability testing, this progresses according to the test and evaluation plan, and also in response to early test findings. If a number of task scenarios were tested earlier in the research phase, they are retested as soon as possible after programming has commenced. Help systems, user manuals, teaching material and tutorials should be developed and tested concurrently with the system. These are described in more detail in Chapter 9. The co-ordination of these various activities is important during the development phase. They are often separated in the sense that manuals may be designed by a different team consisting of technical writers and graphics artists; tutorials may be designed by a team of teachers, and help systems are (unfortunately) often added as an afterthought. This is not very useful and often results in help systems that are either useless or else so unattractive or voluminous that users do not want to use them.

If documentation and other peripherals are designed by other teams, do at least make sure that each aspect of the system which is covered by such other projects is represented at the project review meetings. Testing of all the components must be integrated during the development phase. As screens become available by which realistic user tasks can be partially or completely simulated, try them out in various ways. Heuristic evaluations of each set of such task-related screens aim to test the coherence of these and discover where and how the consistency breaks down (Ch. 5). Doing this will assist in the assessment of where and how real users could get stuck. How well does the help system assist users in trouble to recover from or avoid a tricky situation? How well is each situation described and dealt with in the user documentation? Is it easy to find the information needed in the help system and the documentation respectively? If certain tricky situations cannot be avoided, are they addressed adequately in the teaching materials? Are the problem recovery methods presented by error messages, help information, in the documentation and in tutorials identical? Consistency across different system components is probably the most important aspect of the usability testing program during development, so integrative testing is the central focus at this point.

As soon as it is feasible, trouble-shooting studies should be conducted which span several components. Using the task scenarios, one could, for example, recruit different groups of subjects to complete these in the various media, with one group relying on manuals, hardcopy or online or both, one describing how they would go about doing these tasks using the tutorials, one relying on help, one on the system with as many screens as possible presented on the system itself and the rest shown in paper

'Trouble shooting: where to start?'

form. This will certainly enable the shortcomings to be found in each component and, when rectified, to be tried out in an integrated fashion. A very fine example of such well co-ordinated, integrated testing is given by Gould *et al.* (1987; 1990), on the development of the 1984 Olympic message system.

Summary

This chapter has discussed ways in which usefulness may be assessed and usability evaluation tools may be applied at various points in the systems' design and development phases. Emphasis was given to the feasibility phase because of the crucial issues that should be addressed very early in the process. The feasibility, research and development phases were described in more detail on the basis of two hypothetical systems in an effort to illustrate which usability testing tools could be applied to each of these fictitious systems.

Questions

1. Why should a cost/benefit analysis be carried out during the feasibility study?
2. Why should you study users and the tasks your system aims to support during the feasibility phase?
3. What determines the focus of a feasibility study?
4. What are the steps involved in developing a product concept for a commercial product?
5. What purpose does a business case serve?

6. Why would you choose to design a system from the end users' point of view?
7. Why are time savings made by improvements to a computer system not always relevant to marketing?
8. Why should you investigate other systems available in the field of your proposed system?
9. What decisions are made during the research phase?
10. What do you know at the end of the research phase?

Exercises

1. Assume you were given free hands to design the next generation of ATMs (automatic teller machines). Describe what usability tests could be performed at which stages of systems development and outline the purpose that each test would serve.
2. The hierarchical drugs information system, Pharmanet (Chapter 2) has now been given the go-ahead. List the usability tests that could be applied at various stages of systems development and define what you could gain from each of these.
3. The ticket dispenser prototype mentioned in Chapter 6 is to be fully developed. How could you test usability in the remaining phases of development?
4. You have been asked to redesign an existing system residing in the National Arts Museum in Singapore. The existing system is only three years old, but many treasures have been added to the museum since it was installed which are not mentioned. Touch screen techniques are being used, which will make it difficult to accommodate more information within the present structure, unless such information about the treasures can be fitted into existing categories. At present, menus are presented at four hierarchically arranged levels, and the screen tends to be cluttered with a lot of information. You are free to use taped speech, video and music as well as the touch screen selection mechanism, but speech recognition is not reliable enough to use. The present system allows users to select their preferred language. The budget is almost unlimited in the sense that you can choose whatever platforms you wish, and you are free to perform as much user testing as you want; the only criterion that must be met 100% is usability. Development time is set to two years, but this is flexible. Describe how you are going to tackle the task from a user perspective. How will your investigations proceed? What aspects will you test? Which tests will you apply? When in the development process will you be testing usability?

Suggested further reading

Bewley *et al.* (1990) offer a very interesting example of an actual case study from the early days of usability testing. Their chapter is of interest both as a historical description of usability tests and as a real-life case. It is very readable.

Card *et al.* (1978) give an excellent example of a traditional human factors study using experimental methods for evaluating the relative advantages of different I/O tools.

Gould *et al.* (1990) provide another case study which shows how user-centred design and iterative testing can result in a very usable system which spans multiple languages, cultures and high-usage demands. Their article is both very interesting and readable.

Maguire's (1990) recent report pulls together the literature and expertise associated with designing and using guidelines in graphical user interfaces. It is a nice summary, and is easy to read.

Travis' (1991) book is the most comprehensive and complete book on the topic of colour. The author works through the physics, optics and psychophysics of human vision and applies these theoretical foundations to derive the most effective colour displays. This book is heavy going, quite theoretical and very detailed, but valuable if you are going into details of using colour.

8 Develop a usability test and evaluation plan

> Man can't help hoping, even if he is a
> scientist. He can only hope more
> accurately.
>
> Karl Menninger

A usability test and evaluation plan is a document that specifies the usability goals a given system aims to achieve. The plan outlines in detail how these goals will be pursued, how the project team will assess when the goals and objectives have been attained, and it details the cost and effort deemed necessary to achieve it all. The contents of a test and evaluation plan may be assembled by a specialist human factors testing team, or by the project team which may or may not include human factors experts. At any rate, the details it contains are negotiated and agreed to by the whole project team, and they are approved by the project management as well as by the customer before the project is commenced.

The main purpose of the test and evaluation plan is to ensure that testing is incorporated into the system design and development process, that test results are integrated into the development, and that sufficient resources are allocated to carry out the activities specified in it. In an effort to integrate a program of tests successfully and ensure timely results feeding back into the actual design, the plan must be developed systematically and with a great deal of care. Even though it is impossible to predict exactly what usability defects will be identified or how many iterations of possible solutions will be necessary to reach the usability goals, realistic estimates of resource allocation for testing and evaluating can and must be made. This requires participation of someone with a solid grasp of, and experience in, usability testing, test design, data collection, analysis and interpretation; someone who can also estimate the time and costs associated with conducting various tests, and who can direct and monitor progress in the test schedule. Human factors specialists are trained to do just that, and they should be involved, or at least consulted, in the development and execution of the test program. This person or team would also assume responsibility for designing and co-ordinating the usability tasks, ensuring that the methods by which usability criteria are assessed and put into operation are sound. It is very easy to overlook flaws in the test design, data gathering, analysis or data interpretation, but flaws introduced at any stage can lead to wrong and expensive decisions because the meaning of the the data in some fashion misrepresents reality or may be misread.

The usability test and evaluation plan clarifies and documents what is to be done, how it is to be done, at what stage in the development process, at what cost, and by whom. To do this, usability criteria and goals are quantified and stated in explicit and precise terms. Careful consideration of time and budget constraints, together with a thorough understanding of users and their tasks, as well as their current task environment, is necessary to develop a realistic test plan. Test experts do sometimes get carried away in their efforts to provide perfectly usable systems, because they want to test every possible module, task and aspect of the system before releasing it. In one sense, it is commendable to aspire to perfection. However, the danger in conducting exhaustive test programs is that testers may lose track of the reality that time and money comes in very limited supply. Resources must be used very carefully, although it is difficult to strike a perfect balance between effort, time, cost and benefit to the project of the tests conducted. In order to strike such a balance, it is therefore essential to evaluate the benefits to end users of removing different usability defects. Some defects will not be worth dealing with in

'Planning ahead makes you feel in control of things'

the current version of a software package because the potential benefits from doing so are minor, or they are outweighed by the costs associated with fixing them. Others may require a restructure of some parts of the program which, in turn, could give rise to new usability defects; the removal of very small or very expensive defects would put too much strain on the budgetary and time limits to be justifiable.

A small defect is one that would not be very disruptive to users completing their tasks if it remained in the system; an expensive defect is very time-consuming and labour-intensive for the project team. Removing expensive defects may simply be impossible in the present system life cycle. Instead, a sensible short-term solution could be to apply alternative methods for overcoming and patching up effects of usability defects on user performance. For example, making sure a known defect is flagged in the user documentation and that it is addressed adequately in the help information may provide band-aid treatment that at least forms an acceptable bridge to the future, when the defect is likely to be eliminated. Some software houses would probably prefer not to draw attention to blemishes in their software and therefore choose to ignore defects they are aware of; to us, it would seem more sensible to admit to imperfections by telling users how to overcome them. A list of defects could be placed in the back of the user manual in a place users can easily find, so that major emphasis is still placed on the positive aspects of the system.

Along with estimates of costs and benefits, the impact on user performance of each defect should thus be assessed in order to decide when and how to deal with these. Some kind of 'usability-bug-removal-strategy' or priority scheme must be put in place which is couched in terms of costs (time, effort) versus benefits (impact). Such a priority scheme will be presented in later sections of this chapter.

There is no single 'best' way to go about designing a complete test and evaluation plan. Sometimes, it will suit a given project and project team to start by identifying usability criteria and benchmark tasks; at other times, it will make sense to tackle issues associated with meeting strict time and budget limits first and only then consider which usability goals can realistically be met within these constraints. The issues dealt with in this book, and the sequence in which it is suggested that they be addressed, serve more as a guide for how a test plan might be developed than providing a rigid recipe that must be followed to ensure success. For some projects, it will be appropriate to ignore, or treat lightly, some of the issues presented here. Alternatively, you might find a few of the ideas inspiring for you to develop some of the themes further or add new ones to your own repertoire of project-related skills.

Assuming that a user needs analysis has been conducted by the time a test and evaluation plan is developed, the following should be in hand:

- user profiles of typical primary users and, where necessary, also of secondary and tertiary users (Ch. 2);
- task profiles indicating how tasks are currently completed (Ch. 2); which tasks are to be incorporated into the system and how they are intended to be addressed in the new system, in broad, descriptive terms.

8.1 Integrating results from the user needs analysis into the test and evaluation plan

In reviewing the user needs analysis for the purpose of designing a suite of suitable usability tests for the plan, attention must focus on users and their tasks. The user profiles should give a clear indication of possible choices for hardware/software/I–O tools/dialogue styles, and so on. That is, by knowing enough about the relevant characteristics of the population of primary end users in particular, it should be possible to generate a list of 'acceptable' and 'unacceptable' potential solutions. In terms of hardware, the user profiles may reveal that, for example, 50% of intended end users have poor control of fine motor movements and some 8% are visually handicapped. A system relying on a highly sensitive mouse pointer and tiny icons displayed on the screen would clearly be unacceptable to that particular user population. If a system is being designed for a specialist field in which the bulk of primary users are experts at the tasks to be supported, their specific jargon and conventions should be used as far as possible. By contrast, if a system is being developed for the general public, clear communication is more likely to be achieved by avoiding technical jargon and providing very simple instructions in a step-by-step fashion instead. Such a public system should also be self-explanatory and require no training for occasional users to accomplish clearly identified goals quickly and with a minimum of effort. Where a system is designed for a multi-cultural population, for example, a multilingual user interface could be considered whilst care must also be taken to avoid any suggestion of cultural, racial, political or religious bias or preferences in the information presented. Systems intended to encourage discretionary use should be attractive and inviting, giving the impression that they are easy to use, even if that means adding 'filler' information such as pretty pictures, pleasant music or colourful images which add no information as such, but which have a high aesthetic and entertainment value. Conversely, systems intended for continuous use by experts, as for example in the dental support system (Ch. 7), or Pharmanet (Ch. 2), can afford to be terse and must enable flexible and quick database interrogations.

Knowing for whom one is designing helps to identify those aspects of usability that should be given most attention during the system development. So, the system designed for the visually handicapped should support and maximize user accuracy in comprehending and executing tasks, because user errors are likely to require help. The need to access help, in turn, means that the user must strain his/her eyes to read additional information. In the specialist dental support system, flexibility and speedy task completion are likely to assume a higher degree of importance than making the system particularly easy to learn to use; dentists may be assumed to use it continually, and they want to spend time interacting with the patient rather than with the computer. It is also quite acceptable to expect a training and run-in period in specialist systems, whereas publicly accessible systems really must provide clear and easy-to-follow instructions that users can intrepret without training. Knowledge of the relevant user characteristics as described in user profiles helps to eliminate certain options for system structure, contents, presentation language and interaction styles.

The task analysis plan (Ch. 2) is used to determine which tasks are the most critical for users, which are typical, which ones are most frequently carried out, and to identify those tasks that are likely to be confusing in the new system. Confusion may arise because certain tasks may be presented differently in the new environment and may therefore require users to change well established habits. Some steps within a given task could, for example, be reversed or left out completely. From a usability point of view, it may not be possible to predict how awkward or irritating such changes will prove to be, how long old habits are likely to persist, or whether they are likely to lead to errors which were not observed in the old system. For example, if certain aspects of a task have become automated in the new system, this might unexpectedly cause users to forget to enter details which were never forgotten in the manual procedures in the old system. The effects of changes may thus need to be tested and measured against the benefits conceived to arise from these changes. The user needs analysis comes in very handy when designing the test and evaluation plan because it helps to decide:

- which hardware/software/input/output techniques/dialogue choices can be left out of consideration of possible solutions;
- which other, more viable options could be suggested;
- which 'flags' suggesting usability dimensions should be considered in the usability goal statement;
- generic usability goals; and
- generic list of tasks to be tested during the system development phase, distinguished in terms of critical or potentially confusing tasks which have changed in the new system.

8.2 Developing a test and evaluation plan

This section outlines how a project team may define suitable and measurable usability goals, set usability criteria for the project in the light of the usability dimensions discussed in Chapter 1 (effectiveness, learn-ability, flexibility, attitude). Usability criteria help the project team to decide when a required level of usability has been reached. A suite of very carefully selected tasks may then also be adopted as 'benchmark' tasks. These are the critical tasks by which the overall level of system usability is assessed; performance on these tasks determines when the usability goal(s) has (have) been reached. By specifying benchmark tasks, a start can be made in estimating the costs associated with preparation, conduction and analysis of each. The test and evaluation plan must also indicate when in the development process the various tests should be completed.

'A well-designed plan tells you precisely when you started to run behind schedule'

8.2.1 DEFINE USABILITY GOALS

An overall usability goal states what the project team aims to achieve with the system in broad realistic terms. A usability goal statement is a foundation for a test plan; it helps the design team to focus its efforts by defining what it is aiming for. Goals and priorities should be agreed upon, documented and communicated clearly to all who are in any way associated with a given project right at the beginning of the design and development process. This includes project team, management, customers and users. In order to be effective, usability goals must be concrete, quantifiable, objective and measurable. For example, it is much clearer to say that 'the new system must achieve an overall time saving, taken across all tasks conducted by primary users, of at least 10% compared with the present system' than to state that 'the new system must reduce users' task-completion times substantially'. In this latter statement, no-one knows how much improvement will be considered 'substantial' and by whom. The design team might think that a time saving of 15 seconds on a 130 second task fits the description, whereas the customer might look for a saving of 50% (65 seconds) in the same task. The customer could be unrealistic in his expectations, hoping for the unachievable. The design team could seem to lack ambition by apparently aiming at minute improvements, perhaps in an effort to ensure that they can be absolutely certain to deliver a product which fits its expectations. A saving of 25 seconds could therefore cause the project team to celebrate, and the customer to fume. Instead, when expectations are clarified and stated in precise quantitative terms at the outset, before the project is commenced, everyone knows what requirements the system will meet and targets are open to negotiation and justification.

Negotiations about what is to be improved by how much in a new system must take place very early in the process to ensure that

1. all involved know what must be achieved;
2. all agree with the levels aimed for;
3. the hardware/software platform selected make it possible to achieve the goals within the time and cost limits.

Unrealistic expectations that are dealt with at that point can be adjusted and agreement reached that everyone concerned can accept and live with. Such adjustments are much harder to achieve later, when much of the system is already set 'in concrete', and it is too expensive and time-consuming to modify the software. Also, making it clear beforehand what must be achieved avoids later confrontation. Goal statements saying that a system should be 'easy to learn' or must be 'appealing to users' are clearly unacceptable and must be translated into, or replaced by, quantifiable statements. Customers usually have no idea of how much effort and time may need to be invested to meet their implicit expectations, so they must be told and shown – indeed, encouraging customers to make their expectations explicit helps to reduce these to a level that is realistic and achievable.

Once a global goal has been agreed upon, one can start the more nitty-gritty job of defining which tasks can and should be evaluated in the test plan. Decisions can later be taken as to which ones should be used as benchmark tasks. Thought must be given to the kinds of results one might expect to emerge from every test and task considered for inclusion in the test and evaluation plan. Chapter 6 outlined how the design of an experiment can be adjusted while or before it is pilot tested, to ensure that the findings will be along the lines that make sense and can be applied in the emerging system. The same is true for every other kind of task, test, measurement, iteration or survey – in every instance, the testers must have a reasonably clear idea of the information they can expect to emerge from their tests. Test planning is inextricably linked to data analysis, and interpretation of findings is linked to the statements one can make, as well as to the decisions one can justifiably reach which then feed back into the design process. This is, of course, the crux of the test plan: test results must deliver something useful back into the system development process at the right time. The selection of suitable tasks is therefore of critical importance; unless tests are designed to yield the kinds of results the team is after, they are not worth doing. They may be interesting, or uncover new and fascinating aspects of human behaviour, but unless they yield usable statements that can feed back into, and support decisions to be made in, the further development of the system, they have no place in a usability test and evaluation plan. Naturally, if the purpose of a test is to discover new facets of cognition, different considerations apply, but for a test and evaluation plan guiding the development of a particular computer system, tests must be carefully designed to yield useful feedback to the project team. Feedback need not invariably require changes to be made to the system to be useful. Even a positive statement such as 'no changes are necessary to aspect X, identified by user performance on task Y which met the usability criterion Z' is important feedback.

8.2.2 SELECT CRITICAL, TYPICAL AND POTENTIALLY PROBLEMATIC TASKS

It is normally not possible (nor sensible) to test absolutely every task to be supported by an emerging system throughout the development phase. As stressed before, user performance measured in test tasks must be interpretable in the light of the usability goal or goals. Benchmark tasks must signal the extent to which the project is progressing when measured against the agreed-upon usability goals. Care must therefore be taken in selecting tasks for testing such that they are representative of the range of tasks to be supported and ensuring that critical task demands are met.

The requirement for task representativeness can be met by selecting a suite of typical tasks, or 'user episodes' (Carroll *et al.*, 1991) that cover most aspects of the system, including perhaps, logon/logoff actions and setting or resetting of parameters. Representative typical tasks must be included in a suite of tests. A word processor, for example, should be exposed to users defining formatting styles, opening existing files and establishing new ones as well as editing a number of predetermined features of a document; an e-mail system should enable users to enter and exit the system, to locate and read a message, create and forward a short reply to an individual or a distribution list, and so on.

Critical tasks are those with which a certain level of risk or danger is associated and which therefore must meet very stringent demands on performance from both user and system. Imagine, for example, a train traffic control system in which the barriers on road crossings are not closed with 100% accuracy and perfect timing. Clearly it is not acceptable to risk serious accidents. Similarly, a system which yields information to air traffic controllers about the speed, altitude and direction of approaching aircraft must provide a very clear, accurate and dynamic picture. From a usability point of view, testers must ensure that the information presented on such a screen can be perceived, correctly interpreted and acted upon quickly by the operators. Regardless of which other operator tasks are also supported by the same system, the aircraft identification screen must be absolutely perfect. Decisions which the operator might make after inspecting this screen are, of course, also important, but they are clearly dependent on the initial information being interpreted swiftly and correctly. Unless the initial information is clearly understood on every occasion when the screen is consulted, subsequent decisions based on judgments about the display are likely to be inferior in quality. Operators decide, for example, who is to land on which runway, who will take off next, and who is to cruise around until landing conditions are safe and the relevant runway is cleared. Wrong decisions can obviously lead to terrible disasters. Aircraft identification would thus be a critical task which absolutely must be tested. Critical tasks must assume the highest level of priority in a well designed test and evaluation plan.

The final category of tasks to consider are those that are potentially problematic for users. A heuristic evaluation undertaken of an existing system typically reveals many puzzling system idiosyncrasies that no one had noticed before. One electronic directories system tested in our lab, for example, failed to request user confirmation before carrying out orders issued such as deleting a database entry, and there was no clear indication of how to issue a database search. The ease with which users could delete a database entry was not problematic at all – that was child's play – but the difficulty of recovering a deleted entry, and the annoyance of having to recover entries that were mistakenly deleted would be troublesome. A guess can always be made about the importance each feature might assume for users carrying out typical tasks, but without submitting them to usability tests, one does not know which areas must be fixed here and now and which ones can wait until the next version of the software is planned. In order to test them and support decisions about fixing usability defects, these potentially problematic features are therefore built into task scenarios that represent part of the tests selected for benchmarking.

The list of critical, typical and potentially problematic task features is assembled from the results of the user needs analysis (Ch. 2). Information contained in the user and task profiles should be taken into account and ranked according to its relationship to the usability goal statement when establishing the usability task priority list. Critical tasks belong on top of this list in the category of tasks which must be tested and which must meet the specified level of accuracy and/or speed of task completion. Even with a very meagre test/evaluation budget, the project team must ensure that requirements associated with critical tasks are met. Further down this list comes a selection of 'typical' tasks which may be all inclusive. The trick is to arrange them such that those tasks that can be used to assess how well the system is meeting the demands stated in the usability goal statement, i.e. the benchmark tasks, are placed on top of the typical task list. Tasks which yield no new information in this respect, are placed further down. The final usability task priority list may thus be quite long, containing some redundancies with respect to the information different tasks yield about system usability. There is no reason to avoid redundancy completely; users sometimes do one thing in one context and another in a different task or context. However, funding may not always permit this luxury of testing one issue in several contexts, so, where redundancy exists, this should be flagged.

Once the cost has been calculated of conducting each of the tasks included in the list, judgments can be made on how far the budget allocated to test activities will allow the project team to submit the tasks on the list to testing. The ranking-by-importance allows them to distinguish between the 'must be done', the 'should be done', and the 'budget permitting' tasks; it gives an indication of how priorities should be ranked when designing the task plan.

EXAMPLE: A BASIC ELECTRONIC MAIL SYSTEM (EMS)

Project description:
Your software company has been asked to design an electronic mail system (EMS) for your largest customer who wants an in-house 'bare essentials' system that supports basic elements of a useful EMS. The company is a manufacturer of a wide range (10 000 + different items)

of valves, pistons, rods, tubes, wheels, and many other items used in building hydraulic equipment for the automation of a variety of manufacturing processes. These include food packaging (tins, boxes), electrical household goods, automotive parts, and others. The company has roughly 4000 employees, outlets in 20 countries worldwide, with all its manufacturing activities located in France. All its computing activities (production, ordering, accounting, human resources, etc.) are running on HP 9000 range equipment, and this environment will remain for the time being. Although some of the newer features run in a windows environment, most of the software interfaces with users in the traditional dynamic softkey menu-selection mode, and this is the type of dialogue which all employees know best. Currently, there is no EMS in the company.

At this stage, the EMS is planned to consist of a simple two-level menu hierarchy. At the top level, the user will be able to select one of three main areas, or modes, namely SEND which handles all outgoing messages; RECEIVE which handles all incoming messages, and DIRECTORY which lists all current users and customer addresses. Once a mode has been selected, the user moves one level down to where the 'action' takes place. Selections available at this, the second level, are shown in Fig. 8.1 below. The top row shows the main menu. The second row shows the options available in the SEND mode, the next illustrates options available in the RECEIVE mode, and the bottom row shows options in the DIRECTORY mode.

Note that options are placed such that a given function which might be available in more than one mode is always placed in the same position, that is, it is accessible by pressing the same function key whenever it is available.

Usability goal statement:

EFFECTIVENESS
'Of all users (management, administration, technical, store, sales) 95% must be able to carry out elementary tasks associated with sending and

SEND	RECEIVE	DIRECTORY				
CR/EDIT	POST	SAVE	DELETE	READ	LIST	
		SAVE	DELETE	READ	LIST	
					LIST	FIND

Figure 8.1: The two-level menu hierarchy: main menu (send/receive/directory), secondary menus available within the send, receive and directory modes respectively. (CR/EDIT = CREATE/EDIT.)

receiving messages and locating entries in the directory within one hour on the first occasion when they use the EMS, in their normal work environment.'

LEARNABILITY

'The ability to accomplish the set of test tasks must be based solely on consulting the user manual and help (i.e. without formal training or asking the tester).'

'After using the system once per day for five consecutive working days, the elementary tasks should be completed without reference to the manual, with no more than two errors per test session and by accessing help a maximum of twice. No help is to be given by the tester.'

FLEXIBILITY

Not relevant, as the system is offering very basic and limited features relying on existing principles and techniques, and will be a stand-alone with no electronic links to the other computer systems in the organization. In addition it is designed for a pre-defined reasonably static environment.

ATTITUDE

'On an interval scale ranging from 0 to 100, where the 50 mark is 'neutral', mean ratings across all test users must be within the top quartile (i.e. 76–100%) in a questionnaire seeking users' opinion on:

- likeability of the EMS;
- ease of use (subjective impression);
- their willingness to use it.'

The user profile generated in the user needs analysis for primary users showed that users of the future EMS span the entire range of employees, including management, administrative, sales, technical staff and storemen/women. Apart from the management and administration staff which comprises 20% of all employees, all other staff are occasional users of computing facilities. Their educational level is at roughly final-year school level, and reading ability is relatively low among some of the staff members. User profiles completed for a representative sample of the workers are in hand. The task analysis showed that the EMS needs only to support activities associated with creating/editing outgoing messages, reading/storing/responding to incoming messages, and looking up individuals in an EMS directory. Since orders, invoices and bills are generated, issued and processed in the ordering and accounting modules respectively, it is not intended that the EMS be used for these purposes. Thus it need not interlink with any of the existing computer facilities and modules; the EMS is purely concerned with sending and receiving messages. The only additional feature required is the ability to drop messages, from both the sending and receiving modules, to the fax machine without requiring users first to make a hardcopy of the relevant message. There are no 'critical' tasks in this system, so the tasks listed below include only typical and potentially troublesome ones.

Typical tasks

NO. TASK

NO.	TASK
1.	Logon to EMS
2.	Create a new message
3.	Edit an existing message
4.	Exit from EMS
5.	Delete an existing message
6.	Send/post a message
7.	Read an incoming message
8.	Forward a message
9.	Call up an existing message by its ID
10.	Save an incoming message
11.	List all existing messages sent
12.	Locate a given person in DIR
13.	Scan DIR for a certain country

Potentially troublesome tasks

1. Can the user readily distinguish between outgoing/incoming modes? For instance, 'LIST' exists in all three areas; READ, SAVE, DELETE exist in both outgoing and incoming areas. Does this division cause confusion? That is, does it reduce learnability, effectiveness and positive attitude?

2. Does the fact that the EMS will not provide feedback upon completing a request to 'post' a message create confusion? Feedback was considered by the team and decided to be difficult – since communication is global, the EMS tends to collect messages in batches before forwarding them. Forwarding thus happens at different, unpredictable times. If the user is told that the 'message has been sent', this might not be true and could lower the trust users have in the system when they find out how it actually works. As there is no way they can check the status of a batch currently being collected, it was decided to provide no feedback. To allow interrogation of batch status would be technically cumbersome and thus expensive. However, it is the only area in which no feedback will be provided at least until usability tests convince the project team otherwise; all other system actions result in some kind of feedback to the user, confirming that the relevant action has been completed. Hence, there is a trade-off between system consistency and the need to tell the truth.

Now, the typical tasks are to be ranked in their order of priority.

NO.	TASK	CLASSIFICATION
1.	Logon to EMS	Must be tested
2.	Create a new message	Must be tested
3.	Edit an existing message	Must be tested
4.	Exit from EMS	Must be tested
5.	Delete an existing message	Must be tested

6.	Send/post a message	Should be tested
7.	Read an incoming message	Should be tested
8.	Forward a message	Should be tested
9.	Call up existing message by its ID	Budget permitting
10.	Save an incoming message	Budget permitting
11.	List all existing messages sent	Budget permitting
12.	Locate a given person in DIR	Budget permitting
13.	Scan DIR for a certain country	Budget permitting

8.2.3 IDENTIFY AND SELECT BENCHMARK TASKS

From the list of critical, typical and potentially problematic tasks generated and described above, benchmark tasks can be selected and task scenarios written for each of these. The benchmark task or tasks may comprise several sub-tasks, or it may be a single, comprehensive task, all depending on the nature and size of the system in question. The criteria applied in selecting benchmark tasks must relate to the goal statement, cover critical tasks, and be representative of all tasks to give an indication of overall system usability. Benchmarking is the tool used to gain an impression of the overall level of usability achieved in the emerging system at the time of testing; it is the yardstick which determines when the usability criterion/criteria stated in the goal statement has/have been reached. Task scenarios force designers' attention to the procedural consequences of their decisions (Karat and Bennett, 1991).

Benchmark tasks would nearly always include all the critical tasks where such tasks exist, as well as a range of typical tasks which are representative of the entire system. Selecting benchmark tasks is thus a way of sampling: a subset is taken from a (finite) population of tasks, and usability can be generalized from results obtained in this subset to the population of all tasks in the relevant system. Potentially troublesome tasks should, of course, also be tested, just to make sure that the features they represent do not lower the system usability or – if they do, to attempt getting rid of them and retest them iteratively until they are overcome. However, these types of tasks need not necessarily be explicitly included as independent features in the benchmark task(s).

EXAMPLE: EMS, BENCHMARK TASKS:

Locate and read a mail message (tasks 7, 9)
*Create and send a message (tasks 2, 6)
*Delete an existing message (task 5)
Forward message to distribution list (task 8)
*Enter/logon to EMS (task 1)
*Edit existing messages (task 3)
Find an individual in the directory (task 12)
*Exit from EMS (task 4)

* indicates the 'must be tested' and 'should be tested' tasks identified earlier.

In summary, these are the definitions discussed so far:

- usability goal statement: states precisely, in quantitative terms, the usability criteria which must be met at the time of system release-delivery;
- benchmark tasks: represent an acceptably wide range of tasks to yield an impression of system usability. Used to decide when usability criteria have been met.

8.2.4 TREATMENT OF POTENTIALLY PROBLEMATIC TASKS

As stated earlier potentially troublesome tasks may not need to be explicitly included in the benchmark tasks. However, they must be tested because they can obviously have a significant impact on system usability. Therefore, if they are not explicitly a part of the benchmark tasks, do make sure they are built into the category of tasks that should be tested anyway. To do this, detailed task scenarios should be developed by the test plan development stage. This helps to decide which tasks to submit to which kinds of tests during the development process.

EXAMPLE: EMS, BENCHMARK TASKS:

Locate and read a mail message (tasks 7, 9)
*Create and send a message (tasks 2, 6)
*Delete an existing message (task 5)
Forward message to distribution list (task 8)
*Enter/logon to EMS (task 1)
*Edit existing messages (task 3)
Find an individual in the directory (task 12)
*Exit from EMS (task 4)

(* denotes the 'must be tested' tasks identified earlier)

Overall system goal:
Help to reduce the international communications costs (phone calls, fax and letters) by 20% within 16 months after the EMS has been installed.

Now, the potentially troublesome tasks identified earlier highlighted two problems, namely:

- confusion in distinguishing between two system modes;
- the effect of system inconsistency in providing feedback to the user.

The impact of both of these cannot be stated in the form of an explicit task; instead, impact must be inferred from observations of user behaviour. In order to test for possible confusion between SEND and RECEIVE modes in particular (because these share the most functions), we should thus include at least one, but preferably several, tasks that require users to switch from one area to another. The options as shown in Fig. 8.7 are available:

Therefore, to expose the issue of confusion, we must design tasks that make use of those elements that overlap by being present in two or three modes or areas. SAVE, DELETE and READ are functions common to both SEND and RECEIVE modes, and LIST is common to all three, i.e. SEND, RECEIVE and DIRECTORY. So, we could design a task requiring the subjects to do something to an incoming message, and let this be followed by one that requires an operation which is also possible in the RECEIVE mode but where the task refers to an outgoing message. This sounds complex, so let us use an example couched in a task scenario:

'Your company will no longer be dealing with the FX Manufacture Pty Ltd, since you have ceased production of the specialized casings FX requires. Therefore, remove from the EMS the following items of previous correspondence: Message no. R19 which was sent from FX in Paris on 26 April 1994, and our response to the FX Paris headquarters, S27. Another clerk was instructed yesterday to remove the names and addresses of all the FX representatives which are stored in the EMS. Has this been completed yet? YES /NO (Please circle relevant answer).'

This task comprises three subtasks:

1. delete R19 (in the RECEIVE mode);
2. delete S27 (in the SEND mode);
3. list entries (in the DIRECTORY mode).

Provided this task is given first in the sequence of all the benchmark tasks to be completed, that is, before the subject has been exposed to the EMS and observed how it works, it can be used to test our 'potential troublesome tasks'. If the need to change the mode before issuing the DELETE command does not cause confusion, we could expect the ensuing dialogue to look something like the following:

USER: presses <RECEIVE>
        then <DELETE>
EMS: 'ENTER NUMBER OF MESSAGE TO BE DELETED'
USER: types 'R19'
EMS: 'MESSAGE DELETED'
USER: presses <SEND>
        then <DELETE>
EMS: 'ENTER NUMBER OF MESSAGE TO BE DELETED'
USER: types 'S27'
EMS: 'MESSAGE DELETED'
USER: presses <DIRECTORY>
        then <LIST>
EMS: lists all entries in <DIRECTORY>
END OF TASK!

By contrast, in the next example, the user has not yet realized how the EMS works:

USER: presses <RECEIVE>
           then <DELETE>
EMS: 'ENTER NUMBER OF MESSAGE TO BE DELETED'
USER: types 'R19'
EMS: 'MESSAGE DELETED'
USER: presses <DELETE>
EMS: 'ENTER NUMBER OF MESSAGE TO BE DELETED'
USER: types 'S27'
EMS: 'SORRY, CAN'T FIND MESSAGE S27'

At this point the user has committed an error, because 'S' messages (= outgoing) are stored in the SEND mode, not in the RECEIVE mode.

Now, the user is likely to have detected the rule after this incident, even if it was confusing. However, it is possible that the user has not, in which case the next task should tell us. Let us continue with the confused user who has managed to delete S27 from the SEND area but who has not yet detected the rule. The next part of the task requires the user to list all names in the directory, as the user does not know how many people are working for FX.

USER: (in <SEND> mode) presses <LIST>
EMS: provides a list of outgoing messages stored in the <SEND>mode
USER: presses <LIST> again
EMS: provides a list of outgoing messages stored in the <SEND>mode
USER: presses <DIRECTORY>
           then <LIST>
EMS: lists all entries in <DIRECTORY>
END OF TASK!

Alternatively, if the user has understood the principle and remembers he/she is in SEND, he/she should do the following:

USER: (in <SEND> mode) presses <DIRECTORY>
           then <LIST>
EMS: lists all entries in <DIRECTORY>
END OF TASK!

By including several such mode switches throughout the test session and making sure that all subjects receive the tasks and sub-tasks in the same order to control for EMS experience (Ch. 6), we obtain two different measures which can help us to decide whether or not the mode change issue is confusing. These measures are errors (seeking to obtain information in an incorrect area, i.e. pressing LIST in SEND instead of first moving to DIRECTORY), time and the number of key strokes taken to complete each task. Time is measured in milliseconds as intervals between successive key presses within a given mode, and compared with intervals between successive key presses in different modes. Careful design of the tasks reminds us to ensure that the number of within-mode and between-mode key presses should be identical. These data could be plotted as shown in Figs 8.2–8.5.

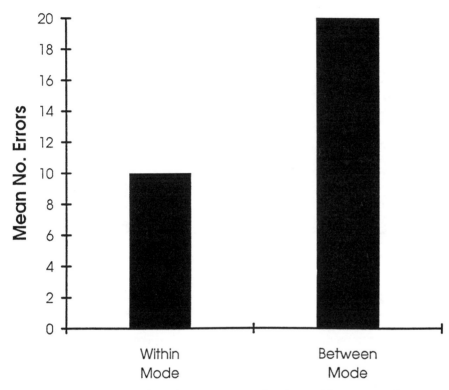

Figure 8.2: Mean number of errors committed within and between modes. Inference: Mode changes are confusing, provided the statistical analysis supports the apparent difference in the two conditions.

First, the error data: Fig. 8.5 shows a plot of time, measured in seconds, of the interval between two successive key presses where one of these occurs just before, and the other just after a mode switch (the between mode condition), compared with key presses that are not associated with mode switches (within mode condition):

Between modes in this example results in longer intervals between two successive key strokes than within-mode in the events occurring early in the test session in events 1–3. By the time they are doing it the fourth time, they seem to have grasped the idea. From this graph we would infer that mode change is confusing, providing the visual inspection of the data is supported by statistical significance in the analysis – if it were not, the graph could resemble that in Fig. 8.5:

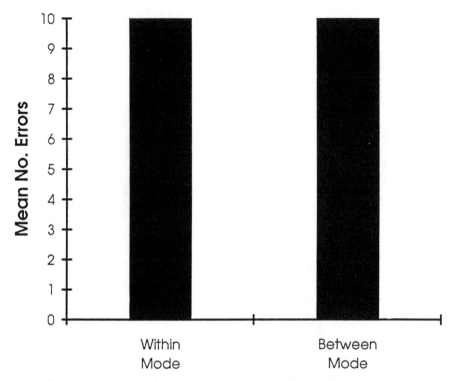

Figure 8.3: Mean number of errors committed within and between modes. Inference: Mode change is not confusing. As the two plots are identical, a statistical analysis is unlikely to yeild a significant difference between the two conditions, even if variation differs substantially between the two distributions.

The two lines are not exactly parallel, but close enough that a statistical analysis would be most unlikely to yield a significant difference between the two kinds of event. We would therefore conclude that the requirement to switch mode was not confusing to subjects.

The second issue raised in the 'potentially problematic' EMS tasks concerned the degree to which a lack of feedback upon users issuing a POST command would be confusing. To test this, several sub-tasks could be included requiring subjects to POST messages at different points in the test session (e.g. beginning, middle, end) to control for EMS experience. Then, the same type of data (errors + some measure of time) could be used to check whether subjects tend to press POST twice or more times when posting a single message. The comparison here would be number of times key presses were repeated unnecessarily versus no repetition (i.e. going straight on to next task).

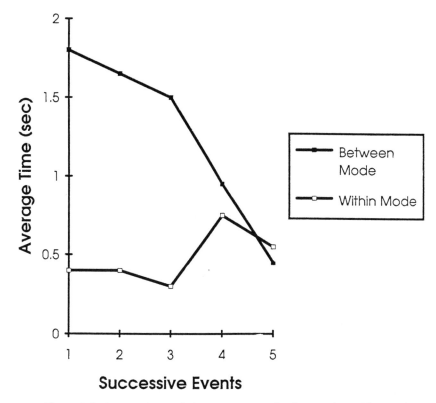

Figure 8.4: Average intervals between successive key strokes within and between modes.

These examples are not exhaustive in terms of the data one could gather, but they make the point that careful design of experimental tasks can yield the information that will tell us whether or not something is confusing or difficult. Note also, that here again, measures of accuracy (errors) and speed (time) are being relied upon.

8.2.5 FIT THE SELECTED TASKS INTO THE DESIGN AND DEVELOPMENT PROCESS

Now that the critical, typical and potentially troublesome tasks have been identified, benchmark tasks determined from the components of the user needs analysis, and a list compiled of typical usability defects, thought must be given to amalgamating this information into some kind of test plan. Chapter 1 identified and described several stages in the design and development process. Chapter 7 discussed which usability testing

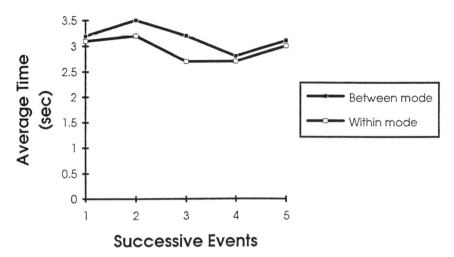

Figure 8.5: Average intervals between successive key strokes within and between modes.

methods might be useful at these various stages. At this point, review that list in order to decide:

1. which tests are most suitable for testing the issues outlined for a given system;
2. when in the design/development process these should be conducted;
3. estimate the time, effort and costs associated with each test procedure.

The usability defect categories identified in the previous section can be useful where there is particular concern about specific issues which should be exposed to testing. Suppose, for example, there is concern about the screen design in a system under consideration or development. Remember the example of aircraft identification presented before in which it was crucial that operators could readily and quickly identify approaching aircraft on the screen. That was one example in which screen design was of extreme importance. While the operators are likely to have an opinion as to how much they like the look of the screen, and while they can comment on how easy it appears to be to use, it is performance that indicates just how effective the screen display is. Usability evaluation of screen design will therefore have to rely on performance measures. It cannot be obtained from interviews or surveys, so these types of tests can both be eliminated from the list of potential usability studies. If one pretends the aircraft identification and decision support system does not yet exist, a heuristic evaluation could not be carried out before at least the prototype stage, so it can be ignored in the early phases of the process. Work your way through the table,

'Hit any key to continue . . . a potentially problematic task?'

deciding for each type of test how or whether it fits into a particular program, and when it would yield the most useful results for the further development of the project. Let us illustrate how such an elimination process might proceed by returning to our EMS example and the sample tasks described earlier:

EXAMPLE: EMS

Task 1 (of 6) designed to cover all the issues of concern in the light of benchmark tasks: Delete R19; delete S27; look up FX members. First, decide on the relevant issues to include from the list of typical usability defects (Ch. 1):

Usability defect of interest in EMS

Navigation	NO: principles are the same as people are used to; only two levels in menu hierarchy
Screen design	NO: softkey menus; no action other than word processing on other areas of the screen
Terminology	NO: same as in postal system; no new concepts introduced
*Feedback	YES: not interview or survey – not knowledge elicitation methods
*Consistency	YES: consider post option; not interview or survey
*Modality	YES: ditto
*Redundancies	YES: identify; ditto
*User control	YES: attitude; not conceptual walkthrough, not laboratory studies
*Task match	YES: generated for current comms habits and postal system

Table 8.1   Types of analyses and where they fit in the design and development process

	Timing of usability study			
	*Fby	Res	Dev	Opn
User needs analysis	Y	Y	N	Y
Protocol analysis	Y	Y	N	Y
Question-asking protocols	Y	Y	N	Y
Repertory grids	Y	Y	N	Y
Multi-dimensional scaling	Y	Y	N	Y
Card sorting	Y	Y	N	Y
Content analysis	Y	Y	N	Y
Heuristic evaluation	Y	N	Y	Y
Contextual inquiry	Y	Y	N	Y
Confirmation studies	Y	Y	N	Y
Cognitive walkthroughs	Y	Y	N	Y
Global usability analysis	N	N	Y	Y
Interviews	Y	Y	N	Y
Surveys	Y	Y	N	Y

*Fby = Feasibility; Res = Research; Dev = Development; Opn = Operation

For the EMS, navigation, screen design and terminology are not of prime concern, but the remaining six issues are. Now, considering the types of tests that are suitable for investigating these issues, we can make the following observations:

Test	Type of usability defect						
	*1	2	3	4	5	6	7
Knowledge elicitation methods	N/A						
Heuristic evaluation	N/A						
Confirmation studies	Y	Y	Y	Y	Y	Y	Y
Interviews	N	N	N	N	N	Y	Y
Surveys	N	N	N	N	N	Y	Y
Contextual inquiries	N	N	N	N	N	Y	Y
Cognitive walkthrough	Y	Y	Y	Y	Y	Y	Y
Global usability analysis	Y	Y	Y	Y	Y	N	N

*1=Terminology;   2=Feedback;   3=Consistency;   4=Modality; 5=Redundancy; 6=User control; 7=Task match

Heuristic evaluation and knowledge elicitation methods are not relevant; the former because no EMS exists as yet in the organization, and the latter because the EMS is very basic in its features and abilities, it is unlikely that a trouble-shooting study other than a global usability analysis will be necessary. This leaves us with a list of three types of tests, apart from interviews and surveys which we will rely on for measurements of attitude. These are conceptual walkthroughs, confirmation studies (experiments and quasi-experiments), and global usability analysis.

Now, since the feasibility phase has been bypassed because the customer actually approached your company, thereby eliminating the need to demonstrate the viability of an EMS in the particular environment, it may be left out of the plan at this stage. The user needs analysis has been completed, so tasks remaining to be done during the research phase include only cognitive walkthroughs. Surveys and interviews will be conducted during prototype and operation once the system is implemented and used, and confirmation studies can be done once conceptual walkthroughs have been completed. Still, as the EMS is very simple, there would appear to be little need for confirmation studies to be carried out at the research phase. These would be more relevant during system development. However, when a prototype is available, a global usability evaluation, confirmation studies and interviews should be carried out.

Tests intended to be carried out in the operation stage are in the 'budget permitting' category. It is the time at which the system is up and running. In this particular project, that is beyond what has been specified within the current framework and represents follow-up studies which are likely to be conducted only if the customer wants to come back for more.

8.2.6 QUANTIFY USABILITY MEASURES IN TIME

At this point, the suite of tasks to be tested has been decided upon, benchmark tasks have been identified, task scenarios have been written to ensure that all aspects of the system that should be tested have, in fact, been included. Decisions have also been made with respect to the types of usability studies that might be conducted, and also the timing, or stage, of software development at which these could yield the most fruitful results to feed back into the further development process. The next job is to quantify the usability measures, so as to estimate the time and resources that will be needed for preparing and running the test program, analysing the results and integrating the findings into the project.

Let us first review very briefly what might be gained from the various types of usability studies before considering when they should be done and who should participate. The discussion here focuses on the EMS, so it should be expanded to include other types of tests suited for your next system.

Chapter 4 showed that conceptual walkthroughs are thinking exercises usually applied to non-existing systems to support certain design decisions. It was claimed that they could help during the research stage, in particular, in determining which of several alternative software/hardware platforms might best suit the user tasks to be supported. During system development, they could be used to talk through tasks in detail to make sure that all information necessary for carrying out the tasks in question is present, clear and unambiguous and that all imaginable situations are considered.

Confirmation studies, also discussed in Chapter 4, are applied to check out the existence and severity of usability defects. They are used to confirm that the usability goals are actually being met, and that defects which might have affected user performance at one point are ironed out and overcome. In this sense, the benchmark tasks constitute confirmation studies every time they are submitted to testing. This does not mean that only benchmark tasks should be included in confirmation studies: any defect detected and addressed through discussions in the project team and/or observation of user performance should be exposed in confirmation studies, even if they are not explicitly a part of the benchmark tasks. Usually, it will not be possible to eliminate all defects because the solution to one problem in one area of the system tends to create problems in another. Where trade-offs have to be made, confirmation studies should serve to evaluate the impact of the decisions in all areas affected by them. This may not be possible during the development phase; if it is not, then assessment of this impact should be made in the global usability analysis.

A global usability analysis is an economical way to allow people with different areas of expertise to inspect and comment on the system. This type of analysis requires at least a prototype, or a fully operational system. By encouraging participants to explore the system fully, trouble spots which were overlooked earlier by the project team and which were therefore not included in the test suite might well be identified.

Interviews and surveys (Ch. 5) are used to assess the attitude towards the system of future potential users. In summary, one can expect to gain the following from the tests:

Cognitive walkthroughs: identify missing steps, information, links, before coding begins and when controversies emerge.

Confirmation studies: confirm that usability defects, perhaps identified in conceptual walkthroughs, exist or, if they have been addressed, that they have been overcome. Confirm that the project is on track and usability goals are being reached.

Interviews/surveys: confirm that all types of users (primary, secondary, tertiary) are satisfied with the product, that its usability is acceptable, and the system provides the outputs users require, in the format they want.

Next, we consider the tasks and measures to be taken in the EMS as well as the resources we will need to run the tests:

EXAMPLE: EMS

Conceptual Walkthroughs:

1. Simple tasks: walkthrough each of the three system areas individually to ensure that:
   (a) necessary information is available to the user to perform every subtask available in each mode;
   (b) access to other, associated systems, e.g. editor, works;
   (c) EMS responses to actions are appropriate, complete and comprehensible;
   (d) this includes error messages, help, confirmation, warning messages.
2. Walkthrough complex tasks that require cross-modal interaction. Create enough tasks so that all links are tested. If time does not permit all tasks to be treated in this fashion, select some at random from the set. Do not merely walkthrough the benchmark tasks, as there is little merit in ensuring that these can be done perfectly without also considering other possible tasks – remember, benchmark tasks are supposed to provide a measure of the overall level of system usability.

Cognitive walkthrough during the research phase:

Ideal case
Simple tasks (N = 13); complex tasks (N = 6)

PREPARATION:
Simple tasks	1	person day
Complex tasks (~ 3 hours per task)	2	person days

CONDUCTING WALKTHROUGHS:
Simple tasks (assume team of 10 people)	5	person days
Complex tasks	10	person days

DOCUMENTING RESULTS, REPORTING OUTCOMES:
Simple tasks	1	person day
Complex tasks (0.5 day per task)	3	person days

SOFTWARE CHANGE DECISIONS BY PROJECT TEAM
Simple tasks	0.25 person days
Complex tasks	0.50 person days

SECRETARIAL SUPPORT
Typing tasks, reports, documentation	1	person day
Total	23.75	person days

This sounds like a lot of time, so let us establish a case for the 'reasonable' and the 'minimum acceptable' set of circumstances as well.

Cognitive walkthrough during the research phase:

Reasonable case
'Reasonable' case (reduction in team size and tasks by 50%)
Simple tasks (N = 7); complex tasks (N = 3)

PREPARATION:
All tasks	1.50 person days

CONDUCTING WALKTHROUGHS:
Simple tasks (assume team of 5 people)	1.25 person days
Complex tasks	2.50 person days

DOCUMENTING RESULTS, REPORTING OUTCOMES:
Simple tasks	0.50 person day
Complex tasks (0.5 day per task)	1.50 person days

SOFTWARE CHANGE DECISIONS BY PROJECT TEAM
Simple and complex tasks	0.50 person days

SECRETARIAL SUPPORT
Typing tasks, reports, documentation	0.50 person day
Total	8.25 person days

Cognitive walkthrough during the research phase:

Minimum acceptable case
Complex tasks (N = 3), evaluated by two people

PREPARATION:
All tasks	0.50 person days

CONDUCTING WALKTHROUGHS:
Complex tasks	0.75 person days

DOCUMENTING RESULTS, REPORTING OUTCOMES:
Complex tasks	1.00 person days

SOFTWARE CHANGE DECISIONS BY PROJECT TEAM
Complex tasks	0.25 person days

SECRETARIAL SUPPORT
Typing tasks, reports, documentation	0.00 person day
Total	2.50 person days

So, total time resources required for conceptual walkthroughs during the research phase would amount to the following person days:

Ideal case	Reasonable case	Minimum acceptable
23.75	8.25	2.50

Assuming we will want to repeat some of this effort during the development phase, we may allocate roughly 50% of the calculated time scale for this. Hence, the total time scale looks something like this:

Walkthroughs	Ideal case	Reasonable case	Minimum acceptable
Research phase	23.75	8.25	2.50
Development phase	12.00	4.25	1.25
Total time allowed	35.75	12.75	3.75

This exercise is repeated for the other kinds of usability studies as well. Basically, one must think through:

- which tests will be conducted;
- when in the process will they be carried out;
- how much time must be allocated to preparations, test sessions, data analysis, reporting, discussing results with the test or project team.

The estimates are unlikely to be entirely accurate to the nearest hour, but they do give an indication of the effort required, and they provide a basis for calculating a reasonable test budget, as well as for determining priorities when adjustments have to be made either in terms of the amount of time, or by replacing certain tests by others along the way as the project matures.

8.2.7 CALCULATE THE TEST/EVALUATION BUDGET

With the figures for usability studies and time resources at hand, it is now a reasonably simple matter to estimate the budget for testing and evaluating the emerging software. Simply review what is to be done at the different stages, translate the resources into actual costs, and the cost side of the plan is complete. Returning to our EMS, we can now say this:

EXAMPLE: EMS
Costs associated with test and evaluation of the EMS.

FEASIBILITY PHASE   (cost of the user needs analysis, i.e. preparing user profiles and task analyses).

RESEARCH PHASE: CONCEPTUAL WALKTHROUGH

	Ideal time (days)	cost ($)	Reasonable time (days)	cost ($)	Min. Acceptable time (days)	cost ($)
Professional ($ 500/day)	21.75	10 875	7.75	3875	2.50	1250
Secretarial ($ 200/day)	2.0	400	0.50	100	0.00	0
Equipment, stationery..		500		400		400
Total ($)		11 775		4375		1650

'Important: sell your test plan and get it signed by the client before you start
usability testing'

DEVELOPMENT PHASE

	Ideal time (days)	cost ($)	Reasonable time (days)	cost ($)	Min. Acceptable time (days)	cost ($)
Professional ($ 500/day)	10.00	5000	3.75	1875	1.25	625
Secretarial ($ 200/day)	2.0	400	0.50	100	0.00	0
Equipment, stationery..		500		400		400
Total ($)		5900		2375		1025

The same procedure is followed for other usability tests intended to be conducted. Calculating costs by considering three different types of situation allows enough flexibility to accommodate any changes to the test and evaluation plan as the project progresses. It allows one to estimate and adjust costs and time resources whilst keeping track of where the money is spent, and how much it would cost if one was to, for example, iterate through another cycle of a particular test.

8.2.8 ESTIMATE THE SEVERITY OF USABILITY DEFECTS

The point of a test and evaluation plan is to ensure that the usability goals and criteria are met with a minimum of effort and at a low cost. Deciding how a system should be tested, what should be done when, by whom, and at what cost fulfils only one part of reaching the usability goals. Since it is not possible to predict exactly how many usability defects will be detected at what stage, or how badly each defect is likely to affect user performance, an index must also be derived for establishing the severity of usability defects. Such an index serves (a) to classify defects, and (b) as a basis for a 'usability defect fixing strategy'.

An explicit strategy is needed because (a) it is unlikely that every problem identified can be solved completely in any one software version, and (b) the impact of trade-offs can be estimated where a solution to one problem may give rise to another. Thinking through the effects of trade-offs one can use the index for assessing the likely effects of alternative solutions. The index presented here takes into account three dimensions of usability defects, namely:

1. the impact on user performance (i.e. how difficult it is for users to continue their task and how long they are likely to spend recovering from it);
2. probability of occurrence (how likely is it that users will encounter the defect?)
3. frequency of occurrence (is it likely that the problem will be encountered only once, very often, sometimes, or hardly ever?).

Each of these variables is given a classification, high, medium, or low as shown in Table 8.2.

These can then be placed in a look-up table which yields the possibilities shown in Table 8.3.

As Table 8.3 shows, each usability defect is given a rating along each of the three dimensions (Table 8.2) which allows us to classify it as critical, high, medium or low in severity. Using such a classification helps

Table 8.2   Dimensions in the usability defect severity index

	Impact	*Probability*	*Frequency*
High	User cannot continue or > 25% of total task-time is spent recovering	All users (100%)	Very often (> 50% of tasks)
Medium	Some impact, user can continue but spends up to 25% of task-time recovering	Some users (up to 50%)	Sometimes/ often (10–49% of tasks)
Low	Users are hardly affected	Hardly any users (<10%)	Hardly ever (0–9% of tasks)

to decide how and when different defects must be dealt with. For example, a team decision might be to remove all 'critical' defects immediately, without further discussion, or all that are labelled 'medium' in which the impact is high (i.e. 5, 7, 8, 9 in Table 8.3), and so on – all depending on time frame, budget, usability criterion, usability goal, and so forth.

8.2.9 DEVELOP A 'USABILITY DEFECT FIXING PRIORITY PLAN'

A usability defect fixing priority plan can be developed through a more detailed impact analysis based on the proportion of total task time users spend recovering from different usability defects. That is, for each task tested in a given usability evaluation session, estimate the percentage of

Example:

Problem	Encountered in task (1–6)	% total task time
1. Help information	1, 2, 4	8.5%
2. Pressing wrong key	3, 6	4.0%
3. Action on feedback	1, 2	2.0%
4. Getting started	1	1.5%
5. Repeating action	1, 2	1.5%
6. Command error	3, 5	1.0%
7. Wrong delete	2, 3, 5	1.0%
8. Create msg error	1, 2	0.5%
Total		20.0%

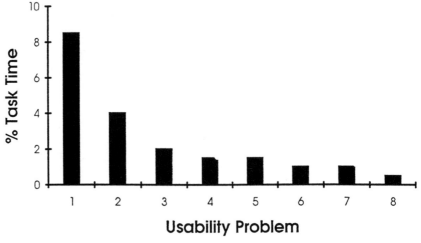

Figure 8.6: Percent of time spent recovering from usability defects in the EMS shown graphically and in tabular form.

time spent coping with and recovering from usability defects, e.g. say the total task-time for six tasks is 80 minutes (= 100%), and the time wasted on recovering from usability defects amounts to 20 minutes (= 25%). The severity index lists every problem encountered in each task; depicted graphically it might look something like the example in Fig. 8.6.

Data presented in this manner makes it easy to see which problems are influencing the test subjects most and from this information, to set realistic usability defect fixing priorities. Replotting the data obtained in different iterations of the test plan, when the software has been modified in response to earlier findings, allows easy comparison of before and after, to see the effect on time wasted on problems of system changes.

Table 8.3 Usability defect index

	Imp*	Prb	Frq	Defect classification
1.	H	H	H	Critical
2.	H	H	M	High
3.	H	H	L	High if early task, otherwise medium
4.	H	M	H	Critical
5.	H	L	L	Medium
6.	H	M	M	High
7.	H	M	L	Medium
8.	H	L	M	Medium
9.	H	L	H	Medium
10.	M	H	H	High
11.	M	M	H	High
12.	M	L	H	Medium
13.	M	H	M	High
14.	M	H	L	Medium if early task, otherwise low
15.	M	M	M	High
16.	M	M	L	Medium
17.	M	L	M	Medium
18.	M	L	L	Low
19.	L	H	L	Medium
20.	L	H	M	Medium
21.	L	H	L	Low
22.	L	M	H	Medium
23.	L	M	M	Medium
24.	L	M	L	Low
25.	L	L	H	Medium
26.	L	L	M	Medium
27.	L	L	L	Low

*Imp = Impact; Prb = Probability; Frq = Frequency

Impact analysis is discussed in more detail by Whiteside *et al.*, (1988). From the impact analysis and the usability defect severity impact index, a table can be generated as shown earlier.

8.2.10 COMPONENTS OF THE USABILITY TEST/EVALUATION PLAN

At this stage, the test plan should contain the following 11 components:

- usability goal statement;
- benchmark tasks;
- task scenarios;
- other tests;
- indication of usability studies to be done;
- timing of tests;
- cost of tests (planned and possible);
- usability defect severity index;
- fixing priority plan;
- impact/benefit analysis;
- noting who takes responsibility for what.

Summary

This chapter has shown one way to develop a comprehensive test and evaluation plan which should serve as a guide to planned usability tests performed throughout the systems development process. First, it discussed how the outcomes of a thorough user needs analysis can assist in deciding what to test when in the process, and selecting the task and user characteristics of most concern in a given system. The notion of usability goals was then introduced and the purpose of these was outlined, followed by a discussion of how to select critical, typical and potentially problematic tasks for inclusion in the task and evaluation plan. The criteria associated with selecting benchmark tasks were outlined briefly, and ways to deal with problematic tasks in the actual test design were highlighted. This was followed by a listing of the most frequently observed types of usability defects, the purpose of which was to support the selection of tasks that touch upon the issues of special concern in a given system. Selected tasks were accommodated within the systems design and development process in order to help the project team decide when in the process different tests ought to be performed. Decisions concerning the timing and the extent of usability tests were then shown to underlie the calculation of the test budget. Three different levels of costs were prepared for each test to give the plan enough flexibility to make details adjustable as usability defects become apparent and additional tests may need to be performed. An index indicating the severity of usability defects was presented.

1. What is the main purpose of a test and evaluation plan?
2. How can human factors specialists help in establishing a test and evaluation plan?
3. What are the components of a test and evaluation plan?
4. Why is it generally undesirable to conduct exhaustive tests on all aspects of a developing system?
5. How does the outcome of a user needs analysis assist in designing a test and evaluation plan?
6. What are benchmark tasks?
7. What is a usability goal, and what does it do?
8. What are the characteristics of usability goals?
9. Why must system goals be stated quantitatively, before a project gets underway?
10. What is the primary criterion for any usability test performed during system development?
11. Which of the three types of tasks usually selected for testing must assume the highest level of priority? Why?
12. How would you rank order tasks in a usability task priority list?
13. What criteria apply to the selection of benchmark tasks?
14. Why is it useful to think through the most typical categories of usability defects before designing usability tests, tasks and studies?
15. Why is it worthwhile to calculate the time/resources/effort necessary for conducting different usability studies/tests/tasks?
16. Why should we calculate the costs associated with different levels of tests (i.e. ideal, reasonable, minimum acceptable cases)?
17. What is the purpose of a usability defect severity index?
18. Why is a usability defect fixing strategy recommended?
19. What are the three dimensions of usability defects?
20. What purpose does an impact analysis serve?

1. In Chapter 7 you were asked to describe all usability tests that could feasibly be performed during different stages of development of the next generation of ATMs (automatic teller machines). Let us now pretend we are taking this development one step further. Using the process outlined in Chapter 7, and your solution to the task in Chapter 6, do the following.
   1. Select an appropriate usability goal statement.
   2. List all user tasks associated with depositing, withdrawing, transferring money from one account to another and making enquiries to one's own accounts.

3. Order these user tasks in terms of critical, typical and potentially problematic ones.
4. Order the tasks in 'must be tested', 'should be tested' and 'budget permitting' categories.
5. Select suitable benchmark tasks, remembering that these should ideally cover the range of typical tasks as well as including the critical tasks (if any).
6. Select from your list of possible usability studies those that will yield the most information with respect to developing the ATM (maximum of three different types).
7. Determine when in the systems design and development process the studies/tests are to be performed.
8. Calculate a usability test budget including at least two extreme costs ('ideal' and 'minimum acceptable').

2. Your project team has just completed a heuristic evaluation, followed by a confirmation study, of a library reference system. All of the usability defects revealed were shown in the confirmation study to cause problems for most users. On average, the time spent recovering from terminology problems amounted to 2.5%, navigation problems to 2.9%, user control problems to 5.1%, and screen design problems to 6.2% of the overall task-completion time. The time frame and budget constraints are such that you cannot possibly fix all of these. Describe how you would establish a usability defect fixing priority plan. Explain which problems would go on top of the plan and discuss why.

Suggested further reading

Eason and Harker (1991) examine the role human factors could play in system design processes. They review design processes and discuss a range of possible contributions human factors specialists could make to it. They show that many different types of contribution are necessary for human factors to be of real value to design, and that these professionals also need to encourage many changes to existing design processes. Their chapter is easy to read.

The short paper by Edmonds (1987) reviews current principles of software design and uses this as a basis for a proposal for defining 'good software design'. He argues in favour of an 'architectural totality' which incorporates the expertise of people from different disciplines into systems design and shows how reliance on engineering skills alone does not lead to successful systems. This paper is short and readable.

Whiteside *et al.* (1988) summarize much of their long experience in practical systems design and development. They describe various usability engineering techniques and show how these have been used in several situations, including ongoing work. They present an analysis of their methods which highlights the shortcomings of these, and which also forms the basis for extending these. The article gives plenty of scope to consider how the authors' experiences may be adapted to the reader's own environment and constraints. Their article is very easy to read.

9 Help, user documentation and tutoring systems

Perseverance is not a long race; it is
many short races one after another.
Walter Elliott

This chapter introduces various types of user support materials which commonly accompany software packages sold in the market place. In particular, help systems, hardcopy user documentation and tutoring systems are discussed in some detail. The chapter serves two purposes: one is to demonstrate the applicability to user support systems of the usability testing tools and techniques introduced earlier, and the other is to outline the purposes these materials serve, might serve, or should serve in the production of well-rounded software packages. In particular, examples show that the value of iterative testing methods is highlighted in help systems and user documentation. The aims of user support systems in general are slightly different from those of other systems; in all kinds of user support, the importance of effectiveness is paramount for determining the value of the system. For example, a help system that fails to assist users in trouble is useless as a form of user support. Similarly, user documentation in which the information users needs cannot readily be located, correctly interpreted or easily applied to a given situation will prove extremely unpopular. Finally, a tutoring system that does not enable users to learn and transfer the product of learning into the environment the system is supposed to prepare the learner for, is not at all effective.

In the discussion of user support material, it is argued that user support is valuable to the extent that it is useful. Naturally, a prerequisite for material to be useful is that it should be usable, but in user support systems, both aspects must be tested. Whereas in other systems, usefulness is assessed by the degree to which it meets the criteria defined and detailed in the user needs analysis, a user support system is effective only when its contents can be applied in another context. That is, information presented in a hardcopy manual, a help system or a tutorial is applied to solve particular problems the user is experiencing. Designing such support systems and getting them right is thus a very special challenge to systems design. This chapter cannot guarantee that your next user support system will be perfect, but it does at least give some hints of what to aim for, what to avoid, and how one might assess the degree to which it can fulfil its intended purpose.

When interacting with a computer system, users encounter problems sooner or later from which they cannot recover without assistance. The very name 'help system' suggests that one of its main objectives is to assist users in trouble. In order to achieve this effectively, the help system designer would need to understand when, how and why users stumble or get stuck during an interactive session. Usability defects may sometimes be inferred from hesitations or longer periods of inactivity, suggesting that the user is uncertain about what to do next. Such defects may, but need not, lead to errors, where errors are defined as incorrect entries or wrong moves made when completing a given task; they reflect user needs in the sense that the information the user requires, when encountering a particular problem or committing a certain error, is not available.

Problems often arise because of a mismatch between the system rules and users' expectations of how the system should work; the reasons underlying such mismatches constitute one type of system weakness. The level of success of help may be measured by the degree to which users consulting help recover effectively from the error or problem encountered. The more accurately user problems have been correctly identified, captured and addressed by the help information, the more successful and hence effective the help facility should be. The objective of a good help system is thus to supply information that users are 'missing' because their model of the system is at variance with the actual system model. The help system is able to meet users' needs by addressing the problems and errors likely to occur in such a way that help information leads to immediate recovery from these.

However, although it is widely agreed that assistance in user problems/error recovery is the most important purpose of help facilities (Alford *et al.*, 1985; Norcio and Stanley, 1989; Ridgway, 1987; Steinhaus and Hammer, 1985; Whittle, 1987), it is not the only possible purpose of help information. Users may, on occasion, seek help for reasons other than requiring solutions to immediate problems. Along these lines, it has been argued that help systems should constitute 'online documentation and tutoring' (Lee, 1987, p. 429), or they could represent a 'dictionary of information about system commands and functions' (Cohill and Williges, 1985, p. 336) which serves both as a memory jog and as an information source to users.

Help systems may well provide information which is also presented in user documentation or tutorials as well as offering dictionaries of system-specific commands and terms. Unfortunately, there are no hard and fast rules for how help systems should be structured, what should go into them, how much information is optimal for which systems, or indeed how information may best be presented in different types of help systems. Nor is it clear how information to be given to users should ideally be divided between help, tutorials, instruction manuals, reference manuals, and whatever documentation may be produced for users. This book does

9.1 Designing useful help systems

'Better no help than a help system that doesn't help'

not aim to solve these problems either; rather its purpose is to highlight trouble-shooting techniques and point to suitable usability testing tools. How optimal help systems should be designed or structured will not be discussed further. Suffice it to say that the usability of help systems is at least related to the degree to which users can readily recover from problems they encounter during an interactive session with a computer system. Help system usefulness is reflected by the extent to which system trouble spots are addressed.

Help systems often fail to fulfil their purpose of assisting users in trouble. Reasons known to account for the failure of help systems to assist users fall roughly into three categories, namely:

1. problems with access to help information and/or exit methods;
2. problems with the actual information provided;

3. difficulties of users to recognize their problem. These are addressed next.

9.1.1 BARRIERS TO EASY ACCESS OF HELP INFORMATION

Navigation through menus
Many help systems are arranged hierarchically, often relying on several layers of menus. Even when users can rely on recognition of terms used elsewhere in the system and select options from menus rather than having to recall commands from memory, they do experience difficulties navigating through such systems (Lindgaard, 1988; Snowberry *et al.*, 1985; Tombaugh and McEwen, 1982). Users tend to forget where in the menu hierarchy they currently are, where they are going and where they came from (Fitter, 1979; Palmer *et al.*, 1988), unless they are provided with cues specifically yielding such information.

In particular, users have been found to lose their way in the top layers of menu hierarchies (Lee *et al.*, 1986; Schwartz and Norman, 1986; Weerdmeester *et al.*, 1985) because the labels describing available options are ambiguously worded (Schwartz and Norman, 1986). One problem with wording menu options is that the full complexity of the system and the information it contains must be expressed in a handful of options; these must be described in sufficiently general terms to encompass everything stored in the entire hierarchy, whilst also being sufficiently specific to suggest clearly what information might be stored at the lower levels along a given path. Two methods may be applied for overcoming navigational user problems: one is to reduce the menu hierarchy to as few levels as possible, perhaps even to a single menu layer providing a large number of options, and the other is to show which options will be coming up at the next level of the menu hierarchy (Snowberry *et al.*, 1985). Increases in menu breadth (many items presented in few menu layers) over depth (few items and many selections/layers) have been shown experimentally to improve performance and reduce error rates (Dray *et al.*, 1981; Seppala and Salvendy, 1985; Snowberry *et al.*, 1983). An effort should therefore be made to design a hierarchical menu structure which is 'broad' rather than 'deep'. Navigational problems occurring in menu hierarchies make it difficult for users to access information stored in help systems.

Although items in a help menu may clearly suggest where particular items of information are likely to be stored, the user needs to understand the nature of the problem he is trying to solve for that information to be useful. The user needs to have a reasonable level of knowledge about the system's functions and capabilities as well as of the potential sources of the current problem. Novices rarely know much about the particular system nor, in many instances, about computers in general. Help information provided in menus does therefore not necessarily help the new user to solve a current problem. Usability testing must be performed even if an 'intuitively obvious' menu structure is designed to accommodate relevant help information.

In addition to sheer navigational problems, it is also likely that the user forgets the question he had in mind when first accessing the help system; the size and scope of a comprehensive help system containing information necessary to recover from all possible user errors may thus be daunting for the user and serve to distract and confuse, rather than to clarify or solve his problem (Steinhaus and Hammer, 1985). The existence of navigational and associated problems suggests that help systems should be reasonably small and compact to be effective.

Commands

In many systems, access to help information is provided by user-issued commands. In order to obtain the right information, the user must know what terms are allowed, what the allowed terms refer to and what information he needs to solve a given problem, access certain data, or recover from a particular error. For users new to a given system, it is unreasonable to expect familiarity with a system's commands. Indeed, it is feasible to argue that the user who knows the name of a command is also likely to know what it does. Even when the full range of commands is presented on a list of keywords, this is likely to be useful for experts only, who already know what these commands do. In order to make keyword lists effective for new users as well, an explanation of the function associated with each command should be provided.

Computer-imposed help

An alternative way to provide access to help information is by letting the system determine when help is needed and then spoon-feed the user. This is not a favoured method, partly because it has been found to be less effective than user-initiated help (Cohill, 1981), and partly because users prefer to be, or at least to feel that they are, 'in control' of the system (Fitter, 1979; Lee et al., 1986; Nickerson, 1981). Generally, therefore, people do not like something that is imposed on them because they have no control, they would be unlikely to read such information which would reduce the effectiveness of help considerably.

Access methods are important for help system success, but it is even more important to ensure that whatever method is chosen is usable. Merely providing information in menus, via lists of keywords, or explanations of how the system works is not enough; one cannot assume that help is therefore effective. No access method eliminates the need for usability testing!

'Automatic help may just turn the user off'

9.1.2 PROBLEMS WITH HELP INFORMATION

Problems with help information have been found to relate to the amount of information provided, the way it is presented, or the vocabulary used.

Problems with the amount of information presented

Help systems are frequently perceived to provide too much information for users to make sense of (Hayes and Szekely, 1983; O'Malley, 1986). Gaines and Shaw (1984) put this point rather colourfully by stating that 'if the user is a little unsure, asks for help, and then has to wait for two minutes while material pours out at his terminal, he will not use the help facility again' (p. 72). Users 'prefer concise and direct instructions' (Houghton, 1984, p. 129). However, clear instructions are unlikely to assist in the problem recovery process unless help system designers can be reasonably certain that the instructions provided actually address users' current problems.

Guidelines have been formulated recommending that certain specified amounts of help information be presented. Unfortunately, several of these guidelines conflict with one another in their recommendations, probably because the empirical basis from which they ought to arise is weak or non-existent. Whereas Steinhaus and Hammer (1985), for example, suggest that 'help system presentation should be short enough that the entire presentation is simultaneously visible on whatever technology is being used' (p. 378), Burke and Wright (1986) suggest that 'users prefer an average of three screens in scrollable help text' (p. 46). By contrast, Ridgway (1987) claims, on the basis of a survey of technical writers, that respondents wanted help to be a 'quick reference, explaining the field that the user was working on' and to be a 'window so that their task context was still present while they were looking at help' (p. 88). However, one could equally argue that the length of any help text must be a function of the complexity and number of problems it addresses rather than adhering to a fixed amount of information. Until more is known about help system usage, guidelines cannot do much to assist help systems designers determine what constitutes an optimal amount of information.

Problems with the help vocabulary

Difficulties in selecting vocabulary that is meaningful to all users is by no means exclusive to words used in help systems. Entering a 'wrong' command in a data retrieval system will result in a 'miss'; misinterpretation of the meaning of options presented in a menu may lead users down an unwanted track; labels presented in a data entry form that fail to convey what information is required may lead to frustration. Vocabulary that fails to reflect its intended meaning to the user cannot be of much help. Unfortunately, it is not always clear how, why, where or when ambiguities arise that will adversely affect user performance.

The issue of naming system functions has received a reasonable amount of attention in the literature, but findings are either unclear or contradictory. It seems reasonable to argue that words with which users are already familiar are more likely to be understood correctly in a system context than unfamiliar, technical jargon. By the same token, uncommon terms tend to be more precise and concise than more common words describing system functions. To the extent that the volume of help information is problematic, it would seem sensible to reduce the verbosity generally associated with commonly occurring terms. Unfortunately, studies in this area cannot really assist in selecting suitable vocabulary for help systems because findings are controversial and/or unclear. Some have found that technical jargon led to better performance than common words (Scapin, 1981; Small, 1983); some have been completely equivocal, finding no performance difference between technical and common terminology (Black and Moran, 1982), and others have found generic words better than technical ones (Landauer et al., 1983). Furthermore, there is little agreement in the literature on what to call things (Furnas et al., 1983) and so, the best method for ensuring the suitability of whatever vocabulary is selected for a given system is by testing it.

Problems with the way information is presented
Nickerson (1981) has suggested that one of the main reasons people dislike computers is the lack of consistency both within and between systems. A lack of consistency may adversely affect learnability and satisfaction. Non-explicit and often not obvious rules underlying system procedures and operations make life difficult in this respect (Kellogg, 1987; Maas *et al.*, 1987).

9.1.3 DIFFICULTIES OF USERS TO RECOGNIZE THEIR CURRENT PROBLEM

Users sometimes find it difficult to recognize the nature of their current problem. People are, according to Aaronson and Carroll (1987) 'very situational. They find help information useless if they cannot immediately see how that information can solve their current problem' (p. 393). This is consistent with Houghton's (1984) claim that help information should be brief. In a similar fashion, one study that focused on 'advice following' by users found that 87% of all requests were for prescriptive advice in a graphics environment (Hill, 1989). The more precisely potential user problems are identified and the more explicitly these are addressed in help systems, the more users should be able to concentrate on applying the solutions presented instead of struggling to identify their problem first.

9.1.4 WHAT MAKES A GOOD HELP SYSTEM?

All of the issues outlined so far should be considered when designing a help system and, in particular, when testing help system usability. In order to assist the planning of a help system, the literature on this topic can be summarized by forwarding a generic 'help system agenda'. From our present understanding of help and the purposes help systems ought to serve, this should:

- be small and compact, presenting a minimum of information;
- give brief instructions;
- consist of as few levels as possible if hierarchical menus are being used;
- provide a list of keywords/commands;
- assist users solving specific problems;
- clearly indicate different system modes, for example, by applying screen identifications;
- present carefully selected vocabulary, ideally tested prior to usage;
- use consistent screen design.

Now then, it is time to put words into action. The development of a help system will be traced through a series of iterations starting with a heuristic evaluation and ending when the help system specifications are handed to the programmers for coding. The crux of the method described here is to show that the help system can be developed and tested iteratively before coding is commenced.

9.1.5 HELP SYSTEM DESIGN STAGE 1:

Trouble-shooting the main system
Assuming that a system already exists for which help is to be appended later, trouble-shooting begins by investigating where, under what circumstances, and why users get stuck during interactive sessions. It is most informative to observe users in action, especially those who are new to the system. They have not yet learned ways to circumvent system trouble spots and areas and so tasks which give rise to user hesitations or errors are relatively easy to identify. If only experienced users were tested, it would be much more difficult to detect the same trouble spots. Experience helps people to develop strategies for overcoming problems so effectively that, even if they are interviewed and asked to assist in identifying trouble spots, they are unlikely to know that problems exist. Ask, for example, an experienced UNIX user about its usability; he/she will no doubt praise it in high tones, noting its efficiency, flexibility and built-in 'intuition'. Yet, there is absolutely nothing 'intuitive' about UNIX or any other computer system; people do not naturally sit tied to computers, and nor is there anything obvious about hitting keys on a keyboard, or about selecting strangely labelled actions by moving an electronic object over a desktop. People do not find it natural at first to press buttons, or easy to interpret the meaning of symbols which, without verbal labels describing them, would be totally cryptic and obscure. But, things with which we become familiar give that warm glowing feeling that signals 'home territory'. When we first learn a new skill using unfamiliar equipment, learning is hard work, frustrating and difficult.

Interview users to identify potential trouble spots, perhaps in a contextual inquiry. In the system used as an example in this chapter interviews clearly revealed that users were invariably seeking to confirm the question, or hypothesis, they had in mind when interrogating the database. This, in itself, is no new discovery; it has long been recognized that human judgments tend to suffer from a 'confirmation bias' which was discussed earlier. However, the rediscovery of this phenomenon was important in the system investigated here, because, as it turned out, users actually expected to be unable to locate target database entries. The database was primarily used to locate the whereabouts of persons who were believed to have vanished deliberately, leaving behind unpaid bills.

Unsuccessful attempts to locate database entries thus confirmed that the target had indeed vanished, rather than leading the user to question the effectiveness of the search algorithm. In some instances, the information requested actually did exist in the database, but it was not located, because searches were abandoned after a single unsuccessful trial. The user's conclusion that a particular entry did not exist in the database was therefore incorrect in a number of cases.

If no host system exists when help is first designed, conceptual walkthroughs mainly enable the project team to identify areas and tasks which are likely to be sites for potential questions or ambiguities in interactive sessions. Much as a project team endeavours to overcome these in the design stage, there will always be some weak spots left that cannot easily be rectified, perhaps because all solutions considered give rise to other questions and ambiguities, none of which might be absolutely trouble free. It is also generally the case that even the most explicit and clear system rules may appear to conflict under certain circumstances which cannot be totally avoided given the very tasks the system supports.

The example used in this chapter to illustrate the value of system trouble-shooting is the EWP (electronic white pages) referred to earlier (Ch. 4). First, let us remind ourselves of how the EWP screen looks (see Fig. 9.1 below).

Outcomes of the heuristic evaluations were summarized in Chapter 4. They were said to fall into two major categories: name field and geographical area problems. These problems were exposed in two subsequent confirmation studies. The results from these experiments

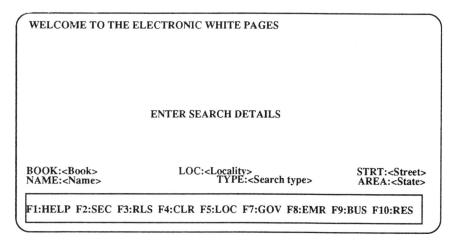

WELCOME TO THE ELECTRONIC WHITE PAGES

ENTER SEARCH DETAILS

BOOK:<Book>   LOC:<Locality>   STRT:<Street>
NAME:<Name>   TYPE:<Search type>   AREA:<State>

F1:HELP F2:SEC F3:RLS F4:CLR F5:LOC F7:GOV F8:EMR F9:BUS F10:RES

Figure 9.1: The EWP screen.

showed clearly that the trouble spots did constitute usability defects, and the list of problems detected in the heuristic evaluation appeared to be complete. This list of specific problems then formed the basis for the information to be presented in the help system.

9.1.6 DESIGNING AND TESTING THE FIRST-CUT HELP SYSTEM

Once a reasonably clear idea has been formed of the types of problems that exist in the system, and one knows where these occur, the next task is to design a help system. In addition to understanding what information needs to go into help, decisions must also be made about the way help is to be accessed, navigated and interrogated. Naturally, it is best to stick with the same system philosophy in help as in the overall system, so that all parts fit and obviously belong together, and so that correct actions, selection and search methods in one part are also correct in another. Some types of information are worthwhile repeating in all areas of help where it is relevant, rather than presenting it once and then designing elaborate interrogation and navigation techniques for the user to get to the information. Fancy techniques may well be designed to enable the user to move swiftly around in help, but lots of movement between different help areas, trying to piece different bits of information together to a coherent and comprehensible solution to a problem, is likely to be confusing. The last thing required of a help system is that it should confuse system users. Besides, some additional text does not eat up a great deal of memory anyway, so redundancy is often more effective than attempts to keep information at a minimum by avoiding repetition. Returning to the EWP example, the following outlines the design of the initial help system.

EXAMPLE: FIRST-CUT EWP HELP
Knowledge of the user problems identified in the heuristic evaluation and confirmed in the previous experiment formed the basis for information to be provided in the help system. It was decided to provide a context-sensitive as well as a browsing help facility. These were first produced on cards with one 'screen' per card. Context-sensitivity was achieved by relating information to the field in which the cursor was located at the time help was sought. The context-sensitive information provided was thus specific to that field. Context-sensitive help was presented on one to three screens depending on the amount of information relevant to that particular field. The first help screen shown was always superimposed on the EWP screen, covering only a small part of this to signal the mode change to subjects and to ensure that they wre not worried about losing the original information when activating help. Such a superimposed help screen is shown in Fig. 9.2 below.
  The browsing part of the help system contained general information about the EWP, information about how to conduct a search, about

F-key functions, the rules pertaining to the various fields and a glossary of the meaning of terms used in the EWP. These various areas were presented in a menu accessible from anywhere within help. At the bottom of every help screen, options available from the current screen were listed together with instructions for how to implement these. Subjects could, for example, exit help, go to the next and/or previous help screen as appropriate or go to the help menu. Help screens were presented on cards because it allowed modifications to be tested before the system was implemented. Each help screen was designed in a 25 × 80 screen format allowing direct transfer from paper to computer once the usability criteria had been reached. Each screen was mounted on a white laminated card, 20cm × 12 cm.

The help system was tested in a quasi-experiment which was an exact replication of the system tasks applied in the confirmation study, except that subjects were free verbally to request help. Upon such a request, the experimenter handed the subject the help screen that would have been shown if help had been implemented. As shown in Fig. 9.2, the subject could then choose the next screen, the help menu, or exit help. Subjects only ever saw one screen at a time, as each was handed back to the experimenter when a new screen was requested or when help was exited in an effort to simulate an online help system as closely as possible. This method yielded findings which gave a clear picture of help system usage. The experimenter's knowledge of the EWP allowed him/her to evaluate (1) whether or not the information subjects needed at any time was provided in help, and when found, (2) the ease of its applicability to the problem at hand. In addition, by considering the problems users encountered, it was also possible to quantify (3) the number of times subjects did not understand the nature of the problem experienced, and

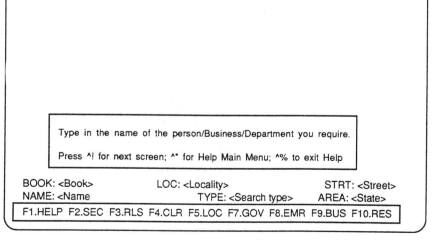

Figure 9.2: Context-sensitive EWP help screen.

the extent to which (4) subjects tended to look for information in areas other than where the experimenter had put it. Hence, the observations gave an indication of the goodness of fit between the experimenter and the user's mental model of the EWP and of help along four measurable dimensions.

Results

The results showed that the number of targets successfully retrieved increased somewhat relative to the no-help experiment, but did not improve significantly. Overall, the help system was accessed relatively infrequently, and subjects read three to four screens on average, every time they accessed help. Help led to immediate recovery in only approximately 35% of cases; ideally, this recovery rate should have been closer to 100%. The most frequent reason for the failure of help to assist users in trouble appeared to be connected with the descriptive nature of instructions alluding to the underlying EWP rules rather than providing explicit statements encouraging subjects to 'do X'. The decision to allude to system rules was made in an effort to assist users gain an understanding of the way the EWP works, and also because the help system was designed to cover a wider range of problems not necessarily associated with the particular targets included in the experiment.

9.1.7 PERFORMANCE VERSUS USABILITY GOALS

The usability criterion for effectiveness required at least 90% of all targets presented in the experiment to be retrieved successfully. This was not reached in the first version of help. Using paper screens, however, made it quick and easy to change them and retest the modified screens. In order to compare user performance directly between iterations, the same experimental tasks should be used so that, apart from recruiting a new sample of subjects for each iteration, the only difference between successive experiments is the modifications to the help system. When selecting suitable user tasks, one must therefore think about how performance improvements may be reflected and how these relate to the usability criterion. When this connection between user problems, tasks, performance measures and usability criterion is made explicit, it is easy to assess precisely when the user problems have been overcome and the help system is good enough. If different user tasks were employed in each new version of help, one would never be certain that the problems had really been overcome because it would be almost impossible to compare performance across different tests. The results obtained in one experiment generally suggest what modifications should be made in the next version.

EXAMPLE: MODIFIED HELP

Findings from the above mentioned experiment prompted three modifications to be made to the help system. One was to eliminate the context-sensitive help facility because subjects were found invariably to go from the first help screen directly to the help menu rather than to explore the contents of context-sensitive help. The second modification was to add information to the glossary about the areas in help in which each of the terms explained applied, i.e. making it more like an index in this sense. Most of the terms were used in several help system areas. Finally, a trouble-shooting menu item was added in which all the major usability defects were summarized, and remedies for overcoming these were provided in point form through brief statements encouraging subjects to take certain actions. This menu option was labelled 'what to do when things go wrong' to signal its trouble-shooting purpose.

The modified help system was then tested on a new sample of subjects but using the same tasks as before. The help system was again presented on cards, with one card serving as a single screen. Results showed that performance improved significantly insofar as most of the targets were retrieved and the usability criterion of 90% correct retrievals was easily reached, as shown in Fig. 9.3.

Help was accessed considerably more often than before. Help system usage reflected the degree of difficulty associated with retrieving entries from the various database sections accurately. Subjects invariably looked for information in the trouble-shooting menu option first.

All in all, the modified help system led to substantial improvements in retrieval performance although the average number of screens accessed each time help was sought was lower than in the previous (Help 1) experiment. This is interesting because the usability defects addressed were precisely the same as before; the one factor that triggered this improvement was the provision of brief statements in the trouble-shooting menu option. Apparently, the information was more readily applied by subjects when presented in short, easily accessible sentences in a clearly labelled menu option. Because the usability criterion had been reached, the help system specifications were given to the implementation team for coding.

In essence, iterations can continue until the usability goal has been reached. Sometimes it takes more than two tests; here we were lucky and the system was small – this is far from always the case.

9.2 User documentation

User documentation covers a broad range of support material including hardcopy user guides, reference manuals, quick reference guides, tutorials and other training material. User support material presented online, such as help systems, error messages and even system prompts are also regarded as user documentation (Horton, 1990).

Much user documentation is under-used or not read at all by the people for whom it was constructed; if people read anything at all, they

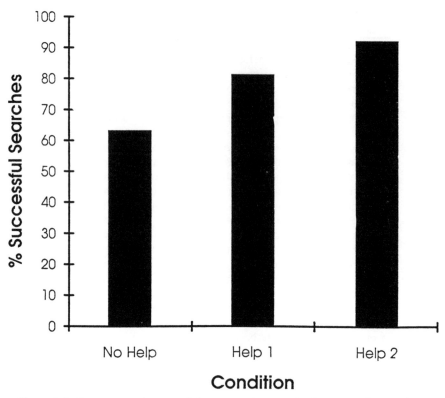

Figure 9.3: Percentage of successfully retrieved targets in the 'No Help', 'Help 1' and 'Help 2' versions.

seem to read only what they absolutely must to get by; they turn to manuals only as a last resort. For that reason, some researchers have recommended that the amount of printed documentation should be reduced (Carroll and Rosson, 1987), or they have created an artificially safe environment (Carroll and Carrithers, 1984). At the same time as user documentation is under-used, it has also been found to be one of the most important factors influencing people to buy a product (Jereb, 1986). Furthermore, when the documentation is considered poor, the software is also likely to be rated difficult to use (Bethke, 1983). This suggests that user documentation serves at least two purposes:

1. it provides users with system instructions;
2. it is an important marketing tool.

The current philosophy in documentation research and design is that user documentation should be produced in parallel with the system it will accompany (Baker, 1988; Brockman, 1990; Wright, 1991). Usability testing of documentation should therefore be built into the overall usability test and evaluation plan (Ch. 8) associated with the development of any given system. According to Wright (1991), there are four clusters of factors which, together, determine the success of user documentation and which should therefore be incorporated into the test and evaluation plan. One comprises organizational factors such as management decisions about who does the writing and the frequency and nature of contact between writers and product developers. Another cluster concerns the time scale within which documentation has to be written and tested. There is a tendency to leave production of documentation until last, which reduces the time available for revision and iterative testing. This is obviously not the ideal way to produce user manuals.

A third cluster is the theoretical rationale which guides decisions about the contents. Decisions about the contents of manuals should be made before they are designed so that the technical writers know exactly what information should be included. Our human factors research team was recently asked to review a new telecommunications product that our company was considering buying off the shelf to retail in Australia. When reviewing the user manual, it quickly became evident that crucial policy decisions had not yet been made, without which the document could neither be structured nor tested in a meaningful way. Issues such as which company owned the product, and whether it should contain information over and above sheer user instructions, for example, had not been addressed. Additional information about related products with which this one could easily be interfaced could prove a valuable marketing strategy but it also increases the size of the manual, and one wonders whether user manuals are suited for advertising. There was no quick reference guide, and the format of the manual was such that it would be inconvenient to carry, although the product itself was intended to remain with the users at all times, stored in their handbags, large pockets or briefcases. The original manual served several implicit purposes, but these had to be specified, ranked in order of importance and made explicit before meaningful redesign and usability testing could be undertaken. The structure, format and layout of user documentation simply cannot be determined before the purpose it will serve has been decided upon.

The final cluster of factors determining user documentation success concerns the resources devoted to documentation. People with different skills in either graphics or technical writing can work most profitably with human factors specialists, linguists and systems designers, but they must be assigned to the particular product to be properly involved.

In addition to all these factors, documentation writers need a thorough understanding of how the manuals and software or other products are to be used, about relevant characteristics of the user population, about the research literature and about the subject matter (Chapanis, 1988) in order to produce effective, usable and useful documentation.

9.2.1 WHY DO USER MANUALS FAIL?

Many good texts discuss user documentation design issues (Brockman, 1990; Doheny-Farina, 1988; Horton, 1990; Simpson and Casey, 1988). Even so, user manuals are still unpopular – why? Traditionally, user documentation has been regarded as 'last minute add-ons' rather than an aspect of systems design that should be integrated with the overall design. Also, there has been a tendency to believe that writing manuals and instructions is so easy that anyone can do it. Where that attitude prevails, the task has generally been given to some unfortunate, unlucky person, often the most junior and inexperienced member of the project team, when the system project is drawing to an end with the launch date approaching rapidly. Alternatively, technical writers might be available but are sometimes recruited so late in the process that they are forced to work under considerable, often unrealistic, time constraints, using specifications that are likely to be outdated. Changes that are made to the system after the initial system specifications have been accepted are often not included; if time does not allow thorough cross-checking of procedures between software, documentation, help system, tutorials and user manuals, these may end up being inconsistent and unsuited as user support (Baker, 1988; Chisholm, 1988).

From the perspective of actual production, several other issues may affect documentation usability and usefulness. These issues include the likelihood that instructions are written for experts, that they are too difficult and technical, and that they assume too much prior knowledge on behalf of the new user who needs information about the system which the manuals support (Simpson and Casey, 1988). The focus of many manuals tends to be on technical matters such as system structure, mechanics or idiosyncratic smart-moves in the software, outlining the methods underlying the various operations rather than helping the user to complete certain user-relevant tasks. Alternatively, different chapters in user manuals may have been written by different people who use a variety of expressions, differ in writing style and discuss the topics at different levels of depth. The resulting user manual is thus a hotch-potch of mixed ideas and metaphors which lack consistency of style, emphasis, layout, and terminology between chapters.

Finally, from the user's perspective, research has shown that users often do not know how to formulate questions. Inexperienced users tend to ask 'why doesn't this work?' or 'what's wrong?' – questions which, without further specification, are unanswerable unless the person asking has considerable knowledge of the system already. Users thus need help in defining clear questions (Wright, 1991) before they can select and apply a suitable solution. Recall that the trouble-shooting option in the modified version of the EWP help system discussed earlier was the most frequently accessed option precisely because it gave clear hints on trouble-shooting activities that were most likely to be relevant. One way to assist users asking more precise questions is thus to provide them with trouble-shooting tools that allude them to different problems that might be the cause of currently experienced difficulties. Checklists can thus be most effective by helping users to think of what to look for.

9.2.2 HOW TO ACHIEVE USABLE DOCUMENTATION?

The concept of 'minimalist' manuals was developed by Carroll and his colleagues (Carroll *et al.*, 1985) who made strong claims supporting the notion that 'leaner' manuals are better than 'fatter' ones. They monitored users who worked with information presented on cards which contained independent modules of instruction. Arguing that users 'learn by doing' rather than by 'reading about doing', they assumed that giving fewer instructions would give rise to more exploratory learning. The authors proposed that guided exploration should help users set appropriate goals, offer advice on how these goals might be achieved, provide checkpoints confirming that users were on the right track, and help users to recover from errors. By adopting the minimalist approach, Carroll *et al.* found that 50% fewer errors were made by 'minimalist' subjects who also recovered more often from these than those given conventional instructional material, and that the 'minimalist' subjects spent 30% less time reading the material. For new users, it thus seems that minimalist manuals may offer an advantage to the extent that these encourage users to interact with the system; apparently, users are more concerned about learning how to do the things they want, at least initially, than about understanding how the system works. This was true in the EWP help system as well: before the trouble-shooting menu was added, 'help' was neither popular nor helpful. More experienced users who are capable of formulating complex questions, may be better served by manuals which provide more information at a level that goes beyond the step-by-step instructions for how to accomplish particular goals (Wright, 1988).

Wright (1983) has suggested stages through which users interact with system documentation. Before reading a user manual, she argues, users formulate questions and look for answers. Obviously, the more vaguely the questions are formulated, the more difficult it is to find the correct answer. During reading, Wright suggests, users comprehend what is written in the documentation, and they create an action plan. Finally, after reading, this action plan is executed and the user evaluates the outcome of his/her efforts. Translated into particular acts or actions, these stages can be summarized into users: locating, or finding, information; understanding it; applying it to the problem or question they were asking.

'The most junior person in the team may not be best equipped to write the user documentation'

Locating information in user documentation

In order to assist users locate information, clear headings and subheadings should signal what information is contained underneath. Indices, tables of contents, use of colour, tabs, indents, symbols or pictures can help readers notice and distinguish different information items from one another. Specific types of messages may be presented in a certain way, perhaps framed in a distinctive manner, using a different font or size for letters, a different colour, or in locations that are easy to find, for example, at the beginning or at the end of chapters. The critical issues associated with assisting users to locate information thus concern the organization of the document, the format, and the actual context.

Understanding information

Problems experienced by documentation users are basically the same as those discussed in section 9.1 dealing with help systems. Vocabulary may be unclear, foreign, or ambiguous. Wright (1991), for example, alludes to asymmetric difficulties with the concepts 'more' and 'less'. People respond faster and are more accurate when making decisions involving 'more' than the same decision involving 'less', and the same is true for many comparative dimensions such as size, length, height and temperature. Noting this first hand, I recently found myself thinking twice about a question which asked me to 'confirm that you don't want X (to happen)' in a statistical package. Answering 'yes' to something you do not want to happen just seemed the wrong way round. The explanation for this phenomenon, Wright argues, lies partly in the more difficult terms being implicitly negative in the sense that short indicates an absence

'Finding the right information can be as difficult as applying it'

of height, whereas long or tall does not denote an absence of 'shortness'. Why this might be so is not clear.

At higher levels of organizing information such as describing a procedure involving several sub-tasks, it is helpful to present these in a step-by-step fashion, outlining the entire procedure in the sequence in which individual steps are completed. Giving insufficient detail can be problematic in the sense that, at some point, the user might be stuck. At the same time, giving too much detail can be equally unproductive because one cannot see the forest for trees, as it were, and users cannot distinguish signals from noise. Lengthy summaries of procedural information can, on occasion, encourage people to try out a procedure before they have all the necessary information and thereby get stuck. It does save space to rely on cross-referencing rather than repetition of information that is of relevance in more than one context. However, it is generally better to state all information relevant to a certain procedure together as a coherent whole even if it takes up more space. The art of good writing is to strike a balance between saying too much and too little to attract user attention and to make explanations comprehensible.

Applying information

Once problem-relevant information pertaining to a given problem has been located, the degree to which it has also been understood becomes apparent when users attempt to apply the information to solve their problem. If ambiguities exist, it certainly becomes obvious once the written text is applied to practical problems. The intentions of a message may well be clear to the author, but it is not always equally easy for others to follow what might seem like simple instructions. A sign carrying the following message was erected next to a lift in a high-rise building some time ago:

PLEASE
WALK UP ONE FLOOR
WALK DOWN TWO FLOORS
FOR IMPROVED ELEVATOR SERVICE

Without looking ahead to the next version of this message, try to paraphrase it in your own words. The intention of that message was to get people who needed only to go up one floor level or down two to use the stairs instead of the lift, thereby leaving the lift free for people going on longer trips. Well, that misfired! What people did was to walk up one floor, then walk down two floors, and finally press the button for the lift, regardless of where in the building they wanted to go. Several iterations of that sign were necessary before the message had the desired effect on people's behaviour, including the following step:

**IF YOU ARE ONLY GOING
UP ONE FLOOR
OR
DOWN TWO FLOORS
PLEASE WALK
(IF YOU DO THAT WE'LL ALL HAVE
BETTER ELEVATOR SERVICE)**

Finally, the wording became:

**TO GO UP ONE FLOOR
OR
DOWN TWO FLOORS
PLEASE WALK**

(from Chapanis, 1963)

This message had the desired effect, but it was obviously far more difficult to achieve the modifications in people's behaviour than first anticipated. The same was true for a sign erected on Australian highways some years ago which read: 'Slow vehicles keep to the left'. The intention here was to reduce the number of serious accidents occurring through hazardous overtaking of slow vehicles by encouraging motorists to use these overtaking lanes. As it happens, no one in Australia drives a 'slow vehicle'. Consequently, the overtaking lanes were not used, and the accident rate remained the same as before. Only when the message was changed to 'Keep left unless overtaking' was the desired effect achieved. People drive happily in the left lane now, and much anxiety associated with sitting behind a large, slow truck, caravan, cattle truck or milk tanker for hundreds of kilometres has been removed from the highways merely by modifying an apparently simple and clear message. In this example, the first message was clear and unambiguous, but local culture and social norms guiding certain kinds of behaviour had been ignored by the road authorities. People apparently feel very strongly about the categories to which they feel they do or do not belong, and that must be considered when writing instructions which aim to modify human behaviour.

9.2.3 EVALUATING AND TESTING USER DOCUMENTATION

By now some of the skills necessary for planning and carrying out a test and evaluation program should have been acquired, so it is no longer necessary to repeat how to apply the tests outlined in earlier chapters. For discussions on documentation usability testing, see Redish and Dumas (1991) or Wright (1988). Instead, a reasonably detailed case history will now be presented describing the procedure and one set of tests performed on user documentation in our laboratory for you to see what was actually done, how it was done, and how the user manual in question evolved through an iterative testing program. Details are adapted from Chessari and Bednall (1990), and the documentation was designed for a certain telephone system.

EXAMPLE: DESIGNING AND EVALUATING THE CENTEL USER MANUAL

CENTEL is a product with up to 20 telephone lines which offers a range of diversions and other facilities. A two-digit number can be dialled to reach any of the lines belonging to a certain group in different geographical locations. Three different manuals had been produced before the human factors team became involved: one contained a set of symbols denoting the various CENTEL facilities, one used verbal descriptions only, and one was an abbreviated version which was structured differently from the two others. The abbreviated version was arranged according to

1. notes on call facilities;
2. how to use call facilities;
3. additional facilities;
4. how to turn facilities on and off;
5. a one-page quick reference guide.

The other two versions were arranged such that all information relevant to a given facility was presented together on 1–2 pages and a quick reference guide at the end.

Heuristic evaluation

Three main aspects of usability were focused on at first, namely ease of location, ease of understanding, and ease of application of information. Ease of location was judged by the distribution and clarity of words used in naming facilities, section headings, the order in which facilities were described, and the overall structure of the manual. Ease of understanding was judged by the clarity and simplicity of instructions, length of sentences and manner of expression, for example, counting the number of negative words, or double negative sentences, and so on. Ease of application was judged by the accuracy and completeness of instructions.

The symbols version was found to be the most appropriate of the three manuals, although several modifications were needed to improve the layout and presentation as well as some of the content. Symbols were, for example, added in places where the underlying concepts were quite simple, few in number and applicable to most of the facilities offered. In terms of layout, it was necessary to space out the symbolic instructions such that they were clearly distinguishable from one another. Also, a consistent layout of information on the pages was necessary to facilitate location of different types of items. Consistency was thus to be introduced across facilities. All irrelevant information was eliminated.

The original manuals were all printed on A4 sized paper. It was decided to reduce this in size, as the manual should be kept near the users' telephone. Also, it was decided to spiral bind it to enable it to remain open hands-free, and to use laminated cardboard for protection. To facilitate location of information in the manual, pages varied in size, with pages at the back of the manual being larger than those at the front. This allowed separation of sections by a tab which was clearly labelled.

CENTEL user guide – new version: experimental trouble-shooting
A CENTEL group setup was used in the quasi-experiment first designed to test the manual. It included three linked telephone lines and one additional external line. Experimental tasks were designed to simulate the way CENTEL would be used in the field as closely as possible. Three types of tasks were included which required subjects to:

1. turn facilities on or off;
2. use call facilities;
3. estimate which facility overrides others.

Some 11 tasks were designed to cover these. An effort was made to avoid using the same terminology in the experimental instructions as in the user guide to estimate the degree to which labels/titles in the guide were suggestive of the kind of information contained behind, or underneath, them. Tasks were presented one to a page to facilitate scoring.

Experimental instructions gave enough details to resemble the amount of information users would have in the field at the time the system was installed. The user manual would be the primary source of information for real users who would not receive any training.

Thirteen subjects took part. All were staff members of the telecommunications company providing the CENTEL services. Due to time constraints it was not possible to recruit actual business people who were the target audience. The subject-group was, however, reasonably homogeneous in the sense that all came from an administrative background and none had any experience with CENTEL facilities prior to the experiment.

PROCEDURE
Prior to commencing the experimental tasks, subjects were encouraged to familiarize themselves with the user guide. Tasks were given in the same order to all subjects, to control for CENTEL experience. At the end of each task, subjects rated the ease of locating, understanding and applying the task-relevant information on a five-point rating scale ranging from 'not at all difficult' at one end to 'extremely difficult' at the other. At the end of the experiment subjects were interviewed to gauge their attitude towards the facilities and the manual.

Two experimenters acting as observers were seated alongside the subject. Usability defects were recorded by both. These included hesitations, the user obviously getting stuck, looking for information in the wrong place, and so on. Time for completion of each task and sub-task was measured, and the number of pages consulted in the manual before and after reaching the correct page was counted, as well as the number of errors in locating and applying information.

RESULTS

Overall, the manual was found to be reasonably usable with two exceptions:

1. 'Call waiting';
2. 'Memory storage' facilities.

Subjects had difficulties interpreting the meaning of 'Call waiting' and with locating the relevant information, as well as with application of instructions for storing information in memory. Interestingly, this was not reflected in the subjective ratings at all which were very high for all tests. The main problem was thus associated with using facilities rather than with turning them on or off, or with assessing which ones were overriding others. Of the 11 tasks, nine were completed by more than 85% of subjects.

ITERATION

Modifications were made to the manual to overcome the problems noted as well as to cater for changes in the product itself. Another group of 13 subjects was recruited and, apart from using the modified version of the user manual, the experimental tasks and procedure remained the same as before. This time, all but one task was completed by more than 85% of subjects. The problem with the remaining task was the application of information. This problem had not been observed in the first experiment. Interestingly, it occurred here because an extra line of text had been inserted to overcome a previously experienced problem. All the smaller problems identified in the previous experiment had clearly been overcome.

The most interesting lesson learned from this example is that one cannot assume that modifications made to a system or a manual necessarily result in improvements in user performance. When changes are made, these should also be tested to ensure that the problems addressed have been overcome (Watts, 1990), and also that the changes made have not given rise to new, unforeseen problems. As in the EWP example of a help system, one should repeat the same tasks and take the same performance measures as well as use a comparable sample of subjects in each iteration.

When it is not possible to simulate a real-life situation, one can set tasks that require subjects to describe how they would carry out various tasks which the manual supports, instead. A typical task would be presented in the form 'If you were to do X task to achieve Y goal, how would you do it using Z system? Describe the steps involved one by one'. Such tasks would give an estimate of ease of location, understanding and application of relevant information as well as of the completeness of procedures described. Comprehension tests can be useful when testing ease of understanding the information presented in a manual; people can be asked to paraphrase the information tested. This is particularly useful when technical, highly specific jargon is used with which typical end users are likely to be unfamiliar. Before conducting a fully fledged usability study and running experiments, it is wise to ensure that the concepts dealt with in the manual are comprehensible to the intended users.

The final type of user support to be discussed here is tutorials. Training materials may be designed and presented in a number of different ways, and it is quite a tricky business to produce effective tutoring systems. This is because it is not well understood how people learn, or how much they learn on a single, or even on repeated, exposure(s). Nor is it clear how they encode, store and retrieve material once it has been learned. Training is one area in which good, solid theoretical knowledge of complex human cognitive capabilities would go a long way towards underpinning decisions about the format, size, scope, structure and layout that an ideal training package should have. Unfortunately, the gap between theory and practice is as wide in this area as in most others so that one cannot even begin to account for much complex human cognitive functioning (Lewis, 1991; Pylyshyn, 1991). Meanwhile, designing tutorials will remain a difficult and messy job, and therefore, usability testing must be relied upon to ensure tutorials achieve their objective in a satisfactory and smooth fashion.

9.3 Tutoring systems

One attribute that distinguishes tutorials from other user support materials such as help systems and user/reference manuals is that learners are generally expected to work through the tutoring systems from beginning to end. This means that tutorials should be written in order of increasing complexity (Jarvinen, 1988), starting with the easiest and ending with the most complex operations and procedures. This approach could thus lay the foundation for the way a tutorial could be structured. However, it is not always easy to determine which are the most complex tasks, and who, amongst all possible users, will be likely to need knowledge of which features at what stage of learning. For that reason, it can be a good idea to include an index in the tutorial package, especially one designed for a large, complex system. It is feasible to expect learners to go through the tutorial in several sessions and return to it at times to refresh their minds, perhaps when the system has not been used for some time, or when they are tackling new tasks on the computer system.

'Tutorial systems are a neat addition to, but not a replacement of, human-human interaction'

There is little agreement about the way a tutorial system should be designed, its layout, contents, size and scope. However, at least people do agree about the purpose tutorials should serve, namely to ensure effective learning as well as effective task completion strategies (Schindler and Fischer, 1986). Unfortunately, it is not clear just what is meant by 'effective learning', and it seems to mean different things in various contexts for different people. On the one hand, it would be reasonable to argue that effective learning should enable learners to generalize what they have just learned to different contexts and other systems. In practice, that is not always the case; users can be highly experienced in certain tasks or in using particular software packages without also being able to transfer their knowledge effectively and with ease from one system to another. Users can, in other words, learn to use a system well without understanding the principles governing its performance (Briggs, 1990).

It is generally assumed that experienced users also have a better understanding of the underlying system logic, and that this 'metaknowledge' helps them to generalize and to further their own learning. It is also assumed that user behaviour necessarily and accurately mirrors user knowledge. However, these assumptions are unfounded and are sometimes shown to be misleading. Berry and Broadbent (1984), for example, found that although subjects were able to operate a simple system to produce a desired output in an experimental setting, they could not explain the variables they were controlling. Furthermore, when instructions about these relationships were given explicitly, this knowledge did not uniformly lead to improvements in user performance. The extent to which people are able to explain what they know may thus not be indicative of their performance when putting that knowledge to use. The relationship between knowledge, behaviour and descriptions of knowledge is likely to be much more complex than is generally realized, and one should be extremely careful about making assumptions about this relationship when designing software – especially tutoring systems and other training material. The practical implications for designers echo the message this book is trying to convey, namely that no material intended to be used by people other than the designer/creator/author/project team should be released without thorough usability testing. Tutorials and other training materials are no exception to this!

Keeping within the framework of tests and evaluations, it is reasonable to adopt the principles suggested in a recent paper (Cannon-Bowers *et al.*, 1991) which seeks to make certain aspects of the training theory and practice explicit. Within that framework, there are three questions which are pertinent to training research, application and design, and which should be guiding the design and evaluation process. These are:

- what should be trained?
- how should training be designed?
- is training effective, and if so, why?

Let us deal with each of these in turn to highlight their implications for the design, as well as for testing and evaluating training materials.

9.3.1 WHAT SHOULD BE TRAINED?

Deciding what should be trained depends on the type of system the training package aims to support, of course. Basically, the decision hinges

'How to train most effectively?'

on an understanding of the nature of the knowledge, skills, abilities and expertise associated with the tasks that are to be taught using the system in question. Indeed, Kieras and Polson (1985) pointed out the importance of distinguishing between task-related and device-related knowledge. On the one hand, they assert, one needs to consider what it is users are doing, as determined by task and job analyses conducted during the user needs analysis, and on the other hand, one must specify how procedures and operations are accommodated within the system. Will users of a system already be experts at the tasks to be supported, or do they need task training as well as system training? How much task knowledge is necessary as a prerequisite for using the system effectively? Where and

'The 'one-size-fits-all' approach may not be effective all-round . . .'

how do users get that training? Through experience on the job, through formal education, short courses, or a mixture of all of these? These types of questions simply must be answered before a tutoring system is planned.

People who are excellent touch typists need not be given much additional background in how to structure different types of documents when learning to use a new word processor (WP); in WP training packages. The major emphasis would thus be on system, or device-related, training rather than on task training. The same is true for many specialist packages. For example, in the dental support system described in Chapter 7, it would be foolish to attempt to show dentists how to run a practice and even to invent new tasks for them, unless the dentists themselves would wish to change what they do when managing their clinics. Similarly, the medical drug decision support system included as an exercise in Chapter 2 would be designed to meet the end users' needs accurately. Both the medical and the dental tasks and system require-ments are extremely well-defined, and task procedures are specific to ensure that the legal requirements associated with handling drugs, especially dangerous drugs, and patients are obeyed. Support systems should impose few, if any, changes to the procedures, and the designer of both the system and the tutorial accompanying the system can safely assume that end users know their tasks well. In systems supporting well-defined tasks with which users can be certain to be thoroughly acquainted, it would probably be quite destructive to provide task-related training material. It is quite probable that end users who are likely to be pressed for time would choose to avoid going through tutorials that seem to teach them what they already know better than the smart system designer anyway!

In other specialist areas, typical learners of support systems may not have the necessary task knowledge for a tutorial system only to teach 'how' goals are accomplished in the particular system. When training operators who will be controlling highly specialized or safety-critical systems, training programs generally focus much more on the contents of the tasks than on how a computer system helps users to complete these tasks. Such operators might include controllers of nuclear plants or people training to monitor telephone or data networks, air traffic controllers, or specialists devising complex scheduling strategies in large production systems, for example, in steel or iron works. Tutorials in these areas are much more likely to constitute a single component in a much larger training programme. Accordingly, the aim might be to enable learners to get 'up to speed' in particular tasks, rather than offering them an interactive overview of the particular system features included in a package.

Clearly, the purpose, the size, scope and nature of the system for which training material is to be designed determines what a tutorial package should contain and how this material should be presented. In addition to distinguishing between task-related and device-related knowledge, one should also distinguish between system-specific and general computer knowledge to be taught. The level of general computer knowledge that end users can be expected to possess is another factor to note. Experts will be annoyed at being confronted with material they know well in a tutorial, and novices are likely to be puzzled about material that assumes a wider general understanding of the system than they possess. Recently, a user support system was designed in our laboratory which brought home the need to consider computer expertise. The system was a large database which would be accessed by people ranging in computer experience from complete novices to hackers. Observing how users formulated database queries revealed that complete novices lacked an understanding of the way a computer searches a database. When a particular search had proved unsuccessful, novices tended to add more characters to the existing search string rather than reducing it to widen the search. Apparently, these users were applying common sense knowledge; in real life, the probability of locating a target increases as more details are provided, but in database interrogations, this is the other way round. If you are asked, for example, to fetch a particular article in a given journal from the library, you will need to know where to find the library, the journal index, the journal, the name of at least the first author, the title of the paper, about photocopy machines, and so on. Clearly, the more accurate knowledge you have at your fingertips, the easier and faster it is for you to fetch the material. The knowledge of how computers work in terms of over-specifying search strings clearly had to be pointed out to people who applied common sense inappropriately.

At the same time, one should not assume that novices will always apply their common sense. In observations of people using the EWP, it was noted that novices had a tendency to search for individuals by entering initials before surnames, e.g. 'N.H.ANDERSON' which was consistent with the details they were given for the target. However, it is contrary to the way they would use the telephone book which was also tested, just to be sure. Apparently, in this case novices attributed far more intelligence to the computer than it had, believing that it knew which part of the character string should be important for the search to be successful. Interestingly, many experts made that same error, but they apparently engaged in a kind of exploratory behaviour aimed to discover the system rules. This was evident in the differing recovery patterns between experts and novices. Whereas experts invariably recovered immediately upon committing that particular error by reversing surname and initials in the very next search, novices took an average of another 4.7 further trials before they recovered. Some even gave up without locating the target at all. Clearly, experts applied their global computer knowledge to solving the problem – knowledge that the novices lacked. At the same time novices apparently thought the computer was smart enough to know the meaning of what they were entering. Evidently, it is very difficult to predict how users will behave.

In terms of deciding what needs to be taught in a tutorial package, it is recommended, therefore, that the issue is divided into task training and device training. Device training should be divided into general computer training and system-specific training, yielding a picture as outlined in Fig. 9.4 below:

It is well worth spending time defining exactly which of the possible holes in people's knowledge your tutorial package will be attempting to fill. It might be worth considering dividing up the package under the above headings if it is intended for a large population of users varying in levels of expertise:

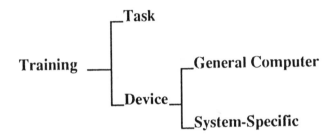

Figure 9.4: A possible way to divide up the training into task and device-specific areas.

9.3.2 HOW SHOULD TRAINING BE DESIGNED?

When designing training material for a particular computer system, it would seem reasonable to assume that material should be presented online to ensure most effective learning. Surprisingly, this is not necessarily so. At least one study has shown that training in a WP tutorial provided online can result in poorer performance than training provided by an instructor or in a hardcopy document (Czaja *et al.*, 1986). Apparently, users experienced extreme difficulties editing an existing document, and their efforts resulted in many errors from which they could not readily recover. The authors believe that the online tutorial promoted a passive learning experience that failed to equip the learners with sufficient understanding of the system's editing functions to apply them to actual documents. Learners were simply following instructions; they were allowed to type only prescribed responses to prompts presented on the screen and were prevented from making errors in the tutorial. By contrast, learners who were taught by both other methods completed certain realistic editing tasks interactively which did not restrict them

'What do you want to know? How should I know? If I knew what I wanted to know, I would ask a dumb computer'

to predetermined responses. Learning by doing thus resulted in a better performance than learning by being told in an abstract teaching environment or in a step-by-step fashion, as Carroll and his colleagues argue (Carroll and Mack, 1983; Carroll *et al.*, 1985; Lewis and Mack, 1981).

However, learning conditions varied in ways other than presentation mode. The reason for the poor level of performance resulting from online training methods may lie in the fact that learners completed different types of tasks during training rather than in the presentation mode as such. Note how difficulties in interpreting results aiming to establish clear cause and effect relationships are omnipresent in the literature! Yet, despite ambiguities, it is still useful to note that online training for a computer system may not automatically provide optimal learning conditions.

The advantage of learning by doing, or guided exploration, has been supported by some, albeit not by all authors (Martin, 1985). Carroll and his associates have advocated a learning method referred to as 'training wheels' for some years now, and it has been shown to lead to more effective learning and more rapid mastering of at least elementary knowledge and skills in word processing. In a 'training wheels' environment, the user is prevented from committing serious errors by locking those parts of the system that might cause serious problems. How the training method affects long-term learning, or whether it actually discourages users from exploring new areas of a system in the longer term, remains to be seen.

On the one hand, Czaja *et al.* (1986) claim that the opportunity to commit errors, as provided by the interactive material presented in the offline training condition, led to better performance than denial of that opportunity in the online material. On the other hand, Carroll and his associates take the opposite view, at least to some extent, claiming that users should be prevented from making errors. Although they advocate learning by doing, users do only certain things and not others. Perhaps the crucial issue lies in providing realistic rather than abstract tasks in a

'Users appreciate a safe learning environment'

tutorial package; maybe, the opportunity to make errors and the decision as to which errors users will be allowed to make are not as central to effective learning as might be assumed.

Another reason for promoting learning by doing is that novices are not very good at asking the kinds of questions that will expand their understanding of how a given system works. Recall that the same observation has been made in the user documentation literature. Novices do not know what it is they do not know and so, they cannot formulate sensible questions. Allwood and Eliasson (1988) and Briggs (1990) both found that user performance on editing tasks did not improve when users were given an opportunity to ask questions, even when they had a certain amount of relevant experience. These findings suggest the same as found in the EWP help system: even with a thorough knowledge of most, if not all, problems users would be likely to encounter, and despite the fact that all of these problems were addressed in the first version of help, it was not very successful. Once it had a quick-fix trouble-shooting menu option, it worked well enough to reach the usability criterion. Users apparently found it difficult spontaneously to identify what the problem was, unless it was presented as a clear example. They could therefore not readily find the correct answer in the original help system.

One limitation to the learning by doing guided exploration, approach is that users might not always discover the best procedure for achieving certain ends, and nor can they always say when a given procedure is most appropriate. In terms of enabling them to ask sensible questions, the guided exploration method might not be the best one to choose. Novices may never be able to ask good questions. They may not be able to invent problems that really explore the system's capabilities or indeed be able to invent problems that demonstrate the advantage of one procedure over another. For that reason, it might be wise to expose the learner to at least some problem-solving tasks in tutorials rather than merely providing worked-out examples (Charney and Reder, 1986).

Access to system rules can sometimes help improve user performance, especially for complex tasks (Stammers, 1986), although, as stated earlier, teaching people system rules does not always improve performance (Briggs, 1990). Similarly, some researchers have found it useful to provide structural displays (Patrick and Fitzgibbon, 1988), maps (Billingsley, 1982) or flow diagrams (Sullivan and Chapanis, 1983) which show the functional and structural relationships of the system. Consulting these before novel tasks have been attempted can lead to improved user learning and performance, as measured in terms of task-completion time and the number of errors committed (Patrick and Fitzgibbon, 1988).

With respect to deciding how training should be designed, the literature cannot help us far if we expect a universally fitting recipe. As with most other complex tasks, it is not clear which solution best fits the problem. However, from the preceding discussion, some tentative conclusions may be drawn that could help us a little towards deriving preliminary guidelines for tutorial design:

- encourage active learning through problem solving tasks;
- encourage learning by doing;
- describe the system rules and set problems requiring these to be applied;
- provide a good index;
- provide an overview map/structural display of the system;
- design the tutorial to start from easy and end with complex operations.

9.3.3 IS TRAINING EFFECTIVE, AND IF SO, WHY?

This section discusses the usability testing, the outcome of same, and the causes for success of a given tutorial system. As was the case in the discussion of user documentation, it will be unnecessary to go through the various tests introduced in earlier chapters to describe which ones might fit into a tutoring system environment. Instead, when you are charged with designing, testing and evaluating such packages, review Chapters 3–6 to remind yourself of the testing tools you could apply to your particular problem. As you have seen, almost any of the tools talked about in this book can be adapted to virtually any testing situation with a bit of skill and imagination. Together with the three principles outlined in this section and the recipe for a test and evaluation plan given in Chapter 8, you should by now be well equipped to go it alone.

Remember to consider the purpose of the tutoring system to be evaluated when you set suitable tasks through which to ascertain whether the package has achieved its objective. Be aware also, that in the case of assessing tutoring systems, you are not merely testing the ability of users to locate, interpret and read information as in user documentation or in help; rather, you are trying to assess the outcome of the skills of someone who has gone through the tutoring system. Evaluating tutoring systems is thus a *post hoc* analysis rather than an assessment of how well users can find their way through the system and interpret its peculiarities. The real test lies in how well learners can put their newly acquired knowledge to use in another system which the tutorial is intended to support.

Usability testing of a tutoring system is thus two-pronged. On the one hand, you will need to ensure that the material provided in the package is clear and makes sense in its own right. This is no different from any other usability testing procedure and program. On the other hand, you will need to assess the effectiveness and applicability of what learners have just picked up. This means that user performance will need to be tested in the host system as well as in the tutorial system to make sure all the critical elements of learning have been adequately covered in the tutoring system. Mentioning a certain point once may not be enough to drive home the essence of the message, or the reason for its importance. Hence, you cannot simply check from the skills on your list from the original analysis of 'what should be taught' to make certain all issues have been covered. Additional illustrative examples or problems might need to be included to consolidate learning.

Testing the learning outcome by measuring user performance in the host system and iterating through modifications to the tutorial system until the usability criteria have been reached, takes care of the 'is training effective?' question. Tackling the 'why?' question is somewhat trickier and requires a certain commitment to research which might not be on the agenda of the company behind you. In order to understand why something works, it would be necessary to test one feature at a time to trace its impact on the outcome. In addition, various features should then be tested in combination with one another to establish patterns of interaction between them as well as the pure cause–effect relationship. It is needless to state the obvious fact that this would require a very elaborate research program. It is very time-consuming to add and test one feature at a time, and the benefits gained from an understanding of the interdependence of a handful of variables may not be generalizable to a wider group of tutoring systems. So, whichever way we look at it, we are unlikely to run out of work in a hurry!

Summary

Three important aspects of user support have been dealt with in this chapter, namely help systems, user documentation and tutoring systems. Each of these was discussed in some detail in an attempt to highlight the purposes each is recommended to serve. Ready-made recipes for achieving a certain level of success when designing these user support systems cannot be given, as the state of our understanding is not yet sufficiently advanced. For that same reason, it is extraordinarily difficult to produce guidelines for the design of user support. Even so, there are certain questions which should be asked when designing and/or testing any form of user support. These were discussed along with some of the traps certain user support systems are known sometimes to fall into, which definitely reduce both effectiveness and usability.

Questions

1. What is the most important purpose a help system should serve?
2. Which prerequisites must be fulfilled for a help system to assist users effectively?
3. What are the main reasons for help systems failing to assist users in trouble?

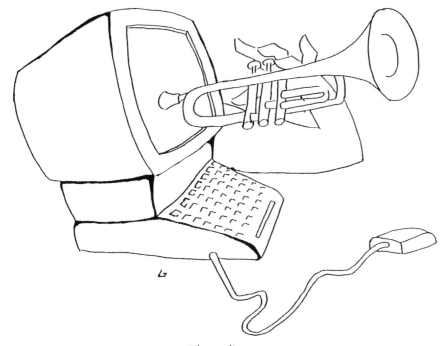

'The end'

4. Why do users have problems navigating through computer systems
   – or even help systems?
5. Where do users mostly get stuck in a hierarchical menu system?
6. How can navigational problems be overcome?
7. Why might it not be a good idea to let the computer decide when a
   user needs help and impose it when such situations occur?
8. What is the best method for ensuring that vocabulary adopted in a
   system or help system makes sense to end users?
9. Which features would make a good help system?
10. Why might it be useful to repeat the same information in several
    areas of help?
11. How do you know when a system or a help system is 'good
    enough'?
12. What is the first decision that should be made before designing user
    documentation?
13. When should documentation be produced?
14. Why do you think user manuals tend to be unpopular?
15. What are new users generally quite poor at doing when trying to use
    manuals?
16. How can the documentation design assist users quickly to locate
    information?

17. What are the most important aspects to test in a user manual usability test?
18. Why should a system, help system or manual be retested after modifications have been made to correct user problems?
19. What is the most important purpose tutorial systems should serve?
20. Which three questions should guide the design and evaluation of tutoring systems?

Exercises

1. Get hold of two user manuals for different brands of similar software, for example, WORD for Windows and WordPerfect, WordStar, or any other WP. Alternatively, you might want to use spreadsheets like Visicalc, Lotus 1-2-3, Excel, statistical packages, graphics software, or whatever you can lay your hands on.

   Without looking at the manuals, set a number of tasks people would typically want to do when using the packages you have chosen. Make sure the tasks cover a wide range of topics, preferably touching on the entire profile covered in the manual. If you chose a word processing package, for example, set tasks including:

   - use of tabs;
   - drawing up tables;
   - reducing the size of text and graphics in an entire document;
   - how to incorporate graphics;
   - footnotes;
   - page numbers;
   - how to draw lines (horizontal and vertical);
   - use of the keyboard instead of pointing with the mouse;
   - how to mark each item in a list with a dot;
   - how to insert mathematical and power symbols.

   Try these tasks for yourself and note down the usability problems you encounter. Remember, in user documentation we are particularly interested in difficulties in locating, interpreting and applying information. In the first instance, you cover the first two points by working with the manual. Later, you might want to check the ease of application on the computer.

   Next, you might like to work in pairs where one person completes the tasks and the other writes down usability problems. When both parties have finished, cross-check the problems you encountered. If several pairs are doing the tasks, check with all pairs to get a complete list of usability defects and an indication of the percentage of users who experienced each problem.

   When the list is complete, make lists of the merits of each manual. Then compare both the good points and the usability defects for both manuals. Based on these lists, outline how you would redesign the manuals to overcome the problems encountered, and think about how and when in the development process you would test for usability.

2. Use the same tasks (add to the list if you like) as above, but this time recruit subjects who have never used the packages you selected. Do not give them the manual, but ask them to complete the tasks on the computer, using help if and when they like. You should recruit at least four people, if possible, to make sure you cover a range of problems.

   While the subjects are working, observe when and why they seek help. How many help areas do they access to get the answer they are looking for? How long do they spend in help on each occasion? Do they browse through help? How, where and when does the help facility fall down? Can people identify their current problem? Do they access help more than once for the same problem? Can they readily apply the information given in help?

   Once you have completed all your observations, do what you did when testing the manuals – write lists of usability defects and help system merits for both systems. How do the two help systems differ in structure, layout and the amount of information given in the different areas of help?

   Compare also the lists of usability problems encountered by people using the manual with those using help. To what extent are the problems the same? Why or why not? Which ones reflect poor descriptions in either help or the manual, and which ones reflect the subjects' lack of understanding of the tasks or the system they are attempting to use? These questions should help you to decide how you can improve the current products.

   Armed with the usability problems associated with help, outline how you would overcome them and redesign the two help systems. Also, outline your usability tests, describing what you would test, how that should be done, and how you would know when your new help system is good enough.

3. Finally, plan a tutorial package aimed at teaching people the basics of the two packages you selected for this exercise. What would you teach? How should the tutorial be structured? How long should it be? Which and how many modules would you divide it into? How would you measure training effectiveness?

Suggested further reading

Brockman's book (1990) summarizes the principles of good writing and readable documentation, and is particularly relevant to people who are responsible for writing user documentation. It is very easy to read but does not provide a great deal of information on usability testing techniques; it concentrates more on achieving clarity and actual presentation.

Bethke's article (1983) gives hints on ways in which user manuals may be tested for usability. It is very practical and readable.

Doheny-Farina's book (1988) gives a comprehensive and yet easy to read summary of research undertaken to date on how to write good documentation. It is a good advertisement for the topic it addresses, and is a good historical overview as well.

Wright is well known for her work in documentation research, and gives hints for writing as well as testing documentation (Wright, 1991). Her paper provides a wider philosophical base for thinking about the role and purpose of documentation. It is very thought-provoking and easy to read, with plenty of material for further discussion in class.

Catterall *et al.* (1991) describe the HUFIT toolset and discuss how it can and should be integrated into the product design process. Naturally, their chapter does not replace the toolset as such. Rather, it should be read as an introduction to the background, the aims and the scope of the toolset. It is very readable.

Answers and solutions 10

CHAPTER 1

10.1 Answers to questions

1. HCI may guide a systematic analysis of people's needs, and it yields methods for testing usability.
2. User models are theoretical representations of the user which aim to predict, analyse and explain human behaviour, in particular to estimate the usability of proposed systems.
3. GOMS models aim to calculate and predict task-completion times for a range of tasks varying in complexity.
4. CCT concentrates on learning and transfer rather than prediction of error-free task-completion times for experts. Hence, CCT examines learners rather than experts, and it predicts learning time rather than success in learning, or error-rates.
5. TAG intends to provide a formalism for modelling the mental representation of an interaction language. It aims to predict the knowledge an ideal user might have of the interaction language.
6. CTA concentrates on functions rather than on properties of processes. It aims to make the relationships between theory, cognitive phenomena, and systems design explicit rather than calculating perfect performance.
7. PUMs aim to enable designers to ascertain whether a user would be able to run/execute the program, thereby enabling the designer to assess the usability of a proposed system.
8. Gould and Lewis emphasize users rather than system functionality; they recommend early focus on users and tasks, empirical measurements, and iterative design.
9. Usability refers to ease of use, measured by how effectively and efficiently the computer can be used by specified audiences and certain tools, for certain tasks in particular environments.
10. Usefulness is reflected in the degree to which a given system matches the tasks it is intended to support, whereas usability addresses issues to do with ease of use.
11. Designers/developers want to be sure that their systems are good; manufacturers want to know that their systems will be better than those of their competitors; marketing and the sales force want to

ensure that the products can live up to advertising claims; customers want to know they are getting the best system to suit their requirements.

12. Legislative requirements are now in force in Europe, and also for the reasons given in question 11.

13. Usability tests may serve to improve an existing system, to compare competing products or measure a system against guidelines and standards.

14. Software relies on psychology rather than physiology, and since we know much more about people's physical dimensions than about how their brain works, it is more difficult to derive software standards.

15. Guidelines are general statements designed to fit a broad range of systems and contexts; they are, with few exceptions, too general to be used in their raw form.

16. Usability testing should take place throughout the systems design and development process.

17. When usability testing occurs too late in the development process, many of the defects identified cannot be fixed because it is too expensive, cumbersome and time-consuming.

18. Usability dimensions enable us to identify measurable usability goals and to quantify usability criteria so that we know when a 'good' system is 'good enough'.

19. Usability defects are problems in the software that stand in the way of enabling smooth interaction between the user and the system.

20. Iterative tests are test-modify-retest cycles in which the same elements are tested repeatedly until the usability goal has been reached. Iterations are necessary because modifications do not always lead to improvements.

CHAPTER 2

1. Designers believe they know what users need because they are users themselves.

2. Designers make assumptions based on stereotyped views of people (users).

3. Users have difficulties verbalizing what they know, they forget that they are the task experts and they rely on designers as 'experts', assuming the 'expert' knows it all.

4. Focus on the users' perspective, develop a detailed understanding of users and their tasks to be supported by the system.

5. System inputs/outputs, attributes and relationships between inputs and outputs. Defines user and system behaviour, that is, it describes what the system will do but not how it will do it.

6. Primary users (end users) interact with the system; secondary users receive outputs from the system but do not interact with it, and tertiary users are involved with the system only in terms of maintenance and longer term IT strategy.

7. A task analysis is a step-by-step comparison of demands of a task on the task performer with the task performer's capabilities, described in terms of operational procedures and knowledge necessary to complete a task.

8. Kirwan and Ainsworth divide task analysis techniques into: task data collection methods; task description methods; task simulation methods; task behaviour assessment methods; task requirements evaluation methods.

9. TAKD aims to identify and make explicit all the knowledge required for executing a particular task successfully and systematically.

10. TAKD seeks to produce a specification of the knowledge required to use a system, or the knowledge a system would need to include to perform a task.

11. TAKD forces analysts to be aware of decisions they make by imposing an explicit way of thinking about tasks and task-contexts in terms of both user and system knowledge requirements.

12. HTA (hierarchical task analysis) is a broad approach to task analysis in which goals are decomposed into sub-goals and sub-tasks from which a series of plans and operations is generated. This forms the basis for establishing when sub-tasks should be carried out to meet system goals.

13. The nature of components is *ad hoc* and lacks formalism which makes it difficult to select the best level of detail at which to describe a given task.

14. The four steps in task analysis are: define the purpose; collect the data; analyse the data; model the task domain.

15. If task analysis outcomes are not verified with the task performers, the chances are that steps have been missed, or that the analyst's understanding does not reflect the way task performers think about their tasks.

16. In whatever form task performers can understand – they must be able to recognize descriptions as the tasks they perform.

17. Otherwise it might not be possible to get permission to be present in the work place; the analyst will ask questions and interrupt the task performers at times.

18. The client may not realise how much time and involvement is required of employees to do task analyses. Making this explicit justifies the analyst's presence and becomes a recognized part of the project.

19. Job analyses help to establish links between tasks and understand constraints as well as competing requirements on users.

20. Knowledge of constraints is important because it helps to exclude possible I/O and other system-related solutions and to arrive at an optimal physical solution.

CHAPTER 3

1. Because we use samples to predict and generalize population characteristics.
2. Random sampling – because this stands the best chance of yielding unbiased data.
3. Independent, dependent and extraneous variables; independent variables are the characteristics we manipulate; dependent variables are what we measure and extraneous variables are what we seek to control.
4. Mode, mean, median. The mode is the least useful.
5. When dealing with a skewed distribution in which a small number of scores contribute disproportionately to the mean.
6. It enables us to compare means and dispersions of scores from different sampling distributions to determine the likelihood that two or more sets of data were drawn from the same population.
7. Because, in many situations, knowledge of scores on one variable enables us to predict the score on another if we know whether the relationship is positive or negative.
8. Reliability means stability and replicability.
9. Because we want to ensure that results obtained on a set of observations are stable rather than being one off, as we tend to use findings for generalization.
10. When measuring the amount of learning or retention from one trial to the next; in split-half reliability tests to see if users really understood the task and the test.
11. Validity is an assessment of the success of a test to measure what it sets out to measure.
12. Because one can never prove one is right.
13. Prototypes allow us to test many aspects of a system and competing, potential solutions very early in the design/development process.
14. Static prototypes do not respond to user input, whereas dynamic ones do (they are 'runnable').
15. Non-interacting, Wizard-of-Oz, hybrid studies and storyboarding; all but storyboarding may be used in usability testing.
16. Field studies give an impression of how things happen in reality, that is, they give context-validity to observations and help fill in gaps, link tasks, etc. One danger is that behaviour may be different when an observer is not present.

17. In field experiments, the experimenter intervenes in the real world setting, whereas in field studies he/she only tries to capture the real situation.
18. Electronic datafiles are likely to show times that are much longer than the average expected. If you are not there to observe what the user does during this time, you miss out on important information that would tell you where to look for usability defects.
19. The main purpose is to convey usability defect severity and ensure someone takes responsibility for fixing them, and that this is documented.
20. A scientific audience must be able to reconstruct your tests and replicate your results.

CHAPTER 4

1. Protocols generate lots of data in a short time without much effort from the evaluator.
2. Protocol data are time-consuming and difficult to code and analyse; they may not give an accurate picture of what is actually happening, and the value of the data depends on the skill of the analyst.
3. In contextual inquiries, the users' work environment is preserved and the method is a mixture of online and retrospective protocols. They form a good basis for generating design ideas which can be manipulated and used directly as design inputs.
4. Task-similarity judgments make explicit relationships between tasks and task-components which may not be tapped by other methods.
5. A heuristic evaluation is an informal, subjective and anecdotal usability analysis which is conducted from the perspective of typical target-audience users.
6. Outcomes depend on what questions the evaluator asks and what he/she decides to test. Hence, the more experienced a usability expert is, the more potential usability defects he/she is likely to uncover.
7. Heuristic evaluations are quick to do, they are relatively inexpensive as they require no data logging equipment or participation by a large number of users, and they uncover a wide range of problems.
8. Several heuristic evaluations are usually necessary. They should ideally be done by usability experts and it is not always easy to distinguish between trivial and serious usability defects. Heuristic evaluations do not therefore test the system in the sense of establishing its limitations.
9. Confirmation studies do not challenge the system. Like heuristic evaluations, they do not establish system limitations.

10. Once a system has been completed and delivered, it is generally too expensive to fix problems and also, the later in the process these are uncovered, the more fixing costs escalate.
11. Different disciplines bring different viewpoints and biases and uncover a wider range of possible usability defects.
12. When they are involved in a design/development project, they find it difficult to think up tests disconfirming system operations; that is, they tend to ensure that the system conforms to their expectations of what it should do – this does not uncover weaknesses.
13. Avoid wasting time fixing trivial problems at the expense of serious ones unless they are easy and quick to fix.
14. Confirmation studies test our hypotheses about the seriousness of usability defects exposed in heuristic evaluations by entering these into tasks and observing user performance.
15. User tasks are designed specifically to test the seriousness and impact on user performance of problems detected in heuristic evaluations.
16. Walkthroughs are structured thinking exercises designed to detect design flaws from thinking through detailed tasks; they are a theory-driven, form-based approach.
17. Critical issues are task selection, actual evaluation process, requisite knowledge and data analysis/interpretation of results.
18. Same as earlier; different disciplines ask different questions and come up with different solutions.
19. Diagnostic rather than analytic tool.
20. Tasks serve largely the same function in a global usability analysis as in confirmation studies, except that, rather than the experimenter measuring the evaluator's performance, the task experience is intended to be integrated into the evaluator's overall impression of the system.

CHAPTER 5

1. The interviewee must have access to the information you require; the aim of the interview must be clear to the interviewee; the interviewer must remain interested but neutral during the interview; a debriefing session must be offered at the end of the interview.
2. Train interviewers to refrain from presenting their own views, from showing signs of disapproval, disagreement or disappointment in the respondent's answers.
3. A semi-structured interview is more focused than unstructured and less rigid than structured ones. It allows for maximum flexibility by including a set of questions in a structured interview, while also leaving room for interviewees to expand on important issues.

4. A probe is a method for stimulating interviewees to give more information. The purpose of probes is to encourage the interviewee to clarify or expand on answers.

5. There are two types of probe: echo and extension. The interviewer either repeats what the interviewee said (echo) or the interviewer asks for more information that extends the respondent's answer.

6. Open ended questions are left to respondents to answer in whatever way and at the level of detail they choose. They are more difficult to code than questions with pre-defined response categories.

7. An interview has a beginning, a middle and an end. First, ask a few warm-up questions, easy to answer, to put the interviewee at ease; then get onto the more complex and difficult questions. Finally, ask another few easy routine questions at the end so that the interviewee feels good about the interview.

8. Write your post interview summary as soon as you can after the interview, while it is still fresh in your mind.

9. An interview is interactive and allows for clarification while it is ongoing; it encourages exploration of issues and ideas and offers room for flexibility; questionnaires are easier to administer but are also more rigidly structured.

10. When planning a survey, you make the research question clear and explicit and then decide what information you are after (define categories) and how this information will be applied to your system.

11. Coding responses and entering the response codes directly onto the questionnaire in the right or left hand margin enables you to enter responses straight from it into the computer.

12. Questionnaires should be structured into categories dealing with different kinds of information. Generally, start with a few brief, personal, non-threatening questions. This makes it look as if the questionnaire is quick to complete, then present the more difficult ones, and finally, a few brief, easy ones – just as in an interview.

13. To use a split-half reliability coefficient, the questionnaire must be quite long so that respondents are likely to have forgotten how they answered questions last time. Long questionnaires reduce respondents' motivation to complete them.

14. The tendency to respond to a long series of questions in a similar fashion, even if this is semantically inconsistent, is called a response–set. It can be avoided by phrasing questions so that sometimes a low, sometimes a high score is consistent with a particular view. This kind of structure forces the respondent to read the questions.

15. Group, individual, telephone and mail are the most common forms of administering questionnaires.

16. People's working memory fades quickly in the auditory mode and we want them to concentrate on the question, not on memorizing response categories.

17. To make sure everyone gets exactly the same information – avoid bias.

18. Feedback paves the way for respondents to participate in future research; people want to know how their data contributed to answers.

19. Enables you to go back for more later.

20. Continuous scales facilitate comparison of responses from different questions, eliminate the need for respondents to translate their judgment or opinion into a numeric statement; finer grain statistical analysis is possible and continuous scales are more likely to detect statistical differences.

CHAPTER 6

1. It is believed that they take too long to generate valid results.

2. Experimental results may fail to meet the experimenter's expectations because the research question may not be suited to experimentation; the question may not be clear enough, ambiguous or too broad; there may be sampling problems, a lack of subject-representativeness; the number of subjects may be too small; tasks may not be suited; data analysis may be inappropriate.

3. The more accurately you define your research question, the easier it is to decide whether a laboratory experiment is appropriate, whether the tasks, subjects, the nature of the data to be collected will enable you to answer the question.

4. Operational questions are phrased so that they can be quantified and measured.

5. Tasks that are too easy are completed perfectly by all or most subjects (ceiling effect); a floor effect exists when tasks are so difficult that no subject can complete them.

6. A control group yields a baseline measure, that is, performance is not manipulated, whereas that for the treatment group shows any effect of the independent variable.

7. Experimental control provides a standard against which to compare the effect of a particular variable; it is also the ability to restrain the sources of variability in research.

8. Counting events; measuring time; noting the presence or absence of phenomena; measuring the level or amount of a phenomenon.

9. The header enables you to identify exactly where in the relevant datafile the data belong.

10. The header specifies the subject, subject-group, condition, task, and other relevant aspects. This is important as data are likely to be combined in different ways once analysis starts.
11. You are likely to miss important events and gaps in the file (i.e. times that are much longer than expected) which cannot be filled meaningfully because, without observing subjects, you do not know what they are doing.
12. If you want to make sure that subjects are fully familiar with the tasks once they get to the experimental tasks, you should train them.
13. Consider what issues the experiment is to address. Start from the general, work towards the more specific; consider tasks, data, data logging methods, data analysis, interpretation, how the data might fit into your system. Consider instructions, training, debriefing, hypothesis, duration of the experiment and the timeliness of the results.
14. Values of the independent variable are generally referred to as experimental conditions.
15. Pilot studies are small-scale experiments conducted before a proper experiment is run.
16. Pilot studies check that instructions evoke the behaviour wanted, that the procedure is fine, that the timing of tasks, data logging tools and data match what is needed to answer the research question. They give you a chance to correct any aspect of the experiment which turns out to be different to that expected, or to make any changes before the full set of data are collected.
17. When briefing subjects, be sure not to give any information about what you are testing and how because people want to deliver their best rather than their natural behaviour.
18. You must ensure that subjects feel good about the experiment and that their contribution was worthwhile.
19. Support for a hypothesis is not validation or proof that it is correct; the test must be fair. Beware of extraneous variables and that variables measured were relevant to the research question.
20. Quasi-experiments do not allow the experimenter to exert the same level of control over the variables as in formal laboratory experiments.

CHAPTER 7

1. Costs/benefits determine whether or not the system ought to go ahead.

2. In order to select the best possible technology and also to provide some basis for calculating costs, users and their tasks must be considered during the feasibility phase.
3. The nature of the system, the environment into which it will be put, the client, whether or not it will be facing competition from other systems, whether it is a follow-on or a new system.
4. Identify the target audience, the target environment, suitable technology and develop a business case.
5. A business case is used to assess the potential success of a proposed system in the market place in terms of the size of the potential target audience and system development costs, and it is a tool with which you attempt to persuade management to allow a system to go ahead.
6. In many specialized systems, the people we are trying to serve are also end users (primary users) and cost savings made by reducing training time, error-correction time, transaction time are calculated on the basis of end users' tasks.
7. Because the people whose time is to be saved may not be able to use the saved time more productively because of other constraints.
8. Other systems soon show whether you may be optimistic about your proposed system's marketability.
9. During the research phase, it is decided which issues should be pursued in more detail; a usability test and evaluation plan is established.
10. We know all relevant details about all classes of users and their tasks, links between tasks, and which ones are suitable for automation.

CHAPTER 8

1. The main purpose of a test and evaluation plan is to ensure that testing is integrated into systems development, that test results are integrated, and that sufficient resources are allocated to testing.
2. Human factors experts are trained to design, conduct and analyse tests and estimate costs and timing.
3. Components of a usability test and evaluation plan are: specification of tests (what tests, done when), costing and timing, who and how much, goal statement, benchmark tasks.
4. They are too expensive, too time-consuming or not necessary.
5. Outcomes of a user needs analysis are user profiles which help to identify those aspects of systems that should be given most attention during the development; a task analysis plan which determines typical, frequent or confusing tasks; this helps to select benchmark tasks.

6. Benchmark tasks are used to gain an impression of overall level of usability achieved in an emerging system; they are the yardstick by which we decide when usability criteria in the goal statement have been achieved.

7. Usability goal states what is to be achieved in broad realistic terms; it forms the basis for a test plan.

8. A usability goals must be concrete, quantifiable, objective and measurable.

9. Goals must be stated in quantitative form to make it clear later when they have been achieved.

10. It must be clear how results from any test will fit into the further system development process.

11. Critical tasks take the highest priority because a certain level of danger or risk is associated with them.

12. Must be done; should be done; budget permitting tasks.

13. Benchmark tasks must signal when usability criteria have been met.

14. To allude to aspects of tasks that could result in any of these; to serve as a conceptual 'hatrack'.

15. To ensure adequate resources are allocated to the test budget from the outset.

16. In case there might be budgetary constraints, during execution of the program, or if we need to balance costs, or if we cannot get the plan accepted.

17. A usability defect severity index helps to classify usability defects according to their impact on user performance.

18. A usability defect severity index helps to identify rank order fixing priority.

19. Impact, probability of occurrence, frequency of occurrence.

20. An impact analysis shows which problems are influencing subjects most; it helps to set fixing priorities that are realistic.

CHAPTER 9

1. A help system should assist users in trouble to recover from errors without fuss.

2. Potential user problems must be anticipated when designing a help system.

3. Mismatches between system rules and users' expectations of how the system should work.

4. Users easily forget where in the menu hierarchy they currently are, where they are going or and where they came from; sometimes they forget the question they were asking when consulting help.

5. Most problems occur at the top level, in the main menu.

6. By providing broad menu structures, allowing users to enter keywords, and searching through keyword lists help to reduce menu navigation problems.
7. Users like to feel in control of the computer; they might not read information imposed upon them which removes this feeling.
8. Test the vocabulary to be used by samples of representative users.
9. A good help system should be small and compact; it should give brief instructions; consist of as few levels as possible if hierarchical menus are used; provide a list of keywords/commands; assist users solving specific problems; clearly indicate different system modes, for example, by applying screen identification; present carefully selected and tested vocabulary; use consistent screen design.
10. It is easier to read all the information that applies to a particular problem in one place rather than moving around, collecting bits here and there.
11. Usability goals should be set for help systems in the same manner as they apply to all other areas of a system, and iterative testing should show when help is good enough.
12. The purpose of user manuals must be determined first, deciding what information to present, how much, how and where it is likely to be used and by whom.
13. Documentation should be developed in parallel with the system itself rather than attached at the end.
14. Manuals are unpopular because they often lack consistency in presentation; often diagrams are difficult to read and relate to the text; manuals are sometimes not accurately aligned to the system. Also, users like to interact with the system – not to read about how to interact with it.
15. New users have difficulties formulating clear questions; they tend to ask 'why does this not work' or 'what's wrong' which does not help in deciding where to look for the right information.
16. Tabs, good indices, clear tables of contents and headings help to make a manual easier to use than continuous text.
17. Usability tests of manuals should ensure that users can locate the right information, that they can interpret it and apply it to problems at hand.
18. Retesting is necessary because solving one problem often creates others that were not foreseen.
19. A tutorial system must enable users to apply the material taught in another context.
20. The three questions guiding tutorial design are: what should be trained; how should training be designed; is training effective, and if so, why?

CHAPTER 2

1. Evaluating user needs for ATMs

Identify users:

Observations: before drafting a user profile, spend a day or so in different locations at different times of day, observing who uses ATMs. Note in particular:

- ages of users (roughly <20 years, 20–35, 35–55, >55 years);
- types of transactions they perform (>1?, deposit? withdrawal? transfer?);
- approximately how long people spend at the ATM (does this vary according to whether or not there is a queue?); and
- possible problems they appear to have.

Interviews: (sample a small subset of people you observe)

- find out how long they have used ATMs;
- what they like about them;
- what they dislike about them;
- where and how they have experienced problems with ATMs;
- whether and how they have overcome these;
- how often they use ATMs;
- whether they use other forms of banking (go to bank, EFTPOS);
- if so, how often; and
- how would they improve the current system.

Source documentation: The bank must have information on who uses ATMs. Get hold of relevant documents and work out the proportion of customers who seem to use them. When these data have been collected, draft a user profile. Then repeat interviews and sample an equal number of people in each age category.

Tasks:

- Simple tasks: deposit, withdrawal, transfer, getting information (balance on all accounts);
- Complex tasks: systematic combinations of two or more of the above in a single transaction.

Tasks to be analysed

- **Primary users:** (bank customers, all ages), from observations, interviews: all simple tasks, at least once and a scenario of complex tasks.

- **Secondary users:** (bank administration staff), from observations, documents, interviews:
  - check daily balance in ATM safe;
  - record of transactions and amounts involved;
  - statistics for weekly/monthly/annual comparison.

- **Tertiary users:** (bank systems staff), sources as for secondary users:
  - record of any technical problem in the past 24 hours;
  - reports on system reliability and performance.

- **Physical constraints:**
  - users range in height (1.20 –ˈ1.90m) – some in wheelchairs;
  - some have corrected vision (large printing or voice output);
  - some have poor hand-eye co-ordination (size of keys, distance between them);
  - some are physically weak (are keys too tight, hard to press?).

- **Environment constraints:**
  - weather conditions change (wet, frost, heat);
  - sun may cause glare (adjustable screen-viewing position);
  - security protection (e.g. enclose ATM in atrium).

2. Task scenarios for e-mail:
Areas of the e-mail system are:

SEND RECEIVE DIRECTORY (main menu)
CREATE/EDIT POST SAVE DELETE READ LIST FIND (next level menu)

Simple tasks (ST) (trying out one main menu item and all relevant secondary options in each task).

- ST 1. (actions required: SEND: FIND/EDIT/SAVE/DELETE/LIST/READ/POST)
  - Message no. S34, written from your company to Ms M Bennett, concerns an order for 5000 steel wing nuts. This number of wing nuts should be 8000 instead, and the message should be addressed to Mr R Green. Please change it accordingly.
  - File the updated order.
  - Previous correspondence from your company to Ms Bennett (S18) is no longer relevant. Please remove it from the system.
  - See whether a reply has been composed to GJ Young of GJ Young and Co. regarding their order for flywheels.
  - Check that the reply gives an indication of how soon delivery should take place.
  - Send it off.

- ST 2. (actions required: RECEIVE: LIST/SAVE/FIND/READ/DELETE)

 – See whether an expected message from M Stewart regarding an order
   for pneumatic valves has arrived.
 – If it has, file it for future reference.
 – Check whether message R12 includes any orders for 1994.
 – If it does not, it has become obsolete and should be removed from the
   system.

• ST 3. (actions required: DIRECTORY: FIND/LIST)
 – Fiona Lewis worked for BMS Engineering in Moorabin, Victoria.
   Please check which street the company is in. The correct street name
   is:..
 – Currently, there is only one company connected to the e-mail
   system in Tasmania and one in South Australia. Please find the
   names of these companies: The names are: Tas:.............................
   S.A.:....................................

Complex tasks (CT) (accessing >1 main menu item and secondary
menu items).

• CT 1. (actions required: RECEIVE: DELETE; SEND: DELETE;
  DIRECTORY: LIST; SEND: FIND)
  Your company will no longer be dealing with the FX Manufacturing
  Company, since you have stopped making the specialized casings FX
  requires.
 – Therefore, remove the following items of previous correspondence with
   FX: incoming message R19, and outgoing message S27.
 – Another clerk was instructed to remove the names and addresses of all
   the FX company's representatives from the system. Has this been done
   yet? YES/NO.
 – Ensure that the last message which was sent to FX, S30, informed
   them that Prime Engineering could act as an alternative supplier of
   their needs.

• CT 2. (actions required: RECEIVE: FIND; SEND: EDIT; DIRECTORY:
  FIND; SEND: EDIT/SAVE)
  The two alterations given below are required to outgoing message
  S24.
 – Check the number of bearings requested in the latest order from
   Thomas Bruckner (message R14) and modify the number promised in
   S24 to correspond.
 – Since S24 was prepared, Thomas Bruckner's company has moved.
   Check the current address, and alter the address mentioned in message
   S24 accordingly.
 – File the updated message so that it can be sent later.

- CT 3. (actions required: RECEIVE: LIST/SAVE; SEND: LIST/POST)
  A telephone order has been placed by John Benson for replacement part number 3361, with written confirmation to follow.
  - Check if the written order has arrived. If so, find the reply which has already been prepared.
  - Find Benson's request and send off the reply.

CHAPTER 4

You obviously need to know much more about your users and their tasks before you can even contemplate an evaluation of the two systems. First, you would therefore conduct a user needs analysis, designing a user profile (remember, consider primary, secondary and tertiary users) and, from interacting with and observing users and reading documentation, you would draft a task analysis plan (Ch. 8). Since the users are experts, you might consider applying some of the knowledge elicitation methods discussed in this chapter, for example, question-asking protocols, contextual inquiry and card sorting exercises, to learn all you need to know about their present tasks.

Equipped with an understanding of users' tasks, you can then work through the systems to sort out just how well each fits the users, their tasks, the environment, and other constraints of the work place. A heuristic evaluation will get you some way towards defining quite a few of the inadequacies of the systems as they are currently presented, and a conceptual walkthrough would help you to identify where and how each is likely to break down. Sooner or later you should expose the systems to user comment, perhaps by trying out some of their tasks included in a confirmation study. User comments, together with their performance data, should enable you to decide on one system, and also give you justification for your decision.

CHAPTER 5

1. Critique of questionnaire
Let us first give you a few hints on the sorts of problems you should identify in the draft questionnaire.

- **Response categories:**
  - too many formats;
  - same-response categories are not kept together;
  - too many open ended questions;
  - Likert scales presented vertically.

- **Response coding:**
  - data coding intentions are not clear;
  - cannot compare responses across scales;
  - data analysis is not clarified;
  - too many actions required (ticking boxes, circling answers, long-hand);
  - sometimes the most negative response is shown first, sometimes it is last.

- **Questionnaire layout:**
  - questions requiring the same type of response are not kept to-gether;
  - category descriptions are not consistent with content;
  - sometimes boxes follow response category, sometimes they precede them;
  - unusual layout of some scales (vertical).

- **Questionnaire structure:**
  - there is no real structure; category names give no indication of content;
  - no clear beginning, middle or end;
  - no consistent alignment of response boxes.

2. Redesign the POSNET questionnaire

DRAFT POSNET SURVEY

SECTION 1. PERSONAL/DISTRICT DETAILS

Family name:...

Given name:...

Work phone number:...

Current position:...

District/Section name:...

District address:...

.... Postcode:.....................

District type:...
(eg. TBS,RES)

a. POSNET has been implemented in your District since:

month .... year ....

b. How many terminals are connected to your POSNET

LAN(s)?: ....

c. How many terminals are **NOT** connected to your POSNET

LAN(s)?: ....

d. How many dumb terminals are there in your District?: ....

e. Does your District use pooled LIDs on POSNET?   Yes/No
(Please circle one option)

SECTION 2. SATISFACTION WITH POSNET

1. How satisfied are you with POSNET in terms of
(For each of the following questions, please circle the answer that best expresses your opinion)

(a) its overall performance?

| Completely dissatisfied | Dissatisfied | Neutral | Satisfied | Completely satisfied |

(b) logon time?

| Completely dissatisfied | Dissatisfied | Neutral | Satisfied | Completely satisfied |

(c) system response time?

| Completely dissatisfied | Dissatisfied | Neutral | Satisfied | Completely satisfied |

(d) reliability?

| Completely dissatisfied | Dissatisfied | Neutral | Satisfied | Completely satisfied |

2. Describe ways in which POSNET has failed to meet your expectations: ....

3. Describe any business processes which might be inhibited by the POSNET LAN: ....

4. Try to outline ways in which POSNET could be enhanced to overcome these problems: ....

SECTION 3. PLANNING AND INFORMATION

(For each of Questions 5-7, please circle one option)

5. Were you or your staff involved in pre-implementation
   planning for the POSNET LAN?　　　　　　　　　　　　YES/NO

6. Are you satisfied with the level of involvement your
   staff have had in the planning of your
   POSNET LAN?　　　　　　　　　　　　　　　　　　YES/NO

If your answer was YES to question 6, go to question 8.

7. Was there sufficient planning
   (a) for the installation of your POSNET LAN?　　　YES/NO

   (b) to meet your business communications needs?　YES/NO

   (c) other (please specify): ....

   　　　　...

SECTION 4. INSTALLATION

8. During the installation of POSNET, how satisfied were you with
   the following:
   (For each of the following questions, please circle the answer that best expresses
   your opinion)

   (a) the programming of the installation?

Completely   Dissatisfied   Neutral   Satisfied   Completely
dissatisfied   satisfied

   (b) the staff who installed POSNET?

Completely   Dissatisfied   Neutral   Satisfied   Completely
dissatisfied   satisfied

   (c) the way they went about their work?

Completely   Dissatisfied   Neutral   Satisfied   Completely
dissatisfied   satisfied

   (d) the amount of time it took to install POSNET?

Completely   Dissatisfied   Neutral   Satisfied   Completely
dissatisfied   satisfied

   (e) the state of the POSNET LAN when it was handed over to the
       District?

Completely   Dissatisfied   Neutral   Satisfied   Completely
dissatisfied   satisfied

Thank you very much for completing this survey. Your responses
will help us greatly to understand just how we can improve our
services to you.

CHAPTER 6

1. Visual list search
Experiment 2: horizontal scanning; alternating dots and dashes, shown in Fig. 10.1

Spaced dots

```
Beecham B.......................................................62
        D.......................................................57
        F.......................................................90
Borland E.......................................................61
        H.......................................................41
        J.......................................................50
        M.......................................................43
Bristow B.......................................................29
        G.......................................................22
        J.......................................................95
```

Spaced dots and dashes

```
Bellamy D.......................................................64
        G-------------------------------------------------------59
        I.......................................................92
Blewett G-------------------------------------------------------63
        J.......................................................43
        K-------------------------------------------------------52
        M.......................................................46
Bradley D-------------------------------------------------------21
        G.......................................................24
        J-------------------------------------------------------97
```

Nonspaced dots

```
Beasley C.......................................................63
Beasley E.......................................................58
Beasley H.......................................................91
Bittman F.......................................................62
Bittman J.......................................................42
Bittman K.......................................................51
Bittman N.......................................................45
Boulton C.......................................................20
Boulton F.......................................................23
Boulton H.......................................................96
```

Nonspaced dots and dashes

```
Beamish A.......................................................61
Beamish C-------------------------------------------------------56
Beamish G.......................................................98
Birrell D-------------------------------------------------------60
Birrell G.......................................................40
Birrell I-------------------------------------------------------59
Birrell L.......................................................42
Bolitho A-------------------------------------------------------28
Bolitho E.......................................................20
Bolitho G-------------------------------------------------------94
```

Figure 10.1: Sample screens with dots and dots/dashes.

If we consider all possible outcomes of our experiment, our data plots would look something like those in Fig. 10.2.

These four outcomes represent the possible ways our data might look, being affected either by both of the variables, by neither, or by one or the other. Actual data are likely to be less clear cut, but, in principle, they will fall roughly along one of the arguments outlined. Plotting data in this way makes you think in more detail about exactly what you can expect from your experiment, given the conditions and the variables you are testing. Doing this exercise is one excellent way to formulate your expectations realistically and make predictions which do not raise expectations to a level the data will not be able to meet, even in the best of worlds.

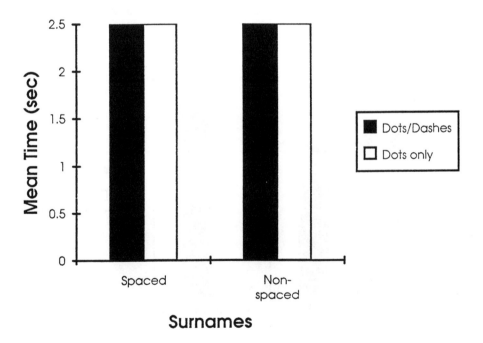

Figure 10.2: Neither of our two variables have any effect on performance. That is, subjects perform equally well regardless of whether surnames are spaced or non-spaced, and regardless of whether lines are filled with dots only or with dots and dashes alternating.

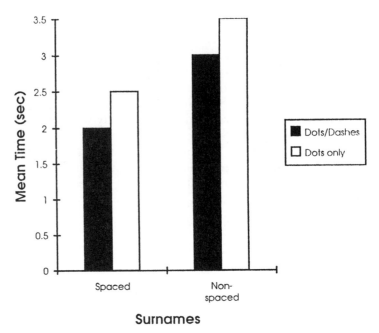

Figure 10.3: Both variables affect performance which is better when dots and dashes are alternating with dotted lines only, and also spacing is better than non-spacing.

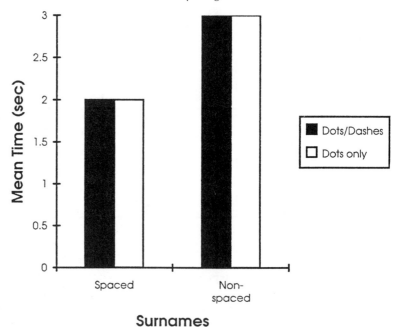

Figure 10.4: Spacing leads to better performance than non-spacing, but alternating lines does not affect performance as compared with dotted lines only.

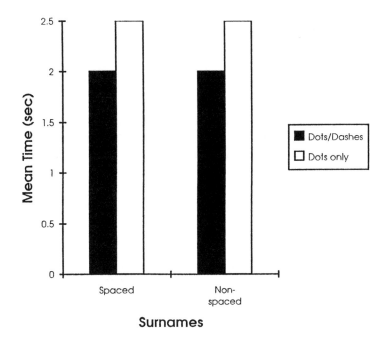

Figure 10.5: Spacing has no effect here, but performance is better when dots and dashes alternate with dotted lines.

For Experiment 3, you again contrast the effect of spacing (versus non-spacing) and inserting a blank line (versus no blank line) between groups of data which belong together. This is shown in Fig. 10.5. As in Experiment 2, experimental design, tasks, measures, subjects and data analysis remain as in the experiment reported in Chapter 6.

Your data plots of possible outcomes would look exactly like the four cases, since you are also testing two variables in the same manner as in Experiment 2. The only difference would be the labelling of the categories as shown in Fig. 10.6.

2. Icon evaluation

Let us assume that the icons have already been designed. Take the entire set, and describe the function hidden behind each in a brief verbal label, using no more than three words to describe each. Then, reproduce every icon and every verbal label on a card, the size of a normal business card, so that you end up with two decks of cards – one containing icons and the other containing verbal labels. Now, write a detailed explanation for each of the functions represented by icons and verbal labels. Take care to avoid using the same words in your explanations as on the verbal-label cards, because your experimental subjects will be matching either verbal labels or icons with the explanations; reading the same words in both explanation and label would therefore be too much of a give-away!

Spaced/blank line

```
Beecham B-----------------------------------------------------62
        D......................................................57
        F-----------------------------------------------------90

Borland E......................................................61
        H-----------------------------------------------------41
        J......................................................50
        M-----------------------------------------------------43

Bristow B......................................................29
        G-----------------------------------------------------22
        J......................................................95
```

Spaced/no blank line

```
Bellamy D......................................................64
        G-----------------------------------------------------59
        I......................................................92
Blewett G-----------------------------------------------------63
        J......................................................43
        K-----------------------------------------------------52
        M......................................................46
Bradley D-----------------------------------------------------21
        G......................................................24
        J-----------------------------------------------------97
```

Nonspaced/no blank line

```
Beasley C-----------------------------------------------------63
Beasley E......................................................58
Beasley H-----------------------------------------------------91
Bittman F......................................................62
Bittman J-----------------------------------------------------42
Bittman K......................................................51
Bittman N-----------------------------------------------------45
Boulton C......................................................20
Boulton F-----------------------------------------------------23
Boulton H......................................................96
```

Nonspaced/blank line

```
Beamish A......................................................61
Beamish C-----------------------------------------------------56
Beamish G......................................................98

Birrell D-----------------------------------------------------60
Birrell G......................................................40
Birrell I-----------------------------------------------------59
Birrell L......................................................42

Bolitho A-----------------------------------------------------28
Bolitho E......................................................20
Bolitho G-----------------------------------------------------94
```

Figure 10.6: Dots/dashes and spaced screen samples.

Subjects: control for aspects as mentioned in the visual list search experiment, and consider contrasting the performance of technical experts with that of technical novices. Use at least two subject-groups: one that matches icons with explanations, and another that matches verbal labels with explanations.

Design: Add 5–6 dummy examples to your list of explanations. The dummy examples, 'filler items,' should be so similar to the real explanations that they introduce an element of uncertainty into the task. The purpose of adding filler items is to make the task somewhat more difficult than a mere choice-by-elimination task. So, your explanation list contains more items than the sample of icons and verbal labels. This is a between-subject design which now looks as follows:

> Subject-group 1: S1–30 match icons with explanations;
> Subject-group 2: S1–30 match verbal labels with explanations.

Data: Compare the percentage of correct matches of icons/explanations with the percentage of correct matches of verbal labels/explanations and analyse statistically (t-test, see statistical texts for details). Also, look closely at which icons/verbal labels are incorrectly matched. Which ones are confused? Are the same items confused when presented as verbal labels and as icons? Are certain underlying functions poorly described in either icon or label, or is there something illogical about the function itself? Once you begin analysing data in detail, you will find yourself asking all sorts of questions that never occurred to you before you conducted your experiment.

3. Error messages

The problem is similar to that in Exercise 2, and can be treated in a similar fashion. Instead of comparing icons with verbal labels, we compare two sets of error messages. You can adopt the same design as before; your list of explanations now outlines the kind of situation in which each error message might be shown on the screen. As before, you should include roughly six filler items which could be confused with actual situations. You could adopt either a between-subject or a within-subject design, and there are statistical arguments supporting either. Your design differs, according to whether you choose between- or within-subject designs:

Between-subjects: as for Exercise 2.
Within-subjects:

> S1–20 Standard error messages → New error messages;
> S21–40 New error messages → Standard error messages.

If you are opting for a within-subjects design, you might want to change around the items in your explanation list randomly and give subjects a different one for each set of error messages. In your analysis, you might want to contrast performance by the order in which subjects matched the two sets of error messages, yielding a comparison of standard/new and new/standard. You would do this if you were interested in determining the effect on 'new' as a function of pre-exposure to standard.

4. UNIX mail

The critical issue here is 'are tilde-escape functions useless'? There are several ways of investigating this, and a few ideas are given here.

1. Design a set of mailing tasks that could be completed using either tilde-escapes or less advanced features. Print these out, each task on a different piece of paper, and ask subjects who must be UNIX users (you might want to define different classes of users, e.g. experts/experienced/new, related to the amount of their UNIX experience) to write down the functions, one after the other, they would access if they were to complete the tasks in UNIX mail. Make sure the functions you include can be achieved either via simple commands or by using tilde-escape commands. Your tasks force subjects to make explicit the actions they would take in the system. The findings should show who uses which functions, and what proportion of functions may be implemented using either tilde-escapes or simple functions. Data interpretation: the smaller the proportion of tilde-escape functions, the more 'useless' they are.

2. Do the same as in (1) above, but sit behind subjects while they interact with UNIX and complete their tasks. You take notes about the functions used and treat the data in the same fashion as described above. Data interpretation: as in (1) above.

3. Produce an electronic data logging tool and do as in (2), except that the system itself yields the necessary data concerning the use of functions, instead of you taking notes. Data interpretation: as in (1) above.

4. You could consider conducting a matching task as in Exercises 2 and 3. Here, you would present each of the UNIX functions, including tilde-escapes, on cards and match these with explanations of possible functions. Data interpretation: to the extent that tilde-escape functions provoke more errors than simple functions, tilde-escapes can be considered 'useless'.

5. Instead of a matching task, you might want to test which of the functions subjects could describe in their own words. Again, give the commands on cards and ask subjects to describe the function of each. Data interpretation: the percentage of all possible functions that are described correctly gives you a measure of the degree of 'usefulness' of the tilde-escape functions.

6. You could give subjects a framework describing how a certain task is to be done in general terms, like 'your boss has asked you to broadcast the message saved in MYFILE to all members on the CHISG.LM.AUS list. The sentence 'the meeting will take place on Wednesday, 19 October 1994' should be replaced by 'the meeting will take place on Wednesday, 26 October 1994' before the message is sent. Whilst allowing the subject to inspect these details throughout, you then also give him/her a set of commands said to have been used by another person doing the same task. Now, the task is to describe what each of the commands would have done to the document. This is, as you can see, just another way of testing what and how much subjects know about the functions of various commands. You would, of course, have several sets of commands, some using tilde-escapes, others, achieving the same things in the document, being simple commands. Data interpretation: the proportion of correct function descriptions tells you the extent to which tilde escapes are used and known (hence 'useful').

We could go on with this; the point for you to note is that there are always many ways in which issues could be investigated; there is never one, and only one, correct way to obtain the data you are after. So, when you design experiments, do consider various options.

5. Hierarchical menu system

Remember, your system is not yet implemented, and it is too bothersome, in the first instance, to program two systems in parallel. Therefore, write out your screens, one by one, using precisely the format the information would be presented in, if it were given on a computer system. Design a number of tasks which exploit the navigation paths. Each task must be carried out in both systems. Now, write the target information (e.g. 'Find out which side effects, if any, could occur by administering DIAZEPHAM 5 mg orally QID in combination with Slow K, 60 mg BD') on a card and work through the necessary screens to retrieve it. Because subjects are likely to 'get lost' in hierarchical menu systems, print out the correct path, screen by screen.

You give subjects the main menu and the target and ask them to tick the option they would select to reach the target. Then you give the next screen in the series, regardless of whether the first selection was right or wrong. Again, subjects select the option they believe would take them in the right direction, and so on, until the target is reached. The data will tell you:

1. the proportion of correct selections;
2. where subjects would have chosen an option that would have taken them in a different direction;

3. the extent to which subjects agreed amongst themselves upon selecting options which, in your system, were incorrect;
4. where your systems would need to be clarified to facilitate navigation;
5. how the two systems compared in terms of usability;
6. and so on.

Now, note that this kind of system would require you to use subjects who are medically trained and who know the subject matter which forms the contents of your database. Try to think of other ways to tackle this kind of problem yourself — and have fun!

CHAPTER 7

1. ATM redesign
First, get a complete list of all possible transactions that are supported by the current generation of ATMs (think back to the exercise in Chapter 2). These are, of course, at the operational stage, while the next generation is in the feasibility phase.

1. **Observation of users in action:** to establish whether, when, or where in performing current transactions users seem to 'get stuck'. Make sure that you observe at least three instances of each kind of transaction.
2. **Heuristic evaluation:** users whom you have observed in action may have been highly experienced. You will need to try every transaction yourself in an effort to work out where you detect potential trouble spots.
3. **Confirmation studies:** from (1) and (2) above you should have a list of potential usability problems. Design quasi-experiments around these, and expose them in realistic tasks. Recruit naive users who are not experienced with ATMs.

During the research phase, evaluate different input/output techniques and vocabulary used in the interactive dialogue, using formal experiments. At the development stage, design the various screens proposed for each transaction.

4. **Conceptual walkthroughs:** going through each transaction, testing user instructions, actions, help information and screen layouts, will help to locate possible 'holes' in the coherence of the user interface.
5. **Confirmation study:** this serves to reassure yourself that the problems you detected earlier have been eliminated. Use the same set of user tasks as in (3) and (5) until you are satisfied that the system works.

Once the ATMs have been installed and are at the operation stage, make certain your predictions concerning usability are shown to be correct.

6. **Observation of users in action:** do what you did at the outset; by observing users you will soon know how well you reached your usability goals. If any further problems are detected at this stage, correct them as quickly as possible and iterate through step (7) and, if necessary, step (6) until you are satisfied with your results.

2. Pharmanet

Since the system was given the green light, a feasibility phase has already been completed. During the research phase, you could do the following:

- **Observation of users in action:** in order to design a system that fits user needs, you will need to understand what information future users need and in which circumstances, how they use the information, and in which order they might want items presented;
- **Conduct surveys, interviews** and design **questionnaires** verifying that what you have observed is consistent with what users think they want;
- **Heuristic evaluations** in which you test the structure of your menu hierarchy as well as the contents; and maybe:
- **Quasi-experiments** using pen and paper tasks before you commit your team to any coding;
- **Conceptual walkthroughs** which take the project team through entire and realistic information retrieval tasks will help to prevent disasters. In particular, test the sense of error messages, help information, screen and system exits, and so forth before programming begins.

During the development phase, you might continue your:

- **Confirmation studies** which serve to verify that you are attaining the level of usability you are aiming for. Iterate through the most representative studies carried out during the research phase, and design further experiments as the need arises.
- **Global usability analyses** which are now due. These should be done by people from a range of different disciplines and backgrounds, including software engineers who have not participated in the project; software engineers from the project team; human factors specialists, and representative end users.

Finally, at the operation stage, you should do some follow-up through:

- **Observation of users in action.** Go out into the field and see how your system is being used, whether new and/or experienced users can readily achieve what they want in your system, and when and where they might have problems.
- **Interviews** of users to get ideas for improvements to the system as well as general comments on usefulness and usability.

3. Ticket dispenser prototype

Considering that this system is already at the prototype stage, you will need to conduct a heuristic evaluation to find out where improvements could be made to the sequence in which sub-tasks fit into a whole, the goodness of fit of relative locations in which different items are placed, in the selection methods, and so on. Depending on the outcome of this, you might need to do a number of confirmation studies to reassure yourself that your understanding of what might be problematic is correct. If major changes seem to be required, redesign the trouble spots, and test these in an iterative fashion. The cycle of redesign/test is repeated until you are satisfied that the usability criterion has been reached.

4. Museum system

First, you will need to observe how people are using, and coping with, the existing system. Notice what information people look for; observe when and where they use the computer and how usage might be related to the exhibits in various areas of the museum. How long time do people spend looking at different areas in the system? Which parts seem most attractive (animation? interactive, exploratory, illustrative tasks? spoken stories? text? text and music? video?). How much interaction is goal-directed information-seeking and how much do people browse? Which areas are browsed for how long? Note also the age and sex of people using the system, and compare the time they spend in a given area of the museum with the amount of time they spend on the computer in that area. Are people looking for in-depth factual encyclopaedic information, or do they want to get their facts via interesting, entertaining stories? Are they looking for background, historical information, or do they seek answers to specific, short questions? Do they seem to find what they are looking for, or are they using the computer merely for fun?

Observations will give you some insight into the merits and disadvantages of the current system, which should help guide the design of the next system. Also, usability problems should be readily identifiable from watching people in action. To complete the picture of current usage, follow up your observations with a chat. Ask users how they find the system, what they would like in a new system, whether they found what they hoped for, what they like best and least, etc.

In addition to observing other people, try out the system yourself in a heuristic evaluation. You must make sure that you know and understand how the entire system works. This understanding is likely to tell you which areas are the least popular, and perhaps why the unpopular ones are not being accessed.

The net outcome of your observations, interviews and heuristic evaluation is a grasp of the purpose users perceive the system is or should be fulfilling, as well as the media people seem to prefer and the suitability for displaying various kinds of information in different ways. You could even consider allowing people to select their preferred presentation medium (e.g. text or speech) as well as their preferred language. Usage will tell you how big different types of information chunks should be, and whether there should be several layers of information. Obviously, the operation stage (existing system) and the research stage (new system) go well together, and combined, they should give you a reasonable idea of what people want.

Short of repeating ourselves over and over, look to Exercises 1 and 2 in this chapter to review the types of tests you might carry out at the various stages. Basically, each one serves a purpose in any system, although it is not necessarily cost effective or even efficient to do them all. The design of a cost effective test and evaluation plan is discussed in Chapter 8.

CHAPTER 8

1. ATM redesign

1. Usability Goal Statement

- **Effectiveness:** At least 90% of new users, selected randomly from the general population, must be able to insert their card, withdraw money from two accounts (savings, cheque), deposit a cheque and request the balance on a nominated account with a maximum of two keying errors within 15 minutes of commencing the test tasks.
- **Learnability:** All operations must be achievable by following the ATM prompts, without reference to a user manual and without asking any questions of the experimenter.
- **Attitude:** Ease of use, as well as likeability must be rated at higher than 75% where 0% is 'extremely difficult' and 100% is 'extremely easy'; the probability of using the ATM again must, likewise, be estimated at 75% or higher.

2. User tasks
1. Insert card correctly.
2. Enter PIN and commence transaction.
3. Nominate a range of accounts (savings, cheque, fixed-term deposit etc.)
4. Withdraw money from any of these.
5. Deposit cash.
6. Deposit cheque.
7. Transfer money from one account to:
   (a) another held by the subject;
   (b) someone else's at the same bank;

(c) someone else's at a different bank;

(d) pay bank fees.

8. Request a statement.

9. Logoff/end session.

3. **Critical, typical and potentially troublesome tasks**
There are **no critical tasks**, but keying accuracy is critical. **Typical tasks** include the range presented above (i.e. 1–9). **Potentially troublesome tasks:**

(a) remembering and keying in correctly the PIN;

(b) follow-on tasks, where more than one task is completed in a single session. Instructions for these differ slightly from the single-transaction instructions with respect to the sequence of keys to be pressed within the transaction.

4. **Order tasks into 'must be tested', 'should be tested' and 'budget permitting'**

1. Insert card correctly	Must be tested
2. Enter PIN and commence transaction	Must be tested
3. Nominate a range of accounts	Should be tested
4. Withdraw money from any of these	Must be tested
5. Deposit cash	Must be tested
6. Deposit cheque	Must be tested
7. Transfer money from one account to	
(a) another held by the subject	Should be tested
(b) someone else's at the same bank	Should be tested
(c) someone else's at a different bank	Budget permitting
(d) pay bank fees	Budget permitting
8. Request a statement	Should be tested
9. Logoff/end session	Must be tested

5. **Suitable benchmark tasks**

Complete a successful withdrawal (tasks 1, 2, 4, 9).

Deposit a cheque in own savings account (tasks 1, 2, 6, 9).

Deposit $ 500 in own fixed term deposit account (tasks 1, 2, 5, 9).

Transfer $ 350 from own savings account to the cheque account of HEARU Pty. which uses the same bank (tasks 1, 2, 3, 4, 7d, 9).

6. **Select usability studies**

- **Observing users in action:** This is preferred over a heuristic evaluation because it is easy to observe a wide range of actual users in action over a reasonably brief period of time, and also because the range of tasks users can perform with an ATM is quite limited, as the ATMs are concerned only with on-the-spot transactions.

Observations will reveal the frequency with which different transactions are issues, any system weaknesses where users appear uncertain or press the wrong key(s).

- **Global usability analysis:** Having observed actual users, it is wise also to include other software designers, human factors experts, potential users, and bank managers in a global usability analysis. This is likely to reveal ambiguities in the prompts, illogical sequences of key presses, and other possible trouble spots, from both a professional and a typical user point of view.
- **Interview users:** In the current version of ATMs, it is useful to ask questions aimed at understanding the people's pattern of usage, e.g. why certain transactions are rarely performed; whether users tend to get all their banking done in one go, or whether they use the ATM several times during a day/week to perform all their banking, what they would like a new system to do for them that they cannot do in the present one, etc. After the new ATM has been installed, it will be useful to know:

  - if any new users have been attracted by it;
  - whether experienced users find it better than the old ATM;
  - what they like best/least about it, etc.

  Hence, a lot of mileage can be gained by asking users what they want, what they like/dislike, what they find easy/difficult, and so on.

7. **When should the usability studies be conducted?**
   The feasibility phase is not included in the program because the bank has already decided to design and install a new ATM.
   Research phase: observing users in action, interviews
   Development phase: not required
   Operation: observing users in action, interviews

8. **Calculate a usability budget, including at least two costs**
   Research phase:
   Observation of current tasks

	Ideal case		Reasonable case		Minimum acceptable	
	Time day	Cost $	Time day	Cost $	Time day	Cost $
Observing users	5	2500	2	1000	1	500
Documenting results, reporting	2	1000	1	500	0.5	250
Secretarial support	1	200	0.5	100	0	0
Interviews						
Preparation	1	500	0.5	250	0.5	250
Conducting interviews	5	2500	2	1000	1	500

	Ideal case		Reasonable case		Minimum acceptable	
	Time day	Cost $	Time day	Cost $	Time day	Cost $
Documenting results, reporting	2	1000	1	500	1	500
Secretarial support	1	200	0.5	100	0	0
Total, research phase	17	7900	7.5	3450	4	2000

Operation phase:
Observing users in action

	Time day	Cost $	Time day	Cost $	Time day	Cost $
Observing actual users	5	2500	2	1000	1	500
Documenting results, reporting	2	1000	1	500	0.5	250
Secretarial support	1	200	0.5	100	0	0

Interviews

	Time day	Cost $	Time day	Cost $	Time day	Cost $
Preparation	1	500	0.5	250	0.5	250
Conducting interviews	5	2500	2	1000	1	500
Documenting results, reporting	2	1000	1	500	1	500
Secretarial support	1	200	0.5	100	0	0
Total, operation phase	17	7900	7.5	345	4	2000

Total usability test budget:

	Ideal case		Reasonable case		Minimum acceptable	
	Time p/day	Cost $	Time p/day	Cost $	Time p/day	Cost $
Total, research phase	17	7900	7.5	3450	4	2000
Total, operation phase	17	7900	7.5	3450	4	2000
Grand total	34	15 800	15	6900	8	4000

2. Library reference system

This problem is a bit tricky in the sense that it could seem tempting merely to order the usability defects according to the percentages given in the exercise. In that view, you would put the screen design problems on top of your priority list followed by user control problems, navigation problems, and terminology problems at the bottom of the list. Note, however, that these percentages are summaries and not raw data; most likely, there were several different terminology, navigation and other problems contributing to these summary percentages – they do not represent one particular problem each. Therefore, you should first go through the actual tasks in which usability defects occurred and list these one by one, complete with an indication of the amount of task-time was consumed by each defect in every task. Next, given that task-time alone does not give the full picture of the severity of a usability defect, rate severity along the impact/probability/frequency of occurrence table presented in the chapter.

Usability defect severity ratings now give the first indication of fixing priorities in the sense that all defects receiving a high rating should go on top of the list. Remember that impact is calculated by time wasted plus the ability to continue the task. This is the reason for rating the defects; users may spend very little time on a very severe problem simply because they are unable to recover at all and continue with the next task instead of overcoming the problem. Such a situation would yield a very short recovery time, but it would also hide the severity of the usability defect.

Next, make up a list containing all the usability defects and an indication of the tasks in which they occurred. It is good economy to put defects that occur in several tasks high up in a fixing priority list. Now, you can arrange the ranking of usability defects in order of fixing priority by placing at the bottom (1) those that received a low severity rating and (2) those that occur very infrequently and were given a low or perhaps even a medium rating; the top of the list, i.e. highest priority are the high rating defects, followed by the defects encountered in most tasks.

CHAPTER 9

No solution is given to the open-ended exercises in Chapter 9.

References

Aaronson, A. and Carroll, J.M. (1987) The answer is in the question: A protocol study of intelligent help, *Behaviour and Information Technology*, **6** (4), 393–402.

Abermethy, C.N. (1984) VDTs and the human factors society – a double-edged-sword, *Human Factors Bulletin*, **27** (4), 1–2.

Ackermann, D. and Tauber, M.J. (eds) (1990) *Mental Models and Human-computer Interaction 1*, Elsevier Science Publishers, North-Holland.

Alavi, M. (1984) An assessment of the prototyping approach to information systems development, *Communications of the ACM*, **27** (6), 556–63.

Alford, J.A., Thomas, J.E. and Witham, B. (1985) A task oriented help system: Human factors issues and activities, in *Trends in Ergonomics/Human Factors II*, (eds R.E. Eberts and C.G. Eberts), Elsevier Science Publishers, North-Holland.

Allwood, C.M. and Eliasson, M. (1988) Question asking when learning a text-editing system, *Int. J. Man–Machine Studies*, **29**, 63–79.

Alves Marques, J., Guimaraes, N. and Pinto Simoes, L. (1991) Images: A user interface development system, *Interacting with Computers*, **3** (2), 131–54.

Anastasi, A. (1976) *Psychological testing*, 4th edn Macmillan Publishing.

Anderson, J.R. (1981) *Cognitive Skills and their Acquisition*, Lawrence Erlbaum & Associates, Hillsdale, NJ.

Anderson, J.R. (1983) *The Architecture of Cognition*, Harvard University Press, London.

Anderson, N.H. (1982) *Methods of Information Integration Theory*, Academic Press, New York.

Andriole, S.J. (1987) Storyboard prototyping for requirements verification, *Large Scale Systems*, **12**, 231–47.

Annett., J., Duncan, K.D., Stammers, R.B. and Gray, M.J. (1971) *Task analysis, training information number 6*, HMSO, London.

Ash, D. and Loeb, M. (1984) Programming and cognitive style, in *Trends in Ergonomics/Human Factors*, (ed. A. Mital), Elsevier Science Publishers, North-Holland.

Bainbridge, L. (1986) Asking questions and accessing knowledge, *Future Computing Systems,* **1** (2), 143–49.

Baker, L. (1988) The relationship of product design to document design, in *Effective Documentation: What we have learned from Research,* (ed. S. Doheny-Farina), The MIT Press, Cambridge, MA.

Barfield, W. (1986) Expert-novice differences for software: Implications for problem-solving and knowledge-acquisition, *Behaviour and Information Technology,* **5** (1), 15–29.

Barnard, P. (1991a) Bridging between basic theories and the artifacts of human-computer interaction, in *Designing Interaction: Psychology at the Human–Computer Interface,* (ed. J.M. Carroll), Cambridge University Press, Cambridge, Ch. 7.

Barnard, P. (1991b) The contributions of applied cognitive psychology to the study of human-computer interaction, in *Human Factors for Informatics Usability,* (eds B. Shackel and S.J. Richardson), Cambridge University Press, Cambridge.

Barnard, P.J. (1987) Cognitive resources and the learning of human–computer dialogs, in *Interfacing thought: Cognitive aspects of human–computer interaction,* (ed. J.M. Carroll), MIT Press, Cambridge, MA.

Barnard, P.J., Hammond, N., MacLean, A. and Morton, J. (1982) Learning and remembering interactive commands in a text-editing task, *Behaviour and Information Technology,* **1**, 347–58.

Barnard, P.J., Wilson, M. and MacLean, A. (1986) The elicitation of system knowledge by picture probs, in *Proceedings CHI '1986 Human Factors in Computing Systems,* ACM Press, NY, pp. 235–40.

Basili, V. and Weiss, D. (1981) Evaluation of a software requirements document by analysis of change data, *Proc. 5th. Int. Conf. Software Engineering.*

Bednall, E.S. (1990) Automatic calling card service: testing and evaluation of the auditory prompts together with comments on other issues concerning the ACCS, unpublished manuscript, Telecom Australia Research Laboratories.

Bednall, E.S. (1992) The effect of screen format on visual list search, *Ergonomics,* **35** (4), 369–83.

Bellotti, V. (1988) Implications of current design practice for the use of HCI techniques, in *People and Computers IV,* (eds D. Jones and R. Winder), Cambridge University Press, Cambridge, pp. 13–34.

Bennett, J.L. (1984) Managing to meet usability requirements: Establishing and meeting software development goals, in *Usability Issues and Health Concerns,* (eds J.L. Bennett, D. Case, J. Sandelin and M. Smith), Prentice-Hall, Englewood Cliffs, NJ.

Bennett, M.J. (1980) Heuristics and the weighting of base rate information in diagnostic tasks by nurses, unpublished doctoral thesis, Monash University, Melbourne.

Benyon, D. (1992a) The role of task analysis in systems design, *Interacting with Computers,* **4** (1), 102–23.

Benyon, D. (1992b) Task analysis and system design: The discipline of data, *Interacting with Computers,* **4** (2), 246–59.

Berelson, B. (1952) *Content Analysis in Communication Research,* Free Press, NY.

Berry, D.C. and Broadbent, D.E. (1984) On the relationship between task performance and associated verbalizable knowledge, *Quarterly J. Experimental Psychology,* **46A**, 209–31.

Bethke, F. (1983) Measuring the usability of software manuals, *Technical Communication,* **29** (2), 13–16.

Bewley, W.L., Roberts, T.L., Schroit, D. and Verplank, W.L. (1990) Human factors testing in the design of Xerox's 8010 'Star' office workstation, in *Human–Computer Interaction,* (eds J. Preece and L. Keller), Prentice-Hall International, Hemel Hempstead.

Billingsley, P.A. (1982) Navigation through hierarchical menu structures: Does it help to have a map?, *Proc. Human Factors Soc. 26th. Ann. Meeting,* Santa Monica, CA.

Black, J.B., and Moran, T.P. (1982) Learning and remembering command names, *Proc. Human Factors in Computer Systems,* Gaithersburg, MD.

Bodker, S. (1989) A human activity approach to user interfaces, *Human–Computer Interaction,* **4** (3), 171–95.

Boehm, B.W., Gray, T.E. and Seewaldt, T. (1984) Prototyping versus specifying: A multi-project experiment, *I.E.E.E. Trans. Software Engineering,* **10** (3), 290–302.

Booth, P. (1989) *An Introduction to Human–Computer Interaction,* Lawrence Erlbaum & Associates, Hillsdale, NJ.

Bostrom, R.P. (1989) Successful application of communication techniques to improve the systems development process, *J. Information and Management,* **16**, 279–95.

Braune, R. and Wickens, C.S. (1986) Time-sharing revisited: Test of a componential model for the assessment of individual differences, *Ergonomics,* **29** (11), 1399–1414.

Briggs, P. (1990) Do they know what they're doing? An evaluation of word-processor users' implicit and explicit task-relevant knowledge, and its role in self-directed learning, *Int. J. Man–Machine Studies,* **32**, 385–98.

Brockman, R.J. (1990) *Writing better computer user documentation: From paper to online,* 2nd edn, John Wiley & Sons, NY.

Brooks, R. (1991) Comparative task analysis: An alternative direction for human–computer interaction science, in *Designing Interaction: Psychology at the Human–Computer Interface,* (ed. J.M. Carroll), Cambridge University Press, Cambridge, Ch. 4.

Brunswik, E. (1955) Representative design and probabilistic theory, *Psychological Review*, **62**, 193–217.

Buckley, P. and Johnson, P. (1987) Analysis of communication tasks for the design of a structured message system, in *People and Computers III: Proc. 3rd Conf. British Computer Society*, (eds D. Diaper and R. Winder), Cambridge University Press, Cambridge, pp. 29–40.

Burch, J.G. (1992) *Systems Analysis, Design and Implementation*, Boyd and Fraser Publishing, Boston, MA.

Burke, K.M. and Wright, W.W. (1986) Making online documentation helpful: Applying what we've learned, *Proc. Nat. Online Meeting*, 6–8 May, New York.

Butler, K.A. (1985) Connecting theory and practice: A case study of achieving usability goals, *Proc. ACM CHI '85*, Elsevier Science Publishers, North-Holland.

Cakir, A., Hart, D.J. and Stewart, T.F.M. (1980) *Visual Display Terminals: A manual covering ergonomics, workplace design, health and safety, task organization*, John Wiley & Sons, London.

Campbell, D.T. and Stanley, C. (1963) *Experimental and Quasi-experimental Designs for Research*, Rand McNally, Skokie, IL.

Cannell, C.F. and Kahn, R.L. (1968) Interviewing, in *The Handbook of Social Psychology*, Vol. 2, 2nd edn, (eds G. Lindzay and E. Aaronson), Addison-Wesley, Reading, MA.

Cannon-Bowers, J.A., Tannenbaum, S.I., Salas, E. and Converse, S.A. (1991) Toward an integration of training theory and technique, *Human Factors*, **33**, (3), 281–92.

Card, S.K., English, W.K. and Burr, B.J. (1978) Evaluation of mouse, rate-controlled isometric joystick, step keys and text keys for text selection on a CRT, *Ergonomics*, **21**. Reprinted in (1990) *Selected Readings in Human Factors*, (ed. M. Venturino) The Human Factors Society Inc., Ch. 23.

Card, S.K., Moran, T.P. and Newell, A. (1980) Computer text editing: An information processing analysis of a routine cognitive skill, *Cognitive Psychology*, **12**, 32–74.

Card, S.K., Moran, T.P. and Newell, A. (1983) *The Psychology of Human–computer Interaction*, Lawrence Erlbaum & Associates, Hillsdale, NJ.

Carmines, E.G. and Zeller, R.A. (1979) *Reliability and Validity Assessment*, Sage Publications Inc., London.

Carroll, J.M. (ed.), (1987) *Interfacing thought: Cognitive aspects of human–computer interaction*, MIT Press, Cambridge, MA.

Carroll, J.M. and Carrithers, C. (1984) Blocking learner error states in a training wheels system, *Human Factors*, **26** (4), 377–89.

Carroll, J.M. and Mack, R.L. (1983) Actively learning to use a word processor, in *Cognitive Aspects of Skilled Typewriting*, (ed. W.E. Cooper), Springer Verlag, New York.

Carroll, J.M. and Rosson, M.B. (1987) Paradox of the active user, in *Interfacing thought: Cognitive aspects of human–computer interaction,* (ed. J.M. Carroll), MIT Press, Cambridge, MA.

Carroll, J.M., Kellogg, W.A. and Rosson, M.B. (1991) The task-artifact cycle, in *Designing Interaction: Psychology at the Human–Computer Interface,* (ed. J.M. Carroll), Cambridge University Press, Cambridge, Ch. 6.

Carroll, J.M., Mack, R.L., Lewis, C.H., Grischkowsky, N.L. and Robertson, S.R. (1985) Exploring a word processor, *Human–Computer Interaction,* **1**, 283–307.

Carter, J.A. Jr. (1991) Combining task analysis with software engineering in a methodology for designing interactive systems, in (ed. J. Karat), *Taking Software Design Seriously: Practical Techniques for Human–Computer Interaction Design,* Academic Press, London, Ch. 11.

Catterall, B.J., Taylor, B.C. and Galer, M.D. (1991) The HUFIT planning, analysis and specification toolset: Human Factors as a normal part of the IT product design process, in *Taking Software Design Seriously: Practical Techniques for Human–Computer Interaction Design,* (ed. J. Karat), Academic Press, London.

Chapanis, A. (1963) Words, words, words, *Human Factors,* 7 (1), 1–17.

Chapanis, A. (1984) Taming and civilizing computers, in *Computer culture: The scientific, intellectual and social impact of the computer,* (ed. H.R. Pagels), Academy of Sciences, New York, pp. 202–19.

Chapanis, A. (1988) 'Words, words, words' revisited. *International Reviews of Ergonomics,* **2**.

Chapanis, A. (1991a) The Business Case for Human Factors in Informatics, in *Human Factors for Informatics Usability,* (eds B. Shackel and S. Richardson), Cambridge University Press, Cambridge,

Chapanis, A. (1991b) Evaluating usability, in *Human Factors for Informatics Usability,* (eds B. Shackel and S. Richardson), Cambridge University Press, Cambridge,

Chapanis, A. (1992) To communicate the human factors message you have to know what the message is and how to communicate it, *Human Factors Society Bulletin,* **35** (1), 3–6.

Chapin, N. (1979) Software lifecycle, *INFOTEC Conference in Structured Software Development.*

Charney, D.H. and Reder, L.M. (1986) Designing interactive tutorials for computer users, *Human–Computer Interaction,* **2**, 297–317.

Chessari, J. and Bednall, E. (1990) *Designing and Evaluating the CENTEL User-guide,* internal report to Telecom Business Services.

Chi, M.T., Feltovich, P.J. and Glaser, A.M. (1981) Categorization and representation of physics problems by experts and novices, *Cognitive Science,* **5**, 121–52.

Chisholm, R. (1988) Improving the management of technical writers: Creating a context for usable documentation, in *Effective Documentation: What we have learned from Research,* (ed. S. Doheny-Farina), MIT Press, Cambridge, MA.

Christensen, L.B. and Stoap, C.M (1986) *Introduction to statistics for the social and behavioural sciences,* Brooks/Cole, Monterey, CA.

Christie, B. (ed.), (1985) *Human Factors of Information Technology in the Office,* John Wiley & Sons, London.

Clegg, C.W. (1984) The derivation of job designs, *J. Occupational Behaviour,* 5, 131–46.

Clegg, C., Warr, P., Green, T., Monk, A., Kemp, N., Allison, G. and Lansdale, M., (1988) *People and Computers: How to evaluate your company's new technology,* Ellis Horwood Ltd., Chichester.

Cohill, A.M., (1981) Information Presentation in Software HELP Systems, unpublished master thesis, Virginia Polytechnic Institute and State University.

Cohill, A.M. and Williges, R.C. (1985) Retrieval of HELP Information for Novice Users of Interactive Computer Systems, *Human Factors,* 27 (3), 335–43.

CORE - The Method (1989) Software Technology Centre, Pembrake House, Camberley, Surrey.

Czaja, S.J., Hammond, K., Blascovich, J.J. and Swede, H. (1986) Learning to use a word-processing system as a function of training strategy, *Behaviour and Information Technology,* 5 (3), 203–16.

Damodaran, L. (1991) Towards a human factors strategy for information technology systems, in *Human Factors for Informatics Usability,* (eds B. Shackel and S. Richardson), Cambridge University Press, Cambridge, Ch. 13.

Damodaran, L., Ip, K. and Beck, M. (1988) Integrating human factors principles into structured design, in *Information technology for organizational systems,* (eds H.J. Bullinger, E.N. Protonotorios, D. Bauwhuis and F. Reim), Elsevier Science Publishers, North-Holland.

Davis, A.M. (1988) A taxonomy for the early stages of the software development life cycle, *J. Systems and Software,* 8, 297–311.

Davis, A.M. (1990) System testing: Implications of requirements specifications, *Information and Software Technology,* 32 (6), 407–14.

Desurvire, H., Kondziela, J. and Atwood, M. (1992) What is gained and lost when using evaluation methods other than empirical testing, in *Proc. HCI 1992,* (eds A. Monk, D. Diaper and M.D. Harrison), Cambridge University Press, Cambridge.

Desurvire, H., Lawrence, D. and Atwood, M.E. (1991) Empiricism versus judgment: Comparing user interface evaluation methods on a new telephone-based interface, *SIGCHI Bulletin,* 23 (4), 58–9.

de Vaus, D.A. (1985) *Surveys in Social Research,* Allen and Unwin, Sydney.

Diaper, D. (1987) Designing systems for people: Beyond user centred design, *Proceedings, Share European Association (SEAS) Anniversary Meeting*, pp. 283–303.

Diaper, D. (ed.) (1989) *Task Analysis for Human–Computer Interaction*, Ellis Horwood Ltd., Chichester.

Diaper, D. and Addison, M. (1992) Task analysis and systems analysis for software development, *Interacting with Computers*, **4** (1), 124–39.

Diaper, D. and Winder, R. (eds), (1987) *People and Computers III: Proc. British Computer Society Human–Computer Interaction Special Interest Group*, Cambridge University Press, Cambridge.

Dillman, D.A. (1978) *Mail and Telephone Surveys: The Total Design Method*, John Wiley & Sons, New York.

Doheny-Farina, S. (ed.) (1988) *Effective Documentation: What we have learned from Research*, MIT Press, Cambridge, MA.

Downs, E., Clarke, P. and Coe, I. (1988) *Structured Systems Analysis and Design Method (SSADM): Application and Context*, Prentice Hall, London.

Dray, S.T., Ogden, W.G. and Vestervig, R.E. (1981) Measuring performance with a menu-selection human computer interface, *Proc. Human Factors Society 25th Annual Meeting*.

Drury, C.G. (1983) Task analysis methods in industry, *Applied Ergonomics*, **14** (1), 19–28.

Dumas, J.S. (1989) Stimulating change through usability testing, *SIGCHI Bulletin*, **21** (1), 37–44.

Eason, K.D. (1984) Towards the experimental study of usability, *Behaviour and Information Technology*, **3** (2), 133–43.

Eason, K.D. (1989) Designing systems to match organizational reality, in *People and Computers V*, (eds A. Sutliffe and L. Macaulay), Cambridge University Press, Cambridge, pp. 57–69.

Eason, K.D. and Harker, S. (1991) Human factors contributions to the design process, in *Human Factors for Informatics Usability*, (eds B. Shackel and S. Richardson), Cambridge University Press, Cambridge.

Edmonds, E. (1987) Good software design: What does it mean? *Proc. 2nd IFIP Conference on Human–Computer Interaction – Interact '87*, Elsevier Science Publishers, North-Holland.

Edwards, A.L. (1976) *An Introduction to Linear Regression and Correlation*, W.H. Freeman, San Francisco, CA.

Edwards, W. (1971) Bayesian and regression models of human information processing – a myopic perspective, *Organizational Behaviour and Human Performance*, **6**, 639–48.

Egan, D.E. (1988) Individual differences in human-computer interaction, in *Handbook of Human–Computer Interaction*, (ed. M. Helander), Elsevier Science Publishers, North-Holland.

Ehrlich, K. and Soloway, E. (1983) An empirical investigation of the tacit plan knowledge in programming, in *Human Factors in Computer Systems,* (eds J. Thomas and M. Schneider), Ablex, Norwood, NJ.

Einhorn, H.J. (1980) Learning from experience and suboptimal rules in decision making, in *Cognitive Processes in Choice and Decision Behaviour,* (ed. T.S. Wallsten), Lawrence Erlbaum & Associates, Hillsdale, NJ.

Elkerton, J. and Williges, R.C. (1985) A performance profile methodology for implementing assistance and instruction in computer-based tasks, *Int. J. Man–Machine Studies,* **23,** 135–51.

Elkind, J.I., Card, S.K., Hochberg, J. and Huey, B.M. (1990) *Human Performance Models for Computer-aided Engineering,* Academic Press, London.

Ericsson, K.A. and Simon, H.A. (1980) Verbal reports as data, *Psychological Review,* **87,** 215–51.

Ericsson, K.A. and Simon, H.A. (1984) *Protocol analysis: Verbal reports as data,* MIT Press, Cambridge, MA.

ETSI, (1991) European Telecommunications Standards Institute, *Draft Standard for Usability Evaluation,* ETSI/STC HF3(91).

Fairchild, K., Meredith, G. and Wexelblat, A. (1989) A formal structure for automatic icons, *Interacting with Computers,* **1** (2), 131–40.

Felix, D. and Kruger, H. (1989) Applying ergonomic principles to the user-interface of ticket-machines in public transport, unpublished manuscript, Eidgenossische Technische Hochschule, Zurich.

Ferguson, G.A. and Takane, Y. (1989) *Statistical Analysis in Psychology and Education,* 6th edn, McGraw Hill.

Fisher, R.J. (1982) *Social Psychology: An Applied Approach,* St. Martin's Press, New York.

Fitter, M. (1979) Towards More 'Natural' Interactive Systems, *Int. J. Man–Machine Studies,* **11,** 339–50.

Forbes, K.D. (1983) Qualitative reasoning about space and motion, in *Mental Models,* (eds D. Gentner and A.L. Stevens), Lawrence Erlbaum & Associates, Hillsdale, NJ.

Forester, T. (1989a) The myth of the electronic cottage, in *Computers in the Human Context,* (ed. T. Forester) Basil Blackwell, Oxford.

Forester, T. (1989b) Computers and organizations, in *Computers in the Human Context,* part 3, (ed. T. Forester), Basil Blackwell, Oxford.

Forester, T. (1989c) Computers and the future, in *Computers in the Human Context,* part 4, (ed. T. Forester) Basil Blackwell, Oxford.

Fountain, A.J. and Norman, M.A. (1985) Modelling user behaviour with formal grammar in *People and Computers: Designing the interface,* *Proc. Conf. British Computer Society,* (eds P. Johnson and S. Cook), Cambridge University Press, Cambridge, pp. 3–12.

Furnas, G.W., Landauer, T.K., Gomez, L.M. and Dumais, S.T. (1983) Statistical semantics: Analysis of the potential performance of keyword information systems, *The Bell System Technical Journal*, **62** (b).

Gaines, B.R. and Shaw, M.L.G. (1984) *The Art of Computer Conversation*, Prentice-Hall, NJ.

Galitz, W.O. (1989) *Handbook of Screen Format Design*, Management Technology Education Pty. Ltd., Melbourne.

Gammack, J.G. (1987) Different techniques and different aspects of declarative knowledge, in *Knowledge Acquisition for Expert Systems: A Practical Handbook*, (ed. A.L. Kidd), Plenum Press, Sydney.

Gardner, A. and McKenzie, J. (1990) The MoD/DTI human factors guidelines, *Computing and Control Engineering Journal*, (March), 71–6.

Gaver, W.W. (1991) Technology affordances, *Proc. CHI' 91 Reaching Through Technology*, pp. 79–84.

Gentner, D.R. and Grudin, J. (1990) Why good engineers (sometimes) create bad interfaces, in *Proc. CHI '90 Conference Human Factors in Computing Systems*, ACM Press, NY, pp. 277–82.

Gentner, D. and Stevens, A.L. (eds), (1983) *Mental Models*, Lawrence Erlbaum & Associates, Hillsdale, NJ.

Godden, D.R. (1976) Probability as preparedness to act: Direct estimation versus indirect measurement, *Organizational Behaviour and Human Performance*, **17**, 147–58.

Gong, R. and Elkerton, J. (1990) Designing minimal documentation using a GOMS model: A usability evaluation of an engineering approach, *Proc. CHI' 91 Human Factors in Computer Systems*, ACM Press, NY, pp. 99-106.

Good, M.C., Whiteside, J.A., Wixon, D.R. and Jones, S.J. (1984) Building a user-derived interface, *Communications of the Association for Computing Machinery*, **27**, 1032–43.

Goodwin, N.C. (1975) Cursor positioning on an electronic display using lightgun, or keyboard for three basic tasks, *Human Factors*, **17**, 289–95.

Gorden, R.L. (1980) *Interviewing: Strategy, Techniques and Tactics*, 3rd edn, Dorsey, Homewood, IL.

Gould, J.D. (1983) Design for usability: Key principles and what designers think, in *Proc. CHI '83 Human Factors in Computer Systems*, ACM Press, New York, pp. 50–3.

Gould, J.D. (1988) How to design usable systems, in *Handbook of Human–Computer Interaction*, (ed. M. Helander), Elsevier Science Publishers, North-Holland.

Gould, J.D. and Lewis, C. (1985) Designing for usability: Key principles and what designers think, *Communications of the ACM*, **28** (3), 300–11.

Gould, J.D., Boies, S.J., Levy, S., Richards, J.T. and Schoonard, J. (1987) The 1984 Olympic Message System: A test of behavioural principles of system design, *Communications of the ACM, 30,* 758–69.

Gould, J.D., Boies, S.J., Levy, S., Richards, J.T. and Schoonard, J. (1990) The 1984 Olympic Message System: A test of behavioural principles of system design, in *Human–Computer Interaction,* (eds J. Preece and L. Keller), Prentice-Hall International, Hemel Hempstead.

Gould, J.D., Conti, J. and Hovanayecz, T. (1983) Composing letters with a simulated typewriter, *Communications of the ACM,* **26,** 295–308.

Gray, W.D., John, B.E. and Atwood, M.E. (1990) An application and evaluation of GOMS techniques for operator workstation evaluation, *Proc. 13th Int. Symposium Human Factors in Telecommunications,* HFT, Turin.

Gray, W.D., John, B.E. and Atwood, M.E. (1992) The precis of project Ernestine or an overview of a validation of GOMS, in *Proc. CHI '92 'Striking a balance' Human Factors in computer systems,* ACM Press, NY, 307–12.

Greif (1991) Organizational issues and task analysis, in *Human factors for Informatics Usability,* (eds B.Shackel and S.J. Richardson), Cambridge University Press, Cambridge.

Grudin, J. (1990) The computer reaches out: The historical continuity of interface design, in *Proc. CHI '90 Conf. Human Factors in Computing Systems,* ACM Press, NY, pp. 261–8.

Grudin, J. (1991) Systematic sources of suboptimal interface design in large product development organizations, *Human–Computer Interaction,* **6,** 149–96.

Grudin, J. and Barnard, P.J. (1985) The cognitive demands of learning and representing command names for text-editing, *Human Factors,* **26,** 407–22.

Hammond, N.V., Barnard, P.J., Morton, J., Long, J.B. and Clark, I.A. (1987) Characterizing user performance in command-driven dialogue, *Behaviour and Information Technology,* **6** (2), 159–205.

Hammond, N.V., Morton, J., MacLean, A. and Barnard, P.J. (1983) Fragments and signposts: User's models of systems, in *Proc. 10th. Int. Conf. Human Factors in Telecommunications* HFT, Helsinki.

Handy, C.B. (1985) *Understanding Organisations,* 3rd edn, Penguin Books, Ringwood, Australia.

Harker, S. (1991) Requirements specification and the role of prototyping in current practice, in *Taking Software Design Seriously: Practical Techniques for Human–Computer Interaction Design,* (ed. J. Karat), Academic Press, London.

Hartson, H. and Smith, E. (1991) Rapid prototyping in HCI development, *Interacting with Computers,* **3** (1), 9–26.

Hayes, P.J. and Szekely, P.A. (1983) Graceful Interaction Through the COUSIN Command Interface, *Int. J. Man–Machine Studies,* **19,** 285–306.

Hayes-Roth, F., Klahr, P. and Mostow, D.J. (1981) Advice taking and knowledge refinement: An iterative view of skill acquisition, in *Cognitive Skills and their Acquisition,* (ed. J.R. Anderson), Lawrence Erlbaum & Associates, Hillsdale, NJ.

Hays, W.L. (1988) *Statistics for Psychologists,* 4th edn, Holt, Rinehart and Winston, NY.

Hewett, T.T. (1986) The role of iterative evaluation in designing systems for usability, in *People and Computers: Designing for usability, Proc. 2nd Conf. BCS HCI specialist group,* (eds M.D. Harrison and A.F. Monk), Cambridge University Press, Cambridge.

Hill, W.C. (1989) Why some advice fails, in *CHI '89, Proc. Human Factors in Computing Systems,* Austin, Texas, pp. 85–91.

Hix, D. (1990) Generations of UIMS, *I.E.E.E. Software,* Sept, 77–87.

Hix, D. (1991) Human-computer interface development tools: A methodology for their evaluation, *Communications of the ACM,* **34** (3), 1974–87.

Hoerr, J., Pollock, M.A. and Whiteside, D.E. (1989) Management discovers the human side of automation, in *Computers in the Human Context: IT, Productivity and People,* (ed. T. Forester), Basil Blackwell, Oxford.

Holtzblatt, K. and Jones, S. (1992) Contextual inquiry: A participatory technique for system design, in *Participatory Design: Principles and Practice,* (eds A. Namioka and D. Schuler), Lawrence Erlbaum & Associates, Hillsdale, NJ.

Horton, W.K. (1990) *Designing and Writing Online Documentation: Help Files to Hypertext,* John Wiley and Sons, NY.

Houghton, R.C. (1984) Online Help Systems: A Conspectus, *Communications of the ACM,* **27** (2), 126–33.

Howard, S. and Murray, D.M. (1987) A taxonomy of evaluation techniques for HCI, *Proc. Human Computer Interaction Interact '87,* Elsevier Science Publishers, North-Holland, pp. 454–9.

Howell, D.C. (1985) *Fundamental Statistics for the Behavioral Sciences,* Dixbury Press, Boston, MA.

Huff, D., (1954) *How to lie with statistics,* W.W. Norton, NY.

HUSAT, (1988) *Human Factors Guidelines for the design of Computer-Based Systems: Human Factors in Requirements Specification,* Vol. 3., HUSAT Research Institute, Loughborough.

Hutchins, E.L., Hollan, J.D. and Norman, D.A. (1985) Direct manipulation interfaces, *Human–Computer Interaction,* **1,** 311–38.

IEEE, (1983) IEEE standard glossary of software engineering terms, *ANSI/IEEE Standard 729–1983,* NY.

ISO, (1990), International Standards Organisation, Draft CD 9241 Part 11: Usability Statements, ISO/TCI159/SC4/N186, 10 August.

Jackson, M. (1983) *System Development*, Prentice–Hall, Hemel Hempstead.

Jackson, W. (1988) *Research Methods: Rules for Survey Design and Analysis*, Prentice-Hall Canada Inc., Scarborough, Ont.

Jarvinen, P.H. (1988) Writing a tutorial manual of a flexible software: The general case, *Proc. IFAC Man–Machine Systems*, Olulu, Finland, 307–12.

Jereb, B. (1986) Plain English on the plant floor, *Visible Language*, **20**, 219–25.

Jervell, H.R. and Olson, K.A. (1985) Icons in man-machine communications, *Behaviour and Information Technology*, **4** (3), 249–54.

John, B.E. (1990) Extensions of GOMS analyses to expert performance requiring perception of dynamic visual and auditory information, *Proc. CHI '90 Human Factors in Computer Systems*, ACM Press, NY, pp. 107–15.

Johnson, P. (1992) *Human–computer Interaction: Psychology, Task Analysis and Software Engineering*, McGraw-Hill, London.

Johnson, P., Diaper, D. and Long. J.B. (1984) Tasks, skills and knowledge, in *Proc. Interact '84*, Elsevier, North-Holland.

Johnson, P., Johnson, H., Waddington, R. and Shouls, A. (1988) Task-related knowledge structures: Analysis, modelling and application, in *People and Computers IV: Proc. 4th Conf. British Computer Society*, (eds D. M. Jones and R. Winder), Cambridge University Press, Cambridge, pp. 35–62.

Johnson-Laird, P. (1983) *Mental Models: Towards a Cognitive Science of Language, Inference and Consciousness*, Cambridge University Press, Cambridge.

Jorgensen, A.H. (1990) Thinking-aloud in user interface design: A method promoting cognitive ergonomics, *Ergonomics*, **33** (4), 501–7.

Kahneman, D., Slovic, P. and Tversky, A. (eds) (1982) *Judgment under Uncertainty: Heuristics and Biases*, Cambridge University Press, NY.

Kak, A.V. and Ambardan, A. (1984) Human-computer interaction and individual differences, *Proc. 1st USA-Japan Conf. Human–Computer Interaction*, pp. 207–11,

Kantowitz, B.H. (1992) Selecting measures for human factors research, *Human Factors*, **34**, (4), 387–98.

Karat, C.M., Campbell, R. and Fiegel, T. (1992) Comparison of empirical testing and walkthrough methods in user interface evaluation, in *Proc. CHI '92, Striking a balance*, ACM Press, NY., pp. 397–404.

Karat, J. and Bennett, J.L. (1991) Using scenarios in design meetings: A case study example, in *Taking Software Design Seriously: Practical*

Techniques for Human–Computer Interaction Design, (ed. J. Karat), Academic Press, London.

Kato, T. (1986) What 'question-asking protocols' can say about the user interface, *Int. J. Man–Machine Studies,* **25**, 659–73.

Kelley, J.F. (1984) An iterative design methodology for user-friendly natural language office information applications, ACM *Transactions on Office Information Systems,* **2** (1), 26–41.

Kellogg, W.A. (1987) Conceptual consistency in the user interface: Effects on user performance, *Proc Second IFIP Conference on Human–Computer Interaction – Interact '87,* Stuttgart, Elsevier Science Publishers, North-Holland, pp. 389–94.

Keppel, G. (1991) *Design and Analysis: A Researcher's Handbook,* 3rd edn, Prentice–Hall, Englewood Cliffs, NJ.

Kieras, D.E. (1988) Towards a practical GOMS model methodology for user interface design, in *Handbook of Human–Computer Interaction,* (ed. M. Helander), Elsevier Science Publishers, North-Holland.

Kieras, D.E. and Bovair, S. (1984) The role of a mental model in learning to operate a device, *Cognitive Science,* **8**, 255–73.

Kieras, D.E. and Polson, P.G. (1985) An approach to formal analysis of user complexity, *Int. J. Man-Machine Studies,* **22**, 365–94.

Kirby, M.A.R., Fowler, C.J.H. and Macaulay, L.A. (1988) Overcoming obstacles to the validation of user requirements specifications, in *People and Computers IV,* (eds D.M. Jones and R. Winder), Cambridge University Press, Cambridge.

Kirwan, B. and Ainsworth, L.K. (eds) (1992) *A Guide to Task Analysis,* Taylor & Francis.

Klayman, J. and Ha, Y.-W. (1984) Confirmation, disconfirmation and information in hypothesis-testing, *Report, Business School of Business, Center for Decision Research,* Chicago, December.

Knowles, C. (1988) Can cognitive complexity theory (CCT) produce an adequate measure of system usability? in *People and Computers IV,* (eds D.M. Jones and R. Winder), Cambridge University Press, Cambridge.

Kolodner,, J.L. (1983) Towards an understanding of the role of experience in the evolution from novice to expert, *Int. J. Man–Machine Studies,* **19**, 497–518.

Labaw, P. (1980) *Advanced Questionnaire Design,* Abt Books, Cambridge.

Landauer, T.K. (1987). Relations between cognitive psychology and computer system design, in *Interfacing Thought: Cognitive Aspects of Human–computer Interaction,* (ed. J.M. Carroll), MIT Press, Cambridge, MA.

Landauer, T.K. (1991) Let's get real: A position paper on the role of cognitive psychology in the design of humanly useful and usable systems, in *Designing Interaction: Psychology at the Human–*

Computer Interface, (ed. J.M. Carroll), Cambridge University Press, Cambridge, Ch. 5.

Landauer, T.K., Galotti, K.M. and Hartwell, S. (1983) Natural Command Names and Initial Learning: A Study of Text Editing Terms, *Communications of the ACM,* **26** (7)

Larkin, J.H., McDermott, J., Simon, D.P. and Simon, H.A. (1980) Expert and novice performance in solving physics problems, *Science,* **208,** 1335–42.

Ledgard, H., Singer, A. and Whiteside, J. (1981) *Directions in Human Factors for Interactive Systems,* Springer Verlag, NY.

Lee, E., MacGregor, J. and Lam, N. (1986) Keyword-menu retrieval: An effective alternative to menu indexes, *Ergonomics,* **29** (1), 115–30.

Lee, W. (1987) '?': A Context-Sensitive Help System Based on Hypertext, *Proc. 24th ACM/IEEE Design Automation Conf.,* 1987, Elsevier Science Publishers, North-Holland.

Lerch, F.J., Mantei, M.M. and Olson, J.R. (1989) Skilled financial planning: The cost of translating ideas into actions, *Proc. CHI '89 Human Factors in Computer Systems,* ACM Press, NY, pp. 121–6.

Levin, I.P. (1975) Information integration in numerical judgments and decision processes, *J. Experimental Psychology: General,* **104** (1), 39–53.

Levin, I.P. (1976) Comparing different models and response transformations in an information integration task, *Bulletin of the Psychonomic Society,* **7** (1), 78–80.

Levin, I.P., Ims, J.R., Simpson, J.C. and Kim, P.K. (1977) The processing of deviant information in prediction and evaluation, *Memory and Cognition,* **5** (6), 679–84.

Lewis, C. (1981) Skill in algebra, in *Cognitive Skills and their Acquisition,* (ed. J.R. Anderson), Lawrence Erlbaum & Associates, Hillsdale, NJ.

Lewis, C. (1982) Using the 'thinking aloud' method in cognitive interface design, IBM Research Report RC 9265 2/17/82, IBM, T.J. Watson Research Center, Yorktown Heights, NY.

Lewis, C. (1990) A research agenda for the nineties in human-computer interaction, *Human–Computer Interaction,* **5** (2 and 3), 125–43.

Lewis, C. (1991) Inner and outer theory in human-computer interaction, in *Designing Interaction: Psychology at the Human–Computer Interface,* (ed. J.M. Carroll), Cambridge University Press, Cambridge, Ch. 9.

Lewis, C. and Mack, R. (1981) Learning to use a text processing system: Evidence from thinking aloud protocols, *Association for Computing Machinery,* 387–91.

Lewis, C. and Polson, P.G. (1992) Cognitive walkthroughs: A method for theory-based evaluation of user interfaces, *CHI '92 Striking a Balance,* Tutorial, 4 May.

Lewis, C.H., Polson, P.G., Wharton, C. and Rieman, J. (1990) Testing a walkthrough methodology for theory-based design of walk-up-and-use interfaces, *Proc. CHI '90 Conf., Empowering People*, ACM Press, NY.

Lim, K.Y. and Long, J. (1992a) A method for (recruiting) methods facilitating human factors input to system design, in *Proc. CHI '92 'Striking a balance' Human Factors in Computer Systems*, ACM Press, NY, pp. 549–56.

Lim, K.Y. and Long, J. (1992b) Rapid prototyping, structured methods and the incorporation of human factors into system developments, in *Proc. EWHCI '92, East-West Int. Conf. Human–Computer Interaction*, St. Petersburg, Russia, pp. 4–8.

Lindgaard, G. (1988) *What's on the Menu – or Better, What Should be on the Menu? A Literature Review and Guidelines for Menu Design*, Customer Services and Systems Branch Paper No. 142, Telecom Australia Research Laboratories, Melbourne.

Lindgaard, G. and Perry, L. (1988) Towards a solution to vocabulary problems in computing: A measure of goodness of fit, *Ergonomics*, **31** (5), 785–801.

Lindgaard, G., Chessari, J. and Ihsen, E., (1987) Icons in telecommunications: what makes pictorial information comprehensible to the user? *Australian Telecom. Res.*, **21** (2), 17–29.

Long, R.J. (1989) Human issues in new office technology, in *Computers in the Human Context: IT, Productivity and People*, (ed. T. Forester), Basil Blackwell Ltd, Oxford.

Lumsden, J. (1974) *Elementary Statistical Method*, University of Western Australia Press, Perth.

Maas, S., Rosson, M.B. and Kellogg, W.A. (1987) User-friendliness, consistency and other hard-to-define principles: Interviews with designers, *Proc. Software Ergonomie '87*, Teubner, Berlin.

Macaulay, L., Fowler, C., Kirby, M. and Hutt, A. (1990) USTM: A new approach to requirements specification, *Interacting with Computers*, **2** (1), 92–115.

Mack, R.L., Lewis, C.H. and Carroll, J.M. (1983) Learning to use word processors: Problems and prospects, ACM *Transactions on Information Systems*, **1**, 254–71.

Mackie, R.R. and Wylie, C.D. (1988) Factors influencing acceptance of computer-based innovations, in *Handbook of Human–Computer Interaction*, (ed. M. Helander), Elsevier Science Publishers, North-Holland, Ch. 51.

Maguire, M.C. (1990) A review of human factors guidelines and techniques for the design of graphical human-computer interfaces, in *Human–Computer Interaction*, (eds J. Preece and L. Keller), Prentice-Hall International, Hemel Hempstead.

Malone, T.W. (1985) Designing organizational interfaces, *Proc. CHI '85 Human Factors in Computer Systems,* ACM Press, NY, pp. 66–71.

Malone, T.W. (1987) Computer support for organizations: Toward an organizational science, in *Interfacing Thought: Cognitive Aspects of Human–computer Interaction,* (ed. J.M. Carroll), MIT Press, Cambridge, MA.

Martin, D.W. (1985) *Doing psychology experiments,* 2nd edn, Brooks/Cole, Monterey, CA.

Martin, J. (1973) *Design of Man–computer Dialogues,* Prentice-Hall, Hillsdale, NJ.

Mayer, R.E. (1975) Different problem-solving competencies established in learning computer programming with and without meaningful models, *J. Educational Psychology,* **67** (6), 725–84.

Mayer, R.E. (1979) A psychology of learning BASIC, *Communications of the ACM,* **11,** 589–93.

Mayer, R.E. (1980) Elaboration techniques and advance organizers that affect technical learning, *J. Educational Psychology,* **72,** 770–84.

Mayer, R.E. (1981) The psychology of how novices learn computer programming, *Computing Surveys,* **13,** 121–41.

Mayer, R.E. (1988) From novice to expert, in *Handbook of Human–Computer Interaction,* (ed. M. Helander), Elsevier Science Publishers, North-Holland, Ch. 25.

Mayer, R.E., Cook, L.K. and Dyck, J.L. (1984) Techniques that help readers build mental models from scientific text: Definitions pretraining and signaling, *J. Educational Psychology,* **76** (6), 1089–1105.

McBurney, D.H. (1990) *Experimental Psychology,* Wadsworth Publishing Co., Belmont, CA.

McCloskey, M. (1983) Naive theories of motion, in *Mental Models,* (eds D. Gentner and A.L. Stevens), Lawrence Erlbaum & Associates, Hillsdale, NJ.

McGregor, S. (1992) Preparing yourself for the legal requirements of usable design, *Proc. Enhancing Usability in Human–computer Interaction,* AIC Group Publications, Sydney.

McGrew, J.F. (1991) Tools for task analysis: Graphs and matrices, in *Taking Software Design Seriously: Practical Techniques for Human–Computer Interaction Design,* (ed. J. Karat), Academic Press, London.

Meister, D. (1986) *Human Factors Testing and Evaluation: Advances in Human Factors/Ergonomics 5,* Elsevier Science Publishers, North-Holland.

Melcus, L.A. and Ferres, R.J. (1988) Guidelines for the use of a prototype in user interface design, in *Proc. Human Factors Society 32nd Annual Meeting,* Human Factors Society, Santa Monica, CA., pp. 370–4.

Miller, L.A. and Thomas, J.C. (1977) Behavioral issues in the use of interactive systems, *Int. J. Man–Machine Studies,* **9,** 509–36.

Mills, R.G. (1967) Man-machine communication and problem solving, in *Ann. Reviews of Information Science and Technology 2*, (ed. C.A. Cuadra), Interscience, NY.

Moll, T. and Sauter, R. (1987) Do people really use on-line assistance?, *Proc. 2nd IFIP Conf. Human–Computer Interaction – Interact '87*, Stuttgart, Elsevier Science Publishers, North-Holland, pp. 191–4.

Moran, T.P. (1981) The command language grammar, a representation for the user interface of interactive computer systems, *Int. J. Man–Machine Studies*, **15**, 3–50.

Moroney, M.J. (1960) *Facts from Figures*, Penguin Books, Mitcham, Victoria.

Moser, C.A. and Kalton, G. (1975) *Survey Methods in Social Investigation*, Heinemann Educational Books, London.

Mosier, J.M. and Smith, S.L. (1986) Application of guidelines for designing user interface software, *Behaviour and Information Technology*, **5**, 39–46.

Murdic, R.G. (1980) *Concepts and Design*, Prentice–Hall, Englewood Cliffs, NJ.

Murray, D.M. (1988) *A survey of user cognitive modelling*, NPL Report DITC 92/87, National Physical Laboratory, Teddington, Middlesex.

Mynatt, C.R., Doherty, M.E. and Tweney, R.D. (1977) Confirmation bias in a simulated research environment: An experimental study of scientific inference, *Quarterly J. Experimental Psychology*, **29**, 85–95.

Newell, A. and Card, S.K. (1985) The prospects for psychological science in human-computer interaction, *Human–Computer Interaction*, **1**, 209–42.

Newell, A. and Simon, H.A. (1972) *Human Problem Solving*, Prentice-Hall, Englewood Cliffs, NJ.

Nickerson, R.S. (1969) Man-computer interaction: A challenge for human factors research, *Ergonomics*, **12**, 501–17, Reprinted in *I.E.E.E. Trans. Man–Machine Systems*, **10** (4), 164–80.

Nickerson, R. (1981) Why interactive computer systems are sometimes not used by people who might benefit from them, *Int. J. Man–Machine Studies*, **15**, 469–83.

Nielsen, J. (1992) Finding usability problems through heuristic evaluation, *Proc. CHI '92, Striking a balance*, ACM Press, NY, pp. 373–80.

Nisbett, R.E., and Ross, L. (1980) *Human Inference: Strategies and Shortcomings of Social Judgment*, Prentice-Hall, Englewood Cliffs, NJ.

Nisbett, R.E. and Wilson, T.D. (1977) Telling more than we can know: Verbal reports on mental processes, *Psychological Review*, **84**, 231–59.

Norcio, A.F. and Stanley, J. (1989) Adaptive human-computer interfaces: A literature survey and perspective, *I.E.E.E. Transactions on Systems, Man and Cybernetics,* **19** (2), 399–408.

Norman, D.A. (1981) Categorization of action slips, *Psychological Review,* **88**, 1–15.

Norman, D.A. (1983) Design principles for human-computer interfaces, *Proc. Human Factors in Computing Systems,* ACM Press, NY.

Norman, D.A. (1984) Cognitive engineering principles in the design of human-computer interfaces, in *Human–Computer Interaction,* (ed. G. Salvendy), Elsevier Science Publishers, North-Holland.

Norman, D.A. and Draper, S.W. (eds) (1986) *User Centred System Design,* Lawrence Erlbaum & Associates, Hillsdale, NJ.

Olson, J.R. (1985) Expanded design procedures for learnable, usable interfaces, *Proc. ACM CHI '85,* Elsevier Science Publishers, North-Holland.

O'Malley, C.E. (1986) Helping users help themselves, in *User Centred System Design,* (eds D.A. Norman and S.W. Draper), Lawrence Erlbaum & Associates, Hillsdale, NJ.

Ostberg, O. and Chapman, L.J. (1988) Social aspects of computer use, in *Handbook of Human–Computer Interaction,* (ed. M. Helander), Elsevier Science Publishers, North-Holland, Ch. 48.

Page-Jones, M. (1988) *The Practical Guide to Structured Systems Design,* Prentice-Hall International Inc., London.

Palmer, J., Duffy, T., Gomoll, K., Gomoll, T., Richards-Palmquist, J. and Trumble, J.A. (1988) The design and evaluation of online help for UNIX EMACS: Capturing the user in menu design, *I.E.E.E. Transactions on Professional Communication,* **31** (10), 44–51.

Patrick, J. and Fitzgibbon, L. (1988) Structural displays as learning aids, *Int. J. Man–Machine Studies,* **28**, 625–35.

Payne, S.J. and Green, T.R.G. (1983) The user's perception of the interaction language: A two-level model, *Proc. CHI '83 Conf. Human Factors in Computing Systems,* ACM Press, NY, pp. 202–6.

Payne, S.J. and Green, T.R.G. (1986) Task-action grammars: A model of the mental representation of task languages, *Human–Computer Interaction,* **2**, 93–133.

Payne, S.J. and Green, T.R.G. (1989) Task-action grammar: The model and its developments, in *Task Analysis for Human–Computer Interaction,* (ed. D. Diaper), Ellis-Horwood, pp. 75–107.

Perlman, G. (1984) Natural artificial languages: Low level processes, *Int. J. Man–Machine Studies,* **20**, 373–419.

Peters, T.J. and Waterman, R.H. Jr. (1981) *In Search of Excellence: Lessons from America's best-run Companies,* Harper and Row, Sydney.

Pfeiffer, K. and Olson, J.N. (1981) *Basic Statistics for the Behavioural Sciences,* Holt, Rinehart & Winston, NY.

Polson, P.G. (1987) A quantitative theory of human-computer interaction, in *Interfacing Thought: Cognitive Aspects of Human–computer Interaction*, (ed. J.M. Carroll), MIT Press, Cambridge, MA.

Polson, P.G. and Kieras, D.E. (1985) A quantitative model of the learning and performance of text editing knowledge, *Proc. CHI '85 Human Factors in Computer Systems*, ACM Press, NY, pp. 207–12.

Polson, P.G. and Lewis, C.H. (1990) Theory-based design for easily learned interfaces, *Human–Computer Interaction*, 5 (2 and 3), 191–220.

Polson, P.G., Bovair, S. and Kieras, D. (1987) Transfer between text editors, *Proc. CHI '87*, ACM Press, NY, pp. 27–32.

Polson, P.G., Muncher, E. and Engelbeck, G. (1986) A test of a common elements theory of transfer, *Proc. CHI '86 Human Factors in Computer Systems*, ACM Press, NY.

Popper, K.R. (1980) *The Logic of Scientific Discovery*, Hutchinson, London.

Pratt, J.H. (1988) Socio-issues related to home-based work, in *Handbook of Human–Computer Interaction*, (ed. M. Helander), Elsevier Science Publishers, North-Holland, Ch. 50.

Pressman, R.S. (1987) *Software Engineering*, McGraw-Hill, NY.

Pylyshyn, Z.W. (1991) Some remarks on the theory-practice gap, in *Designing Interaction: Psychology at the Human–Computer Interface*, (ed. J.M. Carroll), Cambridge University Press, Cambridge, Ch. 3.

Rantanen, J. (1991) User interface management systems and prototyping tools: A state of the art survey and feasibility assessment, *Proc. OZCHI '91, CHISIG Ann. Conf.*, Sydney, pp. 39–46.

Ravden, S. and Johnson, G. (1989) *Evaluating Usability of Human–computer Interfaces: A Practical Method*, Ellis Horwood Ltd., Chichester.

Redish, J. and Dumas, J.S. (1991) Building usability into documentation, in *Proc. 1st Conf. Quality in Documentation*, University of Waterloo Press.

Reichmann, W.S. (1970) *Use and Abuse of Statistics*, Penguin Books, Ringwood, Victoria, Australia.

Reisner, P. (1981) Formal grammar and human factors design of an interactive graphics system, *I.E.E.E. Trans. Software Engineering*, 7 (2), 229–40.

Reisner, P. (1982) Further developments toward using formal grammar as a design tool, *Proc. Human Factors in Computer Systems*, Gaithersburg, MD, ACM Press, NY, pp. 304–9.

Reisner, P. (1987) Discussion: HCI, what is it and what research is needed? in *Interfacing Thought: Cognitive Aspects of Human–computer Interaction*, (ed. J.M. Carroll), MIT Press, Cambridge, MA.

Resnick, L.B. (1985) Cognition and instruction: Recent theories of human competence, in *Psychology and Learning, 1984 Master Lecture*

Series, (ed. B.L. Hammonds), American Psychological Association, Washington D.C.

Richardson, S.A., Dohrenwend, B.S. and Klein, D. (1965) *Interviewing: Its forms and Functions,* Basic Books, NY.

Ridgway, L.S. (1987) Read my mind: What users want from online information, *I.E.E.E. Transactions on Professional Communication,* **30** (2), 87–90.

Rieman, J., Davies, S., Charles-Hair, D., Esemplare, M., Polson, P. and Lewis, C. (1991) An automated cognitive walkthrough, *Proc. CHI '91, Reaching Through Technology,* ACM Press.

Roberts, T.L. and Moran, T.P. (1983), The evaluation of text editors: Methodology and empirical results, *Communications of the ACM,* **26**. Reprinted in *Selected Readings in Human Factors,* (ed. M. Venturino), The Human Factors Society Inc., Ch. 24.

Robson, C. (1990) Designing and interpreting psychological experiments, in *Human–Computer Interaction: Selected Readings,* (eds J. Preece and L. Keller), Prentice–Hall International, Hemel Hempstead.

Roman, G.C. (1985) A current taxonomy of current issues in requirements engineering, *Computer,* (April), 14–22.

Rosenberg, R.S. (1992) *The Social Impact of Computers,* Academic Press, London.

Rosenthal, R.I. (1979) The Design of Technological Displays, in *Processing of Visible Language,* Vol. 1, (eds P.A. Kolers, M.E. Wrolstad and H. Bouma), Plenum Press, NY.

Rowley, D.E. and Rhoades, D.G. (1992) The cognitive jogthrough: A fast-paced user interface evaluation procedure, in *Proc. CHI '92 Striking a balance,* ACM Press, NY, pp. 389–95.

Rubenstein, R. and Hersch, H.M. (1984) *The Human Factor: Designing Computer Systems for People,* Digital Press, Burlington, MA.

Salter, W.J. (1988) Human factors in knowledge acquisition, in *Handbook of Human–Computer Interaction,* (ed. M. Helander), Elsevier Science Publishers, North-Holland, Ch. 45.

Scapin, D.L., (1981) Computer commands in restricted natural language: Some aspects of memory and experience, *Human Factors,* **23** (3), 365–75.

Schindler, R. and Fischer, F. (1986) Effectiveness of training as a function of the teached knowledge structure, *Proc. Man–Computer Interaction Research MACINTER-1,* Elsevier Science Publishers, North-Holland.

Schulert, A., Rofers, G. and Hamilton, J. (1985) ADM – A dialog manager, *Proc. CHI '85 Human Factors in Computer Systems,* ACM Press, NY.

Schwartz, J.P. and Norman, K.L. (1986) The importance of item distinctiveness on performance using a menu selection system, *Behaviour and Information Technology*, **5** (2), 173–82.

Seminara, J.L. (1985) Use of models and mockups in verifying manmachine interfaces, *I.E.E.E. 3rd Conf. Human Factors and Power Plants*, 38–40.

Seppala, P. and Salvendy, G. (1985) Impact of depth of menu hierarchy on performance effectiveness in a supervisory task: computerized flexible manufacturing system, *Human Factors*, **27** (6), 713–22.

Shackel, B. (1959) Ergonomics for a computer, *Design*, **120**, 36–9.

Shackel, B. (1981) The concept of usability, *Proc. IBM Software and Information Usability Symposium*, September, Poughkeepsie, NY.

Shackel, B. (1986) Ergonomics in design for usability, in *People and computers: Designing for usability, Proc. 2nd Conf. Human–Computer Interaction Specialist Group British Computer Society*, (eds M.D. Harrison and A.F. Monk), Cambridge University Press, Cambridge.

Shackel, B. (1991a) Usability - context, framework, definition, design and evaluation, in *Human Factors for Informatics Usability*, (eds B. Shackel and S. Richardson), Cambridge University Press, Cambridge,

Shackel, B. (1991b) Human factors for informatics usability – background and overview, in *Human Factors for Informatics Usability*, (eds B. Shackel and S. Richardson), Cambridge University Press, Cambridge,

Shaugnessy, J and Zechmeister, E.B. (1985) *Research Methods in Psychology*, Alfred A. Knopf, NY.

Simon, T. (1988) analysing the scope of cognitive models in human-computer interaction: A trade-off approach, in *People and Computers IV: Proc. 4th Conf. British Computer Society*, (eds D.M. Jones and R. Winder), Cambridge University Press, Cambridge.

Simpson, H. and Casey, S.M. (1988) *Developing Effective User Documentation: A Human-Factors Approach*, McGraw-Hill, NY.

Slovic, P. and Lichtenstein, S. (1971) Comparison of Bayesian and regression approaches to the study of information processing in judgment, *Organizational Behaviour and Human Performance*, **6**, 649–744.

Small, D.W., (1983) An experimental comparison of natural and structured query languages, *Human Factors*, **25** (3), 253–63.

Smith, S.L. (1986) Standards versus guidelines for designing user interface software, *Behaviour and Information Technology*, **5**, 47–61.

Smith, S.L. (1988) Standards versus guidelines for designing user interface software, in *Handbook of Human–Computer Interaction*, (ed. M. Helander), Elsevier Science Publishers, North-Holland, Ch. 40.

Smith, S.L. and Mosier, J.N., (1984) The user interface to computer-based information systems: A survey of current software design practice, *Behaviour and Information Technology*, 3, 195–203.

Smith, S.L. and Mosier, J.N., (1986) Guidelines for designing user interface software, Report No. ESD-TR-86-278, MTR 10090, MITRE, Bedford, MA.

Snowberry, K., Parkinson, S. and Sisson, N. (1983) Computer display menus, *Ergonomics*, **26**, 699–712.

Snowberry, K., Parkinson, S. and Sisson, N. (1985) Effects of help fields on navigating through hierarchical menu structures, *Int. J. Man–Machine Studies*, **22**, 479–91.

Snyder, M. and Swann, W.B. (1978) Hypothesis testing processes in social interaction, *J. Personality and Social Psychology*, **36**, 1202–12.

Spector, P.E. (1981) *Research Designs: Quantitative Applications in the Social Sciences*, Sage Publications Inc., Beverley Hills, CA.

Stammers, R.B. (1986) Training, generalizable rules and computer data entry tasks, *Proc. Human Factors Society 30th Annual Meeting*, 1460–2.

Steinhaus, C.P. and Hammer, J.M. (1985) Development principles for the construction of help systems, *Proc. Int. Conf. Cybernetics and Society*, IEEE Elsevier Science Publishers, North-Holland.

Stewart, C.J. and Cash, W.B. (1978) *Interviewing: Principles and Practices*, 2nd edn, W.C. Brown, Dubuqne, IA.

Stewart, T. (1991a) Helping the IT designer to use Human Factors, in *Human Factors for Informatics Usability*, (eds B. Shackel and S. Richardson), Cambridge University Press, Cambridge.

Stewart, T. (1991b) Usability and Europe – standards and regulations, People before Technology, *Proc. 3rd Annual CHISIG Conf. OZCHI '91*, pp. 1–8.

Sullivan, M.A. and Chapanis, A. (1983) Human factoring a text editor manual, *Behaviour and Information Technology*, **2**, 113–25.

Sutliffe, A. (1989) Task analysis systems analysis and design: symbiosis or synthesis?, *Interacting with Computers*, **1** (1), 6–12.

Thorne, B.M. (1980) *Introductory Statistics for Psychology*, Duxbury Press, North Scituate, MA.

Tombaugh, J. and McEwen, S. (1982) Comparison of two information retrieval methods on videotex: tree-structure versus alphabetical directory, *Proc. Human Factors in Computer Systems*, Gaithersburg, MD.

Travis, D. (1991) *Effective Colour Displays: Theory and Practice*, Academic Press, London.

True, J.A. (1989) *Finding Out: Conducting and Evaluating Social Research*, 2nd edn, Wadsworth Publishing Co., Belmont, CA.

Tullis, T.S. (1983a) The formatting of alphanumeric displays: a review and analysis, *Human Factors,* **25**, 657–82.

Tullis, T.S. (1983b) Predicting the usability of alphanumeric displays, unpublished Ph.D. thesis, Houston, TX.

Tullis, T.S. (1990) The formatting of alphanumeric displays: A review and analysis, in *Selected Readings in Human Factors,* (ed. M. Venturino), Taylor & Francis.

Virzi, R.A. (1992) Refining the test phase of usability evaluation: How many subjects is enough?, *Human Factors,* **34** (4), 457–68.

Wallsten, T.S. (ed.) (1980) *Cognitive Processes in choice and decision Behavior,* Lawrence Erlbaum & Associates, Hillsdale, NJ.

Waern, Y. (1985) Learning computerized tasks as related to prior task knowledge, *Int. J. Man-Machine Studies,* **22**, 441–55.

Waern, Y., El-Khouri, B., Olofsson, M. and Scherlund, K. (1986) Does computer education affect problem solving strategies? Paper presented at the Work with display units Conference, Stockholm.

Wagner, R.K., Sebrechts, M.M. and Black, J.B. (1985) Tracing the evolution of knowledge structures, *Behaviour Research Methods, Instruments and Computers,* **17** (2), 275–8.

Wason, P.C. (1960) On the failure to eliminate hypotheses in a conceptual task, *Quarterly J. Experimental Psychology,* **12**, 129–40.

Wason, P.C. (1968) Reasoning about a rule, *Quarterly J. Experimental Psychology,* **20**, 273–81.

Wasserman, A.I. and Shewmake, D.T. (1990) The role of prototypes in the User Software Engineering (USE) methodology, in *Human–Computer Interaction,* (eds J. Preece and L. Keller), Prentice-Hall, Cambridge.

Watts, D.R. (1990) Creating an essential manual: An Experiment in prototyping and task analysis, *I.E.E.E. Trans. Professional Communications,* **33** (1), 32–7.

Weerdmeester, B.A., van Velthoven, R.H. and Vrins, T.G.M. (1985) – Keywords for information retrieval on interactive videotex, *Behaviour and Information Technology,* **4** (2), 103–12.

Welbank, M. (1990) An overview of knowledge acquisition methods, *Interacting with Computers,* **2** (1), 83–91.

Wharton, C., Bradford, J., Jeffries, R. and Franzke, M. (1992) Applying cognitive walkthroughs to more complex user interfaces: Experiences, issues and recommendations, in *Proc. CHI '92, Striking a balance,* ACM Press, NY. pp. 381–8.

White, R.R. (1967) On-line software – The problems, in *The transition to On-line Computing,* (ed. F. Gruenberger), Thompson, Washington, pp. 15–26.

Whitefield, A., Wilson, F. and Dowell, J. (1991) A framework for human factors evaluation, *Behaviour and Information Technology,* **10** (1), 65–79.

Whiteside, J. and Wixon, D. (1987) Improving human–computer interaction: A quest for cognitive science, in *Interfacing Thought: Cognitive Aspects of Human Computer Interaction*, (ed. J.M. Carroll), Bradford/MIT Press, Cambridge, pp. 352–65.

Whiteside, J., Bennett, J. and Holtzblatt, K. (1988) Usability engineering: our experience and evolution, in *Handbook of Human–Computer Interaction*, (ed. M. Helander), Elsevier Science Publishers, North-Holland.

Whittle, S.J. (1987) Online Assistance – A Literature Review, Document No. 55112-870228-01TM, AT&T Bell Laboratories Publications.

Williams, M.D., Hollan, J.D. and Stevens, A.L. (1983) Human reasoning about a simple system, in *Mental Models*, (eds D. Gentner and A.L. Stevens), Lawrence Erlbaum & Associates, Hillsdale, NJ.

Williges, R.C. and Hartson, H.R. (1986) Human-computer dialogue design and research, in *Human–computer Dialogue Design: Advances in Human Factors/Ergonomics*, (eds R.W. Ehrich and R.C. Williges), Elsevier Science Publishers, North-Holland.

Wilson, M.D., Barnard, P.J., Green, T.R.G. and MacLean, A. (1988) Knowledge-based task analysis for human-computer systems, in *Working with Computers: Theory versus Outcome*, (eds G.C. van der Veer, T.R.G. Green, J.M. Hoc, and D.M. Murray), Academic Press, London.

Winer, B.J. (1971) *Statistical Principles in Experimental Design*, 2nd edn, McGraw-Hill, NY.

Winograd, T. (1990) What can we teach about human-computer interaction, *Proc. HCI '90 Conf. Human Factors in Computing Systems*, ACM Press, NY pp. 443–9.

Wiser, M. and Carey, S. (1983) When head and temperature were one, in *Mental Models*, (eds D. Gentner and A.L. Stevens), Lawrence Erlbaum & Associates, Hillsdale, NJ.

Wixon, D. and Whiteside, J. (1985) Engineering for usability: Lessons from the user-derived interface, *Proc. ACM CHI '85*, Elsevier Science Publishers, North-Holland.

Woodmansee, G.H. (1985) The vision experience – from concept to marketplace, *Proc. Human–Computer Interaction Interact '84*, pp. 871–6.

Wright, P. (1983) Manual dexterity: A user-oriented approach to creating computer documentation, in *Proc. Human Factors in Computing Systems Conf. CHI '83*, ACM Press, NY.

Wright, P. (1988) Issues of content and presentation in document design, in *Handbook of Human–Computer Interaction*, (ed. M. Helander), Elsevier Science Publishers, North-Holland, Ch. 28.

Wright, P. (1991) Designing and evaluating documentation for IT users, in *Human Factors for Informatics Usability*, (eds B. Shackel and S. Richardson), Cambridge University Press, Cambridge.

Wright, P.C. and Monk, A.F. (1989) Evaluation for design, in *People and Computers V,* (eds A. Sutliffe and L. Macaulay), Cambridge University Press, Cambridge, pp. 345–58.

Wright, P.C. and Monk, A.F. (1991) The use of think-aloud evaluation methods in design, *SIGCHI Bulletin,* **23** (1), 55–7.

Young, R.M, Green, T.R.G. and Simon, T. (1989) Programmable user models for predictive evaluation of interface designs, in *Proc. CHI '89 Human Factors in Computer Systems,* ACM Press, NY.

Yourdon, E. (1989) *Structured Walkthroughs,* 4th edn, Yourdon Press, Englewood Cliffs, NJ.

Index